Village Mothers

VILLAGE MOTHERS

THREE GENERATIONS OF CHANGE
IN RUSSIA AND TATARIA

David L. Ransel

Indiana University Press   Bloomington & Indianapolis

Publication of this book is made possible in part with the assistance of a Challenge Grant from the National Endowment for the Humanities, a federal agency that supports research, education, and public programming in the humanities.

This book is a publication of

Indiana University Press

601 North Morton Street

Bloomington, Indiana 47404-3797 USA

www.indiana.edu/~iupress

Telephone orders 800-842-6796

Fax orders 812-855-7931

Orders by e-mail iuporder@indiana.edu

© 2000 by David L. Ransel

The paper used in this publication meets the minimum requirements of American National Standard for Information Sciences—Permanence of Paper for Printed Library Materials, ANSI Z39.48-1984.

Manufactured in the United States of America

Library of Congress Cataloging-in-Publication Data

Ransel, David L.

Village mothers : three generations of change in Russia and Tataria / David L. Ransel.

p. cm. — (Indiana-Michigan series in Russian and East European studies)

Includes bibliographical references and index.

ISBN 0-253-33825-5 (cl : alk. paper)

1. Mothers—Russia (Federation)—Interviews. 2. Mothers—Russia (Federation)—History. 3. Mothers—Russia (Federation)—Social conditions. I. Title: Three generations of change in Russia and Tataria. II. Title. III. Series.

HQ759 .R34 2000

306.874'3—dc21

00-038908

1 2 3 4 5 05 04 03 02 01 00

Contents

Acknowledgments

Many people helped me with this project. In the former Soviet Union and the Russian Federation, I relied on the assistance and advice of so many people that I could never recall them all. Most important were Olga Glazunova, Tatiana Listova, Inna Peshkova, and Guzel Shugaeva (more about them in the Introduction), my direct collaborators in interviewing the women in the villages. In addition, many people made introductions and traveled with me across Russia to visit villages and informants or they arranged such visits. Others gave advice and encouragement. Among these many people were Sergei Chernov, Nellia and Evsei Gritsevskii, Dolores and Shaukat Galeev, Elena Stepanova, Boris Mironov, Galina Shapovalova, Natalia Gryzyk, Amina and Valentin Teleshov, Ekaterina Danilishina, Tatiana Bernshtam, Guzel Ibneeva, Tatiana Mironova, Tamara Zakharova, and Aleksei Vasil'ev. I also want to acknowledge the invaluable help of archivists and librarians of the following institutions: the State Archive of the Russian Federation, the Russian State Archive of the Economy, the Russian State Historical Archive, the Central State Archive of St. Petersburg, the Central State Historical Archive, the Russian State Library, the St. Petersburg Public Library, the National Library of Medicine (Bethesda, Maryland), the Library of Congress, and the Indiana University Library. All photographs are my own unless otherwise noted. I thank all the women who gave me permission to photograph them.

In the United States, I received advice and assistance from Mercedes Vilanova, Barbara Truesdell, John Bodnar, Tamara Alexandrova, Alice Goldstein, Ellen Dwyer, Laura Engelstein, Gerda Lerner, Nanette Funk, Maria and Clayton Black, and Azade-Ayse Rorlich. My colleagues at Indiana University's Department of Slavic Languages and Literatures, Galina McClaws, Jerzy Kolodziej, and Nyusya Milman, patiently suffered my requests to clarify the meaning of unfamiliar Russian idioms. An Indiana midwife, Mary Helen Ayres, read selected chapters of the book and offered valuable comment. I also profited from comments and corrections by my colleague and Islamist, Nazif Shahrani. Terry Ransel applied her critical eye to the entire manuscript, as did Janet Rabinowitch of Indiana University Press and the copy editor, Anne M. Heiles. I owe a great debt to all these people.

I hasten to add my sincere appreciation for financial assistance in connection with the research and writing of the book. Contributors included the Woodrow Wilson International Center for Scholars, Guggenheim Foundation, International Research and Exchanges Board (IREX), Fulbright-Hays program of the U.S. Department of Education, Indiana University Graduate School, National Endowment for the Humanities, and the Russian and East European Institute at Indiana University.

Note on Transliteration

In the bibliography, I have used the Library of Congress system of transliteration, modified to remove diacritical markings. In the body of the work and the notes, I have in many cases deleted the single and double apostrophes that represent Russian soft and hard signs respectively to ease the reading for those not familiar with Russian spelling. For the same reason, I have deleted some vowel-softening symbols in first names, using, for example, "Lia" instead of "Liia," "Klavdia" instead of "Klavdiia," and "Maria" instead of "Mariia." The proper transliteration is, however, retained in the list of informants at the back of the book.

Village Mothers

Introduction

This study focuses on the reproductive lives of three generations of rural women. It grew out of an earlier investigation into the reasons for marked differences in the success of Russians, Tatars, and Jews in bringing their children through the dangerous early years of life. In late imperial Russia, these peoples suffered very different rates of infant and childhood mortality. Losses were high in the case of Russians, somewhat lower for Muslim Tatars, and very much lower for Jews.[1] I had planned to continue that investigation into the Soviet period using the same sort of materials I had employed in the study on imperial Russia: statistical compilations, medical surveys, and ethnographical accounts. But when I arrived in Russia in the spring of 1990 for four months of research in libraries and archives, I discovered that it was possible (if not yet strictly legal) to do something that had not before been permitted, namely, to go to villages, interview women in their homes, and ask them directly why they made the marriage and reproductive choices they did as well as how they fed and cared for their children. I drafted a questionnaire and, with the help of Russian, Jewish, and Tatar friends, launched into a series of preliminary interviews to test the feasibility of the project and at the same time help me to refine and improve the initial set of questions. The only major difficulty I encountered was finding Jewish informants to interview. For proper comparison, I needed to include only Jewish women who had grown up and reared their families in rural hamlets (shtetls), but it proved difficult to locate Jewish women who had lived in the countryside and survived World War II and the Holocaust. In the few cases in which I was able to find such women, they were not eager to relive, in a detailed interview, the memories of that terrible time. These difficulties and the fact that I had soon accumulated a daunting number of testimonies from Russian and Tatar women persuaded me to limit the study to these two latter groups. The three interviews I was able to conduct with Jewish women have been used here merely to reinforce or comment on more general points or to draw comparisons to the behavior of women in the other communities.

A primary purpose of this book is to introduce into the history of twentieth-century Russia voices of ordinary women of the villages. Until the 1930s the overwhelming majority of women in Russia, 80 percent and more, lived in villages. During the 1930s young women in significant numbers began to migrate from the rural areas in response to the wreckage of collectivization and ensuing famine and also in pursuit of new job opportunities in industrial centers and growing cities. Even so, for another thirty years, until the 1960s, village women constituted a majority of all women in Russia. The lives of this large segment of the population have been little studied. Indeed, until the 1970s it was dangerous for Soviet scholars to study peasant life at all. Some ethnographic accounts have appeared since that time, but the impressions of these people remain for the most part what the Soviet political discourse on the life of rural women left us, images in which they figured as one of two types. There was the "dark" mass that needed to be educated and freed from the ignorance and superstition that made them easy prey for counterrevolutionary forces (often represented as kulaks, priests, mullahs, and other spiritual leaders) or the newly "conscious" agrarian workers who, through example and active political participation, were transforming the village into a productive, socialist community.[2] On the contrary, the women we meet in the pages that follow fit neither of these stereotypes. Their lives were propelled and battered by powerful forces beyond their control, which ranged from the patriarchal tyranny of a household head to civil war, governmental coercion and violence, famine, and world war. But, as we learn from the women's own testimony, amid these storms many of them were able to preserve areas of independent decision that allowed them a measure of personal control and an ability either to act on their inherited norms or to fashion a new set of values appropriate to their time. This ability, if it could not entirely shield them from the despair that attended their personal losses, helped soften the trauma they experienced and gave their lives meaning.

A third stereotype, familiar from Western historiography, likewise fails to find support in the testimonies of the women. This is the unchanging, stolid "eternal Russian peasant woman."[3] Each of the three generations of peasant women we meet in this book differed in characteristic and tangible ways. Each cohort grew up under different circumstances, acquired a distinctive outlook, and expressed a different ethics. Moreover, the women were just as aware as were urban women of the role that politics played in the forces that affected their lives and in the changes they themselves made in response. The public sphere pervaded their private lives and did so in ways that the women understood well.[4]

A second and related purpose of the book is to trace the development of modern medical discourse in obstetrics and pediatrics and show how it entered Russian and Tatar villages, eventually displacing many of the village women's inherited ideas and practices. A transformation occurred in the villagers' reproductive culture (courtship, marriage, fertility choices, birthing, ritual incorporation of new life, early child care), a change that came about during the lives of three generations of women in the twentieth century and that can be followed and marked in the oral interviews of this study. The change was part and parcel of the transformation of the rural order begun by the government and social reformers of the late tsarist era and renewed by the Soviet regime, at first through incentives and education in the 1920s and later with unprecedented ferocity and brutality in the 1930s and beyond.

This is a story primarily about women and how they mediated efforts to alter their reproductive ideas and practices, a story of willing acceptance of some changes and selective acceptance of or outright resistance to others. An important feature of the story is the generational chain of knowledge, norms, and assistance that strongly reinforced inherited practices. But we also gain insight into the power and courage of women who decided to resist the dictates of either their elders or the state and took actions to change their condition.

The book consists of two segments. The heart of the book, chapters 3 through 8, is based on the personal testimony of rural women. They recount how they conceived of and coped with decisions about courtship and marriage, fertility and abortion, birthing assistance, baptism, the death of their children, and the feeding and care of those who survived. The first two chapters are rather different. They follow the chronological narrative form of most historical studies and trace the development of scientific social policy in Russia and the Soviet Union. These chapters provide a necessary background to the personal testimonies of the rural women, for they describe the formation and genealogy of the policies to which the women were responding. Chapter 1 treats the entry into Russia, starting in the eighteenth century, of Western medical discourse on reproduction and child care. It sketches the growing awareness on the part of medical experts and political leaders that the enormous loss of human life in childhood was not an inescapable law of nature but a consequence of human cultural patterns, and it could, therefore, be altered by changes in reproductive and child-care practices. Because eighteenth-century rulers understood population to be a critical determinant of the power of the state, from this time forward reproduction ceased to be a wholly private affair regulated only by religious norms; it became a matter of government concern and intervention as well. The key to change was to be social engineering and education that would convince people to abandon their age-old practices and accept new methods recommended by medical and child-care professionals. These new experts claimed to have freed themselves from magical, superstitious ideas, and stood ready to apply the latest scientific knowledge to the fundamental tasks of human material and social reproduction. This type of formulation signaled a sharp cultural conflict, whose character and complexity became apparent as soon as the new ideas came into contact with the inherited practices of the Russian villagers. In the era of the Great Reforms of the 1860s and 1870s, when an increasing number of Russian doctors and teachers trained in Western scientific thought went to work among the villagers, they were dismayed by the chasm that divided the practices and mental world of peasant women from their own.

It was as if they had entered a foreign country and an exotic cultural landscape. Viewing themselves as cultural missionaries among a primitive people, they shared many of the attitudes familiar from Western Europeans engaged in their "civilizing mission" among the peoples of Asia, Africa, and the Americas.

The task of these Russian cultural missionaries was taken up with increased urgency by the Soviet government, as chapter 2 relates. The Soviets sought not merely to change some practices and to promote public health and hygiene. They were determined to transform the peasant into a worker-socialist who lived in harmony with the dictates of modern scientific thought. They sought, in short, to eliminate the peasantry and replace it with an entirely new kind of people, and claimed to be doing so in accord with reason and the historical dialectic. The implementation of these ideas in the midst of civil war, famine, collectivization, state-directed terror, world war, devastating population losses and material destruction sometimes lacked not only reason but even any coherent motivation beyond the ideological impulse to mobilize and transform rural life. It is not surprising that policy makers paid little attention to the voices and needs of the women whose behavior they sought to change.

It is these voices and needs that constitute the remainder of the book. In a series of topical chapters focusing on different aspects of the reproductive culture, I use the testimony of rural women to illustrate how these villagers responded to new ideas and practices, preserved or altered their inherited practices—in short, how they mediated the entry into the village of modern scientific ideas of birthing and child care. Equally important, the women also explain how they resisted government efforts to force certain changes on them. Chapter 9 considers what these women regarded as their central values and tasks, the actions that lent their lives dignity and meaning, despite the unspeakable horrors and suffering endured by many of them.

Three Generations

The analysis in the topical chapters divides the informants into three generations: those born before about 1912, those born between 1912 and 1930, and those born after 1930. Although each woman led a separate life with individual sorrows and achievements, the members of a particular generation or cohort inevitably shared certain experiences as a group. The great upheavals of world war, civil strife, collectivization, and terror visited the women of each generation at a particular period in their life cycle and consequently shaped their choices and perceptions in some common ways.

The women of the first generation were born before World War I and the revolutions and civil war of 1917 to 1920. They grew up and came into consciousness at the time of these great events and began their paid working lives as teenage nannies or farm workers in the 1920s. They lived on family farms, in a few cases in the large joint families of co-resident married brothers and their children under the overall authority of a patriarchal father. Fathers still ruled their families and family-based farming operations, whether these were individual farmsteads or part of a communal land system. Girls were brought up in religion and instructed to obey their parents unquestioningly. Parents, through their own example and the demands they placed on the girls, early on taught their daughters the necessity and value of hard work. Their daughters had first to look after their younger siblings and help their mothers in the barnyard and garden, and later to take jobs in other homes, sometimes at considerable distance, as nannies and housekeepers. These jobs enabled the young women to provide for their own support and, in addition, to contribute something to their families or to build their trousseaux. For some it was also an introduction to a different way of life, especially so in the cases of those who worked for families in towns.[5]

Most young women of this first generation had the freedom to find their mates either at work or by attendance at parties, dances, and other sites of youthful socializing, but dependence on and ultimate loyalty to the natal family meant that if the father insisted, the daughter would have to allow herself to be married off at his command, as happened to some of our informants from this cohort.

At the time many of these women were getting married and starting families, the upheaval of collectivization (and, for some, subsequent famine) shook their lives. Even though we did not ask directly about this event, one-third of the informants in this generation volunteered stories about how their families had been "dekulakized" and their fathers exiled or killed. The loss of a father and a successful farm worked an especially great hardship on women who were still at home. Apart from the family trauma, it wrecked their chances of assembling an attractive trousseau and dowry. Nevertheless, responses of the women of this cohort to the enforced shift to collectivized farming were far from uniform. For the women who had married before the change and settled into the life of private farming, collectivization disrupted and in some cases tore apart their families and irretrievably ruined their lives. For women slightly younger, memories of the switch to collectivized agriculture were not entirely negative. While virtually all the women of this generation conceded that private farm families had provided more support than early collective farm life for women in their mothering role, several women recalled the work of the collective farm as being easier and more enjoyable than under private farming. They were able to get out from under the exclusive power of the household head and also to work in groups, together with women of the same age from other households. Whatever the stance toward collectivization, the attributes that most strongly characterized the women of this first generation were their adherence to religious norms and devotion to hard work, family, and pre-collectivization community values of mutual support and charity. These were women who in most cases married as virgins and rejected abortion as sinful and odious. They spoke proudly of their natal families' faithfulness to the obligations toward their communities and to people in need.

The women of the second generation were caught in a time of profound change in moral and social values, and they paid a high price psychically and physically. Unlike their predecessors in the first generation who came to maturity before the upheaval of the 1930s and brought to these difficult times a set of loyalties and fixed rules of morality, the women of the second generation came to maturity in the new world of collectivized agriculture and the beginnings of Soviet education and indoctrination. Their values and allegiances were less fixed, and the shifting government policy, terror, and terrible personal losses left them without much faith in anyone or anything. These women married and began their families just before, during, or soon after World War II. They were expected to do all the work of the men who were taken during the terror as former kulaks or recruited and often lost forever in the wars, beginning in the late 1930s against Japan and Finland and later in the 1940s in World War II. At the same time, the government outlawed abortion and exhorted these women to produce a bounty of children for the beleaguered fatherland, and to do so before the government was able to deliver to the countryside the promised support system for new mothers that was to include prenatal care, maternity homes, maternity leave, and pediatric services.

The women of the second generation came of age in a world that had diminished the power of patriarchal family heads and supplanted it with the less personal forces of the Party leader and collective farm chairman. I use the term "fatherland" in the paragraph above and elsewhere (instead of the "motherland" sometimes used by Soviet authorities for emotional effect) to indicate this conscious effort of the Party to displace the power of family patriarchs in favor of a new patriarchy vested in agents of the paternalistic state. Religious values were likewise under challenge from Soviet propaganda and from schooling that encouraged young people to believe in their ability to transform their lives. The women responded to these messages. They were determined not to live as their mothers and grandmothers had: in subordination to a household head, continuously pregnant through their childbearing years and producing a dozen or more children, many of whom would die in early childhood. When the government robbed them of the legal right to control their fertility, they defied the law and obtained underground abortions. This choice inflicted a high cost both physically and emotionally. Many women died from botched abortions. The survivors suffered physical pain from the unregulated procedures. They also witnessed the death of friends and neighbors and imprisonment of the women who provided the services. Finally, they had to deal with the moral sting of abortion because they were not entirely free of the religious scruples of earlier generations about this choice.

What is most striking about the women of this second generation is their lack of attachment to any institutions, large or small. Few had anything good to say about the collective farm or the Party and its national leaders. There was some nostalgia for the later Brezhnev years when conditions briefly improved, but the time before that was remembered as one of continuous suffering, enforced labor, separation from their children, and destruction of their families. The new world of perestroika and capitalism they understood rightly as a return to difficult economic conditions and a threat to their security in old age.

The third generation was composed of women born from the early 1930s onward. They were building their families after the death of Stalin, when conditions on the countryside were improving. More services were reaching village women, and people began to enjoy a small amount of discretionary income. By the mid-1960s, the maternity benefits already accorded state workers were extended to collective farm women. These women had become in some measure "sovietized," that is, included in the social contract that had for some time offered industrial workers social assistance and security in return for their acceptance of the system. These village women were afforded the possibility of restricting their fertility safely through legal abortion, and they felt more comfortable emotionally and morally about this option than had their predecessors. Work discipline on the collective farms and in rural factories was becoming less punishing, and women could choose to spend more time with their children. In short, the government was at last acknowledging farm women's contributions and providing some reciprocity in terms of benefits.

The primary historical reference for the women of this third generation was the one period of relative well-being in Soviet rural life, the Khrushchev and, especially, Brezhnev eras. They could recall from childhood some of the privation and loss that touched the women of earlier times, but their own experiences of courtship, marriage, and child rearing fell into better times. They felt allegiance to the regime that had provided them job security, social benefits, and a comfortable retirement, and naturally resented the loss of this security after the fall of the Soviet regime. These women of the third generation were young enough that they had to be concerned about the future, a future that has for many of them become very tough indeed.

Interview Sites

I want to emphasize the collaborative character of the oral interviews, an essential aspect of research for this book. Although I developed the project and the questionnaire used in the interviews, several others were directly and indirectly engaged in the actual interview process. I conducted only about half of the interviews, and many of those took place in the company of Olga Glazunova, a researcher from the Institute of Archeology in Moscow who had previously surveyed the villages of northeastern Moscow province for artifacts and knew many of the people who lived there. Even when I was interviewing alone, Russian and Tatar friends had almost invariably prepared the ground for the in-

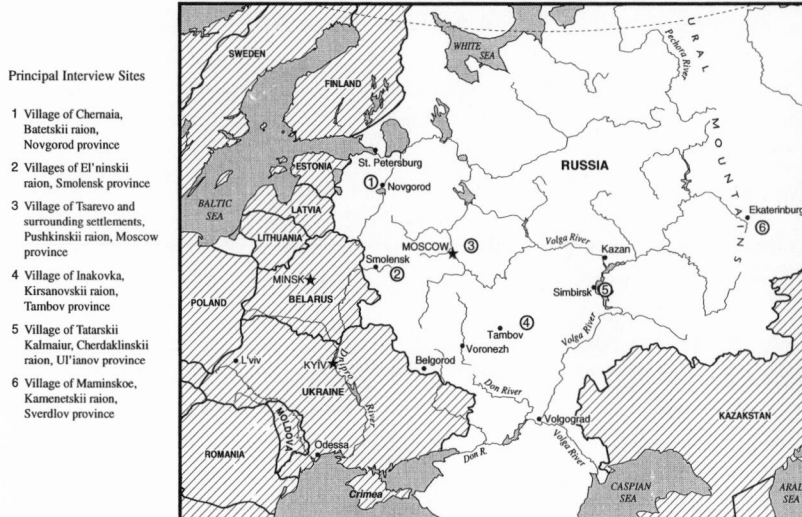

Principal Interview Sites

1 Village of Chernaia,
  Batetskii raion,
  Novgorod province

2 Villages of El'ninskii
  raion, Smolensk province

3 Village of Tsarevo and
  surrounding settlements,
  Pushkinskii raion, Moscow
  province

4 Village of Inakovka,
  Kirsanovskii raion,
  Tambov province

5 Village of Tatarskii
  Kalmaiur, Cherdaklinskii
  raion, Ul'ianov province

6 Village of Maminskoe,
  Kamenetskii raion,
  Sverdlov province

Principal Interview Sites

terviews and accompanied me to the site to provide introductions. Three persons who took the questionnaire to sites where they could spend sufficient time to do thorough investigations conducted the other interviews.

The principal interview sites included six widely dispersed locales. Moving from west to east, the first was the village of Chernaia in Novgorod province. This was also the first village I visited, having made contact with the people there through my friend, the retired folklorist and ethnographer, Galina Shapovalova. Galina had earlier worked with the women in this village in connection with a study of calendar festivals. In advance of our visit to Chernaia, Galina and I took a set of questions to Udel'nyi Park on the northern edge of Leningrad, where peasant migrants to the city had been gathering on weekends ever since the nineteenth century to sing ditties, dance, drink, and socialize together with other country people. After these trial runs, we took a train to Chernaia, which lies about midway between the city of Luga in Leningrad province and the capital city of its own, Novgorod province. The region had once been a profitable linen-producing center, but wartime occupation, a chaotic Soviet farm policy, and the drain of young people from the area had left this industry in ruins—and the villages tied to it in decline. When we arrived in early 1990, the region was populated mainly by elderly women. The one hopeful sign for the area was the revival of folk singing. The nearby cultural center had helped to organize the women into an impressive choir that had resurrected, and was performing, songs the women recalled from their youth. This wonderful sing-

Folk choir from Batetskii District, Novgorod province, 1990

ing group had begun to participate in folk festivals throughout Novgorod province. In this locale, I lived in the home of Anna Zueva, who had served much of her life as a medic, at first in the far north of Novgorod province and later in her home area of Chernaia and its surrounding villages. She was therefore an excellent guide in tracing the changes in medical and social practices in the expansive Novgorod province.

During this first year of the project, I also conducted a number of lengthy interviews with Russian, and even more Tatar and Bashkir, women in and around Leningrad and Moscow, women who were either still in villages or who had grown up and spent much of their lives in villages before moving to urban or suburban centers. With only two exceptions, these interviews and all subsequent ones that I conducted were audiotaped in full and transcribed. The exceptions were the result of a glitch in the tape recorder; these interviews were done in field-note form. (Tapes and transcripts of these interviews and all others used for the study are archived at the Indiana University Oral History Research Center.)

Tatiana Listova, a well-published ethnographer from the Institute of Ethnology in Moscow and my chief collaborator, surveyed the second and third areas of intense contact. In the summer of 1993 she took my questionnaire to the southeastern reaches of Smolensk province, an agricultural region of western Russia and another area that had suffered from German occupation and devastating losses during World War II. The next summer, Tatiana moved to an

Tatiana Listova

eastern district of Tambov province in the black soil region of south-central Russia and interviewed women in two villages there, Inakovka 1 and 2, not far from the city of Kirsanov. Like many others in Russia, these villages had been dying out for years. Although they had boasted 7,000 and 5,000 inhabitants respectively before World War II, at the time of the interviews they contained only about 800 and 500 inhabitants. In the 1950s, according to the head doctor at the local hospital, the villages had produced between 110 and 115 births each year. By contrast, only 12 children were born in 1993. And correspondingly few weddings were taking place: just 10 in 1993. The Tambov province villages were remarkable among those we surveyed for the persistence of religious practice in daily life through the Soviet period and the prompt revival of open religious life since perestroika. A new church had been built in Inakovka and enjoyed a large attendance by the few remaining young people as well as by the old folks.

In contrast to my practice of tape-recording each interview, Tatiana recorded her interviews in field-note form, taking care to note the actual language of key

Olga Glazunova and the author comparing notes during interviewing, 1993

statements. I should add that she also contributed some additional material from the Vologda region and from southeastern Moscow province, offered comments on my work published in Russian, and provided personal insights about conditions of village life and the position of women in the village.

The most intensive interview expedition that I personally conducted took place in the summer of 1993 in northeastern Moscow province in the vicinity of the city of Krasnoarmeisk (formerly Voznesensk). Much less agrarian in character than the other interview sites, this region was dotted with factories and industrial state farms. Many women had worked as milkmaids or other menial workers on collective farms, but some had spent a part of their lives commuting to Krasnoarmeisk to work in factories or had worked on a state fur farm. The villagers in this area were close enough to Moscow to be able, especially after transport improved in the 1960s, to visit the metropolis on occasion to trade products or purchase scarce goods.

The summer of 1993 was also the time that interviews were done in the village of Maminskoe in the Urals. Maminskoe lies about 90 kilometers southeast of the city of Ekaterinburg in the Kamenetskii district of Sverdlovsk province. It was settled about 200 years ago and currently has 4,000 inhabitants. The villagers are primarily occupied with agriculture and animal husbandry, although early in this century the settlement boasted a large brick factory as well. Maminskoe has good connections both to Ekaterinburg and to the city of

Mullah of Tatarskii Kalmaiur
and his wife, Roza, at home,
1999

Kamensk-Ural'skii on the southeast. In recent years, the character of the village
has been changing, as young people depart from the village and urbanites buy
summer cottages there. Inna Peshkova, a retired journalist from Ekaterinburg
who has long had a summer cottage in Maminskoe and is familiar with many
of the women living there, conducted the interviews. All these interviews were
tape-recorded.

Finally, our Tatar village interview site was in Ul'ianovsk province, about an
hour's drive southeast of the provincial capital city of Simbirsk/Ul'ianovsk.
Tatar friends of mine from Moscow took me to Simbirsk in the summer of 1990
so that I could do some interviewing there and then find an appropriate village in the countryside for study. After I conducted a couple of interviews in the
city, we borrowed a Soviet jeep (known as an UAZ) and drove eastward, looking for minarets on the skyline. This is how we found the village of Tatarskii
Kalmaiur, which lies in the rich black soil of a large peninsula formed by Volga
River reservoirs. This large, prosperous village was split between a population
of Tatars and Chuvash (a Turkic people of Christian religion). According to the
mullah, the area had been settled after the Pugachev rebellion of the late eighteenth century. Tatars have lived there continuously since that time, and all of
our informants had been settled in the area for generations. They are known as

New timber mosque in
Tatarskii Kalmaiur, 1990

Mishari Tatars, and the Tatars of the Kazan region farther north (and they themselves) consider their dialect or tongue a coarse brand of the Tatar language.
The Kalmaiur Tatars and Mishari generally do not otherwise distinguish themselves from other Tatars. The Kalmaiur Tatars are Muslim—and they held to
their religious practices throughout the period of Soviet rule, despite being deprived of clergy and a place of worship.

When I drove there in July 1990, they had just completed building an impressive timber mosque under the direction of a mullah who had arrived the
previous year from Kazan. It was in this mosque that I conducted my interviews
during that first brief stay, posing as a Finn to protect my friends from the descent of the provincial police that would have followed news of an American in
the village. It turned out that the arrival of any foreigner at that time was enough
of a sensation that I was unable to do interviews one-on-one. Instead I had to
be satisfied with a group interview at which an ever-greater number of onlook-
ers kept appearing. This provided a start, and in 1993 Guzel Shugaeva, an anthropologist trained at Moscow University (whose family had purchased a summer cottage in Kalmaiur where Guzel was a regular visitor), conducted more
fruitful, detailed, and one-on-one interviews. Guzel recorded her interviews in
a very structured format, entering responses separately to each question in the

Guzel Shugaeva

questionnaire, noting carefully the actual language of key statements, and including as well the Tatar names used by the women to describe particular acts
and rites.

I should add that I use the term "Tataria" in the title of this book to signal that
reference is made to Volga Tatar women generally and not just those who live
in the present-day Republic of Tatarstan. The bulk of interviews were done with
women whose home villages lie outside the boundaries of Tatarstan. Indeed, 68
percent of Tatar citizens of Russia reside outside the Republic of Tatarstan.

Oral History Practice

A confession: When I started the oral-interview stage of this study, I had had
no training in this method beyond what Mercedes Vilanova, director of the
Barcelona Oral History Program and a fellow scholar at the Woodrow Wilson
Center in 1989–1990, was kind enough to teach me in a few hours of conversation. Although she wisely encouraged me to go after large questions or even
life interviews, I did not feel I had sufficient grasp of this open-ended interview

style to perform it well. I was more confident initially in pursuing a focused study of reproductive and child-care issues (later, I did try the life-interview approach in a separate investigation of small-town industrial workers). The trouble with a focused set of questions, however, is that they assume the significance of the researcher's agenda and may limit the informant's ability to communicate what she believes are the most important or defining experiences of her life. Were marriage, fertility choices, birthing, and care the defining aspects of the lives of rural women in twentieth-century Russia? The study did not ask that question and cannot answer it. The interviews do nevertheless make clear that for many of the informants the great political and social upheavals of the century were as important as marriage and children in where they ended up in life. Of course, the macro events and micro histories of each life constitute a single whole and cannot be disentangled. Decisions about when and whom to marry, how many conceptions to carry to term, whether to work or stay at home with small children, plus the hardships or blessings of losing a spouse, all these choices and conditions were bound up with the larger political and social disturbances of the time.

Memory is the archive in which oral historians work. Oral interviews create historical documents. Although the documents sometimes merely add material to that already available from articulate actors who have produced written works of their own, oral historians most often produce records of the actions and thoughts of people who do not leave written accounts of their lives. The oral histories therefore introduce new voices and, ideally, new information and perspectives. Working with memory, however, presents problems. Memory is fragile. People quickly forget matters that are not regarded as significant or that lack emotional impact at the time they are experienced. Memory is also malleable and suggestible. Remembered events and stories are mentally and orally rehearsed by their bearers and undergo embellishment, extension, and contraction in the retelling. Informants may consciously or unconsciously present as their own experience stories that belong to others or that they have heard in regard to themselves or others. Furthermore, memory is selective. In short, the archive of memory in which oral historians work is a complicated, fluid blend of past and present.

Textual sources are not necessarily more reliable. They manifest some of the same characteristics as oral accounts, the more so the further the writer is removed from the events or original thoughts being recorded. Written memoirs are notoriously problematic, since their authors consciously and continuously select and suppress information in order to advance a particular self-presentation. They avoid the probing that an oral interviewer applies to those regions of memory an informant may wish to avoid or suppress. In other words, issues of memory are an inherent aspect of all historical research, and they concern research using oral history no more or less than other types. Nevertheless, oral historians grapple with some distinctive issues related to the peculiar interactive and temporal features of this research approach.

In regard to the interactive aspect, I have already mentioned that my own more-or-less fixed questionnaire guided each interview. I went into the study with the assumptions of a middle-class Western researcher that marriage, child-bearing, and child rearing would be central and shaping events in nearly every woman's life. This imposition tended to confine the conversations to subjects and stories closely related to these issues and to exclude detailed consideration of other events and stories that may have been of equal or greater importance in an informant's ultimate destiny and identity. In a few cases, this indeed became apparent. Some of the informants with whom I spent a great deal of time (even living in their homes in a couple of cases) made it clear in recorded and non-recorded conversations how important other events had been in shaping their lives. Anna Zueva, with whom I stayed in Novgorod province, for example, was more interested in discussing her life behind enemy lines with the partisans in World War II than in answering my interview questions. It soon became evident that her wartime experiences were more important in creating and sustaining her sense of self than were her contributions as a wife and mother. The advantages of a fixed research agenda, which allows an investigator to focus on a limited set of questions, has therefore to be weighed against the potential exclusion of interesting, possibly even decisive, experiences affecting an informant's life.

Interviews are affected by the temporal context in which they take place. I will have more to say about this in chapter 9, which sums up attitudes of the women of these three generations at the time of the interviews. But it is worth noting that even in the course of collecting interviews for this study, the context shifted in ways that undoubtedly affected the character of the interviews. When I began interviewing in 1990, the position of rural people was not nearly so foreboding as it became in subsequent years. Certain aspects of perestroika, the opening of the country to the rest of the world, the legalization of small business, and especially having permission to practice religion openly had created a positive mood, a sense of new possibilities for personal fulfillment. By the time we renewed interviewing in 1993, conditions had changed significantly. Informants and hosts in the villages frequently complained about the rapid erosion of their savings and expressed fears for the future. By the next year, conditions had deteriorated still more. Tatiana Listova found the villagers in Tambov province to be terribly concerned about the coming winter. The price of coal had risen to the point that adequate supplies were beyond the reach of pensioners. Supplies of gasoline were insufficient to carry out the usual plowing and planting that summer. Many feared they would have to leave their homes in the winter and accept shelter in public institutions. Just how much this changing context affected the interview process is difficult to say, since some informants were by nature more optimistic or philosophical than others. In interpreting the materials from all the sites, I tried to keep this dimension in mind. Current conditions provide the context for stories of the past and cannot help but color the information conveyed. This can perhaps best be seen in the fears and sense of betrayal expressed by informants. But these conditions and attitudes were also significantly inflected by each woman's generation and accompanying set of expectations, a point to which I return in chapter 9.

Another consideration is language. A peasant woman is unlikely to speak to urban-based researchers in the same manner she would address her friends and family. But just what the character of this difference might be is difficult to judge. Some of the questions we posed and issues we addressed might never ordinarily be mentioned in the presence of the women once they passed a certain age. Indeed, some informants told us that they had never, and could not possibly, talk to their children and grandchildren about sexual intercourse, contraception, abortion, and the like, even to offer advice. Other questions would never arise in a context similar to the one we had created for the interview. It is probably not very helpful to ask how authentic were the voices we captured. The forms of expression used by informants varied quite a bit by age, education, location of the interview, and person of the interviewer. More educated and younger women included a greater quotient of Soviet public discourse in their language, whereas older women in more remote locales used more concrete forms of expression, images from folk tales, and, in a number of cases, stories of the influence of dreams on their choices and way of thinking about problems. By asking about behavior more than about feelings or political stance, we may have reduced the number of responses freighted with ulterior motives and political language. But we could not avoid such responses altogether, as we were in some cases asking about behavior (e.g., abortion and potential child neglect) that was criminal at the time informants may have engaged in it.

What was most surprising and gratifying was the willingness of most women to cooperate in the interviews. When I first considered doing the project as an oral-interview study, I feared that women might either refuse to participate or, even if they agreed, be reluctant to discuss the details of their reproductive life with a man, and a foreigner to boot. I was sure that the difficulty would be greater with Muslim women than with Russians. But these expectations proved quite mistaken. Only a handful of the women approached for interviews turned me down, and Muslim informants were, to all appearances, every bit as cooperative as Russians. Differences in willingness to talk about particular topics were greater between generations than between confessional groups, the oldest women in both communities being more reserved about discussing intimate matters. Most interviews were arranged beforehand through family members or trusted acquaintances, and the informants could thereby be reassured about the scholarly character of the exercise. In most cases, too, interviews took place in the home of the informant so that she could feel comfortable and in control.

Even unannounced interviews proved successful. When Olga Glazunova and I spent a few days wandering from village to village in northeastern Moscow province, knocking on doors and asking for interviews, most of the women obligingly spent an hour or more responding to our questions. Only a small number begged off on excuses that they had urgent work to do or had recently suffered a death in the family that left them emotionally exhausted. A few women, it is true, answered our questions reluctantly, evidently believing that they had to do so, even though we assured them that participation was voluntary. One of these inquired more than once why on earth we needed such information. "Is it that you want to arrest me?" she asked. Later, she inquired again about where we intended "to write such nonsense." When told, she responded, "Goodness! Holy Mother in heaven! And I'm going to go into the history books. Me and my children will be there." Still concerned, she asked that we not use her last name.[6] More poignant was an interview with another woman from the same region who was wonderfully helpful and candid. She gave us information that went beyond our questions, telling of the mistreatment of her and her husband by the authorities, of her feelings of guilt about the death of her children. She became agitated as she related her stories, and seemed to be refreshed by the chance to tell about the things that had happened to her and her family and her feelings about them. Toward the end of the interview, after she had disclosed the details of her underground abortions during the war, where they took place, how much she paid for them, she suddenly caught herself and exclaimed: "So, that's it, that's all. Oi! Maybe you are going to arrest me now. What I have lived through, what I did. It's all true. Yes."[7]

These allusions to possible arrest were exceptional, and I mention them merely to indicate some villagers' continuing suspicion of outsiders, especially outsiders who appear in the village unannounced. The last part of this second woman's statement and the rest of her very candid interview were far more typical, namely, her obvious relief at being able to tell the story of her sufferings and regrets. Oral history is sometimes used for therapeutic purposes; it provides a forum in which old people can review and integrate their experiences with that of the community at large while contributing to a larger historical account of their time and place.[8] Though not in any sense an objective of this study, this therapeutic element was active and helpful. It was clear that many of the informants had not been asked, even in their families, about the side of their lives that we were studying. For some, the chance to talk about such experiences was welcome and salutary. The idea that they were contributing to a scholarly study likewise seemed to give women a sense of satisfaction. The time was right. It was the early 1990s and the lid was off. The fear was gone for many, and the opportunity to give voice at last to their hurts and grievances clearly appealed to many informants. As Nancy Ries pointed out in her book on Russian talk of this period, it was a time of litanies and laments. Stories of suffering created value, identity, and moral authority.[9]

This type of talk also affected my interviews. When I first began, before my questionnaire became more fixed and less open-ended, I would start off an interview with questions about the informant's most and least pleasant memories of her youth. It usually took urging to elicit a positive memory. Most often, a woman's response to the first part of the question was that there was nothing pleasant about her childhood and youth or, if something nice happened, it was quickly cut short by a terrible misfortune. The second question, about unpleasant memories, released a flood of talk about the many losses, wrongs, privations, abuses, and accidents she had suffered. Even so, as will be seen in chapter 9, these misfortunes did not necessarily define an informant's life. The women often articulated a notion of a life properly led, measured their actions against this standard, and said that they felt satisfied they had done what was right, so far as the harsh circumstances of their times allowed.

Child Welfare before the Revolution

From the late seventeenth century onward, Russian political and religious leaders lived in the world of European ideas. Accordingly, concerns about child welfare that had been gaining strength in Europe since the fifteenth century began to find expression in Russian legislation in the seventeenth century. In Russia, the laws were informed by populationist ideas about the strength of a nation corresponding to its numbers, and rulers at first sought to achieve a larger population by stopping infanticide. The government inflicted ferocious penalties on women who killed their infants to avoid the shame of illegitimacy or to limit family size.[1] Such women were subjected to prolonged, painful execution. In the early eighteenth century, Peter I supplemented the existing negative sanctions for child murder with positive measures to save children. In 1712 he issued a decree calling for the establishment of institutions to care for abandoned and illegitimate children. These were not care institutions of the modern kind that attempted to stand in for missing parents and provide opportunities for advancement but simply a means for preserving young lives that could be used to build the strength of the state. The boys who survived went into military service; the girls, into factories or other work in support of the state or its servitors.[2]

Enlightenment

Later in the century, Empress Catherine II revived and extended the work begun by Peter I. The concern of her government about population growth found expression in her famous "Instruction" to the Legislative Commission of 1767–1768, which contained a startling assertion:

Art. 266. The peasants have generally from 12 to 15 or 20 children by one marriage, but rarely does a fourth part of them attain to the age of maturity. Wherefore there must certainly be some evil, either in their diet or in their manner of life, or in their education that is so destructive to this hope of the state. How flourishing would be the situation of this empire if it were possible by wise institutions to avert or prevent this fatal ruin.[3]

Although the source of these impressionistic statistics is not clear (possibly they were based on sketchy analyses of vital statistics done by Mikhail Lomonosov and other scholars at the St. Petersburg Academy of Sciences), Catherine could have added that death rates among Russians generally, not just peasants, were quite high in the imperial period. Population counts done in urban locales in the nineteenth century and family records of some members of the nobility and merchant class from the late eighteenth century confirm that losses of young children were often well over 50 percent.

Even before writing her Instruction, Catherine had launched a program to gather in and save unwanted children. This effort drew on the humanist impulse of the European Enlightenment and began with the assumption (later shown to be mistaken) that most of the unwanted and abandoned children were born out of wedlock. Instead of punishing unwed mothers, the idea was now to protect them from humiliation and the motivation to kill or abandon their children. Catherine established large urban foundling homes that accepted children without asking questions of the mothers (or others bringing in children). Catherine also furnished her foundling homes with associated lying-in hospitals and schools for midwives.

The collaborators in this project hoped that most of the children left at the foundling homes would be not merely saved but also educated in urban institutions, that they would become productive city dwellers. Yet the difficulties of keeping even a small minority of the children alive in the large urban homes soon forced administrators to farm the children out to village women for wet-nursing and rearing. Eventually, hundreds of thousands of children deposited at the homes ended up in the countryside. While this policy provided substantial supplemental income to village women who nursed and cared for the babies, it did little to improve the survival rate of the children. Fewer than 20 percent lived to maturity. This unfortunate child-welfare regime did not improve until the 1890s, when a major reform increased the time infants were able to spend with their biological mothers.

Catherine II's reign was also the time when manuals for birthing and child care first appeared in Russia. Early in her reign, the imperial foundling homes prepared a guidebook compiled from "the best writers about the upbringing of children from birth onward," a work that enjoyed at least six printings between 1766 and 1768.[4] A few years later, Dr. Semen Zybelin, a 1759 graduate of Moscow University who completed several years of study at Leyden's medical college, published two lectures that addressed the question of population growth and offered advice on how to care for infants and give them a better chance of surviving childhood. He spoke about a practice that has been a concern of Russian doctors ever since: the early introduction of solid food. "The common people usually on the second or third day after delivery," Zybelin wrote, "begin to give the babies heavy, thick food indigestible by infants," and this "more than any other cause leads to their illness and death."[5] Zybelin mentioned the idea, later reported frequently by Russian doctors working among the peasants, that people believed milk by itself to be insufficient nourishment and thought that the more solid food a baby ate, the faster and stronger it would grow. Zybelin's advice to rely on breast-feeding alone was in line with the emphasis in European medicine on natural feeding, as was that of other Russian medical writers of this time.[6] Zybelin's writing was also based on his own large clinical practice and keen powers of observation. He advised that mothers continue nursing until the baby teeth were fully grown, or for about 22 months, even though they could begin to introduce age-appropriate solid foods as the teeth emerged.[7]

While Zybelin was a clinician and professor (indeed, the first Slavic professor on Moscow University's medical faculty), another doctor from this era who shared his views was better known as an experimentalist. Dr. Stanislaus Pinas Ely, an official of the Medical Economic Chancellery, member of the Free Economic Society, and leading Freemason, supported his views against artificial feeding by working out the chemical properties of nonmaternal milk and its containers. He first described the principal contrivance for such feeding.

> In various provinces of the Russian empire, in cities as well as the countryside, and even in this glorious imperial capital, I have remarked with exceeding sadness that many infants, deprived of the breast, are fed by means of a device, which is quite harmful to their health and inevitably causes not only very many severe but even fatal childhood illnesses. This device consists of the following: they take a cow's horn, and, turning it over with the wide hole on top and the narrow point on the bottom (through which they bore a hole), they fasten a cow's teat onto it and then, pouring milk into the horn, they place it in the infant's mouth. This device is everywhere in Russia known as the horn [rozhok].[8]

Ely then did experiments on the acidity of artificial nipples and the chemical effects of horn-bottles and calculated the probable death rate of babies fed on the horn at about 70 percent. He was also critical of wealthy people, who, shunning the horn-bottle of the common folk, resorted instead to expensive containers made of silver and lined with copper. Ely's experiments with these devices convinced him that they, too, caused harmful changes to the milk and often brought death to the infants fed with them.[9]

This was also the time that Russia boasted its first native specialist in obstetrics, Dr. Nestor Maksimovich Maksimovich, better known as Maksimovich-Ambodik after Empress Catherine tagged him with this Latin nickname meaning "twice said" as a jest about the doubling in his patronymic and surname. Maksimovich went to school at the Kievan Academy, planned for a career in the law, and got his first job with Catherine's Legislative Commission. But, soon after, he developed an interest in nature and went abroad for seven years of study, principally in Strasbourg, where he took special courses in obstetrics. On his return to St. Petersburg, he was appointed to the State Medical Collegium and taught obstetrics to students at hospitals in the capital, eventually earning the title of Professor of Obstetrics. Among other works, Maksimovich produced a magisterial six-volume study of pregnancy and childbirth.[10] Appended to the final volume was a separate work designed for Russian doctors. It contained the latest scientific advice on how to recognize common misunderstandings about pregnancy and childbirth and avoid mistaken medical practices that often led to injury or the death of mothers and babies.[11]

Toward the end of Catherine's reign the first Russian medical magazine, the *St. Petersburg Medical News,* apparently trying to reach a larger public, published a lengthy article spread over several issues about the care and feeding of infants.[12] Apart from this article and the work of the foundling homes, however, child welfare in Catherine's era was largely a conversation among a few Western-educated scholars and officials. They extended their knowledge through clinical and experimental work while making some initial efforts to inform the small community of educated people in the major cities of the Russian empire. But as to touching Russian birthing and child-care practices at large, they had about as much effect as a stone skipping across the surface of an ocean. Government officials and the public still understood birthing and child care as wholly private acts and saw government action as possible only in connection with the prevention and punishment of child abandonment and murder, that is, when families denied protection to their offspring. The few people who gave thought to the question of Russian birthing and child-care practices more generally felt helpless before the size of the task and the difficulty even of obtaining sufficient information to assess the problem. In his experiments with his own clientele, for example, Dr. Stanislaus Ely collected data about the subjects' age and cause of death. But he remarked that to get similar information about Russia as a whole would, in view of its size and variety of climates and peoples, be even more difficult than to do so for all of Europe.

Demographic data did nevertheless become more abundant in the next era, the early nineteenth century, and scholars began to offer more detailed analyses of the population problem and high rates of childhood death. Using vital records for the years 1798–1806, Karl German, a German immigrant and member of the St. Petersburg Academy of Sciences, calculated that only 55 percent of Orthodox subjects attained age six and fewer than 50 percent made it to age ten. Another statistician worked on the St. Petersburg data and found that over 40 percent of children in the capital died by age five.[13] Growing knowledge of the high level of child death prompted further efforts from state officials to act where they could for the improvement of birthing and early child care. Alexander I's despotic favorite, Aleksei Arakcheev, for example, imposed a plan of regulated birthing and child care on the military settlements under his control. The plan called for birthing by experienced midwives who had trained with a doctor (and, in a reference to granny midwives, it strictly forbade the use of "decrepit old women with poor eyesight"). In regard to child care, the plan prescribed daily washings, breast-feeding until nine to ten months, no use of bottles or rag pacifiers, no swaddling, and no rocking or covering of cribs.[14] In other words, it sought to overturn most of the characteristic practices of child birth and care among the peasantry in Russia that doctors then regarded as particularly harmful.

In 1833 the Free Economic Society, a civic organization enjoying tsarist patronage, launched an international contest soliciting essays on how best to improve the survival chances of young children. A very lucrative monetary prize and medal attracted eighty-four entries. Reportedly, the judges were disappointed with the essays because none of the authors was sufficiently well acquainted with Russian peasant life to be able to propose workable solutions.[15] Even so, seven essays were singled out for recognition, and the grand prize went to Dr. I. R. Lichtenstedt, whose essay was published by the Free Economic Society in 1839. Using the vital records collected by the various bishoprics of Russia, Lichtenstedt worked out a reasonably accurate mapping of childhood death rates in the country, indicating mortality of somewhat under 50 percent to age five in the western provinces and greater than 50 percent in the eastern, southeastern, and far northern provinces, a breakdown that in broad outline fit with later, more thorough and sophisticated analyses. Like most of his contemporaries, Lichtenstedt tended to be pessimistic about the general issue of high childhood mortality, thinking that nature overproduced and then eliminated large numbers of all species and that humans were as subject to these laws as others. Demographic historians today sometimes refer to this understanding as the "wastage" theory of high fertility and high infant mortality. Lichtenstedt nevertheless separated what he regarded as "natural" causes of death from controllable ones. Controllable causes included an early introduction of solid food, poor nutrition in the mothers, the desire of people for fewer children (which led them to starve their infants or turn them over to wet nurses on such poor pay that the women had no incentive to feed the babies), bottle feeding, bad air, a lack of hygiene, congenital diseases such as syphilis, superstitious practices, excessive cradle rocking, and a reluctance to consult doctors. This list replicated some complaints of earlier Russian doctors and anticipated many objections of doctors working among the common people later in the century. Lichtenstedt also made some important behavioral observations. He recorded, for example, that many people regarded infant illness, especially convulsions, as something holy and untouchable. Equally dismaying, no doubt, were his discoveries that peasants recognized midwives and older women more than doctors as experts on infant care and that even when peasant families resorted to a doctor, they rejected the use of prescribed drugs, saying that *"they do not wish to torment the child to no purpose."*[16] These observations might be credited as the beginning of a cultural anthropology of parenting in Russia. They testify to Lichtenstedt's effort to understand the underlying spiritual and social determinants of peasant behavior and to a dawning appreciation of peasant childbirth and care as grounded in a cultural order different from that of urban professionals.

Lichtenstedt could not avoid mentioning the chief expression of child welfare in Russia at the time, the imperial foundling homes. He was enough of a politician to praise the achievements of these tsarist institutions, but he added that he preferred the German (Protestant) policy of holding fathers responsible for the children they produced and not giving parents the option of depositing illegitimate or unwanted children at the doorstep of the state. Even if his solution led to an increase of infanticides, he wrote, it was preferable to the foundling homes, which were an encouragement to immorality. He also criticized the use of private wet nurses by those who could afford their services and seemed to believe (mistakenly) that the practice was exclusive to Russia.[17]

The ultimate solution, according to Lichtenstedt, lay in education. He proposed the establishment in every province of midwifery schools and of societies to report on neglected children. Although his proposals for education, trained midwives, and greater supervision did not produce practical results at the time, they did point in the direction of future action.[18]

Professor Stepan Khotovitskii, another contributor to the contest,[19] likewise focused on external manifestations of what urban doctors then regarded as poor child-care practices, such as heavy swaddling, bad air, overheating of babies on the stove, feeding them crusts of bread and herbal medicines in their first few days of life, or infrequent bathing. Like Lichtenstedt and his late-eighteenth-century predecessors, whose studies were based on statistics too crude and rounded to reveal the association between mortality and seasonal occupational factors, Khotovitskii was not able to probe the complex links between economic issues, seasonal epidemics, and infant deaths that became central to later assessments. Moreover, the discoveries of bacteriology were still decades away. Doctors of the 1830s continued to think in terms of miasmatic theories of disease. Foul air, decaying refuse, and excesses of heat or cold were considered primary causes of disease. It is worth noting, too, that although these medical writers recognized a difference between their own practices and those of the common people, they did not express their advice and criticism in harsh, combative language that branded the peasants as a dark, backward herd nor did they describe them as some horrible departure from normal humanity. These men represented the scientific and technical professionals of the Enlightenment age, professionals who, no longer accepting the chaos of life, believed that life processes could be subjected to human control and thus improved, perhaps ultimately even perfected. Yet since the practices and mortality of their urban and even privileged clientele were not so different in this age from those of the peasants, they did not see peasants as altogether alien and did not refer to them in the stereotypical and patronizing language that became common later on.

New Observations and Missionary Zeal

By the 1860s and 1870s, Russian scholars were acquiring a fuller appreciation of the social and cultural causes of infant mortality. An increasing number of medical-topographic surveys were conducted of specific locales and peoples, and this type of study allowed for a clearer understanding of the processes affecting health. V. S. Snigirev completed such a medical dissertation in 1863 on the province of Stavropol, in which he emphasized the importance of cultural factors and drew telling comparisons between different peoples. He observed that Armenians living in Stavropol province supported themselves mainly by commerce and were better educated than other groups, and the Armenian women there stayed at home to take care of their infant children. Consequently, they did better than the Russians with their children. "The sphere of activity for an Armenian mother is family life; for a mother not to nurse her own infant is as much a rarity as it is for a Russian mother to feed her child exclusively on the breast. [Armenian mothers] do not suffer dire need and therefore do not abandon their children and hire themselves out as wet nurses." Here Snigirev was repeating Lichtenstedt's mistaken notion that among European peoples private wet-nursing was something only Russian women did. In fact, the practice was quite common in France and most of the other Catholic countries of Europe. Snigirev likewise mentioned the success Jews had with their children and quoted a Prussian study to this effect. He was working against prevailing ideas that a high rate of infant mortality was inevitable and arguing that the economy and culture were strong determinants. He found his best evidence in the high rates of infant death among Russians in the summer months, which he linked directly to the need of Russian women to do field work at that time and therefore either to nourish their babies inadequately or put them on indigestible solid foods. Unfortunately, he remarked, Russian mothers took pride in the fact that they could subject their infants to extremes of temperature and an early introduction of solid foods.[20] This explanation on the part of peasant mothers would be noted subsequently by many other doctors, and I heard it even in my interviews with women about the children they had in the first half of the twentieth century. They seemed to believe that their practices inured children to hardship and that, while many died, the survivors were extraordinarily hardy.[21]

Snigirev summarized his important findings in an article that appeared in 1867 in the influential journal *The Archives of Forensic Medicine and Social Hygiene*. Again, he spent much time on social and economic issues, which he saw as associated with the incomplete emancipation of the serfs and the slavish position of women in peasant society. To strengthen his point that social conditions affected health more than did circumstances of climate or resources, he added comparisons with the Baltic region. This area he argued, despite its poor soil did better than Russia in preserving infant life because of its better communications, working conditions, and cultural development.[22] Comparative analyses of this kind were to appear in increasing numbers in the 1880s and afterward (see later discussion).

About the same time as Snigirev was writing, an archpriest responsible for towns and villages in northeastern Novgorod province published an enormous study on fertility and infant mortality. In this work, printed by the Russian Geographical Society, he detailed vital records for the years 1835–1855, including breakdowns by social class. The author, Father F. V. Giliarovskii, found the death rates for children to age seven in the small towns of the region to be about 50 percent (a bit better overall for peasants and merchants than for Old Believers and ordinary townspeople [*meshchane*]).[23] His work was idiosyncratic and couched in a condescending and moralistic language that set the tone for some later medical studies made by crusading populist and rural public-health (*zemstvo*) doctors. For example, Giliarovskii lambasted mothers among the townspeople (*meshchanstvo*) because of what he regarded as a fashion for avoiding breast-feeding. "I have seen that young mothers of the towns in full health and able to nurse their children deny them the breast and as a result either give birth yearly or suffer terrible mastitis but, even so, generally deprive their children. Despite such bitter experiences, I know that such a fashion is growing each year."[24]

But if he disliked the women of the towns, his characteristically populist stance allowed him to sympathize with peasant women, whose enslavement to the rhythm of the agrarian cycle cruelly interacted with the rhythm of their fertility. He was the first to observe the powerful effects of the relationship between procreation and seasonal work requirements. He pointed out that the high frequency of conceptions in the post-harvest season of celebration yielded a high number of births in the following year just at the time of heavy work in the fields. Some village women, Giliarovskii lamented, had several abortions in a row because the anticipated births would have interfered with their work. As a result, they ended up not being able to conceive at all, debilitated from the aftereffects of abortions, and shamed for not having had children. The women who conceived in the fall and chose to carry their babies to term delivered the children just before the field-work season and consequently had to leave them at home all day without breast milk and often without much supervision. In this connection, he related stories of neglected babies being eaten by pigs and falling victim to other grim fates. Because the mothers were not nursing, Giliarovskii continued, they conceived soon again in a cycle that produced another baby at the start of the next work season. In short, the women were pregnant much of the time and suffering this burden and its attendant illnesses, plus they gave birth too often, and most of the babies died.[25] Indeed, by Giliarovskii's calculations, 80 percent of babies born in the summer months did not live out the year.

Giliarovskii's counts also revealed an appalling loss of life among the women themselves. One-seventeenth, or nearly 59 per 1,000, of the women married during the twenty-year period of his survey died in childbirth. And this counted only deaths directly associated with birthing. Quoting the Russian proverb "The coffin lid does not close for a birthing mother until forty days pass," Giliarovskii calculated that about again as many deaths occurred to mothers in this post-natal period, so that the actual risk of maternal death for a woman in the region was somewhat greater than 10 percent through the course of her child-bearing years.[26] It is not surprising then that Russian women commonly said their "last farewells" to family and friends before delivery.

Giliarovskii's study with its rare statistics, strong point of view, and vivid stories created a sensation at the time of its publication and was honored with the Zhukovskii Prize and Small Gold Medal of the Russian Geographic Society. It also exerted a powerful influence on subsequent medical writers, many of whom cited his work and even adopted his language in building their own portrayals of rural misery.

Other local studies of central Russian lands during this period added to the growing impression in urban society that the peasants existed in a different, loutish reality and that Russia's salvation required a civilizing mission. A zemstvo doctor, Mikhail Shmelev, published a study in 1868 based on his practice in Iaroslav province. Though looking at the entire range of public health issues, he focused on high rates of syphilis and untreated gynecological disorders and the problems they caused for fertility. Like many other zemstvo doctors who sympathized with the plight of peasants, he nonetheless was distressed at their "ignorance, poverty, and coarse manners" and emphasized the need to civilize them. Villagers, he commented, gave no special consideration to pregnant women. Assistance at birthing "consisted mainly of supporting the mother under her arms and dragging her around until she lost consciousness, shaking her, and grabbing whatever part of the baby first appeared and pulling it out with not the slightest thought to the course and process of birth, and other similarly barbaric methods."[27] After giving birth, he added, the mother enjoyed little time to recover. As far as feeding infants, Shmelev dismissed this discouraging issue with the comment that it consisted solely in "the most ignorant and most harmful stuffing of a child full of all kinds of, and primarily unsuitable kinds of, victuals."[28]

Other investigations of central Russian rural populations were producing equally dismaying information. P. A. Peskov, author of a major and often cited study of a township in northern Moscow province in the 1870s, bemoaned the poverty and ignorance that was behind the high mortality statistics and, again like Lichtenstedt and Snigirev, attacked the foundling-home policy of hiring rural women as wet nurses. Peskov stood aghast at the spectacle of wet nurses picking up nurslings at the foundling homes and then selling the babies and accompanying pay booklets to women without breast milk, therefore ensuring the early death of the fosterlings. Peskov dubbed this practice "a special type of disgraceful commerce that reminds one of pagan times or even prehistoric conditions."[29] He nevertheless associated the largest share of the infant deaths with epidemic levels of diarrhea and dysentery that were especially virulent in the summer months and therefore correlated with the infant mortality peaks in that period. Like others, he cited the lack of basic hygiene and such "false ideas" as the use of cow's milk, the need to feed kasha and other foods to babies because mother's milk alone would not suffice to nourish an infant, and the need for babies to observe fasts as adults did, to name a few.[30] A year after Peskov's study, Pavel Griaznov finished a medical dissertation on Cherepovets district in the northern lakes region, just west of the city of Vologda. He blamed the high rate of infant mortality there on "the lack of a sensible diet for babies from the very day of birth. Whenever a mother has to go away to work or even when she is busy at home, the babies are fed cow's milk that has often soured through a putrid horn or given a 'chaw' [zhvachka] of moistened bread or kasha wrapped in a rag. Nearly daily in my zemstvo practice I have to examine dozens of children who have enlarged stomachs and are suffering from intestinal catarrh." Griaznov added that Giliarovskii had seen babies left alone with this type of chaw or rag pacifier tied to their hands. Mothers are so ignorant, he continued, that "they react with surprise when you tell them that a month-old baby should not be fed with bread and kasha. In the four years I have spent in the district, not a summer has gone by without widespread epidemics of bloody flux in the children."[31]

The "chaw" that Griaznov referred to is usually called zhvachka or soska in Russian and misleadingly translated nowadays as "pacifier," perhaps because it has been replaced in recent times with the familiar rubber or plastic pacifier that is also known as a soska. The rag soska was meant to pacify but to do so by feeding the infant. As earlier comments reflect, Russian peasant women considered the soska part of the normal dietary regimen and regarded it as an essential contribution to a baby's growth. Not surprisingly, Russian doctors were alarmed to learn that the soska was used almost continually in the summer when the mother's help was needed in working the fields. Many times it was the child's only source of nourishment from early dawn until the return of the mother in the evening.[32] The gap separating peasant culture and urban medical society can be measured by their different readings of a sign associated with this practice. The soska often putrefied and left around the baby's mouth a moldy residue that doctors believed to be a sign of the pathogens causing the summer diarrheas fatal to many infants. Village women reportedly interpreted the residue as a positive sign that the baby was receiving the nourishment it required. They referred to the mold as a "flower in the mouth" and said that the baby's mouth was "blossoming."[33]

Not all doctors blamed the heavy toll of infant death on the soska. Some populist doctors sympathized with the lot of the peasant mother and argued that this ubiquitous device of infant care was less harmful than its critics believed. V. I. Nikol'skii, who published his medical dissertation in 1885 on conditions in Tambov district of Tambov province, was such a writer. He liked to use peasant life as a foil for criticizing urban practices, and contrasted the "abnormal and sickly" life of educated women with the sound, natural life of peasant women. He not only repeated the commonplace that educated women were subject to all sorts of nervous disorders not found among the peasantry but also claimed that peasant women were "incomparably more valued" than their urban counterparts. Further, he compared the bride price paid for a peasant woman to the dowry the bride's family paid upon an educated woman's marriage It said to him that peasant women had value for which their parents had to be compensated, whereas urban women had to pay men to accept them! He could not deny the coarse personal relations among peasants, but contended that they

> do not limit the full respect a peasant woman enjoys as a person, whereas in our refined world behind its gallantry and courtesy lies a complete and thinly veiled contempt for women. The fabled "woman question," which enjoys so much attention from the privileged classes, the common people settle once and for all by the very simplest division of labor, from which definitively and clearly flows the rights and obligations of each sex.[34]

Nikol'skii nevertheless had to admit that this ennobling labor was the source of many physical, if not emotional, disorders. Like others, he saw that the rhythms of agrarian life worked an especially great hardship on a woman's childbirth and child-care obligations. Referring to the heavy work of weeding and tying sheaves under the hot summer sun that women did just at the time they were most likely to give birth, he remarked:

> Pregnancy does not excuse peasant women from weeding and harvesting equally with other workers. Birth in the fields is no rarity. Muscular effort, exhaustion, and poor diet undoubtedly affect the fetus. . . . After delivery a woman here usually returns to field work and the heaviest labor after just three days, something that is done even after pathological births! It is clear that her milk cannot meet even minimal standards. The situation for a woman in the field is familiar to everyone: heat, intense work, unbearable thirst, and foul drinking water.[35]

These conditions of life and work were the culprit, according to Nikol'skii. He mentioned Peskov's view that epidemic disease caused the loss of infant life but rejected it, writing that the only epidemic in his region was childhood diarrhea, which strictly speaking was not an epidemic disease but a result of everyday practices (*byt*) and socio-economic conditions, in other words, the poor care and feeding to which other medical writers were more and more pointing.[36]

As for the soska and the diseases associated with it, Nikol'skii contended that a mother had little choice. She had to care for the entire family and do all the domestic work, in addition to field tasks, and "it is not surprising that she uses [the soska] for the sake of something to occupy the baby and keep it from crying so that she can have at least a moment's peace. For this, the soska is a godsend." He felt that too much was attributed to the soska; people were even proposing that the zemstvo should distribute rubber pacifiers to replace the rag version. While Nikol'skii refused to defend the peasants' right to their soskas ("Nothing could be more repulsive," he remarked), he pointed out that these rags were used year-round, not just in the summertime. The cause of high infant-mortality rates must lie somewhere else: in hunger, poorly prepared food, and foul water, he believed.[37]

For all Nikol'skii's sympathy for the peasant woman as a mother, he had nothing but anger and contempt for her in the role of midwife. "No words can describe how they torment each birthing mother," Nikol'skii raged.

> Every birth is an act of torture inflicted by the *babka* on the mother, an act which is provided for in the code of criminal law but not unfortunately for this particular case. This is not the place to describe these shocking manipulations, beginning with cramming the mother's braid down her throat, insistent walking of her to the point of collapsing in suffocation, and ending in the tearing of the umbilicus or the prolapsing of the uterus at a breech birth when several *babki* together use their hands to pull out the baby with all their strength, having thus conspired in a counsel for the most certain death of the mother.[38]

The ferocity of this attack was not unusual. Many Russian doctors wrote in similar terms, using the worst examples of village birthing care. It is interesting to note that criticisms of this type were being leveled at the same time by obstetricians in the United States and elsewhere against midwives in their communities. The motives of U.S. doctors, however, seem to have been rather different. Studies about midwives and obstetricians in the United States stress the importance of the two groups as competitors for the business of birthing.[39] In Russia, financial motives played less of a role. Russian physicians did not expect to earn money by treating villagers. They thought of themselves as cultural pioneers on a mission to uplift the common people and bring them into the modern world. Their satisfaction came from changing what they saw as the peasants' barbaric, primitive existence and from their feeling of superiority over the "dark" people whom they infantilized and pretended to be guiding to a new and better way of life.

Finally, it should be noted that these local studies gained impact as a result of broader concerns in post-reform Russia about loss of control, death, and degeneracy.[40] The medical surveys referenced here arose from and reinforced these concerns. These and other health studies prompted new efforts by the government to understand the underlying causes of mortality. One such effort was a commission established in January 1886 under the direction of S. P. Botkin by the Ministry of Internal Affairs to investigate this question. The Botkin Commission in turn asked the newly formed Society of Pediatricians in St. Petersburg to act as a subcommittee for looking specifically at infant mortality in the villages and the cities. Although the commission identified the many causes of mortality in different sectors and age groups of the population, it did not produce an explicit program for dealing with them other than to propose the establishment of a Central Office of Public Health.[41] It would take further discoveries of grim losses of life among Russian children to provoke society and government into more concrete efforts. Undoubtedly the increasing number of studies that began to appear on the extraordinarily high mortality rates among Russians as compared to other peoples of the empire were an important impetus to greater action.

Comparative Studies

In the next few years, a number of health studies came out that treated regions of the country containing large populations of non-Russian peoples. The studies not only documented in more convincing detail than before the staggeringly high mortality of Russian children but also the much lower mortality of the neighboring non-Russian populations such as Bashkirs, Tatars, Votiaks (Udmurts), and Jews, whom many educated Russians thought of as miserable, dominated, and backward. These revelations carried a special sting in this age of growing ethnic-Russian nationalism.

Similar studies of the Baltic region showed unfavorable comparisons of Russian and non-Russian child mortality, but most Russians probably did not find it surprising that these peoples would have better success with their children.[42] They lived to the west in an area dominated by German culture. The results of detailed studies of mixed Jewish and Russian or Belorussian populations, however, were more embarrassing. The earliest of these that appeared from the late 1880s to 1905 were more anthropological than medical and did not contain startling revelations about mortality. Among them were the huge study of Jews in the southwestern provinces by P. P. Chubinskii and a smaller work by M. Berlin.[43] These authors provided valuable information about child care, diet, living conditions, and customs but did not collect vital records for use in comparing Jewish demographic experience with that of their neighbors. Even when scholars began to produce medical-topographic surveys of areas of large Jewish settlement in the late 1880s and 1890s, their ignorance of cultural practices and demography led them to accept absurd reports of vital records that erased the significant differences between the infant and childhood mortality of Jews and their Orthodox neighbors. For example, the authors of three otherwise useful studies of the cities of Mogilev and Minsk took at face value reports that Jewish families were producing from 170 to 210 boys to every 100 girls, a statistical anomaly produced by the failure of many Jews to register the births of their daughters. Jews could not, however, avoid registering the deaths of their daughters, and, accordingly, these studies showed the proportion of childhood deaths to births to be much higher for Jews than it actually was.[44] The only study from this period that got it right was I. Feitel'berg's survey of the Baltic coast city of Windau in Kurland, which reported on a small population of Jews and Christians of three denominations (Orthodox, Lutheran, and Catholic) in the years 1879–1893. As later was found to be the case nearly everywhere, Jewish infant mortality in Windau proved to be one-half that of the Orthodox and also well under that of the Lutherans.[45] A few years later, when the extensive and detailed information of the first all-Russian census of 1897 at last allowed a thorough and sophisticated comparison of the success of various ethnic groups in caring for their children, it became plain that Jewish infant and childhood mortality in European Russia as a whole was substantially less than half that of the Orthodox, mainly Russian, population and below that of all other groups as well.[46]

Researchers who assembled these figures had difficulty explaining them. They knew that a large majority of Jews lived in poor sanitary conditions and often in difficult economic circumstances as well, not to mention the threat of brutality from their non-Jewish neighbors. To give just one example, even where the number of people per household among Jews was twice that of the surrounding Christian population, the mortality differentials held.[47] In the absence of measurable conditions that would explain the extraordinary success of Jewish parents, some observers, including writers who in other respects were not complimentary to Jews, suggested cultural explanations, noting that Jews looked after their children better than others and made sacrifices to bring sick children back to health. "They are devoted to their family and very loving of their children," wrote one anthropologist.[48] Dr. Koshelev found that the Jews in Mogilev lived no better in economic terms, and probably worse, than their neighbors but that they took much better care of their children and always saw to it that sick children received medical assistance.[49] "Evidently," wrote one team of analysts, "a big role is played by a combination of all those factors known under the general term of civilized behavior, including internalized civility and civility of the spirit, because in outward appearance with regard to nutrition, clothing, cleanliness, housing, and the like, the Jewish masses exist on a rather low level."[50]

If the Jewish success could be explained somehow by a distinctive civility and greater use of medical doctors, what about the Muslim peoples of the Volga? It turned out that they, too, had comparatively low rates of infant mortality. For Orthodox peoples of the empire as a whole in 1896–1897, infant mortality ran to 284 deaths per 1,000 live births (rates rose to nearly one-third for the provinces of predominantly Russian settlement), while for the Muslim population it was 166.[51] The contrast was most striking in the very regions where

Russians and Volga Muslims lived in close proximity. It could therefore not be explained away by better climate or resources, or more healthful environments for the Muslims. In Penza province during the 1880s the infant mortality rate for Orthodox peoples outside the city of Penza was 342 per 1,000 live births, while for the Muslims it was 140.[52] In Kazan province at the end of the century, mortality among the Orthodox in the first year of life was 304 per 1,000; among the Muslims it was 161.[53] These figures at first struck Russian doctors working in the region as so improbable that they did special checks for accuracy. One of the first to do so was Sergei Ershov, a physician trained at Kazan University and working in a Volga district of mixed Tatar and Russian settlement. He conducted a thorough review of the vital records for his villages from the 1850s into the 1880s, including a comparison of 1858 cadastres with the household lists from 1884. Finding a close correspondence in all the registers, Ershov concluded that "the very low figures shown for the deaths of [Tatar] children are not a result of shortcomings or omissions in the records."[54] Later studies of Tatars in Astrakhan and Penza provinces included similarly detailed checks and likewise found the records to be accurate.[55] It can be added that the figures also meet basic modern demographic checks for authenticity such as age-appropriate sex ratios and comparisons of census data with household and family lists. The mullahs, who kept the registers of fertility and mortality for the Muslim peoples, evidently did their work conscientiously.

The doctors who worked in the areas of Tatar settlement came to their assignments with stereotyped preconceptions that colored their descriptions of the people. In most cases, they viewed the Tatars as alien and stubbornly committed to their way of life, despite three hundred years of living under Russian rule. They sometimes expressed thinly veiled contempt for what they saw as the Tatars' easy-going style, alleged inability to manage farms efficiently, and lack of interest in agricultural work. Tatars, according to these sources, were more inclined to do animal husbandry, artisanal work, and petty trading. They were sometimes referred to as "the Jews" of the eastern half of the empire.[56] N. I. Teziakov, who did a study of infant mortality in Saratov province, even found the Tatars there to be living in dire straits, usually half-starving and "in dirty conditions."[57]

This last comment is unusual. Even writers who did not particularly like Tatars almost uniformly gave them high marks for cleanliness. Nineteenth-century writers noted the Muslims' ritual cleansing five times a day before prayer. They referred even more often to the regular (daily or at least weekly) washing down of floors and furniture in Tatar homes. The steam bath was also in frequent use, and in these baths Tatars plucked out the hairs from their underarms and, in the case of females, from their pubic area.[58] So, a cult of cleanliness reigned, which extended on the one side to whitewashing of homes several times a year and on the other to small daily tasks such as milking, during which women wore "large aprons, cleanse[d] the udders with warm water, and cover[ed] the milk pail with a clean towel."[59] This well-attested neatness continues to be an important identity marker for Tatars to this day. Many of my Tatar informants took pride in the fact that they kept their homes and themselves much cleaner than did the Russians or Chuvash with whom they were acquainted. With regard to the question of infant mortality, however, it is far from clear that this tidiness would have had much of an effect in protecting children from disease agents in the environment before the introduction of water filtration and antisepsis.

What quickly became apparent to nineteenth-century observers was the striking difference between Russian and Tatar feeding of their infants, a difference that by itself seemed fully adequate to explain the much greater success of the Tatars in keeping their infants alive. A. E. Romanov was one of the earliest writers to comment on this when he was doing yearly reports in the 1880s on illness in Penza province:

> According to [Muslim] law, as a mullah explained to me, Tatar women are obliged to breast-feed their children for two years, and they actually follow this rule. Moreover, if their breast milk is adequate, Tatar women will feed the children exclusively on the breast, not using any surrogates. In contrast, Russian mothers breast-feed no more than a year and from the day of birth begin to use solid foods such as kasha, chewed-up bread, cow's milk, and the like. Sticking out of the baby's mouth continually is a soska made from a cow's teat or a rag filled with chewed bread. It is understandable that this kind of feeding, especially in the summertime when high temperatures quickly putrefy these substitutes for breast milk and babies are left for whole days at a time or even a month in the care of old grannies or little girls, creates favorable conditions for the development of diarrhea.[60]

Sergei Ershov, in his study in Kazan province, observed that Russian mothers sometimes gave up breast-feeding in the first weeks after birth. Burdened by work, he wrote, they could give only snatches of time to their children. "In some villages of Sviiazh district (especially those lying closest to the Volga River), it is even accepted as customary that [Russian] mothers will nurse their children for only two weeks, and then they go on to being nourished with chaws made from black bread, kasha, biscuits, and even cakes [prianiki] (as a treat)." The result of the different regimens of Russians and Tatars was easily seen in the first-year mortality rates for this district, which were 175 per 1,000 for the Tatars and 432 per 1,000 for the Russians (as high as 467 per 1,000 for Russians in one Volga township).[61]

Even writers who criticized Tatar women for indolence confirmed the point about their attention to child care. For example, Ivan Blagovidov, who published his medical dissertation in 1886 on the native peoples of Simbirsk province, told of the supposedly soft life that all but the poorest Tatar women lived. They stayed at home and gave most of their thought to eating and cosmetics. Their main occupation, Blagovidov seemed to complain, was child care.[62] Another doctor, who worked among the prosperous Tatars of Astrakhan province, noted some other circumstances that may have contributed to their success with their children, including a low level of illegitimacy, better economic conditions than the Russians, and no baptism (and thus no exposure to the cold in the early days of life); but he, too, recognized that all these matters paled in comparison to the differences between Russian and Tatar feeding and early child care.[63]

The medical researchers found a number of things particularly interesting about the Tatars. First, they seemed to be free of the grip of seasonal cycles that affected the other ethnic groups and that were especially devastating in the case of the Russians. Tatar births occurred more evenly throughout the year than did the Russians and did not show the typical Russian peak of births in the summer months when disease agents harmful to infants were most active and could carry away the greatest proportion of children. Second, the researchers were impressed with the apparent lack of correlation between economic conditions and success in child survival. Even where poor Tatar families lived in the same vicinity as better-off Russian families, the Tatars did much better in bringing their children through the first year of life. In other words, the two ethnic groups lived in self-enclosed systems of fertility, early child care, and mortality that seemed to be little influenced by their shared climate, topography, and environmental resource base or by one another's practices. Sergei Ershov pointed out that in some of the villages he studied half the inhabitants were Russians and half Tatars, and despite this closeness, in the summer "every single Russian child suffers from diarrhea, while the Tatar children are all healthy." And the explanation, according to Ershov, was obvious. "The Tatar mothers strictly avoid bottle feeding or solid food. Only in cases of extreme need do they use the so-called *al'va*" (a "soska" made of fresh ingredients and heated before use, making it less pathogenic than the type employed by the Russians). He added that Father Giliarovskii had many years earlier made the point about this harmful Russian practice of using cow-teat soskas as feeding devices.[64] M. M. Kenigsberg, who worked among the mixed ethnic population of Orenburg province, likewise marveled at the differences between Russians and Tatars; he rejected the findings of some other studies that tried to show a correlation between mortality and such objective measures as levels of ground water or humidity. How could all these common variables be given weight, he asked, in light of such large differences between two ethnic groups who live side-by-side? "This phenomenon can be attributed, in our view, exclusively to the fact that the Quran requires Muslim women to feed their children only on the breast for two years, and they strictly adhere to that rule."[65]

Additionally, doctors working among the Eastern Finnic peoples likewise reported a lower infant mortality among these peoples than among the Russians. The Finnic peoples did not do nearly so well as the Muslims and Jews because their practices in many respects resembled those of the Russians. But they were more consistently breast-feeders and resorted less often to the soska.

From the 1880s onward, reports on conditions in Russian villages and on the contrasts between Russians and other peoples of the empire played an increasing role in public discussions at medical congresses, both local and national, and in the medical press and social welfare press. The Pirogov Society of Russian Physicians, which held biennial congresses starting in 1885, included a session on infant mortality as a permanent feature of its program.[66] The issue came up regularly at provincial congresses as well, where many of the findings about the differential outcomes for the various nationalities were first reported and analyzed.[67] The accounts of care in Russian villages became more specific and vivid. Take the report by one of the best-known zemstvo physicians and public spokespersons, Dmitrii Zhbankov. He told about child care in the summer of 1883 in the village of Bol'shoe, where 71 families had small children. In 25 of these families, Zhbankov wrote, parents left their children for the whole day in the care of girls aged six to eight; in 31 families, they left them with an old male or female relative "who very often was half blind or barely able to move"; in 6 families, they hired an old woman to watch the children; and in 9, they took the children to the fields with them. "With small variations," he declared, "you can see the same thing in June, July, and August in every village in Russia." In another account, Dr. M. N. Ovsova, who was fighting yearly epidemics of summer diarrhea among the children of Kostroma province, portrayed a similar scene of entering a village during the season of field work and finding not a single able-bodied person. She walked into a home and saw that "on the bench by the crib lies an old woman suffering from dropsy, the oldest member of the family. In the corner by the door lie two girls, one seven and the other nine, and next to them is a mug with soured kvas. In the crib a baby is crying itself hoarse. The old woman is barely hanging onto the line for rocking the crib, while next to the infant bobs a soska filled with kasha."[68] When reports like these were contrasted with the more positive accounts of how Tatars, Jews, and Finns looked after their children, the medical community's anger rose. How could it be, the doctors and popular press wanted to know, that the minority peoples of the empire were doing so much better than the Russians themselves? The observations on the strikingly different results quickly became a rhetorical weapon in the fight to gain more resources for improving the condition of Russian families. Typical was the stance of Dr. Nikol'skii in his study of Penza province. The statistics on Muslim infant mortality, he wrote, "constitute a living reproach to our populace. These results are after all obtained right here within the borders of Penza province, and therefore should be attainable for the rest of the population as well. And if this is so, how many innocent victims are perishing as a result of our negligence and inattention? Is this not a form of child murder and are we not guilty of failing to extend assistance to the dying?"[69]

The difference in the results among minority peoples also persuaded the doctors that the carnage of Russian children was not caused primarily by economic conditions. They understood the high mortality rate as a matter of stubbornly maintained "irrational" feeding practices that appeared in all the families, whether prosperous or poor. Speaking for many others, Dr. Kenigsberg concluded: "The infant soska, chaw, and their accompaniments can be found everywhere, even in wealthy families, despite simultaneous feeding by other means, even including breast-feeding. . . . In wealthy merchant homes, we have encountered the most shocking ignorance in regard to the care and feeding of their infants. There is also a deeply rooted conviction in the majority of the population that you should not try to cure young children because everything is caused by teething. So, this is why we say that *mental poverty* and *parental ignorance* play at times *a bigger role than poverty*."[70]

A lengthy, statistically sophisticated, and detailed report appearing in 1902 on infant and childhood mortality in Moscow province left no doubt that the problem was not only acute but also as evident in this backyard of the ancient capital as anywhere in the country.[71] Government leaders and the medical community were by now fully convinced of the need for action to improve the situation, but it was difficult to know what might be effective. If the cause of high death rates among children lay in deeply rooted cultural practices reinforced by seasonal work rhythms, the solution would have to include a transformation of the villagers' way of life. But just how would one begin such a process?

Village Obstetrical Care and Summer Nurseries

The one approach to combating infant mortality in the villages that had been tried with public support before the end of the nineteenth century was the provision of trained midwives to the villages. Initially, the only institutions in Russia to train midwives were urban hospitals and, above all, the foundling home medical wards, which had begun educating them during Catherine II's reign. These institutions were the source of the few trained midwives who reached the countryside in the first half of the nineteenth century in response to requests from military settlements, reformed state peasant communities, and a few landlords.[72] Additional midwife training became available during the reform era of the 1860s and 1870s when schools of midwifery were established in some provincial towns. Most of the students came from towns and were expected to go into urban practice, but in the case of a few zemstvo-sponsored schools, efforts were made to direct the graduates to service in the countryside. When it turned out that few of the graduates were interested in careers in the village, the sponsors came up with the quaint idea of recruiting young peasant women for the schools. They insisted that the women continue to wear peasant dress during their courses of study in town so that on completion of their studies they would be able to reenter village life just as before, except that they would now be educated in scientific obstetrical practices. For a number of reasons this scheme did not work as expected. Despite the hopes of the sponsors, the young peasant trainees were more inclined to use the opportunity as a route out of the village than to return to a life of service among the peasants. Trained midwives, whether of urban or rural origin, found little demand for their services in the village. Peasant women preferred older, experienced women to assist them at birth, women who knew the prayers and spells critical to a smooth delivery and healthy child. Moreover, traditional village midwives did not limit their services exclusively to deliveries, as did trained midwives. The traditional midwives were not above accepting the additional responsibility of helping out around the house in the first hours and days after delivery. Resistance also came from the zemstvo's male peasant delegates, who objected to taxes for such services and did so in the colorful, contemptuous language with which rural men sometimes referred to women.

> Our women give birth like cows in a barn or in some other isolated place and often when they are out mowing hay 30 versts or so from home. Right after giving birth the woman will take the newborn in the hem of her sarafan or shirt and bring it home by herself. [An old woman then takes her and the baby through all the usual rituals] but in any case, like a cow, she drops a baby and gets up and goes; cows don't need a trained midwife, and so why should our women?[73]

Another impediment was that medically trained midwives had difficulty demonstrating their superiority even in the purely medical aspects of birthing. Birth was a natural process, and in most cases it went smoothly whether or not the midwife had hospital training. If complications arose, the medical midwife was in no better position than the traditional village midwife to handle the situation. She would know not to intervene heroically and do harm, as some village midwives did, but the opportunity to demonstrate this skillful reserve was rare enough that the advantages she offered over the traditional ways were hard to perceive. These observations prompted proposals to recruit from among traditional practicing midwives and give them a short course in hygiene and proper methods of delivery, but this approach, too, yielded poor results.

After these false starts, the early years of the new century brought proposals to have obstetrical services dispensed not by women specializing in midwifery but by ordinary medical staff, such as a female physician's assistants (fel'dsheritsy). These women would be able to establish a reputation as effective healers through their normal medical practice and thus eventually win the trust of birthing mothers as well. The proposals and efforts to implement birthing assistance for the Russian village were accompanied by vigorous debate at medical congresses and in the press, but the ultimate impact was small.[74] By the turn of the century possibly as many as 2 percent of rural births were assisted by medical personnel, and progress beyond that point continued to be painfully slow, right up to the end of the imperial period.[75]

Efforts to keep children alive once they were born started much later than the programs for training midwives, but once such efforts got going, they developed rapidly. A zemstvo doctor from Perm, N. A. Russkikh, began agitating

in the late 1890s for the creation of national and international organizations
dedicated to reducing infant mortality. In 1904 he won the support of the Pirogov Society of Russian Physicians and the Russian Society of Public Health for
the establishment of the All-Russian Union for Combating Infant Mortality,
which opened in December of that year. Even earlier, starting in 1901, charitable societies began organizing urban milk kitchens; modeled on West European and American institutions and known as "Drop of Milk," they provided
not only fresh milk for infants but also advice to mothers on child care.[76]

The preferred method of assisting villagers became the establishment of
summer nurseries. This solution arose logically from the observation that the
rhythm of rural work and fertility produced the largest number of births in the
summer, just when the babies were least likely to be fed and cared for by their
mothers. Even before Dr. Russkikh's union was formed, some rural nurseries
had been set up as isolated acts of individual charity. Princess Boriatinskaia
started one of the first nurseries on her estates in Riazan province in 1890. The
idea soon caught on with a number of zemstvo doctors, who established summer nurseries in their own regions and then reported on them at medical congresses and in books presenting detailed statistical findings of their impact.
Among the most active promoters of summer nurseries were Dmitrii Zhbankov, Nikolai Teziakov, Zinovii Solov'ev, and P. Kudriavtsev. A large study by
Kudriavtsev appearing in 1900 about his work in Simbirsk province was a key
text. Its first 200 pages surveyed the creation of summer nurseries up to that
point, and the rest of the study presented detailed descriptions and statistical
analyses of the efforts in his region. A. I. Shingarev, a well-known zemstvo physician and spokesperson for the peasantry of Voronezh province, likewise fostered a network of summer nurseries in his region.[77] These efforts, however,
remained scattered and uncoordinated until after the upheavals of the Russo-
Japanese War and Revolution of 1905.

The mood of educated society in the years leading up to these events was
increasingly radical, and Dr. Russkikh and his allies were at first accused of
favoring "small deeds" that lent support to the tsarist system—rather than joining a frontal assault on it. But after the failure of the 1905 effort to topple the
tsarist government, more people recognized the need for action on a small
scale, and Russkikh's union gained support.[78] A number of other locally organized efforts ensued, and finally, in 1913, Professor Karl Raukhfus succeeded
in establishing a national organization under the patronage of Empress Alexan-
dra: the All-Russian Guardianship for Maternal and Child Welfare [Vserossiis-
koe popechitel'stvo ob okhrane materinstva i mladenchestva]. In accepting imperial
sponsorship, Raukhfus had to turn his back on many of his medical colleagues
who still refused to cooperate with the imperial regime. But tsarist backing
came with an immediate infusion of one million rubles in royalties and donations.[79] These large resources enabled the Guardianship to develop an impressive network of child welfare agencies in a short time. By 1917 nearly 800 summer nurseries serving 46,000 children had been established, a level of activity
that would not again be reached until 1925 under the Soviet regime.[80]

The Guardianship, whose purpose was to protect children in some degree by educating their mothers, also promoted an active publication program that included guides to proper child care and similar works.[81] The emphasis was very much on reaching the common folk, as one of the leaders, Dr. S. Ostrogorskii, explained in turning down a manuscript about reproduction among the privileged classes. The Guardianship, Ostrogorskii pointed out, wanted to direct its resources to "the poorer, little educated strata of the population, where we still encounter a total lack of knowledge about the care of infants and frequently complete ignorance and all imaginable harmful preconceptions. We therefore believe that we should turn some rays of light on that dark mass by producing appropriate and accessible brochures."[82]

Despite the efforts and resources of the Guardianship, its late start and the demands of the war limited its impact. The leaders hoped to be able to extend the organization's activities by joining with the efforts of the zemstvos, but when they did a survey in 1917, they found that a large majority of district zemstvo offices had failed either to develop or to continue operating summer child-care facilities.[83] So the villagers of Russia, well into the second decade of the twentieth century, were still caring for their children as they had in centuries past. The results were a continuing high mortality, running in some locales to rates as high as have ever been recorded anywhere. For example, soon after Professor Raukhfus announced the founding of the Guardianship, he received a letter from a village priest in Perm province. The priest, Aleksandr Malinovskii, wrote that as a seminarian he had heard lectures about basic medicine and hygiene, and in his job had soon after encountered in "the dark Russian people" all the problems he had heard about. As pastor, he was especially distressed by the tribute his flock paid each day in infant death. His carefully constructed tabulations of vital records from his village for the years 1902 to 1913 revealed an infant mortality rate (deaths to age one) of 55 percent, including an appalling rise in the final two years to over 70 percent! His plea for financial and other support to combat this misfortune received a courteous but unhelpful reply.[84] Others who, like this village priest, read in the press about the efforts to combat infant mortality, including promotion of summer nurseries and other assistance to mothers and children, might well have wondered if the reports were mere rhetoric. This was apparently the view of the writer Anton Chekhov, himself a doctor by training and a man who followed the medical press. In his play the *Cherry Orchard*, Chekhov had the student Petr Trofimov ask accusingly: "Show me where are all of our nurseries, about which we are constantly hearing so much? In actual fact, they don't exist at all."[85]

The efforts were real, as archival correspondence and other evidence confirm, but they were pathetically small compared with the size of the population and, at best, brought assistance to a tiny fraction of villagers even in those districts where nurseries existed. The reality of life for village mothers remained largely unchanged in the early decades of this century. Nearly half the children still died before age five, and the result was a weekly offering at the altar of virtually every village church in central Russia, a scene poignantly evoked by writer Nina Berberova, in speaking of a village north of Moscow where she lived as a girl: "Every Sunday in the chapel there stood a row of small coffins containing the bodies of newborn infants—six, eight, sometimes even more. The infants were all alike, somewhat similar to dolls, somewhat to Easter suckling pigs."[86]

From early modern times into the twentieth century, Russian elites shared with other educated Europeans the growing belief that the high loss of life in infancy and childhood was not inevitable. At first, charitable and public agencies limited their efforts to gathering in abandoned and unwanted children, for this was the most scandalous and seemingly controllable arena of child loss. Only with the advent of the Enlightenment technicians of human improvement did public officials and medical reformers begin to promote changes in the behavior of intact families. They worked to preserve the lives of infants, for example, by pursuing campaigns in the late eighteenth century to encourage medically assisted births, improved hygiene, and breast-feeding. Leading Russian physicians studied in the West and returned home eager to foster improvements in childbirth and child care, as the work of Semen Zybelin, Nestor Maksimovich-Ambodik, and others attests. But their ideas were available to only a small segment of Russian society, the educated elite.

Until the middle of the nineteenth century, many physicians in Russia accepted the high toll in infant and childhood death as a normal and natural consequence of species reproduction. But increasing evidence of much-reduced childhood mortality in Western countries eventually made clear that much more could be done in Russia as well. Increasing contact with the life of Russian villagers taught Russian physicians that the underlying cause of teeming death among children was a social, economic, and cultural nexus highly resistant to change. Its culturally determined character became unmistakable when physicians produced studies of neighboring peoples, such as Tatars and Jews, who lived in identical climatic and economic conditions yet suffered much lower infant mortality. Because the beliefs and practices that brought high death rates to Russian children were deeply imbedded in the rhythms of rural life and the seeming need of villagers to fully deploy both the productive and reproductive capacities of women, the stage was set for a broad assault by urban specialists on village culture. Their assault was coded in an opposition between the light of knowledge and reason and the dark ignorance of the common people, the language of intense cultural conflict. Although the language was already well established in tsarist times, efforts to mobilize against the cultural system of the village began late, only on the eve of World War I, and did not go far before the fall of the old regime. But the Bolshevik successors to the imperial government took readily to the same language of cultural confrontation—and even more eagerly to the project of transforming and ultimately obliterating Russian village life and the beliefs and practices that sustained it.

Soviet Efforts to Transform Village Mothering

The efforts begun before the Revolution to improve maternal and infant care in Russia's villages collapsed during the Civil War years but were renewed by the Soviet regime once it got a firm hand on power. Public health doctors who had been active before the revolution in zemstvo medicine or other government agencies in many cases continued their work for women and children under the auspices of the new regime. And the Soviet government's pronouncements in favor of health care for all citizens corresponded to the hopes workers in the idealistic, populist programs had had in the past. Progress lagged, however, and not until the mid-1920s did efforts to reach the villages with summer nurseries and information about childbirth and child care match even the token levels that had been attained under the tsarist regime. To the very end of the decade, the actual delivery of obstetrical services and even child care in the summers remained woefully small in relation to the total village population. The two principal impediments to more rapid progress during the New Economic Policy era were the lack of state resources for investment in social services and the apparent loss of idealism in the medical community, whose younger members did not share the populist spirit of the prerevolutionary zemstvo physicians. In the late 1920s, as a consequence, only about 10 percent of villagers had access to maternal medical services, while the vast majority of women continued to give birth and bring up their children in the same way as Russian villagers had for generations.

The most visible feature of the efforts to improve village maternity and care in the 1920s were press campaigns designed ostensibly to educate village women and mobilize them to act in their own behalf. Both Soviet and Western historians have written about these campaigns in glowing terms and reprinted the posters and other artifacts that accompanied them.[1] But these energetic campaigns, scripted as stark oppositions of the light of modern science and the dark ignorance and superstition of village women, did little to alter the conditions in the nation's villages. In using established intelligentsia constructions of peasant ways of thinking, the campaigns, though designed in hopes of changing village practices, may have been more important in convincing urbanites and aspiring rural communists that the Party and government were capable of managing Russia's renewal.

The breakthrough in medical care for women and children in the villages came only after the upheavals of the early 1930s, when the reorganization of rural life and direct intervention of the state sped up the cultural transformation in the countryside. Even so, it took many more years for regular obstetrical and child-care services to arrive to much of the country, because the personnel for such services had first to be lifted mainly from the village population itself and trained. Not until after World War II did services reach a majority of rural districts. Still more time passed before the government could break the chain of intergenerational, female child-rearing knowledge that continued to foster such practices as the rag pacifier, early introduction of solid food, the hanging crib, and swaddling. Such fundamental spiritual requirements as baptism and equivalent Muslim rites resisted transformation altogether, and these continued in Soviet rural society to the end of the regime.

Office of Maternal and Infant Care

The nearly three years of civil war that followed the October Revolution disrupted or destroyed what few child-welfare institutions had been functioning under the tsarist and Provisional Government regimes. Remaining activity consisted of local ad hoc efforts to assist birthing mothers, refugees, and abandoned children. True, within three months of the Bolshevik takeover in October 1917, an Office of Maternal and Infant Care (Okhrana materinstva i mladenchestva), or OMM, was organized under the People's Commissariat of Social Welfare, but in the midst of war this supposedly national office had difficulty mounting anything more than local relief efforts in and around the large cities. During the course of 1918, the OMM absorbed what was left of the pre-October Guardianship for Maternal and Child Welfare and began to revive it and other urban childbirth and child-care facilities left over from the old regime.[2]

The director of the OMM, Vera Pavlovna Lebedeva, and her co-workers were eager to consolidate their institutional base and get to the work of transforming the medical and childbirth culture of the country and to attack the problem of infant and maternal mortality. Progress was hampered, however, by the OMM's lack of resources and a stable institutional foundation within the new governing order. Its responsibilities were at first divided between the Commissariats of Social Welfare and of Education, then shifted to two others, the Commissariats of Labor and Health. The leaders of the OMM fought against this parceling up of its work, and in May 1920 finally won approval to concentrate all its operations under the Commissariat of Health.[3] Having achieved a more solid administrative position, the OMM was able to begin building institutional networks. In December 1920, it convened the first All-Russian Conference of Maternal and Infant Care. The meeting took place in conjunction with the Congress of Working Women; the two organizations shared many concerns.[4]

Officers of the Women's Section (*Zhenotdel*) of the Party were important collaborators with the OMM, especially in supporting outreach to factories and in publicizing decrees issued by the government and Party that encouraged efforts on behalf of mothers and children. But the reality of the OMM, as of other welfare operations, was decline from the prerevolutionary period. Even in Petrograd, the most developed locale where, before the Revolution, nearly 90 percent of births took place in maternity wards, the rate fell in two years to about 70 percent. The reason, Dr. A. Shuster reported to the OMM in 1920, was the lack of transport and especially the lack of heat in maternity facilities.[5] If conditions were poor in the large urban centers, a few miles outside of Petrograd maternal and child welfare services faced near-total collapse. Dr. Marshak from the Detskoe Selo[6] district southeast of Petrograd reported having just a handful of maternity beds, one maternity shelter, and two pediatricians to serve the densely populated district. A doctor from the city of Luga, farther south, lamented that his far-flung district was served by two obstetricians and one pediatrician, doctors who did not even live in the district but rode in from Petrograd. He added that not a single OMM institution was operating and that welfare activity, such as it was, consisted of the distribution of milk. When questioned about this specific activity, the doctor further admitted that milk distribution had been available only in the summer and that the milk was spoiled and came not from public but from private sources.[7] In short, nothing was functioning. Even where welfare facilities were operating, conditions were far from rosy, as may be judged by complaints about the most elite of such institutions, the former imperial foundling home in Moscow. Reports there told of neglect by the medical staff and of mice and worms being found in the cereal fed to children and midwives.[8]

A common practice of Soviet leaders during their first years of rule was to seek popular approval by advertising programs and issuing decrees to implement them, even when they knew that most of the decrees were unenforceable. The OMM was no different. Officials and delegates at the first conference of the OMM in December 1920, for example, proposed expansive plans for developing a modern welfare program. This was a key item in a Soviet modernization that included scientific authority, industrialization, and a fully developed bureaucratic welfare state. OMM officials looked to a new day when all women would have access to modern gynecological and obstetrical care and when housework and child-rearing responsibilities would be communally supported and conducted by professionals. Of course, they understood that the great majority of women in the Soviet Union still resided in the countryside and were subject to patriarchal power and an agrarian cultural system that had to be transformed before such boons could be realized. The OMM officers and medical staff agreed that the objective had to be not merely changing a few practices but initiating a systematic assault on village culture. They would have to eradicate or transform virtually every aspect of traditional birthing and care, starting with what they considered the most obviously harmful practices and their associated "superstitions." Their catalog of "barbarous" practices echoed those that Russian physicians since the eighteenth century had condemned and zemstvo doctors in the next era had struggled against. Peasant women gave birth alone, hidden in some out-of-the-way spot, or they were delivered by untrained granny midwives who had no idea of sound hygiene or what to do in difficult births. Birthing mothers were walked to exhaustion or, in difficult births, suspended from a ceiling beam. Babies were swaddled tightly, breast-fed on demand rather than on a doctor-approved schedule, or otherwise nourished with the rag soska, "chaws," or horn bottle; they were rocked in their hanging cribs to the point of stupefaction. This was the "dark" world of the peasant *baba,* the supposedly ignorant and superstitious village woman, one of two prominent images of rural women in Soviet discourse.

Because the OMM had only limited means to conduct this transformation, it relied on mobilizing support among the citizenry, engaging the help in particular of the "conscious" activist woman, the other prominent image of womanhood in Bolshevik rhetoric. One of the first such efforts was a "Week of the Child," running from September 26 to October 3, 1920. To judge from reports in Petrograd province, the home of the OMM Institute, the results were not impressive. The official in charge of Luga district wrote that requests for food aid during the week had yielded a mere one pound of groats.[9] At Detskoe Selo, the week featured inspections of child-welfare institutions, lectures on illnesses and on maternal and child care, plus an excursion for women to Petrograd to look at nurseries, prenatal dispensaries, and the OMM Museum on Vasilevskii Island.[10] One wonders what the forty-two women who took part in the excursion (workers at children's homes, nurseries, and a hospital as well as housewives) thought of the facilities in the city, many of which were in desperate condition. Soon after the excursion, the head doctor of the Vasilevskii Island maternity home warned his employees that wood to heat the facility was virtually gone, in part due to pilfering by the staff, and that if patients started to freeze in their beds, he would close the home and lay off all personnel.[11]

The Petrograd district, the rural area immediately adjacent to the city and containing 80,000 inhabitants, was served in 1921 by twenty-five doctors of every kind (some of whom were in private practice) and only one trained OMM nurse. Maternity beds were in better supply, about fifty of them being scattered through the district in public and private facilities. Summer nurseries did not yet exist and were apparently not in great demand because of the non-agrarian character of much of the area. Few teachers trained in hygiene were available, and many of the women who worked in child-care facilities were illiterate.

According to Dr. Brazhenikova, head of the OMM office for the district, disease was rampant among children in institutional care, and the health of children generally was poor. During the "Week of the Child," she reported, they examined all the children in institutions and all the children of some villages and found that a majority suffered from anemia, swollen glands, and bad teeth.[12]

After the Civil War, matters improved in the largest cities, where the OMM was able to concentrate on putting prerevolutionary facilities back into operation. It was hoped that after reestablishing services in the major centers, the agency would have the resources to expand gradually into the countryside where the greatest number of women still resided. But, contrary to expectations, activists soon had to adjust to a new and much narrower field of activity. The advent of the New Economic Policy dramatically limited what the OMM could hope to accomplish. Budgetary constraints not only put a stop to plans for institution building. It put the program into reverse. In 1922 the OMM was forced to curtail much of its activity, close one-third of its facilities, and accept the fiction that many of its responsibilities were being transferred to local authorities. It was obvious to everyone, however, that local bodies were even less capable than the central government of providing the services needed by mothers and children.

In adjusting to the New Economic Policy (NEP), OMM leaders found that one of their biggest challenges was the imbalance between live-in (*zakrytye*) institutions such as children's homes or shelters for homeless mothers and children and the service (*otkrytye*) facilities such as prenatal dispensaries, milk kitchens, nurseries, and kindergartens that were essential to deliver on the revolutionaries' promises to provide benefits to women and families generally— and not just relief operations for the most needy. Another crucial function of the service facilities was to provide sites at which women and girls would be educated in hygiene and modern methods of childbirth, child care, and upbringing; this type of education was thought to be the most effective means of lowering the shocking rates of infant mortality. The NEP frustrated this mission in two ways. First, it caused radical cutbacks in government funding for health services, and likewise annulled a number of benefits specifically aimed at pregnant women and new mothers, including a so-called dowry for newborns (a packet of clothing and baby-care items), supplementary food for pregnant women and for children up to age three, and free milk allocations. Second, the market mechanisms of NEP, the return of men from the Civil War, and discrimination against women in hiring threw large numbers of women out of work.[13] The combination of decreased benefits and decreased employment pushed ever more women and children into shelters for the homeless, and these costly live-in institutions soaked up an ever larger percentage of the declining health and welfare budget.[14] The OMM leaders understood that the live-in facilities, while of some help in combating infant mortality, were narrowly based and expensive relief operations that would never be able to exert the kind of broad impact which service and educational outreach facilities would have in advancing the cause.[15] They needed therefore to seek out means to turn around this downward spiral.

One tactic to compensate for the loss of government support was the creation of a Commission for Cooperation with the OMM, an auxiliary body under the authority of the OMM that started in the summer of 1922 to help generate funds and build greater outreach. The commission obtained money through the sale of some OMM assets, contributions from public organizations, lotteries, and income from artisan workshops that it organized by drawing on the skills of unemployed women. The workshops specialized in the needle trades, such as making lingerie, belts, blankets, and mattresses among other things, and the commission even won a government contract for repairing tents.[16] But this limited expediency, helpful though it was, could not answer the problem of educational outreach and services to women generally.[17] For this the OMM had to resort also to the devices that figured prominently in other Bolshevik propaganda campaigns: posters, exhibits, magic lantern projections, health manuals and other publications, and more "Week of the Child" drives. Print media were the most prominent means it used, and, although the agency began with puny print runs of its posters and magazines, by the end of 1920s it was publishing in numbers sufficient to make contact with a substantial portion of the female population in provincial towns, if not in the far larger rural areas.[18] The main periodicals the OMM used to reach activists in the countryside were *Krest'ianka* and *Krest'ianskaia gazeta*. Later it attempted to reach villages directly with education and at least temporary services, above all medical check-ups and summer nurseries, in the hope of gaining a foothold from which to begin the transformation of the maternal and child-care culture. Initially, however, the work had to rely on the printed word and images.

Language of Bolshevik Modernist
Assault on Village Women

If linguistic and other signs were going to substitute for building a solid institutional base, words and images had to be powerful enough to prompt voluntary actions in pursuit of the goals of the OMM. The organization's language replayed the themes of prerevolutionary doctors and represented a renewed assault of modernism and professional medical authority on village beliefs and practices. The OMM language especially aimed at the village women's world of knowledge and mutual support. Bolshevik modernism might be a more accurate term for the language deployed in the OMM and other Soviet campaigns of this time; going beyond the standard modernist images of the light of scientific knowledge and professional expertise illuminating the dark corners of popular ignorance, it added to the modernist vocabulary appeals to class hatred, contempt for compassion, and attacks on female bonding and trust.

The leaders sought allies, unpaid volunteers who were willing to assist in the effort to define and then destroy the old world of village beliefs and practices. They found these allies in the educated or semi-educated, opportunistic, and upwardly mobile rural dwellers who became known as "village correspondents."[19] These people were one component of a larger project, of "worker and peasant correspondents," designed to mobilize the eyes, ears, and pens of ordinary people sympathetic to the Communist cause. These were people willing to testify to the accomplishments of the regime in their workplace or locality and also to report on the shortcomings of their neighbors and the local leadership or on instances of actual resistance to Party and government objectives. To become a correspondent, an aspirant filled out a questionnaire and often also submitted a short biography telling of his or her interest and qualifications for such a role. The biography was usually couched in the form of a conversion story, similar to those offered by new candidates for Party membership, and it resembled standard stories of religious conversion. A common version featured the aspirant wandering in ignorance, making the wrong choices, acting against her own and her people's interests until she saw the light of reason and progress represented by the new regime. In another version, the aspirant might simply appeal to the crushing oppression she and her family suffered, thereby validating her qualifications to speak for the downtrodden.[20]

It was with people such as these—ambitious or aggrieved residents of rural areas who wanted to make a mark on the process of change—that the Party and the OMM were able to create the impression of a link between the center and the village. In time, the exchange of information between the centrally produced journals and the villages that had access to them did animate some village women to act on their own behalf and to cooperate with the OMM and other government offices to introduce new services.

The presentation of material in the press was not, of course, an unblemished mirror of the feelings of the local correspondents, let alone the peasant men and women whose lives they were describing. The issues about which the correspondents wrote were signaled at Party meetings and in the publications themselves. Particular issues or campaigns were highlighted at particular times. Even so, writers sometimes could spontaneously and independently identify events and examples they chose to describe. But whatever they offered, the letters that arrived in the offices of *Krest'ianka* and *Krest'ianskaia gazeta* were edited before they were published. The editors sought to fit the contributions into the framework of their current campaigns, and they might trim a letter back to a specific illustration and then stitch in from another part of the letter a slogan or formulaic phrase in support of a particular theme.[21]

The one thing the aspiring correspondents did not seem to need much help with was "speaking Bolshevik." They adopted easily the metaphors and stereotypes of the Communist press: the priest secretly conspiring to return the old regime, the kulak exploiting his neighbors, the evil babka undermining efforts to bring modern ideas to the village, the "dark" women in need of the light of the Party to guide them toward equality and freedom. It was these images and types that enabled the correspondents to write, and although they often got off on tangents of angry recrimination for the ills of the village, they did so in the language given them by the Party press.

The plot line of letters and stories about innovation coming to the village emphasized the initial resistance of the forces of darkness, whose interest it was to keep the villagers in ignorance. In the case of child-care or maternity improvements, these forces were personified as folk healers, granny midwives, priests, and male bosses who did not want to allocate resources to help women. Superstition and the inertia of established practice also frequently figured in the stories. Accordingly, efforts by the forces of light to start nurseries inevitably were said to have met with mistrust on the part of mothers. By dint of unflagging efforts by activists, however, eventually the resistance is overcome. And after seeing what a positive contribution the summer nurseries or other child-care initiatives made to the lives of the children and peasant women themselves, they are convinced of the rightness of the forces of light and eagerly seek a renewal of the nurseries the following year.[22]

Among the issues mentioned most prominently as causing initial hesitation were fears that a nursery would cost money. The villagers believed they would be assessed for the service and that if they did not pay up, their children would be confiscated. Some were said to believe that the village children would be registered as communists at the very least, and possibly even taken away to the city for indoctrination; if that happened, there was little expectation that the youngsters would be returned.[23] Concerns about payments were indeed justified: resources for supporting the summer nurseries had to come from local budgets. That was why the OMM was pushing campaigns in the first place. A correspondent from Karelia, Alla Piiraiunen, wrote: "I have to say that the people here are poor and fear any extra assessments. We explained that we would get the money with parties and plays, and they would supply only basics, such as milk and wood. It took quite an effort to calm them down and reassure them."[24] Not surprisingly, priests were accused of being behind much of the misinformation that was causing resistance. An activist from the Pskov area explained that although they initially signed up thirty-three children for a nursery in her district, when a doctor came to examine them for final admission, few of the previously registered families appeared: a priest had convinced the parents that they would have to pay ten rubles each to get the children back in the fall.[25]

Priests reportedly also were succeeding in convincing villagers that the nurseries were going to turn the children into atheists. A writer from Kursk province lamented this supposed misconception and, equally, its unfortunate class locus. Villagers were telling her, "We won't bring our children there. They teach them not to pray to God." And then the correspondent added, "The worst part is that [this vicious propaganda] is being said by the poor peasants on whose behalf we created the nursery-playground, for we wished to help them in the difficult time of summer field work and hunger. How powerful village darkness still is!" (This disclosure of class ingratitude was struck by the editor at the publishing house.)[26] In Muslim villages, parents were said to resist nurseries because they feared their children would be fed pork in them.[27] The concerns about indoctrination, it is worth pointing out, were scarcely misplaced. Indeed, other reports by correspondents openly boasted of using the child-care facilities to introduce children to tales, songs, and stories of the Revolution and Lenin—the myths of the new regime intended to replace religion.[28]

The rest of the story told by the correspondents at the prompting of their editors was about how activists won the hearts and minds of the people by demonstrating the benefits of nursery care and other services. Peasants were suspicious of anything that they did not see operating in practice, a correspondent from Ivanovo-Voznesensk wrote. "We tried to convince them that a nursery was better than a seven-year old nanny," a writer elaborated, but no real cooperation came from the villagers until activists lined up assistance from a number of administrative organizations and set up the nursery themselves. Once set up, as these stories invariably went, at the end of the two-month life of the nursery, the village women had only one concern: how to extend the period of the nursery's operation.[29]

An important purpose of this letter and many others that were eventually used in one or another publication was to provide advice on how to overcome practical problems. They addressed such issues as obtaining funds, wood, food, recruiting the right kind of nursery supervisor (someone who could talk to peasant women in their own language, po krest'ianski, was one recommendation), and even, when all else failed, how to take matters into one's own hands. A correspondent from Moscow district told of fruitless meetings in which women of her village fretted about who would give them a nursery. Finally, a seventy-four-year-old activist said: "You do it yourselves. The men wanted a tractor and they got together and made it happen. Are we any worse? We have our hands and our fields. All we need are horses and we can plow fields . . . to earn money for a nursery."[30]

The letters also functioned as petitions for redress of grievances or appeals for assistance. Indeed, as time went on, this function took on increasing importance. Throughout history, ordinary Russians have sought some path to a "higher instance" that could respond to their needs and overrule local power holders who were treating them unfairly. Petitions to the tsar are the best-known forms of this appeal. Once correspondents found that the publication offices of the peasant journals could provide a service of this sort, they seized the opportunity. Most of the letters received by the journals are not therefore in the conveniently located archival files of the publications that received them but in the myriad government and Party repositories to which the editors sent them for action or reply. At the height of the letter flow from 1924 through 1926, the publication office of the peasant journals had to request a hundred additional staff from various government commissariats to sort the letters and move them to the appropriate offices.[31]

First Try: Mobile Dispensaries

Reports from the countryside made clear that it would take more than agitation to gain the attention of rural women. Tangible assistance programs were needed. Once the OMM leaders began to recover from the ruinous budgetary cutbacks of the first NEP years, they planned outreach to the villages in the form first developed by charitable institutions in tsarist times: nurseries during the summer work season and mobile medical teams to give check-ups to mothers and children. Here, they believed, were services of immediate benefit to village mothers and their children that could also significantly help in meeting the two main challenges of the OMM work. First, the provision of day care, proper food, and clean surroundings for children in the summer months would reduce substantially the high rates of infant and childhood mortality that occurred in that season due to poor feeding, accidents, and neglect. Second, the mobile dispensaries and summer nurseries could serve as sites for educating mothers in the proper care of themselves and their children. Once the mothers came to understand the benefits of these facilities, they would be eager to cooperate with other efforts at improvement and to learn about and exercise the political and social rights that the revolution had won for them.[32]

A push for action of this kind began in 1924, spurred by the call at the Twelfth Party Congress at the end of 1923 for "all-round assistance by the city to the countryside" and a renewed "common effort with the peasantry" (*smychka s krest'ianstvom*). The message was reinforced at the next year's congress, which demanded "every possible cooperation with the peasant masses." The OMM mustered what resources it could from its own budget and at the same time signaled activists in the countryside to request assistance from local bodies in conformity with Party directives about assistance to the villages.

Although the campaign began in 1924, difficulties in organizing and finding resources delayed most action until the following year. Even then, efforts remained sporadic. In the relatively well-staffed Leningrad region, the best the OMM could do in 1925 was to send out small teams of traveling medics who stayed a week or two in a particular township and then moved on. Dr. L. O. Sverdlova took such a team to the northeast part of Leningrad province beginning in the spring of 1925 and offered some sobering observations. Only about half of the pregnant women they examined were healthy. The children were even worse. In one township, the team looked at 90 children age 0–3 years and found only 12 in good health. Of the 25 children age 3–13, three were healthy. The rates of infant mortality were appalling, as bad or worse than the staggering death tolls reported by Father Giliarovskii for mid-nineteenth-century Novgorod province. In one locale, of 19 children recently born, only 3 survived, and these were ill. In several other villages Sverdlova visited, she found similar losses. In one, of 45 recent births, 35 of the babies had died in the first months of life. "In another, during the two weeks prior to our visit 20 women had given birth, and now only a few of the babies remain alive; but, in compensation," she remarked dryly, "the village's cemetery was adorned with fresh little graves." These results, she wrote, "can only be attributed to the darkness and ignorance of our women." Wherever she went, Sverdlova tried to leave behind OMM cells composed of any literate women she could find. They were given literature and urged to gather the village women together at least twice a month and somehow "wake them from their heavy slumber."[33]

Later in the summer Sverdlova visited a township about thirty kilometers from her medical station in the district capital. There she ran across a situation common enough in many parts of Russia and distressing to this medical missionary: the women either did not speak Russian at all or spoke it so poorly that communication was difficult. She had evidently entered a Finnish- or Karelian-speaking region. "This township is a primitive outback where the women are very dark and ignorant," Sverdlova remarked, using her two favorite words for characterizing peasant women. Describing the conditions she found so discouraging, she then repeated almost word for word what ethnographers and rural doctors had been writing about village Russia for the past 100 years:

> A mother is forced to leave home for work early in the morning and returns late at night, leaving her baby in the care of a child eight or nine years old or with an utterly blind old man. It is very difficult to describe the miserable conditions in which the infant exists, lying all day long in a stuffy or even smoke-filled house in a hanging crib next to the oven, a chaw in its mouth so that he does not cry.[34]

Here, she emphasized, is where the OMM needs to help out by establishing summer nurseries at which "these boorish women" could receive instruction in child care and that would also serve as centers of enlightenment.

Again, in the same terms as her predecessors, Sverdlova described the sorry lot of the pregnant woman: "She has to work up to the very last minute before labor, and because of her darkness and ignorance that are deeply rooted in prejudices about the evil eye causing harm to a birth mother and her baby, peasant women do not ask for help but give birth alone in a barn or go off to the other side of a lake or deep into the forest." She noted that a trained midwife had tried to start a practice in the township but could not attract enough business to make a living because of this peasant attitude toward birthing. As for the children in the township, like elsewhere, a substantial majority suffered from rickets and other diseases. On the positive side, Sverdlova could report a good turnout for their talks and dramatizations done with exhibitions and slides. But she worried about follow-up in an area with almost no literate women and almost no schools so that the younger generation was growing up as illiterate as their elders.[35]

Another team led by Dr. D. Kuritsina was active in June 1925 near the district center of Lodeinoe Pole. The villagers in this area had more experience with medical practitioners, even if they still believed in witches and spells, Kuritsina remarked. The women gladly brought their children for check-ups, and even wanted to leave them at the medical station while they went to work. So it was clear that a summer nursery would have been welcomed here, but the medical team did not have resources to do it properly. The examinations of the children also revealed the need for regular professional care and observation, since the children were in no better shape here than elsewhere. Only 10 percent of the 220 examined proved to be "relatively healthy."[36]

Kuritsina made an important observation about where the OMM needed to target its efforts: "I think it is necessary to work with the young girls," she wrote, "because they do a lot of the child care. A baby is with them more than with its mother." She went on to tell about how she made a rag doll and used it to show the girls the proper way to handle and care for infants, and she believed that she had some success, as a visiting nurse who followed up three weeks later found that these young nannies retained some notion of what Kuritsina had taught them.[37] The greatest challenge for the medical workers were the grandmothers and other older care givers. The medical staff found that they sometimes had to threaten police action to get the old women to stop feeding the babies chaws and other harmful foods. When it came to the hanging crib (zybka), however, everyone opposed the medical workers—young girls and grandmothers alike. Doctors had long considered this device dangerous and debilitating. Babies could occasionally fall out of this high crib and be crippled or die, and doctors for some reason decried even more what they regarded as the stupefying effect on the child of being continually rocked in the crib. Peasant women, for their part, thought it cruel to deprive a baby of this comforting motion and wondered why the doctors wanted them to torment their babies. In any event, Kuritsina had identified the three-generational pattern of the Russian child-care culture. Child care was usually taught to young girls by their grandmothers, skipping a generation and consequently building in a strong conservative bias that kept alive and powerfully reinforced the beliefs and practices of the past.

A team working in the opposite end of Leningrad province, the southwestern district of Gdov, found the situation no better. Dr. L. L. Burshtein, the team leader, reported on finding there, too, the early introduction of solid food, endless crib rocking, heavy swaddling, covering the crib with dark cloth, and fear of exposing infants to the outdoors or to fresh air indoors even on warm, sunny days (they thought it caused colds), in short, all the practices the doctors considered baneful. Even the smell of peasant homes offended this urbanite. "In the homes it is stifling," Burshtein wrote, "and each has it own characteristic smell. When you approach the crib, you are assaulted by the stench of urine and baby excrement."

The practices of the peasants constituted a true culture of child care, for, as Burshtein discovered, they were common to all the villagers and not just a particular stratum of them. After describing baby care in the Gdov area, Burshtein added:

> I say this not only about poor homes, in which I generally offer my counsels with a heavy heart, knowing how difficult it will be for a mother to act on them when her little hut is full of children, each one smaller than the next, and hunger and privation peek out from every corner, but even in prosperous homes where the rooms are clean and bright, snow-white curtains grace the windows, you still find the baby lying in filth, stinking of urine, and kept under three layers of crib curtains, tightly swaddled and with the ever-present pacifier in its mouth.[38]

As for giving birth, most women in this community delivered their babies kneeling on a dirt floor on dirty hay, according to Burshtein, and without any assistance but that of a granny midwife. In this community not far from major urban centers, there was not a single medical midwife available, even though some eight hundred children were born each year.

The best Burshtein could report was that the team seemed to be making some progress on the issue of cleanliness. They noticed that after lectures, people tried to find a clean shirt for their children and improved their use of the crib.

More lasting success was reported by a team that had the opportunity to work closely with peasants in a single locale for a long period of time. This team set up a pediatric dispensary in the village of Iotanino (Volkhov district) in early spring, and it continued working for nine months to examine all the children in the surrounding area. According to the account of its leader, Dr. Nikolaeva, the peasants initially greeted the team with mistrust, making it clear that they did not welcome the service or even understand the point of bringing healthy children in to be examined by a doctor. Again, the strongest challenge came from the old women of the village, who were often heard to say something like, "We gave birth and brought up our children just fine without you." They had to be reminded, Nikolaeva remarked, that although they had given birth to many children, they brought up fewer than half of them.

By June, the report declared, the team was enjoying greater trust and seeing an increasing number of office visits, including requests of treatment for adults as well children. The team also opened a nursery for twenty children and was able to keep them healthy, which stimulated interest among the people of a neighboring village in also having a nursery. Although at the time of Nikolaeva's report most of the children still suffered from skin diseases and other ills and were inadequately nourished, she thought that the dispensary had become accepted by the peasants and she wrote that, indeed, they "are now afraid that we might decide to close it."[39]

The first year was an opportunity for the OMM physicians and activists to acquire some experience of conditions in rural areas, to assess the scope of the need, and to make plans for future work. The stories they told contained many of the same elements that appeared in letters and stories from activists in the countryside, archived or printed in *Krest'ianka* magazine. Wherever efforts were undertaken to bring medical assistance and especially nurseries to the villages, women were said to be suspicious at first, and local male supervisors unhelpful, yet in time trust developed. By the end of the stay, mothers were clamoring for continued services and even offering to contribute to them personally. So, this way of describing the interaction between peasant mothers and activists was a well-established narrative form shared by village correspondents and medical workers alike.

Push for Nurseries

The Third All-Union OMM Congress met in Moscow in December 1925 and assessed the results of the previous year's work. Much attention was devoted to the countryside.[40] Although OMM director Vera Lebedeva believed that her agency's primary objective should be to establish medical facilities wherever possible, the experience of 1925 convinced many OMM workers that summer nurseries were their best means of reaching peasant women. Dr. N. F. Shtiftar spoke for these people in her speech to the congress. She pointed out that the idea of preventive care was altogether new for the peasants and very difficult to get across by treatment and lectures alone. The reports she had received about educational efforts in the villages uniformly noted that the peasant audiences listened politely to presentations, "but left the meetings convinced that none of what was said was of much use to them; they could not imagine applying such advice in conditions of village life, amid grinding poverty and backbreaking labor." In contrast, Shtiftar continued, the village nurseries taught by example and in a familiar setting. "Even in a facility set up in village conditions and outfitted primitively, a mother could learn many things that she could do for her child, things that she was not doing now out of ignorance."[41]

This message was echoed by Commissar of Health Nikolai Semashko in his circular of February 1926 to provincial and regional health administrators about that year's campaign. He noted that the OMM Congress found summer nurseries to be one of the most important means of influencing the peasantry and urged that activists begin well ahead of the summer season's field work to prepare and encourage an expansion of nurseries. Semashko added that local organizers should heed the resolutions of the congress and focus on keeping the nurseries open for a minimum of three months, increasing the percentage of infants and children up to age four in the nurseries (older children had been a large component, whereas infant and early childhood mortality was the government's chief concern). They should ensure that poor and middle peasants be served unless they were loafers who did not engage in field work.[42] Vera Lebedeva also joined the chorus with a circular that urged women activists to mobilize all possible resources in the fight. "[We need to see] pressure from the female peasant masses on the township and regional committees," she wrote, "so that they will allocate the means essential for the establishment of maternal and child-welfare facilities, such as more maternity beds in hospitals, an increased number of traveling medical midwives, village nurseries, and dispensaries." Though still emphasizing the medical facilities as priority, Lebedeva also stressed the value of nurseries for engaging and organizing local women activists (*delegatki*). They could be trained to assist the local village women who were having babies. By helping these women with chores, the activists would build solidarity and could use the practice of mutual aid and the promise of summer nurseries as a year-round theme for organization. "The nursery campaign is senseless," she argued, "without the wide participation of *delegatki*. The nurseries are an important part of the new village, and township organizers should develop work in and around them for involving *delegatki*. Work should start on the nurseries long before they are to open. They should be made into cells of collective life." She also urged that the material base of village operations should be strengthened by attracting help from other locally active groups such as child-assistance commissions, the Red Cross, "Friends of Children" cells, committees of mutual aid, and the like.[43]

There could be no doubt that the leadership's purpose with the OMM facilities in the villages, especially the nurseries, was not simply to improve child survival and maternal health but also to use them as vehicles for changing the whole peasant way of thinking and acting in the world. "Educational-sanitation" work was to be one of the essential elements of nurseries, as a directive from this time indicates:

> Since dispensaries in the villages are few, this educational work should be concentrated in the nurseries. If a nursery is not doing this, it is not fully meeting its obligations. It would be good if a special room could be attached to the nursery for a library or exhibit for this work, to hold conversations with mothers. . . . Taking into consideration that questions of a sanitary-educational character are closely tied to the conditions of everyday life, that is to societal issues and likewise political questions, it is essential to address and illuminate these matters during conversations with the women.[44]

In short, summer nurseries in the villages had become the preferred site of educational work with peasant women in regard not only to health issues but also to larger social and political consciousness-raising.

Krest'ianka and other publications aimed at activists interested in the countryside cranked up the volume of stories and letters on summer nurseries and similar facilities, such as supervised playgrounds for children past infancy. Three genres were prominent in carrying the message. One featured personal stories of tragedy and success. The main character in the stories of tragedy was the village *babka*, a term that referred variously to women who served as granny midwives, abortionists, and healers of women and young children.[45] The babka was blamed for inflicting pain and death on women and children. In her role as midwife, she was accused of continuing all the useless and harmful practices of the past, such as isolating the mother, placing her in filthy conditions, reaching into her with dirty hands, the results of which were allegedly 40,000 to 50,000 deaths by childbed fevers each year. Abortions by these *babki* crippled large numbers of women, and writers often followed condemnations of abortion by a call for more emphasis on contraception and production of contraceptive devices, a controversial stance even in the 1920s and one that later was condemned.[46] A few items were also included about women who had seen the light and transcended the past. These stories contained the key elements of the model didactic tale of female consciousness-raising. For example, there was Aunt Marfa, a much beloved granny midwife (*povitukha*) who realized that she did not have the training she needed to help her patients. She decided that she had to go to a two-month medical training course in the city. But when she turned to the patriarchal village head for financial assistance, he responded with derision. Undeterred, Aunt Marfa gathered the women of the village and convinced them to act as a pressure group to get the needed support—and she ended up with the wherewithal to attend the special midwife course.[47] The same cast of characters appeared in many tales: the patriarchal village power structure that impeded enlightened change was confronted and overcome by women using organization and self-help to make needed reforms. A second genre included straightforward reportage on the growth in the number of summer nurseries, dispensaries, and playgrounds, plus a series of columns starting each April and continuing into the height of the field-work season that told about preparing for the opening of summer care facilities and offered step-by-step advice on how women could cooperate to organize such facilities in their own locales with a minimum of help from official agencies. Finally, a third type offered a series of articles with up-to-date medical advice. This series began with a tough attack on babki and then proceeded to lessons on how to nurse infants, when to begin solid food, how to properly care for infants, the importance of sunlight and fresh air, and how to avoid malaria and rickets. Each lesson was accompanied by pictures, often the traditional Russian lubok-type popular woodprint, that contrasted proper care and the harmful practices associated with the babka.[48] The publishing house likewise continued its behind-the-scenes work of forwarding complaints to local governing bodies and requesting responses to problems pointed out by correspondents.

Whatever the hopes of OMM leaders, the guidelines for use of the nurseries ran into difficulty when the workers tried to apply them in the countryside. A closer look at activities in Leningrad province demonstrates the point. A detailed report on Kingisepp district southwest of Leningrad noted that the idea was first to seek financial backing from the provincial health ministry and then to agitate for contributions from mothers in the villages targeted for action. Activists were able to get help from the ministry and also succeeded in drafting child-care workers from among students at a technicum for training physician's assistants and midwives. But when it came to finding help from among the women in the locales being served, financial aid and work support was less forthcoming. Local women expressed some interest in having child care, but did not offer to contribute more than a few rubles. Where nurseries were active, the work with the children reportedly went well. The children were said to have gained weight, and in good weather they played outside all day in a yard and sand pile. Nurses examined the children, gave vaccinations against small pox, and taught basic hygiene, such as washing hands before eating, using the chamber pot, cutting hair, and trimming nails. Again, however, the mothers, who were the primary educational target, had neither the time nor evidently the interest to be indoctrinated with new ways of doing things. "The period in which nurseries function," the district health officer wrote, "corresponds to the time of agricultural labor, when mothers are not always available even on Sundays. Moreover, we have not yet outlived the torpor of village life . . . in which women demonstrate little initiative in their own behalf."[49]

The same kind of situation confronted Dr. Brianskaia, who took a medical team to the village, or perhaps better, small town of Voznesen'e, on the south end of Lake Onega, a transfer point for the Onega Canal. Brianskaia was working for the Red Cross in cooperation with the OMM. Her team arrived on July 19, 1926, and stayed until mid-October. Despite resistance from the township supervisors, who refused to provide housing, the team was able to set up in a school while local Zhenotdel organizers spread the word of their arrival and encouraged women to come for check-ups. This opportunity for one-on-one visits with some of the mothers was considered a success, except that each visit proved to be very time-consuming. "You have to talk to every mother about things that in the city were known long ago, even by women of very little education," Brianskaia wrote. "Here you have to speak of the harm of the hanging crib and swaddling, about chaws and cow teat nipples, and show that they should not give an infant the breast on demand fifteen or so times a day and the like." The team could even report some success in seeing a large number of babies for check-ups. In the three-month period of work, the team saw 360 children, many of them more than once. But they could not stick to their program of doing strictly well-baby care and education, as planned, since families called them for home visits to sick children. The team realized that their authority would quickly evaporate if they failed to respond to such requests. "The healthy ones they say they'll look at, but as soon as one gets sick, they leave it without help," would be the reaction, Brianskaia feared.[50] Here, as elsewhere in Russia and in poverty-stricken regions throughout the world, every effort at preventive care or education-based public health was in danger of being swamped by the need for outpatient treatment for the sick.

Brianskaia's team was continually frustrated in its central purpose of making regular, instructional contact with the pregnant women and mothers of the community. Prenatal work with pregnant women proved to be especially hard. Brianskaia reported that "Our work in Voznesen'e came at the height of the field-work season when it was very hard for a peasant woman to go to the doctor unless she was too sick even to stand up."[51] As for meetings after work hours, these, too, were nearly impossible to organize because the women were just too exhausted after a day of field work or barge hauling.

Milk kitchens were another service the team could not operate as proposed. The team's guidelines provided that it should furnish milk to families based on a rough means test, which permitted assistance only to day laborers or large families earning very low wages. But Brianskaia soon learned what Dr. Burshtein and other medical workers going to Russian villages for the first time had also discovered: The care of children had very little to do with the wealth of their households. It was a pervasive cultural pattern controlled by the rhythms of female work and long-held ideas about infant needs.

> [O]ften we had to think not so much about the material position of the parents, since in the best case the mother, when she goes to work, leaves her child in the care of some old woman or an eight-year-old nanny, and they begin feeding the infant from as early as two weeks of age on semolina kasha or biscuits. Biscuits and the cow teat are the true bane of babies in Voznesen'e. I have a number of infants who nearly every Monday show up with diarrhea and vomiting. You start in talking with the mother about how important it is to keep her child at least a little while on a proper dietary regimen until he is completely well, but at the same time you know perfectly well that as soon as the child arrives home, it will again get fed in the best case biscuits, or even bread and potatoes; so, these children had to be fed from the milk kitchen until they got well, plus a visiting nurse had to go to their homes and convince the eight-year-old nanny not to feed the child anything extraneous.[52]

It was clear that the approach had to be general if the goal was to change beliefs and practices and not simply deliver a few services on a temporary basis.

This was the situation in a large community located along an important transportation route. The real countryside beyond was scarcely touched. Brianskaia's instructions also called for outreach to the surrounding villages. But this work was stymied from the start for lack of assistance from local people: "If by chance I got out to one of [the other villages], I could see maybe twenty persons, talk with the mothers, but that was the limit of my contact. I was not able to return a second time to any village nor to warn people when I might be coming. So the work had an entirely haphazard character." She actually was able to visit only three villages in the entire period of her stay, not counting a few trips to nurseries in Oshta, which like Voznesen'e was another large community on the Onega Canal.[53]

The final act of these expeditions to the countryside was a purely political event at which the team brought together as many women as they could possibly induce to show up and have them sign onto a petition that would confirm for provincial officials and sponsoring organizations that the team had done its job well and, equally important, that would exert pressure on local officials to continue and even expand the work of medical assistance to the community. Brianskaia, who had complained in her report about a lack of cooperation from the township committee, happily announced that fully forty-five women came to the meeting and supported the following resolution:

> During the dispensary's brief stay in our village, we became accustomed to it and learned a great deal about things we had no idea of earlier. We much regret that we were not able to take greater advantage of the good and useful counsels, especially the proletarians, who also received some material support in the form of milk and bottles for weak children. We are surprised that our township committee could not provide housing for such a useful and necessary institution. We mothers request the cooperation of the township committee in seeing that if a permanent dispensary cannot be opened, then special days be designated at the hospital for the reception of children only and that scales be obtained for weighing them. All of us are very satisfied with the treatment of our children who went to the dispensary; they clearly improved. We ask that in the future you do not forget us and again come to our village, and we ask that the township committee open a dispensary in our village with a female doctor.[54]

The language and agenda were more likely to have been Brianskaia's than those of women she had earlier described as not knowing what even uneducated, big-city women had long understood. But the women who turned out for the meeting were undoubtedly those who most appreciated the benefits that the medical team had delivered and were willing to support efforts to continue the service. The final sentence is expressed in a popular idiom, and its request for a female doctor comes across as both genuine and understandable.

In Gdov district the results were mixed. At the beginning of the year, the OMM instructor there, V. Khramchenko, found that township organizers assigned to work among women were responsive to the message about nurseries, and she was able to obtain help from township executive committees in finding space to house children. By the summer of 1926, sixteen nurseries were operating in the district, and information had also arrived about seven more begun on private initiative, although the OMM did not know much about them. Virtually all the nurseries, however, faced familiar problems: inadequate financial support from official bodies, an inability or unwillingness on the part of peasant families to themselves pay for the programs, and, linked to this lack of financing, difficulty in recruiting trained personnel to staff facilities. The staffing problem was affecting not only the summer nurseries but had even caused a termination of well-baby and maternal care at a long-established, year-round dispensary.[55]

The OMM ran into one further difficulty in Gdov, namely, outright hostility and direct resistance among the peasants of one township to the nursery program and the political education associated with it. Predictably, officials attributed such resistance to "terrible backwardness" (*strashnaia kosnost'*) of the populace in that area. But in more sober moments, they also acknowledged that difficulties sometimes stemmed from their own rules, such as the preference in admissions to the nurseries for poor and middle peasants. Some townships admitted only the children of poor peasants, and this policy, in the bureaucratese of the officials, "evoked a negative attitude on the part of the population and somewhat impeded the collection of voluntary contributions."[56] Indeed, other reports suggest that the bias in favor of poor peasants may have stigmatized the nursery operations and undermined support for them in some locales.[57]

Still, the concluding report on the summer's work was upbeat. In 1926, this second year of an all-out effort for summer nurseries in the villages, the Leningrad OMM could announce that 102 programs were serving more than 2,000 children. The year before they had fielded less than half this number: 43 nurseries serving 1,005 children.[58] Officials also claimed to take heart at the large number of villages in the program that had passed resolutions noting their desire for the nurseries to continue again the next summer, two townships even offering to use their own means and personal efforts to help out.[59]

This jump in the number of nurseries in Leningrad province was similar to that for the Russian federation as a whole. Starting with only 125 summer nurseries in 1922 and rising to no more than 524 in 1924, the first big campaign of 1924–1925 more than tripled the number in Russia to 1,853 in 1925, and the second campaign raised the total substantially again to 2,924 for the summer of 1926.[60] But the advent in the last years of the 1920s of the drive toward industrialization meant giving less attention to the countryside, at least in the short run. Nurseries continued to be of importance, but the focus shifted to supplying industrial sites. The slogan became "The more factory smoke stacks we have, the more nurseries we need." In the countryside, emphasis moved to creating nurseries on the small number of state and collective farms, here too using slogans that emphasized productivity more than the fight against infant mortality (for example, "Summer nurseries help to raise crop yields").[61] In any case, the lack of resources and personnel in the late 1920s stunted the earlier, rapid growth of village summer nurseries.[62]

Medical Profession

The lack of trained specialists willing to serve in rural areas long remained an impediment to advancing the work of the OMM. Just when the campaigns of the mid-1920s on behalf of summer nurseries, dispensaries, and other efforts to reach villagers began to enjoy some success, their development was frustrated by the difficulty of recruiting qualified personnel to staff rural facilities. Again, my most complete data are from Leningrad province. The difficulty occurred throughout the country, however, and in most places it was probably worse than in Leningrad province, which was relatively well supplied with educated people. The fact that most of the district officials in Leningrad province were nevertheless complaining about this problem gives some measure of its dimensions. Reports from the large Luga district, for example, told of the declining number of medical midwives active there in 1926; when current people left the work, new candidates did not appear to fill the positions.[63] Likewise, in Gdov district, the longstanding OMM work at a dispensary was dying out in 1926 for want of qualified staff.[64] Even when candidates could be found, they were often the least-skilled people in their profession and sometimes did more harm than good. One doctor was so disliked that the activist women of the village labeled her with epithets normally used by doctors to describe peasant women. This letter came from the women of a village in Luga district:

> In late August [1926] you sent us a doctor, V. I. Stokhovskaia, but from the very start of work Dr. Stokhovskaia behaved not as a doctor should but like a loutish, dark, and stupid village woman [*derevenskaia baba*]—and we don't actually have such women here. The doctor treats the people rudely, argues with patients hourly, and in the presence of patients chews out the staff, makes a row with the physician's assistant and often insults the patients and poorly examines the children. We women and delegatki . . . reported this to the [township supervisors] and got no results, and so we are coming to you to ask that you immediately remove that doctor or we are not going to take our children there anymore, because we don't get anything except insults and wisecracks from Dr. Stokhovskaia.[65]

Staffing problems affected not only areas like the Luga district, which lay a great distance from the city of Leningrad. Even within the Leningrad district, the immediate suburban region surrounding the metropolis in which most villages were a short ride from Leningrad or a city or factory served by a hospital, a large majority of village women continued to go without medical care. They delivered their babies just as they had in the past. "Unfortunately," the district health officer wrote in 1926, "our work is impeded by the lack of experienced workers willing to go to the village."[66] Matters had not improved a year later when the OMM had to inform its activists in the countryside that it could not provide specialists and organizers to every district, and it would be "a very long time" before it could do so.[67]

This difficulty in recruiting medical staff to the countryside may seem remarkable in view of the longstanding commitment of Russian physicians to rural community-health service in the nineteenth century. Idealistic doctors had gone in large numbers into the zemstvo medical service starting in the 1860s, and the leading professional organization for doctors, the Pirogov Society, was dedicated to the model of community medicine. Despite an exodus of physicians from zemstvo positions following the upheavals of 1905–1906, as late as 1913 nearly 30 percent of Russia's doctors were working in rural areas. By the 1920s the proportion in the countryside had declined to 22 percent, and it continued a rapid fall until the period from 1926 to 1930 when it fluctuated between 14 and 18 percent.[68] Anton Bol'shakov claimed that the proportion had actually dropped to 10 percent in the mid-1920s, and added that while "the villages were being emptied of doctors, the cities had a mass of unemployed physicians."[69] He was right. There was no shortage of physicians; the cities had an oversupply. In fact, nearly 9 percent of the physicians in urban areas were out of work, yet they refused to take positions in the countryside. They preferred to change professions or accept low-level jobs as laboratory technicians rather than leave centers of cultural life and serve in the provinces.[70] Agitational pressure to convince doctors to move into vacant positions in rural areas seemed to have little effect. In the period from October 1926 to January 1930, when such pressure was being applied, the unemployment rate for urban physicians declined only 1 percent, and it is by no means clear that the reduction was the result of physicians taking jobs in the countryside.[71]

The idealism and commitment of doctors in the nineteenth century to community medicine was not shared by the new generation. The usual explanations that life was difficult in the countryside were not convincing. Conditions in the 1920s were scarcely any worse than they had been in the late nineteenth century. Something else had happened: a decisive shift in doctors' sense of identity, professionalism, and purpose. It is difficult to pinpoint the exact causes of the shift, but some observations may be helpful. It has to be kept in mind, first, how much the nineteenth-century movement for community medicine had owed to the ideology of populism that dominated the intellectual life of the 1860s through the 1880s. Political activists and writers in that era believed that Russia's future depended on the peasants, for they formed the overwhelming majority of the population. Populists idealized the peasants and thought of them as naturally communal and socialistic. The peasants, they believed, being uncontaminated by the artificiality of urban life, were ultimately capable of serving as the foundation of a harmonious social and political system that would be truly Russian in its shape and values. Advocates of community medicine, though less idealistic and radical than the leading populists, nevertheless shared with them a belief in the common people's underlying goodness. Furthermore, like the populists, they were opposed to centralization and state control and believed that Russia's afflictions and the social ills that underlay them could most effectively be cured not by state-directed development but by furnishing resources directly to doctors and others working among the people.

As the influence of populism declined toward the end of the century, the medical field was also being altered by new discoveries in bacteriology, technology, specializations, and imported models of professionalism. Some doctors were developing private practices on the fee-for-service model. Others were convinced that centralized, government-supported organization of public health would be more effective in improving the health of the people than the locally based zemstvo provision of general practitioners.[72] When the dust settled from the Revolution of 1917 and the civil war that followed, this centralized model of research and health delivery was ascendant. Moreover, the new prevailing ideologies of liberalism and Marxism were urban-centered and associated Russia's salvation not with supposedly innocent rustics but with the people who had left the countryside to create a new life in the cities as professionals or workers. The prestige of community medicine, bound as it had been to ideas of populism and individual rather than corporate action, no longer had a hold on young physicians; this ideal was of little use in recruiting the workers needed for rural medical services.

A New Revolution

Starting in the late 1920s, the massive mobilizations accompanying the first Five-Year Plan and the policies of rapid industrialization and collectivization of agriculture accelerated the pace of change in maternal and child-health services. Many writers have seen this period as a time when women lost ground. They were asked to give up the idealistic hopes of the revolution for more individual freedom and personal development and to relinquish the promised communal support in household tasks and child care. Instead, women had taken on the double burden of participating in the work force plus motherhood and home care, and, if ambitious for advancement, a third burden of after-hours study and organizational involvement. Elite women may have experienced the revolutionary push of the 1930s as a loss of this kind, but women in rural Russia found this period marked by both losses and gains. Those women whose families resisted collectivization or who themselves just happened to be in the way when reprisals were carried out suffered terrible personal and material losses. The families of at least one-third of the women we interviewed had suffered such losses. Indeed, every family that had enjoyed some measure of autonomy lost it. But for some farm women (as well as for many women working in industrial enterprises), the 1930s also initiated the delivery of family support services. I want to emphasize that this was just a beginning, a promise of what was to come, because it took a long time for services to appear in many villages. Of the villages we surveyed, toward the end of the 1930s a few had received medical services, maternity leaves, or rudimentary summer child care facilities; others had to wait until well after World War II, in some locations until the 1970s. But the government, at the time it launched collectivization, decided to sponsor these services. It was clear that if the state was to recruit women into the work force and at the same time maintain their essential reproductive contributions, it had to provide more by way of maternal and child care. The change was grimly ironic: the government coming to the support of women and families at just the time it was destroying so many of the most resourceful rural families through "dekulakization" and the failure to assist famine victims. It was this very damage the government did to farm families that necessitated substantial new inputs into the agrarian sector in support of women's productive and reproductive roles.

The decision to push for full-scale collectivization in late 1929 turned the spotlight on the condition of health services in the countryside. At a meeting hastily called on the last day of November 1929, Commissar of Health Semashko confessed that this area of work had been lagging badly. He was confronted there by representatives not just of the health services but also of the State Planning Commission, the Commissariat of Lands, and the agencies in charge of state and collective farms. Excuses that it was difficult to recruit personnel were no longer acceptable, and the health officials had to commit to the rapid development of maternal and child health-care facilities in the countryside. Priority was to go to large state farms, machine tractor stations, and regions of full-scale collectivization, and if personnel could not be found in other ways, child-care and health workers would be recruited from the ranks of collective and state-farm women themselves.[73]

To ensure that these changes occurred, the entire medical community had to be brought on board, including specialist researchers, who previously had shown little interest in social problems. The consequences of the decisions made at the Commissariat of Health for these specialists can be followed in the dramatic changes that then ensued in the leading professional periodical on women's health, the *Journal of Obstetrics and Gynecology* (founded in 1887). Here was a scientific periodical that, like many others being published since the nineteenth century, had scarcely been affected by the Revolution of 1917 and its aftermath. Soon after the Revolution, it is true, the journal had been forced to cease publication for a time because of staff disruptions and paper shortages, but as soon as the editors could reassemble their staff and locate adequate supplies, they resumed publishing the same menu of exclusively clinical and professional articles they had carried in the prerevolutionary era. The orientation strongly leaned to curative medicine rather than toward the new regime's goals of education and preventive medicine, and its heroes were practitioners and teachers of the earlier era, some of whom opposed policies of the Soviet government.

All this changed suddenly in 1930. The periodical's very first issue that year carried the text of a talk given by I. F. Makkaveev to the Leningrad Society of Obstetrics and Gynecology in which he delivered a stinging indictment of the members for their focus on clinical and curative medicine and their lofty indifference to the welfare of mothers in particular. To the extent that social medicine had made any headway, he declared, it had been left to pediatricians, whose focus was on the children and not their mothers. The medical society had been satisfied to stand on the sidelines when it should have been taking a leadership role, Makkaveev asserted. He then outlined a course of action that would bring work on maternal welfare into greater prominence.[74]

In the next issues, the editors cleared a third of the journal's space for articles on social medicine, and their writers worked up plans for delivery of health services to the people on a scale not contemplated earlier. Among the studies that appeared soon after were "Protection of the Health of Women and Children in State and Collective Farms," "Maternal Mortality: Constitutional, Social, and Daily Life Factors," "Abortion in the Village," and "Information about Untrained Granny Midwives Today." By the next year, 1931, the editors had added a separate section on "Social Gynecology and Obstetrics." Although in its first year, this new section took third place behind the perennial first two sections, "Lead Articles" and "Clinical and Experimental," this order soon changed. The 1932 volume reversed the positions of the social and clinical sections, placing Social Gynecology and Obstetrics just behind the Lead Articles.

By 1932 the pressure from Party radicals everywhere was intense, and angry accusations were the norm. The journal started off the year with a lead article titled "Against Rotten Liberalism in the Medical Press," which took to task many writers on women's health for their false views or neglect of important issues. Some were accused of not paying attention to the social conditions that affected women's growth, illness, and difficulties with birthing. Others were blamed for stressing that biology was destiny. Doctors were said to have exaggerated the importance of motherhood in a woman's life and underrated women as workers; they had distorted the effects of work on the female organism, thus undermining women's struggle for equality, which could best be achieved by altering the conditions of work rather than relegating women to the domestic hearth. Concerns allegedly expressed by doctors about the effects on mortality of unhygienic conditions that women faced in industry, the editors declared, simply flew in the face of "precise and irrefutable data we now possess about the significant decrease in mortality generally and infant mortality in particular, especially in industrial centers."[75]

This attack on doctors was part of a broad assault on persons and agencies that the government believed were not doing enough to facilitate the entry of women into the work force. The industrial work force was the initial area of concern, but as soon as the collectivization drive got under way in earnest, the inadequacy of services in the countryside became glaringly apparent. Dr. D. A. Glebov of the State Obstetrics and Gynecological Institute in Leningrad had taken a lead in using the *Journal of Obstetrics and Gynecology* to promote the rapid expansion of medical services, and he soon was rewarded with its editorship. Glebov had first looked into conditions in the state and collective farm sector and reported early in 1930 that despite the efforts in the past decade, only 12 percent of births to peasant women were attended by any medical assistance. Even this figure, which he apparently got from materials for the Five-Year Plan, seems inflated in view of the little progress that had been made in the 1920s. Glebov acknowledged the woefully small number of facilities, noting that the Five-Year Plan had called for only 1,000 year-round institutions. But 40 percent of the farms were suddenly collectivized, and even though the health departments were adding 2,000 nurseries, 500 dispensaries, and 1,500 midwife stations, these facilities were "drowning in a sea of unfolding socialist construction in agriculture." He emphasized the need to expand the number of midwife stations, first of all, and then to push toward year-round nurseries for state and collective farms so that these enterprises could be supported like other industrial operations and fully use their female work forces.[76]

In December 1930, the All-Russian Conference on Medical Services to Collective and State Farms convened and declared that the medical offices in the countryside had to take responsibility for OMM work in their locales and that large state farms, Machine Tractor Stations, and regions of heavy collectivization had to provide milk kitchens, mobile dispensaries, permanent nurseries, and even mobile nurseries to bring nursing children to mothers at work in the fields. A few months afterward, in April 1931, the All-Russian OMM Conference met amid the heavy pressure of an enlarged attendance by representatives of trade unions and Party offices. Strong emphasis was placed on services that would free mothers for work, especially providing curative as well as preventive care services and setting aside quarantined spaces in nurseries so that sick children could be cared for and thereby reduce the absenteeism rates from work for the mothers. This second point was highly controversial, since mixing sick and healthy children at care facilities was scarcely good public-health practice, and the expense of staff and buildings for separate care facilities was not trivial.[77] It also conflicted with the emphasis up to this time on preventive medicine. But the preventive approach, like many other well-intentioned efforts of the 1920s, had to give way to the sheer pressure to expand the work force as rapidly as possible. And this was not a time when doctors or anyone else could safely raise practical or ideological objections to Party policy. The measures were passed. To the extent they were implemented, they primarily affected industrial areas and not the countryside, where improvements of any kind were slow in coming amid the wreckage inflicted by the collectivization drive and the famine that came in its wake to large areas of the country.

Slogans at the OMM Conference signaled the changes going on in the country. Although primary attention went to the industrial regions and large construction projects, the countryside was not forgotten. The agrarian sector was itself being mechanized and industrialized, for large investments of machinery had to be directed to the collective farms to make up for animal draft power lost during the collectivization drive. Accordingly, a key OMM slogan for the countryside was "A Tractor in the Field, and Nurseries in Daily Life." More ominously, other slogans emphasized the responsibility of medical personnel. They were no longer to think of themselves as educators and supervisors of care facilities but were to take an active part in the treatment of every sick child, assuming responsibility for the youngster's recovery and well-being. Prominent slogans announced, for example, that "The Doctor and Nurse at the Dispensary Are Accountable for the Life and Health of the Children in Their District" and "We Shall Thoroughly Investigate Every Death of a Child to Ascertain Its Causes and the Guilty Parties."[78]

After the end of the first Five-Year Plan, the governing council of the Commissariat of Health met in April 1933 to review a report by a team of investigators on the status of maternity care in the Russian republic after more than three years of strenuous effort to expand services. The number of maternity beds was reported to have increased substantially (from 19,987 to 31,330) during the plan period, which ran for four years, January 1929 to January 1933. Industrial centers supposedly saw a 43 percent rise from 12,994 to 18,620, while for the countryside a 73 percent growth was claimed, from 6,973 to 12,110. But these achievements, like much else reported about the Five-Year Plan, were gross exaggerations. Many of the supposed maternity beds were actually being used for other purposes, not the least for an increasing number of abortions. The investigating team disclosed that an order of the Commissariat in November 1931 to remove abortion beds from maternity homes had not been carried out. They added (in a sentence struck from a later draft) that "the number of abortions being performed in maternity homes is exceptionally high," a situation that in the cities was limiting the time birthing mothers could stay at the homes, and in the villages was causing a significant reduction in the ability of the homes to provide birthing.[79]

Sanitary conditions were another area of concern. From Samara to Leningrad, the team had run into "intolerable conditions" of intermingling in the care facilities of sick and healthy women and children. Indeed, in all the maternity facilities in the city of Leningrad, save for the State Obstetrics and Gynecological Institute itself, there was no system for separating birthing women with fevers and those without, so that "all are examined at admission in the same room and in the maternity home in Smolny district even on the same table." If sick and healthy people were mingled, the team continued, so too were the linens, which were not only inadequately supplied to many facilities but were also washed together, infected materials with uninfected. And this occurred not just in remote areas but right on the outskirts of Moscow because few hospitals had two separate cleaning operations.[80]

As for providing the rural areas with increased maternal and child-health facilities, according to the investigators very little progress had been made because most local health officials failed to appreciate the importance of midwife stations. Consequently, not only was the number of such stations altogether inadequate, but those that existed were operated poorly. They noted further problems, including a very weak development of birth assistance to women in their homes and a virtual absence of record keeping. "In a majority of places absolutely no records are kept, and in the remainder the records are primitive." It seems, too, that the midwives had very little medical backup or guidance. "In a majority of cases," the report stated, "there is no supervision or inspection of the stations by doctors."[81] To make matters worse, the governing council of the Commissariat of Health was having difficulty winning the cooperation of its branch offices, whose administrators were accused of not doing enough to prepare adequate numbers of medical midwives in technicums and short courses and of not upgrading and recertifying the skills of current doctors and midwives. Indeed, the regional offices were outright refusing to cooperate on some matters, for example, defying an order to organize separate, independent offices for maternity care, an order that they actually succeeded after a time in rolling back.[82]

The second half of the 1930s saw increased pressures and responsibilities for the OMM as the Soviet government adopted strong policies to encourage population growth. The growth of fascist regimes in Europe and especially the Nazi takeover in Germany had brought to power parties that were ideologically anticommunist and militaristic. These parties promoted pronatalist strategies for building the human resources required for industrial growth and military success. While the Soviet government belittled these efforts abroad by comparing them unfavorably to its own policies for protecting mothers and children, it felt menaced by the growing power of the fascist regimes and apprehensive about the steady decline in fertility at home, a decline that since the late 1920s appeared ever more closely linked to an increasing number of abortions. So, it soon responded with vigorous pronatalist measures of its own.

Starting in 1935, the government banned abortions in the case of a first pregnancy. In the same year, it extended the maternity leave and benefits introduced in the 1920s for women in the industrial sector in part to collective farm workers, thus reducing the disparity in the treatment of working class and peasant women. These so-called "decree leaves" gave collective farm women one month off before birthing and one month after at half pay. Officials touted the leaves as not only a great social boon but also a breakthrough in supervising the health of rural women, who now would have to appear for a check-up in order to be registered for the leave.[83] This enthusiasm, if not entirely out of place, was premature. The arrival of these benefits was much delayed in many places, and while farm women gladly sought this registration, many went only for the single check-up required to obtain it, after which they reverted to self-care and even traditional birthing.

The All-Russian Congress of Soviets in January 1935 also called for a further rapid expansion of OMM facilities. The aim was to enlarge the network of dispensaries for women and infants so that by 1937 every district (*raion*) would have at least one. At the same time, the congress approved the new policy of installing maternity homes on collective farms, using means provided by the farms themselves. And it called on the Health Commissariat to increase the number of midwife stations in the countryside as well, to furnish them with qualified staff and augment midwife services for home births.[84] The inspiration for maternity homes at collective farms had come from the Ukrainian republic, where, between 1933 and 1935, more than 400 such facilities had reportedly been created. Russian OMM officials were, however, reluctant to push this program too fast for fear that poorly equipped and managed collective-farm maternity homes "could discredit the service in the eyes of the population right from the start."[85] This concern was not misplaced, as doctors' reports attest. We also learned from the village women interviewed for this study that conditions in rural maternity homes in the mid-1930s were so unappealing that many mothers who at first used them returned to home birthing for their subsequent children.

The best-known pronatalist measure from this time was the Family Law of June 1936 that outlawed abortion in all cases except when the life or health of the mother was threatened or serious genetic disorders might be transmitted. It should be kept in mind that although the abortion ban was what made this law famous and produced controversy and opposition, the legislation included much more, as its title makes clear: "An enactment on the banning of abortions, increase of material assistance to birthing women, establishment of state assistance to large families, expansion of the network of maternity homes, nurseries and kindergartens, strengthening of criminal punishment for non-payment of child support, and changes in legislation relating to divorce." Unlike the abortion ban, these other measures were not only acceptable but even popular with most women, and we look next at the efforts to implement them.

But first it should be pointed out that, despite the draconian abortion ban and the promised improvements in support of motherhood, the law did not achieve its intended effect for long. The first two years of the law registered an increase in fertility as women planning on abortions suddenly found that option closed to them and had to give birth. But very soon women started to limit their fertility again, either by applying contraceptive techniques, returning to self-abortions, or establishing personal networks for obtaining illegal abortions. By 1938 the birthrate stopped rising and resumed its pre-1936 downward trend. Even the temporary rise in fertility during the first two years was not as productive as hoped because it was accompanied by an increase in infant mortality. Illness and death rates from dysentery and summer diarrheas rose sharply in 1936, and in early 1937 they jumped enough to scare the Russian Commissar of Health, P. G. Sergiev, into issuing a series of lengthy orders for a major mobilization of all medical, sanitary, and child-care facilities to bring the crisis under control. The jump in death rates of infants and small children in this period was substantial enough to undercut much of the gain in fertility.[86]

Results of the Late-1930s Efforts

The law banning abortion initially reduced the number of abortions sharply and continued to hold down the number of legal abortions. But women refused to give up the right to control their fertility and, since the government now discouraged other contraceptive methods as well, soon established networks for obtaining illegal abortions. Assistance came from sympathetic medical workers, but many non-professional practitioners also contributed. Our interviews with village women of the generation whose childbearing years fell in this period of the abortion ban revealed that virtually every village had a person (most often a woman) who performed illegal abortions. Indeed, it was just this generation of village women who first began resorting to abortions on a large scale.

The women either used the services of an underground abortionist or simply performed self-abortions. How many abortions actually occurred is impossible to know, since only a small proportion of them came to light and were registered by the authorities either as legally approved procedures (about 8 percent of total known abortions) or as treatment sought for botched illegal abortions (about 92 percent). These two known counts amounted to 426,434 cases for the Russian republic in 1938; they rose nearly 9 percent to 464,246 in 1939.[87] The actual number must have been several times this amount.[88]

Enforcement of the law against illegal abortionists was weak, if one can judge from complaints filed by reviewing bodies. A report in 1940 by the director of the State Obstetrics and Gynecological Institute in Leningrad, Dr. E. E. Polotskii, criticized medical personnel for not giving attention to this matter and insinuated that they were themselves implicated in sheltering abortionists. "The number of criminal underground abortions established as such is laughably small," he wrote. "Of the 490 incomplete abortions registered in Luga hospital in 1938, only three led to criminal accusations, in 1939 of 514 only four did. The reality, of course, is several tens of times greater." There was even a case, Polotskii added, in which a woman dying of a botched abortion gave the address of the abortionist, and nothing was done about it until two years later when the woman's daughter filed a complaint.[89] Defending themselves against similar accusations from central authorities, medical workers across the country complained of the difficulty of determining a spontaneous abortion from an induced one when women showed up for treatment. They argued that they could only know for sure if the women actually confessed to an illegal abortion.[90] Statistics in Polotskii's report about the few convictions obtained against abortionists suggest why the hospitals and medical workers were not turning in the perpetrators: a substantial number of the convicted abortionists were themselves physicians or other medical workers.[91]

Later we will hear from the women themselves why they refused to knuckle under to this law and made not only defiant but life-threatening decisions to take control of their fertility. It is worth mentioning here, however, one general indicator that undoubtedly figured importantly in making such decisions possible, namely, the substantial growth during the 1930s in the education of rural girls. Four-year primary schooling was made compulsory in 1931; as early as 1935 girls had become nearly half of rural pupils. By the end of the decade the percentage of rural women under the age of fifty in the Russian republic who were literate was approaching 80 percent.[92] Soviet education modeled a world in which people could create a better life for themselves through individual initiative and collective action, and young women understood that they could scarcely achieve anything better if they lived as their mothers had, giving birth continuously through their childbearing years and rearing a large family. They rejected the government's effort to turn reproduction into an obligation of citizenship.

A second aspect of the 1936 law was a promise to expand the number of maternity beds throughout the country. Cities and industrial centers were to gain 11,000 more beds in the next three years, and the countryside 32,000, half of which were to be established and supported primarily by collective farms. These years did see a substantial increase in the number of maternity homes and beds in the provinces whose information I was able to check. Soviet scholar E. M. Konius claims that by 1941, two years beyond this period, the number of maternity beds for the USSR as a whole had reached 141,873 and that 66,261 of these were serving villages. This figure for the villages, if accurate, records an impressive, more than fivefold increase over the 12,110 maternity beds reportedly available to rural dwellers at the end of the first Five-Year Plan in 1933.[93] But it is also a measure of how poorly served the countryside remained. While 70 percent of the population resided in the villages, they were served by less than one-half of the country's maternity beds. Equally important, the state of the facilities in the countryside did not inspire confidence in either the authorities or many of the rural women themselves. Evidently, maternity homes had been established quickly to meet plan targets but had not been furnished with adequate fuel, linen, and other supplies. Some homes enumerated in the plan achievements did not function at all and existed merely on paper. Either they were too poorly equipped to provide service or had failed to recruit midwives because the collective farms charged with sponsoring them refused to provide support and housing.[94]

The doctors who visited rural maternity homes on inspection tours painted disheartening pictures of conditions there. One report comes from a team traveling through the eastern reaches of Leningrad province near the city of Babaevo in bitter cold, sometimes on horseback, sometimes in an open truck with no hay to insulate them against the wind and chill. The birthing facility the travelers visited proved to be no place to warm themselves:

> This maternity home makes a rather sad impression. Despite the fact that, according to the midwife, a large number of women are very close to delivery [na snosiakh] and the decisive season is approaching, the home was far from what you could consider outfitted. It was quite dirty, and the cold was such that it was hard to stand there even in your overcoat—and that was the actual delivery room. The premises had probably not been refurbished in fifteen years. Dirt was everywhere and the plaster was falling off, a singularly neglected building.[95]

From the other side of the country, in Stalingrad province, came a report in 1940 of a maternity home that had been opened three years earlier on a state farm:

> Fuel for the winter has not been secured. The lighting is done by kerosene lamp, and the kerosene is poorly supplied, and frequently is not available at all. The midwife [a sixty-five-year-old woman] lives right in the maternity

home, not in separate quarters, and all the doors are open [between her quarters and the other rooms]. The home is wretchedly furnished, the beds are iron without netting, the mattresses filled with straw. A *Rakhmanov* [obstetrical] bed[96] is available but it is not used as intended, and women give birth on an ordinary bed. . . . Guidelines for her work are provided, but the midwife does not make use of them. Women who come in for check-ups are examined on the same couch as birthing mothers. Disinfection of bedpans and cleaning of oilcloths are done improperly. No bast scrubbers or brushes for washing hands are in the maternity home.[97]

Another concern of the inspector and her superiors was that the midwife merely performed births and did no home visiting, which, in view of her advanced age, is not surprising. But it meant that essential outreach work was not being done to identify pregnant women and follow up after delivery on care of the baby. These criticisms were not limited to the two reports cited here. Similar complaints were being leveled at thirty maternity homes in Moscow province.[98]

In sum, facilities were being put in place rapidly but haphazardly. As a consequence, health officials had many complaints about poor supplies, inadequate staff, even about thoughtless spacing of maternity homes and midwife stations. Some were right next to hospitals and therefore hardly used, and others were far from populated areas and therefore also underutilized. In addition, midwives were often unable to perform much of the work they were expected to do. In some cases, such as the elderly midwife in the Stalingrad state farm home, the midwife was physically unable to carry out the duties; in many other instances, midwives were continually called on to perform such services as first-aid or pharmacy work, so that they had little time to check up on pregnant women and arrange for deliveries. Officials expressed fear that women who had once gone to a rural maternity home or midwife station were reverting to home births with the notorious granny midwives. Indeed, women of this generation, as we learned from interviews, were doing just that because of the discomforts and difficulties associated with birthing in these cold and poorly supplied rural facilities.[99] At home, a woman would usually be better fed, could keep an eye on her other children, and feel more comfortable. It is likewise a mark of the mutual trust and cooperation of village women that they continued to provide and to use the services of granny midwives at a time, as we also learn from the interviews, that these traditional caregivers were being mercilessly persecuted by the authorities. Health officials, for their part, emphasized the occasional tragic side of such a choice. In expressing concern in his survey of Leningrad province about how "pregnant women were escaping the attention of midwives [who were distracted from their main task] and still turning to the *babki*," Dr. Polotskii reported that "in Borovichi hospital a birthing mother died from infection after giving birth at home with a babka, even though a midwife station, we discovered, was only ¾ of a kilometer away."[100]

Despite the many problems pointed out by inspectors and officials, it should be kept in mind that a large number of facilities were being put in place during this period, facilities that would provide the foundation for a more effective development of maternity services for rural women after World War II.

Two other areas of care for mothers and children saw little growth in this period, at least as far as the villages were concerned. These were the expansion of dispensaries and the provision of child-care facilities, nurseries in particular, but also kindergartens and supervised playgrounds for children. Dispensaries were not given priority in the 1936 Family Law, and it is therefore not surprising that they received less emphasis in the following years, despite the long-standing commitment of the health services to unifying prenatal and postnatal office visits and examinations with the birthing services. Although Konius printed statistics showing a steady rise in the number of dispensaries for the USSR as a whole—from 2,148 in 1928 to 4,384 in 1937—the large Russian republic counted only 1,904 women's or combined women's and children's dispensaries in 1938 (half of which served the countryside), and officials expressed deep concern about their work.[101] Dr. Polotskii's report included inspections of four district dispensaries in Leningrad province, and of these only the Novgorod city dispensary received anything like passing marks. Yet even it had failed to do adequate outreach to women or to coordinate its efforts with maternity homes, two supposedly key features of dispensary work. Other facilities did not perform even the most elementary tests, such as urine analysis or Wasserman tests.[102]

Officials at the Commissariat of Health in Moscow expressed the same concerns about dispensaries in most of their provincial cities, especially about the failure of these institutions to perform outreach to women in their districts.[103] Close to home, in Moscow province itself, of twenty dispensaries surveyed in 1939 only eight did outreach and pathology workups. Five did no kind of educational work.[104] In view of this lackadaisical performance, it is probably not surprising that the number of visits to dispensaries declined in the late 1930s at a rate considerably in excess of the decline in the birthrate. In Moscow province, for example, the number of visits to dispensaries fell by 30 percent from 1938 to 1939, even though the number of births declined by only 5 percent.[105]

To compensate for the failing work of the dispensaries, health offices dispatched doctors and young teachers from the medical institutes to provincial towns, factories, and farms for educational outreach. The reports these outreach workers submitted suggest the status of care facilities and the difficulties of educating women outside the large cities. OMM doctors who made trips within Leningrad province expressed satisfaction with what they were able to accomplish in Pskov district, but in this instance staff support was exceptionally good and the doctors were primarily visiting urban hospitals and factories. The doctors sent out to rural areas told a different story. A team led by Dr. Levidov that visited a set of collective farms reported on a typical situation. The local organizer seemed to have had no idea that the team was arriving, and four hours had to be wasted while everything was being arranged on the spot. The visitors were then supposed to travel six to eight kilometers to the collective farms but ended up going twice that distance, much of it on horseback after their car bogged down in the snow. Finally, late at night, when about twenty-five people could be assembled for a lecture in a freezing room, it turned out that 70 percent of them spoke only Finnish and stared blankly at the lecturers. Levidov figured that the rest of the audience understood little more, since they had few questions after the lecture. The session ended at 11 o'clock, and the doctors had to spend the night in the same unheated room. This kind of work, Levidov angrily remarked, was a "profanation," utterly worthless. "It has to be approached with some sense of realism."[106]

Several other reports mention the same lack of organization and correspondingly fruitless efforts to contact and educate the people, even though the doctors appeared to be committed and doing their best under difficult circumstances. For example, on a trip to the Lisii Nos area (northwest of Leningrad along the Gulf of Finland) the team nearly got into a slugfest with a local boss who refused them entry into the hall where they were supposed to give a medical lecture sandwiched between a collective farm's accounts meeting and a movie. Apparently the chairman of the village council, who had arranged the lecture, had vanished on a spree; the next in command did not "cotton" to outsiders, whether or not they flashed documents from the big city. Even the local police were unable to budge him.[107] It should nevertheless be noted that in other places where the doctors were able to make direct contact with ordinary collective farmers, they commented on the peasants' positive response to them and also on the concern the peasants expressed about the health of their children, evident in the many questions they posed about specific illnesses and how to prevent and treat them.[108]

Unlike dispensaries, nurseries were an important element of the 1936 Family Law. The legislation called for a doubling of nursery spaces by 1939 both in the urban, industrial, state-farm sector and in the collective farm sector. An astonishing figure was projected for the collective farm sector of a half million new, year-round nursery beds and 4 million new summer nursery beds.[109] It is hard to find reliable figures for the country as a whole, but certainly nothing on this scale was actually achieved or even approached. Figures printed in the 1950s after Stalin's death recorded a growth in the total number of year-round nursery beds (urban and rural) from mid-1936 to 1941 of 213,577.[110] Summer nurseries in total were reported to have under 2 million spaces as late as 1954.[111] Indeed, in the late 1930s, despite the terror (or possibly because of it) the number of nursery beds in some places was not growing but declining. For example, Leningrad province, while reporting an increase in the number of spaces in urban, year-round nurseries from 3,645 in 1935 to 7,654 in 1939, experienced a major reversal in the countryside. There spaces in year-round nurseries dwindled from 10,931 to 7,441; in summer nurseries they plummeted from 42,314 to 28,189. There was some shifting of population from the countryside to the cities during this period but nothing comparable to the changes in nursery spaces, and, in any case, this period saw a loss of 13,606 nursery beds overall at a time when the population of the province (not count-ing the city of Leningrad) was on the increase.[112]

The provision of other child-care facilities such as children's homes, kinder-gartens, and supervised playgrounds was likewise lagging. Information about developments in this area was so poor that in composing his report in 1940 for Leningrad province, Dr. Polotskii had almost nothing substantive to say. "I do not have proper figures for the province," he wrote. "But the fact that Novgorod district, for example, did not shy away from reporting that it had no informa-tion on the state of kindergartens and supervised playgrounds or about their development before 1939 says a lot." The establishment of kindergartens was running far behind plan, as much as 80 percent behind in Novgorod district, Polotskii lamented. In thrashing about for explanations of the calamitous con-dition of child-care facilities, Polotskii pointed to the lack of concern, insuf-ficient space, inadequate supplies of equipment and linens, poor sanitation, and lack of supervision. "It is hard for me even to offer concrete proposals about what to do," he sighed, "but it is clear that the situation has to be radically reorganized."[113]

The War Years and After

As Polotskii's reports and the others indicate, on the eve of World War II conditions for maternal and child welfare fell far short of the promises of the mid-1930s. During the war, many of the facilities and resources assigned to OMM work had to be reallocated to relief efforts, including medical services and evacuation operations. The need to rely more heavily than ever on women for the work force did nevertheless compel a boost in the provision of child-care services.[114] After the tide of war turned and the frightful toll of human losses was assessed, the government issued new legislation to encourage women to meet the country's need to replenish the population. Women who were bearing a much heavier burden than before of industrial and agricultural production were now admonished to give renewed attention to their reproductive contri-bution. The Family Law of July 1944 on "increased state assistance to pregnant women, large families, and single mothers" promised a one-time subsidy for a third child (before the war, subsidies were paid only after the seventh child) and a continuing subsidy for subsequent children until age five. This was the law that also established the well-known "Heroine Mother" awards and other prizes and medals for women who produced large numbers of children. The subsi-dies, having a pronatalist intent, were to be paid only for children born after 1944. In effect, the many war widows with large families could not claim a sub-sidy unless they remarried and had children or were willing to have children out of wedlock.[115] A highly controversial aspect of the law (once Stalin died and controversy was tolerated) was its denial of paternity suits against men who fathered children out of wedlock, a provision that returned the country to the family regime of tsarist times, recreating once again a de facto status of illegitimacy for the children.[116]

After the war, the OMM had first to attend to the reappropriation and restaffing of its facilities, which had been converted to war and relief efforts. Its progress was often remarked on in the internal memoranda by the number of institutions that had been reconverted from wartime purposes and returned to normal functioning. A report on the Russian republic in 1947 laments that the Ministry of Health was not only far behind in fulfilling the promises of the Family Law of 1944 for providing nursery spaces but moreover that the number of spaces had actually declined by sixteen thousand from 1945 to 1946. The plan for summer nurseries in the countryside was only 60 percent fulfilled, and several hundred child-care institutions and maternity beds had still not been converted from wartime uses.[117] Even where facilities were up and running in the late 1940s and early 1950s, infant and maternal mortality occasionally surged because of breakdowns in prophylactic measures. On the whole, however, illness and death rates were trending downward as the provision of services slowly increased and spread into rural areas and as the qualifications and technical support of medical staffs rose.[118] One continuing area of concern for the authorities—and a clear sign of women's continuing defiance of the law in the interests of controlling their fertility—was the rising rate of illegal abortions. In the city of Moscow, more than 60 percent of the gynecological beds were occupied by women suffering from the aftereffects of botched abortions. In the surrounding province, 50 percent of the beds were used for hospitalization of such women, and the increase in illegal abortions in villages was galloping along at 5 percent a year (to judge from the records of women seeking treatment for incomplete abortions).[119] Not until 1955, after the death of Stalin, was the right to abortion restored and the conditions ameliorated that had been crippling and hospitalizing hundreds of thousands of women each year with underground abortions.

After Stalin's death, the Soviet leadership shifted emphasis in family policy and seemed to regard women's reproductive contribution less as an obligation of citizenship to be enforced by draconian laws than as a personal choice to be encouraged by incentives. Maternity benefits for women working in state enterprises were increased at the beginning of the 1960s, making them eligible for paid leave for eight weeks prior to and eight weeks after a birth. A woman could also choose to take additional unpaid leave until her child attained one year of age. In 1965, similar benefits were extended to collective farm women.[120] Maternity services also improved, largely because of improved communications and transportation that allowed an increasing percentage of rural women to reach central hospitals for prenatal and birthing services and dispense with the local, small maternity homes and midwife stations. These measures, plus further refinements in leave benefits over the next two decades, nevertheless did little to stem the declining birthrate in the European parts of the Soviet Union. In rural areas the demographic crisis was exacerbated by the outflow of young women in the 1970s. Having become educated, and yet still barred from mechanical work by stubbornly defended sex role stereotypes, young women had few options on the farm. They moved to the towns for employment rather than take menial and dirty jobs in livestock handling or field work. This change brought in its wake a "bride problem" in the countryside. Where the young men could not find women to marry, they followed the women into the towns.[121] By the 1980s many villages were seeing no marriages or baptisms for years on end, and population of the countryside began to age and die out.

This sketch of Soviet efforts to reach village women and eventually transform mothering is intended to provide a background against which to view the testimony of village women themselves about their lives, reproductive choices, and mothering practices during the first two-thirds of the twentieth century. The government and Party activists in the fields of women's affairs and health looked on rural women as wholly incompetent in their mothering roles. They viewed them as people subject to superstition and under the sway of ignorant, old midwives, folk healers, and priests whose ideas and practices were harming mothers and their children. Activists first tried to mount educational campaigns through the press and in visiting lectures, but they soon realized that only by delivering medical and child-care services to the villages could they hope to make headway against the established regime of birthing and care. The chapters that follow look into various stages in the lives of young rural women and assess what in their ideas and practices changed and why, which practices became sites of resistance to the assault by the government and which the women chose to relinquish in favor of new ways of dealing with marriage, fertility, and child care. The chapters trace a natural sequence of courtship and marriage, of choices about fertility, birthing, baptism, infant death, child care, and illness.

Courtship and Marriage

A central objective of Bolshevik family policy was the transformation of marriage. The first decree on family law, issued within weeks of the October seizure of government, abolished the requirement of a religious service for marriage and made the act a matter of simple civil registration. The intent was not merely to end religious control of this key social institution but also to free marriage from other constraints affecting the choice of the two individuals involved, including the power of the parents, especially the household head. The new policy soon won acceptance in urban areas and, in time, in the villages as well. Unlike baptism and abortion, traditional forms of marriage-making (such as obligatory matchmaking, the bride-price and bride-show,[1] dowry, and the religious ceremony), reflecting the nature of the institution as a sacred and material contract between two families, did not become sites of resistance to the new regime.

It is far from clear, however, that legal change and the accompanying Communist Party promotion of it were key influences in bringing a new form of marriage-making to the village and, thus, implicitly an instrument for undermining patriarchal power. Among Russians (and somewhat less so among Tatars) the conditions under which partners met and made choices about marriage had been slipping from parental control well before the Bolsheviks came to power. The Revolution, the Civil War, violent reorganization of village life during the 1930s, and World War II all removed large numbers of men from their families and temporarily rendered moot the question of male power in these families. Women were left to fend for themselves; they had to learn to manage their own affairs, including the finding of mates and making of marriage arrangements.

As early as the reign of Peter I, the government decreed that no one could be forced into a marriage against his or her will, although this law probably had little effect beyond the privileged classes.[2] The power of village household heads to force their children into marriage or to prevent a marriage choice by their children continued through the era of serfdom. Serf owners sometimes demanded that household heads marry off their daughters so as to create the largest possible number of production units (understood as a married pair of working age).[3] The abolition of serfdom, however, brought in its wake an increased incidence of young women working outside the family farmstead, a much greater movement of young men and women generally between rural and urban locations, and an accompanying diminution of the power of household heads. In these circumstances, parents were less able to control the choice of mates for their children. Despite the trend to greater personal choice before the 1917 Revolution, the traditional forms used in contracting a marriage, including matchmaking and a religious ceremony, continued in Russian villages until after the collectivization of agriculture—and in many places until after World War II. By the 1950s and 1960s, however, these old forms had likewise faded. More recently, since the collapse of the USSR, church weddings have returned, but not other traditional components of weddings, including formal courtship, matchmaking, and displaying proof of virginity.

Russian Courtship and Matchmaking

Nearly all the Russian women whose first marriages occurred in the 1920s or early 1930s, that is the earliest generation of informants, socialized with young men in their communities before marriage and took an active part in choosing a mate. Cases in which fathers refused to consider the wishes of their daughters and forced them into unwanted marriages were exceptional. Indeed, their parents evidently expected them to do the principal work of finding and agreeing upon a husband-to-be before the rest of the family was brought in to make the wedding arrangements through the traditional matchmaking negotiations and affirming rituals.

For several women of the first generation, traditional youth parties, such as the *posidelki,* remained the primary site of youth socializing and mate selection. Posidelki were evening gatherings organized by village girls in the winters. They would use an unoccupied house or rent the home of a widow in order to talk and sing together while sewing, knitting, or doing other household crafts. The village boys stopped by and joined in with instrumental accompaniment, songs, and dancing. Kissing games were a part of the merriment. As the evening wore on, some couples might pair off to become better acquainted. Aunt Valia (born in 1902, married in 1923) met her husband at these parties during the yuletide.[4] She recalled the parties as the great enjoyment of her youth. Olga Mal'tseva, too, remembered the posidelki in her Novgorod province village with fondness. "We would rent an empty house somewhere and meet there to enjoy ourselves and to dance." A club did not appear until 1949. The parties in her village were known as *supriadki* because the girls did hand spinning for the most part. After they tired of spinning (or just felt lazy, Olga remarked), they would relax by dancing to the music of a concertina, the favorite folk instrument of the day. They especially liked the Yuletide parties. At these, no spinning was required, and the young people just had a good time for two weeks. "We would ride from village to village on horseback. In those days [just before collectivization of agriculture], there were plenty of horses. Now there's nothing to ride on, whereas then we had so many horses. We'd ride to nearby villages, and then they would ride over to see us. We had great fun in those days." When she and her beau had made their choice (it was 1931, and she was eighteen years old), the matchmaking began. "Father didn't force any of us into marriage [Olga had four sisters]. All of us found our husbands on our own. [Then] the matchmaker [the mother of the proposed groom in her case] came. My husband's father had died young. The groom came with his mother and . . . his cousin. Then we had the wedding, a church wedding. The church was lovely, and we had the ceremony there."[5]

Only two of our Russian informants experienced a union arranged by family and matchmakers with little participation of the bride. Praskovia Kurkova, the oldest of our Moscow province informants (born in 1899), was about twenty-three years old and working as a cook at a local children's home (one of those established to care for the millions of homeless children spawned by revolution and war)[6] when a female co-worker proposed that she consider marriage to the co-worker's brother. Praskovia had just two opportunities to get acquainted with the man during evening visits he made to her at her family's garden plot before the co-worker and another woman arrived to do the official matchmaking. The wedding, though agreed upon in the summer, did not take place until the traditional nuptial season in the fall, after the harvest was in. In another respect, however, the wedding departed from the traditional norm: no vodka was served. Because Praskovia invited orphans from the children's home, the wedding celebrations included only beer, mead, and sweet liqueur.[7]

This was the first of two marriages for Praskovia, who evidently had even less choice in the second. After having two children in quick succession with her first husband, she lost him to death in 1927. Her father-in-law then forced her into a second marriage with a widower. Collectivization of agriculture had not yet occurred, and the family, which was engaged in private farming, needed an able-bodied man to help with the work. The head of the family therefore found a widower and arranged for a match to be made without consulting Praskovia.[8] So long as the context of farming had not shifted from the established household-based system of production, women like Praskovia, with few resources and children to support, could be used by the household head to meet the needs of the family unit in whatever way seemed reasonable.

Another case of forced marriage among the women of this earlier generation is accompanied by a poignant story about the helplessness of young women when confronted with ugly rumor, fears of shame, and the power of fathers. Lina Buldakova was born in 1907, and grew up with nine siblings in a family headed by an industrious and morally stern father. Her father had established a good reputation with landed upper-class families in the region of northeastern Moscow province when as a young man he worked for many years as a groundskeeper for a noble landowner. Later, he set up on his own, operating a successful farming and bee-keeping operation. When Lina was twenty years old, she went to work as a servant for the daughter of a former noble landowner. She was there for two months when she received a letter from her father:

> Insolent daughter! You are no daughter of mine, and I am not your father. The door to my house is barred to you. Do not come home anymore.

As she soon learned, a female cousin of hers had gossiped that Lina had gone away to get an abortion, a rumor her father for some reason was willing to believe.[9] Lina sobbed all day, and when her employers returned in the evening, asked to be released to return home. They proposed that she go to a hospital and obtain certification of her innocence, but Lina could not imagine that a paper would placate her father and decided to start out immediately for home, a long journey that brought her to the house at 11 P.M. Everyone was surprised to see her. Her father, already asleep, awoke and dragged her out the door by her hair, shouting "You're no daughter of mine!"

Her mother and siblings complained about her having no place to go in the middle of a cold night, and her father relented only enough to let her stay in an adjoining unheated hut until 5 A.M. when he threw her out of there as well, saying that he would not have even "a whiff of her around here." Her mother, too, thought the worst of her and cried, "Daughter, how could you have ruined yourself in this way!"

Lina went to the church but found it closed. On the way she passed the hospital and thought to herself "I'll go to church, say a prayer to my guardian angel, and then go the hospital, get certification of my virginity, and lie down in front of an oncoming train." After church, Lina went to the hospital but was too embarrassed to allow a pelvic exam, fearing that her father would hate her even more for having exposed her sex organs to a doctor. But, finally, she gave in (the doctor was a woman), received her medical certification of virginity, and went home trembling to face her father. When he had read the certificate, he came to her with heavy step, fell on his knees, and embraced her legs. "Daughter, forgive me," he said. "It was fortunate that you arrived home at night yesterday. Had it been in the day, I would have killed you. I had even got out a hatchet to do it, I wanted to kill you . . . to chop off your head."[10]

Once reconciled with Lina, her father sought revenge on the cousin who had defamed her and humiliated the family. He insisted that Lina get a proper forensic certification from the hospital (the one she already had was not adequate for legal action). When she returned with her brother to the hospital and found that a young male doctor had replaced the female doctor who had earlier examined her, she was unable to go through with the pelvic exam. After much wrangling, she finally gave in only to learn that, in addition, she had to have a further exam performed by a forensic specialist in Sergiev Posad. There an older male doctor examined her and provided forms in triplicate—Lina reported that she kept a copy of that form to this day. The doctor admonished her not to show mercy for the perpetrator of this slander. Lina said, "But she is my own cousin." The doctor answered, "Even so, don't excuse her. File suit in the usual way. What cause did she have to defame you like that?"

When Lina gave her father the forms, he wrote some further information on them and filed suit. Lina sat all that day again at her usual place at the corner seat of the family table, feeling too nauseous to be able to eat. Her father was outwardly very kind and considerate. But in the evening, matchmakers arrived with a groom for her. Lina continued, "I had never before seen [this man] in my life, not once. He was seven years older than me. Can you imagine? And he was an orphan. He had no father. He was very poor, didn't even own a horse, had but one bad cow and two sheep." Her father liked the fellow. He managed a small farm while also working as a bookkeeper and shop attendant, earning a 45-ruble wage in addition to what the farm produced. Her father said that the family was large, and they had to make room by giving Lina away in marriage. And so the arrangements were made. The groom and his matchmakers came on horses decked out with special trim for the occasion. Villagers stared in the windows to observe the proceedings, as was the custom in those days—all the while, Lina said, she sobbed, tears flowing in abundance. They were marrying her off not just to a poor man but to a man seven years her senior. This was a double misfortune for a young Russian woman before the modern age, who, ideally, married a man with resources and community respect who was about the same age or even a bit younger.[11]

It is not surprising that in retelling her story Lina dwelled on the poverty of the farm rather than the income from her husband's job, for Lina had the primary responsibility for managing the farmstead, and her husband's job did not last long. He soon lost his work, and later his life, for his unyielding opposition to the government's policy of collectivization.

Lina's story contained well-rehearsed elements of melodrama. I suspect she had told it many times to close friends and family members, for she related it without much prompting on our part. In it, she exhibits her victimization effectively, her innocence, courage, and claim upon our sympathy. Her stance tells us something important about the power of fathers in their households before collectivization, when they were still present and in full control of their property and dependents. But her story also serves as an explanation of why the conditions of her marriage differed from those of her peers—and so it tells us by implication of the weakening power of fathers generally to decide the fate of their children. In other words, Lina's marriage is the exception that proves the rule.

Lina will appear again later in this book because she is articulate and observant. But I want to finish briefly here the story of her marriage. Her husband, although he came from a family that had been forced (in his boyhood) to take up begging after the death of the father, proved to be enterprising and successful. He also had sufficient courage to resist the drive to collectivize farming, so that he, like Lina's father, was arrested as a kulak and exiled for a time. Then, again, in 1941 at the outbreak of the war, a car pulled up in front of Lina's house and took her husband away and sentenced him without trial to eight years on the basis of article 58 (a broad and liberally applied statute on political crimes). He was never heard from again. Lina received a paper in 1944 confirming his death while in prison, but she and her daughter assume he was shot soon after his arrest.

It is important to emphasize that hasty courtships and forced marriages were not typical among women of this first generation. Most of our informants worked either at home and became acquainted with boys at local evening parties or worked off the farm as nannies or even in factories. Olimpiada Bakhmesterova (born in 1902) did both. Because her father died when she was young, she started work early, was a nanny for nine years, and then worked in a factory before marrying. She saved enough money to build a house as a gift to her new husband.[12] Anastasia Shishanova, who worked at home on her family's farmstead, was married in 1928 to a neighbor with whom she was well acquainted before the matchmaking. Both families were independent farmers, his family also working as smiths. The prospective groom's mother and eldest sister-in-law appeared one day at Anastasia's home to ask on his behalf for her hand, and matters were arranged quickly.[13] Elizaveta Nikolaeva worked away from her village in the city of Tver as a nanny for a physician's assistant and his seamstress wife before going home in 1926 to marry at the age of twenty-one. She had a falling out with the man to whom she had been betrothed (he decided "to kick about the world"), but she soon found another to her liking.[14] In short, these women of the oldest generation were in most cases able to make their own choices about marriage. Although the traditional forms of matchmaking continued, they were simply a means of carrying through with decisions that had already been made informally.

Russian Village Weddings and Dowry

Finding a mate was one thing, arranging the wedding another. The traditional wedding described by ethnographers was a protracted affair that could last a week or more.[15] Wedding practices varied considerably from place to place, but typically included the visit of matchmakers, agreement on exchange of dowry or gifts and distribution of responsibility for the costs of the wedding, laments sung by the bride-to-be together with her girl friends, mutual visiting of the families, parties in their homes, a church ceremony, and, after the Revolution, civil registration. The culmination was usually an intense two-day house party, village procession, church ritual, and sexual consummation.[16] For this study on childbirth and early child care, we did not do a detailed inquiry into changing marriage practices but asked only about salient elements, such as the church ceremony and dowry.

For most of the older informants, weddings included a church ceremony. The women who reported in any detail on this aspect of their lives noted that they had a "proper two-day" wedding celebration with a church ceremony.[17] Even Maria Somova of the Tambov region, who married through civil registration because of her husband's opposition to religion, explained that "almost everyone else at that time did have a church wedding."[18]

Despite the independence of most of the women in finding a mate, the details of arranging the wedding continued to be made in the traditional way by matchmakers, usually members of the families concerned. The principal task of the matchmakers was to work out payment for the wedding. The central point was the actual expenditures for the wedding festivities and related activities, not dowry or "bride-price," which, if they had ever been of major significance in Russian peasant life, had lost importance after the serf emancipation in the mid-nineteenth century.

Although dowry can sometimes be an important part of marriage in traditional society, the Russian term for dowry (*pridanoe*) most often referred to what might better be described in English as a trousseau: clothing, linens, and other basic inventory needed for setting up as a new family. Brides seldom brought to a marriage the substantial amounts of money, land, or animals implied by a "dowry." In some areas of Russia, marriages in the past also called for the payment of bride-price (*kladka*). The groom's family had to compensate the bride's family for the loss of her labor. The bride-price was one of several mechanisms employed by villagers to maintain a rough equality of resources among the households in a community and thus enable all the families to contribute to the community's taxes and other obligations. But this practice seems to have died out following the abolition of serfdom and subsequent decline of the communal system. At any rate, it was not mentioned by our informants, even those from Tambov province where, according to Steven Hoch, bride-price was a common feature of peasant marriage contracts during the serf era.[19]

The dowry items mentioned most often by women of the older generation were linens, dresses, and household utensils, though for the better-off families gifts also included a bed and furniture. The financial condition of the households naturally played an important role. Of the women from Moscow province, Anastasia Spiridonova (married in 1928) had a larger than usual dowry: "I was outfitted properly, very well. I brought furniture; let's see, there were . . . three or four chairs, a table, a trunk full of clothes I had made. Yes, I was very well outfitted."[20] Keep in mind, too, the surprising case of Olimpiada Bakhmesterova, whose marriage gift to her husband was a new house. But, typically, the dowries were modest. Zinaida Shumkova, married at age eighteen in the difficult year 1933, regarded her dowry with scorn. "What kind of dowry?" she responded to our question. "It was rags and tatters [*khudoe-rvanoe*]. What kind of dowry was there?! Almost nothing at all. Grandma gave a pillow, [another] grandma gave some lace trim for the bottom of the bed [*podzor*]. My aunt gave a towel. The other aunts gave pillowcases. There weren't even any blanket cov-

ers. We only got blanket covers after I was married. . . .What else was there?
. . . sheets, four pillowcases or, no, eight of them. Also four pillows so that there
would be a change. And someone else gave something or other."[21] Although
matters were not much better for Anisia Gureeva, who married in Riazan province in 1931, she described her situation in more positive terms. The wedding
took place in the old way of the pre–collective-farm era. "We had a church ceremony. Mother didn't prepare a large dowry but just had linens, a mattress, a
featherbed, pillows. There's no way not to have these things. It was expected."[22]

Among the women from a village in the Urals, the picture was much the
same, except that in addition to linens, mattresses, and the like, the trousseau
might include sturdy footwear or a sheepskin coat. On this western edge of
Siberia, extra-heavy clothing was of vital importance. A custom that survived in
this area until after World War II was the display of the items contributed by the
bride and her family. Aleksandra Gibert, married at age eighteen in 1939, reported that "earlier, after all, we sewed everything ourselves, and then it would
be hung up for display at the time of the wedding. This display was obligatory.
The bride would sit there beside the groom, nails were driven into the wall next
to them, and people hung up towels."[23] Anna Panacheva, married at age nineteen in 1947, likewise said that while her dowry was nothing like those of
women nowadays, she did have a mattress, pillows, and embroidered towels,
the last of which were hung up for display.[24] The bride's skill at handwork continued to be valued until very recent times.

In the black-earth province of Tambov, the dowries for the women of the
older generations sometimes included more substantial items. Maria Somova,
like most of the other informants from this generation and place, listed the
usual contributions of a bed, featherbed, pillows, blanket, and clothes.[25] Not
everyone was this fortunate. Maria Abramova, who married in the drought year
of 1933, said that people could not provide dowries then, and she just had
her bed brought over to the home of the groom's family.[26] But some women from
this area could boast dowries that included money or land. Anna Reutova,
married in 1929, said that her "father gave seven *sazhens* of land[27] as a dowry,"
in addition to the usual household items.[28] Another woman, who married in
1934, reported that her dowry provided some cash in addition to a bed and a
trunk with the usual items. She also mentioned that wealthy villagers included
animals, such as heifers and sheep, in their dowries.[29]

The older women in the Tambov villages told of one other aspect of traditional marriage that they knew of from their mothers but that they had not had
to suffer themselves, namely, a public display of the bride's bloodstained shift.
It had been a common practice for the bride to have to give up her shift right
after the sex act was performed on the first night of marriage, and the groom's
family then displayed it around the village on a plate, usually accompanied by
much noise and merriment.[30] But even for the oldest informants, this practice
was merely a memory. "I was chaste when I married [in 1934]," said Praskovia Krivolapova, "and so were, I suppose, all the brides, [but] mother related

how earlier on they had carried around the bloodied shift on a plate."[31] Pelagea Nikulina, married in 1930, told the same story. "I was a virgin when I wed, although by then they were no longer checking one's virginity."[32]

Wartime and Postwar Marriage

The younger generations of Russian informants, those who married in the late 1930s, the war years and after, had a different experience of youth and marriage than did their elders. The younger women were more educated (many having completed elementary school) and had grown up or at least gone through adolescence after the collectivization of agriculture. Decisions about the marital partner were almost entirely their own; parents and matchmakers were little involved. Most significantly, mentions of church weddings disappear almost entirely from the comments of these women, despite the somewhat improved conditions for church work during and after the war. Most of the women of this generation were either satisfied with civil registration (plus the usual family celebration) or accepted it in preference to the trouble and expense of a religious ceremony in a distant church.

Something new appears in the reports of these younger rural women: divorce. Although divorce had been legal and infamously easy in principle since the early days of the Soviet regime, it was mentioned only once or twice by women in our interview sample from the earlier generations.[33] Divorce was, however, an important part of the experience of our younger informants, several of whom exercised this option to end unhappy marriages. Keep in mind that this cohort also lost many husbands to death in World War II (starting with the East Asian and Finnish wars in the late 1930s). Taken together, early death and divorce produced a high incidence of marital breakup in this generation (an important influence on these women's fertility histories to be discussed later).

A brief summary of the marital experiences of informants of this generation from Moscow and Novgorod provinces will indicate the change. The oldest person was the most casual about marriage. V. I. Zaitsev (he and his wife were interviewed as a couple) was working as a village teacher in the late 1930s when he met his future mate. "Was matchmaking involved?" we asked. "Oh no," he responded, "It was all very simple. . . . She just moved into my apartment. We had gotten acquainted. She had a job as a bookkeeper. So, well, we started living together . . . making our meals together."[34] Nina Novozhilova married in 1946 after meeting her husband-to-be in the large factory at Kraznoarmeisk. She was then thirty years old and had been doing factory work since her mid-teens. There was no mention of matchmaking.[35] Anna Zueva, a village medic, was working far from home in the north of Novgorod province when she met and married her first husband in the late 1930s (he died soon after in the Winter War with Finland). "My parents weren't involved. By this time, young people decided this without the parents, independently." And what about your daugh-

Anna Zueva and Olga
Mal'tseva, Novgorod province,
1990

ter, I asked. "Yes, my daughter as well did not ask permission to marry. But my
granddaughter, in contrast, did ask permission. She would come to visit and
show her fiancé. It indicates that she was a bit smarter—and that conditions
had changed."[36] Anna seemed to mean by this last comment that children no
longer felt a need to reject their parents' values. Antonia Larshina married at her
state farm in 1948 at age twenty-five, had two children, and then divorced.[37]
Anastasia Kuzina, who rather unexpectedly married a man seven years her senior in 1941, reported cryptically that "We got married out of grief." She then
explained: "We scarcely knew one another. He had not been to my house [and
was living elsewhere]. He came home April 29 because his father had died. He
had in a way come home to grieve. We felt sorry for him . . . then on May 3 my
father died. At that time, my brother was in the army. Here at home we were
all girls. No one else. So, he latched onto us. He had just buried his father, he
was experienced . . . already along in years. He was born in 1916, and I wasn't
born until 1923. Well, my relatives took a liking to him. All my aunts and un-
cles were saying, 'Look, Nastia, are you going to find anyone better? Go ahead

and marry this fellow.'" Just a few days later, on May 24, Anastasia and the man went to the government bureau and registered their marriage. They did not have time for a wedding celebration of any kind; indeed, they had little time at all to enjoy married life, as the German invasion began less than a month later on June 22, 1941, and Anastasia's new husband was called up for service.[38] As another example, Nina Gracheva married in 1949, had one child, divorced soon after, and only remarried ten years later in 1961.[39] In none of these cases was there any mention of matchmakers or a church wedding.

A similar picture can be seen in the Smolensk and Urals villages. Of the seven women of this younger generation from Smolensk province who told about their weddings, none spoke of using matchmakers or having a church ceremony. The oldest, Elena Sorokoumova who married in 1937, said that her parish church had been closed, and people were not willing to travel the more than fifteen kilometers to the next available church.[40] After the war, as well, weddings in this region were rarely accompanied by a church ceremony. The same was reported by the Urals villagers we interviewed. The four Russian women who were married after the war all made love matches.[41] One mentioned that, although matchmakers were employed, she and her fiancé had been well acquainted and in agreement about the marriage beforehand.[42]

The Tambov villages, characterized as they were by a stronger persistence of traditional ways, are worth dwelling on more. Experiences there were varied. Anna Mikhaleva, who was scrupulous about observing religious practices associated with the birthing and upbringing of her children, was more casual about marriage. She and her groom did not have a religious ceremony when she wed at age twenty-three, a year after the end of the war. She said that church weddings were not customary at that time. She reported that her children, too, did not have church weddings because they were members of the Komsomol (although she did not specify when, they most likely married in the late 1970s and early 1980s). She noted that religious weddings had again become popular since the end of Communist rule.[43] Natalia Mikhaleva, who was from the same village as Anna and had married eight years later, insisted on a religious ceremony as part of her two-day wedding. She believed there was a good reason for a church wedding: "Children born of parents not married in church were regarded as illegitimate." Like the previous informant, she remarked that her children, despite her beliefs about illegitimacy, married without a church ceremony, whereas nowadays church weddings had again become the norm.[44] Antonina Abramova had her first marriage in 1955 without a church ceremony. Having lost her husband five years later when he was decapitated in a drunken brawl, she remarried after another nine years, this time in a church wedding; she had changed her mind about the importance of this aspect of nuptials.[45] Anna Kasiakina, who married at age twenty-two in 1961, did not have a church wedding. "Not everyone was getting a church wedding in those days. Our church had been closed, and we would have had to travel to Kirsanov. Of course, it would have been better to have a church wedding."[46]

The youngest informant in this generation from the Tambov villages, Aleksandra Krivolapova, made an especially unfortunate choice when she decided to marry in 1968 at age nineteen—and she did so as the result of magical thinking not uncommon in village life. She came from a large and spiritually close family, which was not financially well off, however, because her father's parents had been "dekulakized" and brought to ruin in the 1930s. She remembered her father as industrious and as a non-drinker, her mother as a devout woman who kept their home clean and wholesome. The father worked as a shepherd, and the mother as a servant until after the war when she began giving birth to and caring for eleven children. Aleksandra described her parents as strict but also loving and supportive. Her own marriage proved to be very different:

> I lived with mother in a joyous family life. There were never any arguments, just warmth, cleanliness; mother taught us to be kind to one another. Then I got married, and it was as if I had fallen into a hole, an unfriendly family. The parents were drunkards. I wasn't eager to marry Vasilii. He just completely wore me down. And my mother tried to talk me out of it. He was older than I, had already been divorced, and I didn't find him attractive; he wasn't at all like us. But he hung around me all the time so that people would start to talk about us [being intimate]. During the Christmas holiday, we did some fortune telling by placing soap, matches in the form of a well, and a towel under my pillow. I then had a dream in which [Vasilii] took water from a well and gave it to me to drink. I told mother about this, and she said, well, it's clear that you are destined to marry him. And we also were asking his name on the street. You take a pancake in your teeth and ask a name, and that year I was told that I said the name Vasiatka [Vasilii]. And so I got married at age nineteen; [it happened] as if out of desperation.[47]

Aleksandra's mother insisted on a church wedding, and the marriage took place very much in the old way, even though the year was 1968. "We first registered at the government office, then had a church ceremony. The party for the wedding took place a week later, and only then did we start to live together." Here we see a survival, common until the Revolution, of the decisive importance of the pre-Christian dinner and party phase of the wedding, which as much as the church ceremony or the civil registration (introduced by the Soviets) determined the time when the couple could start conjugal relations.

Provision of a decent trousseau, let alone a dowry, was difficult for the women who married from the 1930s onward. The notion that a trousseau of some kind was a necessity continued, but the poverty of these young women as a result of collectivization and war (which in both instances included the loss of many fathers) often made it impossible for them to meet the expected standards. Women reported having contributed some linens and other household items, if only on a very modest scale. One woman remarked that her dowry of thirty-six pounds of flour was considered princely in view of the fact that she married in May, a time of the year when flour was running low.[48] But this gift, presented in the relatively good year of 1937, was unusual. A woman from the same region who married two years later said that her fiancé demanded a dowry of more than five hundred pounds of grain. When she refused (not being eager to marry), he decided to marry her without a dowry.[49]

Tatars: The Older Generation

The stories of Tatar family life and marriage in the imperial era speak of the strict separation of the women, in some cases even veiling of them, the costly bride-price (kalym) demanded for a marriage contract, dowries and the like.[50] These practices, described by officials and travelers such as Mil'kovich, Dr. Karl Fuchs, and others, were difficult to confirm in our interview sources. Earlier writers had had their eyes mainly on wealthy urban or aristocratic families that no longer exist and whose descendants did not turn up in our limited sampling. Even so, the stories of the very oldest Muslim women in our project bear the imprint of the traditional way of life found in the nineteenth-century sources.

Accounts of nineteenth-century life for Volga Tatar girls make clear that they received instruction in Arabic script for the purpose of reading verses from the Quran and prayers. In line with Muslim ideas of a fairly strict separation of the sexes, girls were taught apart from the boys. The boys studied with the village mullah, while the girls were trained by his wife (abystai).[51] In return, the children were expected to do household chores for the clerical family.[52]

At an early age, girls began work as nannies at home or, as they became older, helped out at other tasks. For poorer families, this would involve field work; for better-off families, work around the house. Female socializing remained confined to sewing bees with other young women, gatherings from which boys were excluded. Only during major festivals such as dzhien was social mixing of the sexes permitted. Tatars practiced village exogamy, as they were encouraged by their clerical leaders to seek mates unlikely to augment the blood relationships among the families of the village.[53] Young women might therefore have little opportunity to influence the choice of their spouse. In any event, they were unlikely to be able to reject a match arranged by their parents.

Negotiations for marriage included a wide range of gift giving between the parties, which began at the first approach to the matchmaking when the prospective groom or his petitioners offered small gifts to key members of the prospective bride's family. The chief contributions were, however, the meger (or mekher, Arabic: makr) and the dowry. Nineteenth-century sources also mention kalym or bride-price, which for wealthy families could amount to a large sum whose accumulation sometimes delayed the wedding for many months. We asked all the Muslim women we interviewed about bride-price and found that, while they were familiar with the concept, few of them reported its use in their experience. The most recent reference to bride-price, and that a vague one, related to a wedding in 1935.[54] Meger was more often involved. It was a money or property payment that may initially have gone to the parents of the bride (even if, according to the Quran, it properly belonged to the bride as security in the event of divorce). By late in the imperial period, *meger* seems often to have gone toward expenditures for the wedding festivities and preparation of the dowry.[55] As in the Russian case, a large part of the dowry was what would better be termed trousseau: essential clothing and household items. Parents or relatives of the bride might, however, also contribute livestock.

After the families agreed on the exchange of gifts, the actual marital union could take place. The key ceremony was the performance by the mullah of a prayer or oath known as *nikiakh* (Arabic: *nikah*). This ceremony, equivalent in meaning to the Russian Orthodox church wedding, might precede the festivities connected with the wedding dinner (and in Soviet times secular registration of the marriage) by some days, but performance of *nikiakh* was sufficient for the bride and groom to start their life together as a married couple.

In turning now to the interview material, I should mention that about half of the Muslim subjects came from one large Tatar village to which we gave close attention. The others (with one exception) were interviewed in a variety of urban locations to which they had moved as grown-ups from Muslim villages.

The oldest village woman about whom we collected detailed information was born in 1889. She was the only daughter of a well-to-do farmer, and when she married, about 1909, her family provided a substantial dowry: two cows, a horse, forty sheep, a trunk containing housewares, plus clothing and bedding. The match, which was arranged by the mother of the groom, was uneven in several respects. The groom was nineteen years older than his bride, had been married twice before, and had two children from the first marriage (his second wife had died in her first childbirth). Moreover, he was not wealthy and could afford at best a small bride-price. Perhaps his status as a soldier, or some kinship or personal characteristic, made him a desirable match for the bride's family.[56]

A second woman of the oldest generation, Giuldzhamal Tukhvatullina, born in 1896 and married for the first time in 1911, was likewise the only daughter in a family of means. The marriage of this fifteen-year-old girl to a man sixteen years her senior was arranged by the parents of the groom without her knowledge. Her family informed her about it three days later. Although she opposed the decision (according to the story she told her daughter, our informant), her parents insisted on the match. They provided a dowry consisting of one cow, two sheep, plus a large amount of clothing, pillows, featherbeds, quilts, and downy kerchiefs. The groom did not pay a bride-price. After having three children with this husband (who died in 1921), Giuldzhamal lived as a widow for seven years and then remarried, this time as a second wife. The first wife of this new husband had been incapacitated by a bladder fistula, and one of Giuldzhamal's tasks was to care for the ailing first wife. Polygamy, though permitted by Islamic law, was not common among the Volga Tatars and may have been largely confined to situations in which the first wife could no longer manage her responsibilities. Our informant knew of only four cases in her large village of men bringing a second wife into the home.[57]

A male informant from another village, Rakhmet Suleimanov, reported that his wealthy, and later violently "dekulakized," father had four wives, of which his mother was the fourth and was treated as a servant. He told how she was expected to pull his father's boots off when he returned to the house. It was also her job, when he wished to smoke, to roll a cigarette for him, light it, and place it in his mouth. A well-to-do Tatar father before the 1930s could evidently demand exceptional outward signs of respect from members of his household, signifying his patriarchal authority.[58]

A third woman, the current matriarch of her village, Khatima Nizamova, was born in 1903. She claimed (in her interview with me in 1990 and again in a follow-up interview with Guzel Shugaeva three years later) that she was well schooled in the Quran, having studied for ten years. When I asked if she actually attended a formal school emphasizing religious training (*medressa*), she answered, no, that she had studied with the wife of the mullah.[59] This was the usual practice for Muslim girls, but schooling normally lasted only long enough for them to learn the most often recited prayers in Arabic.[60] Interestingly, the oldest women among our informants could read Arabic script when they often had little other book learning.[61] Although Khatima may have exaggerated her scholastic attainments (other women in the village disputed the story of her lengthy schooling), she clearly took great pride in what she regarded as her own and her family's special devotion to traditional Islamic learning. Her mother, she reported, had a thorough knowledge of the Quran and actually served the community as if she were a mullah.[62]

I should point out that the interviews took place at a time of religious revival in this village. A mullah had come in the past year from Kazan, and the community had just completed a large, solidly built mosque. Claims to special status as a bearer of traditional religious knowledge, especially in view of the new mullah's evident educational limitations, could be expected to bring a certain amount of positive recognition and respect.

Khatima recounted her life as very happy until age seventeen. She was the oldest of seven siblings and probably considered special because, in addition to being the first child, she was a surviving twin, her brother born at the same time having died two months later. (A few years later her mother had another set of twins, and again lost one of the pair soon after birth.) Just as Khatima reached maturity, the Civil War and famine of the early 1920s brought disaster on the Volga. Famine struck twice, first in 1921 and again in 1923. By 1923 her father and her eighteen-year-old brother were dead. The father was apparently either away from home or incapacitated before that, because sometime in 1922 Khatima's mother had in desperation given away her five other children, everyone except Khatima herself, to a children's home in the town of Melikesa (later Dimitrovgrad), and they were never heard from again. Soon after, she married off Khatima. The match was a good one in material terms, as the groom's family, despite the difficult times, could boast two horses and a cow. They gave Khatima's family gifts of clothing and footwear, while her dowry consisted of a calf, a coat, shawl, and bedding.[63]

Khatima's groom was a neighbor and just two years older than she. So, they were well acquainted before the match was made, and the families were in agreement. Contrast this to the case of the first two women from this oldest group whose husbands were sixteen and nineteen years older than they. The same is true of Khatima's own mother, whose husband was twelve years her senior, as well as of the parents of the next woman we shall meet (who were separated by thirteen years) and of one further woman (Sharifa, described later) from this older group.[64] In the case of the other Tatar informants, women married from the mid-1930s onward, the ages of the spouses were somewhat closer, but husbands' ages still exceeded wives' by an average of more than six years, which was distinctly different from the pattern typical in Russian marriages.

The process of traditional courtship and marriage in the Tatar village was best described by Garifabanu Abdullina, who was born in 1908 and married in 1928. Just like young Russian women, Tatar women organized evening get-togethers at an available house, Garifabanu reported. But stricter rules about separation of the sexes in Islamic society dictated different procedures. In the case of the Tatars, the women covered the windows with towels before beginning their sewing work, singing, and dancing. The young Tatar men, in contrast to Russians, were not allowed into the house to join in the party but had to stand out in the street.[65] When it came time for a woman to marry, the father of the prospective groom approached her parents and negotiated the arrangements. Her side provided gifts to her new parents-in-law; in the case of Garifabanu's marriage a towel to the father and wool kerchief to the mother. Her dowry-trousseau consisted of two sheep (one given by her father, the other by her brother), a winter coat, regular coat, dress, and downy kerchief. In return, her father, mother, and brother received gifts of clothing. The groom's family also paid a special bride-price in a formal ceremony. As Garifabanu explained, the men of the families called for a gathering (*giziat kabul*) to which they invited the mullah. When everyone was in place, the prospective mother-in-law handed the bride a tray on which 50 rubles lay wrapped in a shawl. The mullah then inspected the tray to confirm the agreed-upon sum.[66]

Sharifa Ialisheva, the youngest Tatar informant from the generation married before full-scale collectivization of agriculture, suffered an especially painful forced marriage. Her anguish stemmed from the glimpse she had enjoyed of an entirely different and marvelously liberating life of the city and of the healing arts, for which she had a talent (she later became a skilled folk healer). Sharifa was born in a village in Mordovia where her father worked as a teacher. When I asked for the happiest memory of her early life, she answered unhesitatingly that it was her move to Leningrad at age eighteen (in 1930). She stayed with relatives there and found work in a hospital. Sharifa came from a tradition-bound village in which the Muslim women were not permitted to visit the mosque or the bazaar. Women stayed around home and had to cover their hair when they went out, although, by the same token, they were not expected to do field work. Her escape to the big city was exhilarating, and she could think of nothing more wonderful than the opportunity to stay forever in Leningrad. But within two years, her father summoned her home. She resisted, he insisted, and finally she had to give in and return to her native village. Her father had arranged her marriage to a man much her senior who had four children of his own. The saddest thing that ever happened to her, she asserted, was this forced marriage to a man for whom she had no love. She wept for days until her eyes were huge swollen lumps. In Leningrad she had known freedom and independent work, and then suddenly she was hurled back into a remote village and a life with a man she did not know and whose many children she had to rear. In addition, she complained, he kept her pregnant so that she had seven births of her own (of which four survived), plus a number of secret abortions.[67]

In contrast to the Russian women of their generation, the stories told by these older Tatar women portray them as helpless against the power of their parents. The choice of their husbands and the timing of their marriages were out of their hands. Their stories also reveal the greater hold of earlier ways of life in other respects. Livestock continued to play an important role in exchanges that accompanied marriage contracts, possibly an echo of the central place that livestock sales, and especially horse trading, had long occupied in Tatar life. Even polygamy could still be found. The older Tatar women probably had a higher degree of literacy than did their Russian counterparts, something they took great pride in. But this literacy was of a special kind: the ability to read the Quran or, at the very least, prayers in Arabic. Since the available Arabic texts were religious works, this training, too, acted more as a reinforcement of established norms than as a potential opening to new worlds through access to written knowledge.

Tatars: Since Collectivization

The younger Tatar women, those born since 1917 and marrying from the mid-1930s onward, had a very different experience of courtship and marriage. Every one of them had at least a few years of secular education. Several of them received an education that went well beyond the elementary level. Mariam Gimadeeva, for example, was born in the village of Kalmaiur in 1918 and completed a seven-class basic schooling before going on to medical training in Kazan, where she became a licensed midwife. She met her husband-to-be in medical school—he was training to be a military doctor—and they married in 1939 in the town of Bugul'ma (in the southeast corner of the Tatar republic), where she had her first work assignment. This modern marriage included no matchmaking, dowry, or bride-price.[68] Although Mariam was unusual in her achievements, the Tatar women of this generation who stayed in the village were also much more independent than the older generation in choosing their mates and the timing of their marriages.

The new type of education was undoubtedly important in this shift. Perhaps even more important were the changeable and arbitrary methods by which this new education was introduced. Two considerations are worth noting here. First, while the generation of women born after the Revolution received a basic secular education, changes in cultural policy robbed this education of some of its value. Zukhra Pozdniakova grew up in a dirt-poor village in Mordovia, so impoverished that when her father brought her at age four a white-bread roll from town, it was such an oddity that she rejected it and asked for her usual potatoes. Her language training, done partly at a religious school, partly at a secular one, included four classes of Arabic, four of Russian, and four of Tatar: in other words, not enough of any of them to become truly proficient.[69] Government-mandated changes in the alphabet likewise complicated learning for Tatars. Tatar language was first taught in Arabic script. Then, in the 1920s, the government ordered a shift from Arabic to a Latin alphabet of the kind introduced in modern Turkey. But after a few years, it mandated a further change from Latin letters to Cyrillic. A Tatar lawyer from St. Petersburg told me that these changes resulted in "the loss of an entire cultural stratum. At the home of my father-in-law," he remarked, "there is a large bookcase filled with books—and some are no doubt of great value—but no one can read them because they are all in Arabic script."[70]

The chaotic language training limited what ambitious young people could achieve. Fina Iurenieva grew up in a Bashkir village and received encouragement from her parents to strive for a higher education. She went to the village school for seven years and then had to transfer to a neighboring village, fifteen kilometers distant, for further schooling. This meant having to rent a room with an old woman in that village for the week, for she was able to return home only on weekends. But after all her preparation, she failed the exam for entry into an institute of higher education, an event she experienced as deeply humiliating. "Why humiliating?" I asked. "I had desired it so, and it was expected," she said. "First, it was a matter of national pride, and then also [pride] among my peers." The problem: the exam was given in Russian, but Fina's schooling had been in Tatar. To complicate matters further, her own language was Bashkir. "In our region, the teachers instructed in Tatar, we conversed half in Bashkir, half in Tatar. Where we grew up, where we lived, there was no pure Tatar language. It was a mix."[71] As with Fina, many Turkic women lacked a stable language base of their own, and if they wished to go on to higher studies, they had to compete by taking exams in a foreign language. After a number of detours, the determined Fina did finally acquire a postsecondary education and became a teacher of mathematics and physics.

In the village of Kalmaiur, all the women of this younger generation attained at least four classes of basic schooling (under either the Latin or Cyrillic regime). A number of them had seven or eight classes, and a few were able to go further. Roza Fakhrutdinova (born in 1933), for example, completed three years at the teachers' college in Melikesa and returned home to work as a leader in the Pioneers program at the local school.[72] I have already mentioned Mariam Gimadeeva, who finished midwife schooling in Kazan.

The second consideration in regard to the shifting methods of language training is the arbitrariness with which the alphabet and language changes were imposed. The intervention of the party-state in such matters directly assaulted the authority of the mullahs and the traditional education provided in Arabic script. The closed cultural world that supported the power of the male village leaders was under attack. This imposition of language at once revealed the weakness of the village authorities to resist fundamental changes in the form of written expression and also handed to young women a linguistic key to knowledge far beyond the Quran and other religious texts to which they had been limited. The disorderly form in which secular education reached these women, while it may have impeded their advancement in some respects, also weakened the village patriarchy, opening to young women a route out of the village.

More than educational achievement undercut the power of fathers to make marriage decisions for the Tatar women of the younger generations. Because the change occurred just following the drive to collectivize agriculture, the importance of this event can hardly be denied. Collectivization was an assault on the powers of independent households; in this sense it was a direct attack on the authority of fathers as the heads of those households. Whether fathers went along with collectivization or opposed it (and were exiled or killed), their power was diminished.

The actual loss of fathers altogether was equally an influence. Whether the catastrophe was collectivization or another of the disasters of this century—wars, famines—many men died before their time and were not around to affect the marital decisions of their daughters. Rkia Kamaletdinova, born in 1922, lost her father in 1941. When she married in 1946, the negotiations had to be handled by her older sister (their mother was alive at the time but incapacitated). Because of the family's poverty, it could not provide a dowry or even much of a wedding. Senior family members simply gathered at the bride's home for the performance of *nikiakh*.[73] Zeinab Gimatdinova lost her father in 1930 when she was just seven years old. The next year she had to start working alongside her mother at the collective farm so that they could earn enough to support themselves and her younger brother and sister. When Zeinab married in 1955, her mother and the older brother of the groom conducted the negotiations. No fathers were alive to approve or disapprove. Zeinab's marriage was unusual in that she was 32 years old. Her husband was 13 years her senior and had three children from his first marriage to a woman who died in childbirth. The marriage involved gift giving and a trousseau in the usual way, and the husband even won a kind of dowry by acquiring Zeinab's house when her mother, soon after the wedding, moved to Tajikistan to live there with her son.[74] A third woman born, like these others, in the early to mid-1920s, Zatia Bagautdinova, also lost her father early, an invalid from World War I. His death in 1930 forced the family to sell its livestock, including a horse and a cow, to survive, and even then Zatia's mother had to send her at age seven to baby-sit in return for her food. When Zatia was seventeen, she went to the city of Kolomna as nanny for a family of the village who had moved there. She married at age twenty-two in 1947. The negotiations were initiated by the groom and his aging mother, and Zatia's mother had to give her agreement to arrangements that included a trousseau (pillows, drapes, bedding, tablecloth) and gifts for the bride (silk shawl, shoes, a dress). No bride-price was asked, and evidently this aspect of marriage negotiations, rare enough earlier, had by World War II almost completely died out. Her groom was ten years her senior, the war apparently having delayed his settling down.[75] These three women all had secular education: Rkia received secondary schooling; Zeinab, four classes (enough that she later served as deputy to the raion committee); and Zatia, six classes of Tatar schooling in the Latin alphabet. But, for better or worse, they also did not have to contend with the demands of fathers in their wedding plans. The resources available had their fathers survived would doubtless have given them an advantage in the marriage market, but their fathers' wishes also would have had to receive consideration.

For Tatar women whose families had moved to the city, the role of the parents in marital decisions was less pronounced, even if normatively no less required. Fakhiza Suleimanova was born in a village in 1930 and moved with her family to Simbirsk/Ulianovsk when she was seven. The city was not large then, she said, and she knew most of the Tatars of her age group. The young people met at evening parties and got acquainted. In contrast to what she thought of as the traditional village way of doing things, in town the couples first found one another and only then did the parents become involved. "It is not like [Central] Asia," she remarked. The man she decided to marry lived right down the street. When he came with his sister to ask for her hand ("You had to have parental permission," Fakhiza stressed), her father threw them out of the house, saying that his daughter was too young to marry. At age 24, Fakhiza was scarcely too young in the usual sense of the word. But she was younger than a sister who had not yet found a husband, and this was an impediment. "It was not right to leave an older daughter behind," said Fakhiza.

"That's important," I agreed, "but how did things work out?"

"I went and got married anyhow."

"With your father's permission?"

"No, I disobeyed his injunction."

"But did he then come to the wedding?"

"Of course, he came. He was there."

In the city, it is clear, the father's word could no longer be decisive. Despite the opposition of Fakhiza's father to her wedding plans, the usual arrangements were made for her marriage. When I asked about bride-price and dowry, she said that her mother had told her stories of how in the village her family was

Fakhiza Suleimanova
showing her embroidery and
Quranic verses, Simbirsk,
1990

able to demand a certain amount and quality of gifts from the groom. Now-adays, however, the families work out a gift exchange in accord with their means. "A dowry is prepared for each girl, including pillows, linens, bedding, but there is no bride-price among us. Exchanges are just negotiated by the two families: we will give such and such of this approximate value, depending, too, on how many relatives are involved, how many sisters, so as to know what to give to whom, and the other side is expected to give gifts of comparable worth. A brother might get a shirt, someone else some cloth for a dress; at that time it might be calico, which was very expensive."[76]

In the villages, money continued in some cases to play a part in marriage arrangements, perhaps when additional persuasion was required. Nurania Bad-rieva contended that money was a factor in her marriage, which took place in 1955. The first effort to make a match with her came from the prospective groom himself, but Nurania rebuffed the proposal because she did not love him. The young man then tried a more traditional approach. His parents came the second time, money was promised and received, and Nurania's mother ordered her to marry the suitor. The dowry provided by Nurania's family included three geese, three sheep, plus clothing, drapes, and other household items. This marriage and one other from the same year were the first since the 1920s in our sample to include livestock, indicating a return of relative prosperity to the village. By the mid-1950s, families were evidently replenishing sufficient animal stocks following collectivization and war to be able to spare some by way of a dowry.

In Nurania's story of her marriage, the father's role was, again, unfilled, even though her father was alive at the time. It was her mother who handled the negotiations and "ordered" her to marry the man in question. Her father may have been absent from the village much of the time, for he worked as a horseback rider at the Hippodrome in Simbirsk. The movement of fathers (and children) to off-farm work is another influence in the breakdown of parental power over the children's marriage choice, even if the story told by Nurania described her mother's power as sufficient to overturn her objections to her suitor.[77]

This family represented a remarkable mix of modern and traditional characteristics, showing how unreliable these classifications become for fixing the realities of life in Russia. When Nurania's mother and father decided to marry, about 1920, her parents refused to accept the offer of the matchmakers. The groom then "stole" her away, an expression that referred to an elopement. Exchanges of the usual gifts evidently patched up relations between the families, and the dowry even included a horse for this man who earned his living at horsemanship.[78] Love seemed clearly to play a role in this marriage in a way not evident in other marriages of the Tatar women of the older generation. To Nurania, one of the children of this romantic relationship, the lack of love for her suitor was the reason for turning him down. Her mother, however, denied to Nurania a choice based on love that she had exercised for herself.

Despite this anomalous case, the movement of Tatar women toward the Soviet and modern norm of increased independence in the choice of their mates was unquestionable. Education, the weakened power of the fathers, mixing of the sexes had all arrived in the changeover of a single generation from the 1920s to the 1950s. Sofia Teleshova (born in 1950) expressed this shift concisely in response to my asking if the women in her family were kept separate when visitors came to her home: "No, no, not in our age group. But at my grandmother's that is what happened. At my parents, no."[79]

Fertility Choices

Russian and Tatar rural women usually married young (between the ages of eighteen and twenty-three) and began their childbearing soon after. But each of the three generations of women surveyed for this study managed its reproductive contributions in different ways.

Fertility, including rural fertility, declined rapidly in Russia during this century, beginning at very high rates (close to what demographers call "natural fertility") and falling by 1970 to levels comparable to those in Western industrialized nations. The context in which this decline took place was unusually brutal, punctuated as it was by World War I, the Revolution, the Civil War, forced collectivization of agriculture, forced industrialization, and World War II, which claimed 27 million dead in the USSR and heavily skewed the proportion of men and women in the adult population. The context was furthermore shaped by government policy. Important in this regard were the liberalization of marriage and divorce laws soon after the Revolution plus the legalization of abortion in 1920.[1] This trend was reversed in the mid-1930s by a pronatalist policy that granted subsidies to large families, limited options for divorce, and outlawed abortion in all but cases of grave medical danger. These measures were to be accompanied by the provision of improved medical services and child-care facilities, but, as was detailed in chapter 2, villagers saw little or none of this until after World War II, in some cases not until the 1970s. The ban on abortion was lifted in 1955, but the ban and other pronatalist measures had done virtually nothing to increase fertility. The birth rate continued its descent into the late 1960s, when it stabilized at a low level. This chapter is concerned with how these changes were experienced and understood by the women who lived through and, indeed, were causing them.

First Generation

The first generation, the women born before about 1912, was close to the nineteenth-century practices and outcomes. These women typically gave birth from six to twenty times and lost about one-third of their children before age five. A few of the women had access to a maternity home, but most of them gave birth at home with a village midwife, and many of them reported at least one birth while at work in the fields. Women in this generation did heavy household, garden, and even field tasks right up to the onset of labor. Most of the women spoke of their vulnerability at the time of giving birth and the need therefore to conceal knowledge of the birth from outsiders. Otherwise, the birth could be hard and endanger both mother and child. Here we encountered, in almost all the women, concerns about the evil eye to which birthing women and their children were especially susceptible until their ritual acceptance or reintegration into their communities through baptism or churching.[2]

The birth rates in this generation make clear that few of the families were exercising fertility control. To questions about barrier methods of contraception, most of the women confessed that they had known nothing about such things. However, virtually all of them had learned from female relatives or friends that prolonged breast-feeding reduced the chances of getting pregnant again, and they attempted to achieve this result. But several reported that their menstrual cycles started right up and they again became pregnant sooner than expected. A couple of women of this generation divulged having strictly adhered to a religious prohibition of no sex on certain days of the week. Maria Malikova (born in 1913) would not consent to sexual relations on Wednesdays, Fridays, or Sundays. The contraceptive effects of the practice were evidently minimal, for she had seven pregnancies, despite several years of separation from her husband during the war.[3] The mother of Aleksandra Krivolapova likewise observed such prohibitions, yet had eleven children.[4] A few other women mentioned similar prohibitions but understood them as limited to the eves of Sundays and major religious holidays.[5]

The other option for limiting births, abortion, was unacceptable to most women of this oldest generation. Of the sixty women born before 1912 about whom we collected information, only three had abortions, insofar as we could determine.

The reports from and about these women of the oldest generation are remarkably consistent. They entered puberty during and just after the period of civil war, when family law underwent radical reform. Although medical centers often lay at some distance from villages and abortion was still not available on demand (a special board had to certify that the procedure was warranted, and peasant women were given a lower priority than working-class women in the application process), it was not these formal impediments but their strong religious beliefs that kept the women of this first generation from seeking abortions. The few among them who obtained abortions did so outside the law.

Most women born before 1912 regarded abortion as a sin and did not resort to it. Anisia Gureeva (born in 1911) lived in a village in the southern reaches of Moscow province. She had her children between 1932 and 1946, and consequently ten of her childbearing years fell into the period when abortion was banned. But the legal shifts made no difference to her; rather, she said that she could not imagine having an abortion under any circumstances. "It is an unforgivable sin," she stressed. "The Scriptures say that women who murder the children inside them are like serpents who devour their young. I don't think there was any of that disgraceful stuff going on in our village."[6] In our interviews in the villages of Smolensk province, women from the oldest generation reported the same strict norms. "My mother had eleven children and did not do any abortions," Efrosinia Ruleva related. "She feared the sin of it."[7] Another woman said of both her mother and mother-in-law (women born about the turn of the century), "They didn't do abortions, regarded it as a sin."[8] Anna Varfolomeeva explained her mother's categorical rejection of abortion in the same terms. "She would say, 'How can it be that people would murder a soul? That's just like killing a living person. Our Lord won't permit the killing of children.' People were religious in those days; they all prayed and feared committing a sin." Varfolomeeva added that her mother also had a healthy appreciation for the physical dangers of abortion. She explained that in those times, abortions were done primarily by village midwives because the neighbors were not keen on going to hospitals—and "we children might have ended up as orphans."[9]

In the Smolensk region the one woman from this age group who had resorted to abortion suffered oppressive feelings of guilt. Her life, she said, had been hard. Of the five children she had borne before the end of the war, three had died. After the war she gave birth to another child, which survived, and then began having abortions, for an eventual total of seven or eight. "I can never be forgiven this sin in the life to come. It is said that, in that life, frogs will suck on the breasts of women who have gotten abortions. And I did not go to the church to seek repentance." She tried to ease her feelings of guilt by laying some of the responsibility on the conditions of her life and on her husband.

> Our family was already large before the war, and life was hard. My husband wanted me to get the abortions. I was very fearful and understood that this was not the right thing to do. And it was terrifying to go to the hospital. I had never before had any reason to go to a hospital. In each instance, my husband's brother wrote a note to a doctor he knew at the hospital in Terino asking him to help me get an abortion, because, you know, it wasn't really permitted just to get one.

She went on to relate a story of her feelings of humiliation about abortion and her efforts to hide the truth from other members of her household.

> I concealed the first abortion from everyone in the family. I didn't say anything about where I was going. But one of my sisters-in-law somehow figured

it out and said, "Oh, so you sort of went off to get yourself an abortion." And I was so ashamed to admit this that I started showing her my skirt and all so that she could see that it was clean [no blood stains], and then I went out and loaded manure onto the wagon in order to show how healthy I was. As a result, I got pretty sick. . . .

Sometimes people ask me about my life and want to know if my husband treated me well. I think that if he had cared about me, he wouldn't have sent me to get abortions.[10]

Other women of this generation whom we interviewed in the villages of northeastern Moscow province expressed equally strong religious opposition to abortion. Only one told of having abortions, and she said, "This was sinful, sinful, sinful! I went to church. I prayed for forgiveness."[11] In the preceding chapter, we saw the story of another woman whose father had banished her from her home for life and even confessed to wanting to kill her when her cousin spread a rumor (subsequently proved to be false) that she had obtained an abortion while working as a nanny in a distant village.[12] Religious sanctions and the shame associated with a father's loss of control in this area of family life were still powerful.

A woman in a Urals village seemed to distinguish between having an abortion and attempting to abort herself. Born in 1911, this woman was the mother of six children, three of which died young. When asked directly about abortion, she gave the expected answer that she had not known about abortion and had not had one. But at another point, when asked a more general question about contraception ("Weren't there any means back then to protect yourself from pregnancy?"), she let slip: "[Oh, yes] I ate powders, and soap, also some kind of herb. . . . And, sinful to say, I would take falls." Then she added immediately, "Don't write that down. . . . That was, after all, after my husband started cheating on me."[13] Although she held to the norms of her generation in not seeking out an abortion from a hospital or an underground practitioner, she did attempt to induce abortions by every folk method she could think of after her husband ceased to love her. She recognized that these efforts were shameful but she felt justified in personal terms. Her story was poignant, for unlike many others of her generation, she had risked much for the man she loved, having gotten pregnant by him and eloped when her parents refused to consent to her marriage. Later, when the family had reconciled, her husband left her to run around with other women.

Anastasia Shishanova of this generation admitted to a similar experience. Although at first she claimed "not generally to have had any abortions," she subsequently related how after her final child in 1939, she was overburdened with children and work and then found herself pregnant once more. Her cousin, a woman skillful in folk remedies, promised to bring her a potion that would take care of things without an abortion. Anastasia was relieved. "I was so terribly afraid of abortions. And, well, well, well, gramps [her husband] would never allow it." Her cousin delivered the vial of medicine, and when her husband was away on a job, she took some of the potion and got horribly sick. Her husband came home in the evening, saw her in pain, found the vial, and realized what had happened. He threw the vial away outdoors and demanded that she go nowhere and drink nothing, adding that they would be able to bring up children if they had them. The potion seems nevertheless to have done its job because Anastasia reported no subsequent births, even so continuing to think of herself as someone who had never had an abortion.[14]

The Tambov villagers also reported ignorance of contraception and strong resistance to abortion in the oldest generation. Maria Somova (born in 1905) said that when she lived for a time in the city of Tambov, she had heard of a few abortions being done. But she added, "In our village women gave birth to as many babies as came. We didn't know about contraception and didn't ask anyone how you might do it—and we considered abortion a terrible sin. . . . One woman gave birth seventeen times, and only five children remained alive. . . . but they tried to bring up all of them."[15] Maria was acquainted with the birth practices and outcomes in her village because her mother was a respected granny midwife there. In one respect, her story diverged from those of other Tambov women of this generation. While they reported not practicing contraception or having abortions themselves, they had heard about some abortions occurring in their villages. According to Maria Abramova (born in 1911), the women who did the abortions were specialists of a sort in this trade and not regular midwives, as is sometimes believed. "We had babki in the village who did abortions in secret. A few women died from such abortions, but no one ever turned in the babki. Midwives would not do abortions; midwives were God-fearing folk, and abortion is a sin. It's like murder not to let a living being come into the world, for it receives a soul right away at birth [pri rozhdenii]. They say that those who do abortions are like snakes. I myself didn't have even one single abortion."[16]

Marfa Malikova (born in 1910) described in detail the moral and physical pressures experienced by women of her generation. She gave birth nine times and lost four of her children in infancy: "If I named them Nikolai, they died quickly." (After two dead Nikolai-named sons in her second and third births, she gave up on the name for a while, trying it again for her seventh child, who also died.) She went on:

> I gave birth often because that is how things worked out. My husband didn't want to use contraception, and I didn't know how to do it, was just stupid. And there wasn't anyone to get advice from. Mama likewise didn't know how to do it. You couldn't have an abortion either. It was strictly forbidden back then, you could even be convicted.
>
> It happened that someone or other would die who secretly got an abortion with a babka. It seemed like everyone knew which of the babki were doing such things, but everyone kept quiet about it. And then, recall, we were believers. We feared God. Abortion is such a sin. In our village, one girl had an abortion; she was unmarried. She went to take communion and had to confess to it. The priest started berating her about how she could have sinned so.

My mother was a village midwife, but she did not do abortions because it would have been no less a sin for her. Even to consider having an abortion was a sin. One time I thought about it myself. Life was really hard, lots of children, we were hungry. Then I had a dream. I was breast-feeding the children and, no matter what I did, could not give them their fill; they appeared to be completely black. Then I woke up and thought that's what would happen to them [if I had an abortion]. No, I'm not going to do that.

She added: "In those days, people feared God and felt shame in front of their neighbors."[17]

Another woman of the same surname, Maria Malikova (I mentioned her earlier as having abstained from sexual relations on Wednesdays, Fridays, and Sundays), also spoke of the importance of a dream in dissuading her from having an abortion. She related this story about being pregnant with a fourth child, her daughter Anna, in 1949:

I started to talk with the other women working in the field with me about how one might abort a child without going to the doctor; well, there, you see what a sinful soul I was. You know, I was the oldest one there and didn't know anything.

Then I had a dream: I was running through a field and coming toward me was dear old St. Nicholas [starichok Mikolai-ugodnik]. He led me to a tumbledown shack, and inside were boards with tiny children lying on them wrapped in white rags. He said, these are aborted children [vykinutye spetsial'no deti], they will lie here until the Second Coming. Then I looked in my apron and saw a girl. The old man handed me a knife, saying "Take it, stab her." She was so chubby (and, it turned out, [my baby girl] was born 5 kilo 200 grams, even though I was poorly nourished and had to work a lot). And I answered "No, I won't do it" and was refusing. He said, "Then why do you want to kill the one inside you?" He explained to me that they would cut out the baby in just this way. He told me that "as many children as there will be I should let them enter the world." Perhaps that was a sign. [Of course], if a miscarriage happens accidentally, it is not a sin.[18]

When this woman was pregnant with her last child at about age 44 and encountered a problem with bleeding, her doctor proposed abortion, but she again decided to continue the pregnancy and with much prayer got through a difficult birth.

Abortion was obviously not unknown to women of the oldest generation. These last stories were from women in the most religious of the villages we studied. Yet they had sometimes considered abortion, even if, ultimately, religious dictates, moral scruples, and physical fears caused them to reject this option.[19] It should also be kept in mind that our interview sample contained a conservative bias. Most informants were women who chose to stay in the village. Those of their generation who had left for a life in the city were likely to have been more daring in other respects as well, more modern and willing to risk abortion if it promised some benefits. That being said, the women of this generation who remained in the countryside, apart from a few exceptional cases, consistently reported that they practiced neither contraception nor abortion. As one of them remarked with a smile, "Back then, we did not economize like today when they have one or two. Then it was one hundred!"[20]

For her generation, family size was limited not by abortion but by the death of children. Child death rates in Russia right into the 1890s were as high as rates ever recorded anywhere, and women were inured to this loss. They were taught not to mourn the death of small children. "Don't cry over dead children," they were told. Value was placed on the health of the working woman more than on the child. Maria Malikova reported that her grandmother not only advised her not to grieve for dead children but also suggested she take the best pieces of food for herself, not leaving them for the children.[21] Among the means these women had for coping with frequent infant death was a kind of emotional and moral distancing, a triage of sorts to manage the multiple hardships and losses they faced. They knew how to read signs on an infant's body that foretold whether the child was fated to live or to die. They then "labeled" the dying children in ways that placed responsibility for them more in God's hands than in their own.[22]

Second Generation

The next generation of mothers, women born between about 1914 and 1928 and whose childbearing years fell in the late 1930s through the 1950s, had a much different experience. These women made changes that their mothers were unable or unwilling to make, and the women of this generation of change suffered the moral uncertainty that accompanies a shift in values and aspirations. They gave birth during high Stalinism, when medical services began to reach the villages (or transportation reduced the time and effort required for villagers to seek medical attention in nearby towns). It was also the time when abortion was outlawed.

Most of the women of this generation had some births at home with the help of a village midwife, usually their first births, and later births in a hospital or maternity home.[23] About one-third had all their births in such a medical facility. This change meant that more women were able to enjoy rest just before and after delivery. Some of the women could take advantage of a paid leave from work, thanks to the pronatalist policies of the time. Medical births also gave them access to information about hygiene, modern child care, and vaccinations. Although many mothers still lost a child or two to illness or accidents, the survival rate for their children was much improved over the rate during their mothers' generation.

A much different attitude toward children accompanied these changes in birthing and child care. The women wanted fewer children, they said, because life was harsh. Forced collectivization of agriculture had altered the context for childbearing and child rearing. If the government's assault on the village and reorganization of rural life ultimately brought the women some medical services and maternity leaves, initially collectivization made matters worse by removing some of the protections that independent farm families, especially large families, had been able to provide birthing women in the past. But this was not the key. The women reported that they could not live as their mothers had. Terrible as their own lives were, they saw their mothers' uncontrolled fertility and large families, despite the frequent loss of children, as unacceptable, and they were determined to bring their own fertility under control. The comments to this effect that we heard from our informants corresponded well with responses given by peasant women in a survey published in the early 1930s about the reasons village women sought abortions. The top three responses, accounting for nearly two-thirds of the reasons, included: "hard material conditions," "pregnancy and children interfered with work," and "too many children."[24]

Contraception was not an option for most of the women. Apart from prolonged nursing (a luxury few of them had time for), the women claimed to be ignorant of contraception. Only one-sixth admitted to practices such as coitus interruptus or condoms. What this generation resorted to on a large scale was abortion, despite its illegality and the existence of powerful religious norms against it in peasant society. A village medic, Anna Zueva, herself a peasant who learned medicine at a vocational school in the 1930s, told me that when abortion was outlawed, "fertility all the same declined. Many women did not give birth. They learned how to do abortions on themselves." "Weren't there a lot of mistakes, even deaths?" I asked. "In our area there weren't a lot of deaths," she replied, "but even so, every week I had to send about two women to the hospital with hemorrhaging. They would explain that they had either jumped down from a machine, or leapt over a ditch, or lifted a large load. Well, that's what I wrote on the referral. Some years later after that law was abolished, they told me the truth, that they all had actually scooped out themselves."[25] Anna, though wife of the collective-farm chairman and obliged to enforce government policy, sympathized with her village women's violation of the law to control their fertility. She herself wanted and had no more than one child. She told me that only one woman in her village had a large family, nine children, and when Anna visited her, the woman often wept uncontrollably about her horrible life.

The doctor who ran the local hospital for the Tambov villages told a story similar to Anna Zueva's. "After the war, and especially in the 1950s, there were a lot of abortions. It was, of course, against the law, and we were obliged to keep records on the number of illegal abortions. Criminal abortions were mostly done by babki, but all that was done in secret and the women kept silent about it. Still, many were botched, and we had to send women who were hemorrhaging to [the town of] Kirsanov."[26]

Abortion imposed a high moral cost on the women of this middle generation; in most cases they expressed the same disapproval of abortions as did the older women. Yet most of the women in this second generation admitted to having abortions either legally, after the ban was lifted in the mid-1950s, or, more typically, illegally with the help of either a village abortionist or a doctor practicing in secret or by performing abortions on themselves. For example, Anna Kirsanova (born in 1920) reported that after having four children, she decided not to have more. Her husband was not well. "I didn't know how to practice contraception—there was no one to teach me about this, and pills weren't available." Her husband, she claimed, practiced withdrawal, but this proved far from effective. "So I had to do ten abortions. . . . I did them myself at home. I simply injected boiled water, squirted in two syringes, and it did the job. I never once went to the hospital to get it done." She knew that "abortion is an unforgivable sin" but saw it as necessitated by the conditions of the time. "I didn't do them, you know, to have a good life."[27] Efrosinia Ruleva (born in 1915) confessed to having had two abortions, the first with a village abortionist, even though she knew it was "harmful and a great sin. But nearly everyone was getting them, since there was nothing to eat. My mother had eleven children and did no abortions. She feared the sin of it. But I was beyond worrying anymore about it," she sighed, "even if I died."[28]

Within the stories often lie compelling personal testimonies about individual hardships and achievements in difficult times. Elena Bobkova told of having three abortions (in 1948, 1949, and 1952) all within the ban period. Two were done secretly by a doctor in the closest city. "I paid the doctor 10 rubles, a lot of money in those times. Someone took me in secret to that back-alley doctor; you couldn't just show up, you know. She, too, you understand, was afraid." Then she described a third abortion done by a woman in a nearby village. "She reached inside me with dirty hands, one hand slipping inside and the other pressing down on top of my stomach until I started bleeding. Many women died in this way, but no one turned her in."[29] Praskovia Korotchenkova had her three abortions done in a hospital after the ban was lifted, but she knew about the women in villages who did abortions. In one, she said,

> There was a woman who was a really skilled abortionist. And in our village, too, there was one woman whose sole occupation was this. She pushed a rubber object into the womb and caused an inflammation. Three women died after being aborted by her, but they refused to reveal before they died who had done their abortions—they wouldn't turn her in. Well, you knew what you were risking. But abortions had been outlawed and so what could you do about it but go to one of these village abortionists. . . . My mother, after getting an abortion from a village woman, went to the hospital to get cleaned out. A police officer came to question her about who did the abortion (but, of course, she didn't reveal a thing).[30]

Like other women her age, Korotchenkova believed abortion to be sinful. "They say that in the afterlife they bring you the fetus on a plate and force you to eat it. You have to beg God's forgiveness on fast days, Wednesdays, and Fridays. . . . If my mother had survived to be with me, she would have helped me out [at home], and I would've given birth [rather than done abortions]. Now instead I have had to live all these years in a state of sin." When Korotchenkova spoke of the abortionists, she revealed the opprobrium that her generation still attached to these women.

> It is an even greater sin for those who perform the abortions on others, that is the village women who do this for a living. One such woman died and when they took her to the cemetery, they suddenly noticed that a huge number of worms were crawling after her; and they crawled right into the hole dug for the grave after the body was placed in there. These [worms] were her "abortniki" [i.e., the fetuses she had destroyed in the course of her work].[31]

The references to village abortionists appeared in many of the interviews. For the women in this second generation, the village abortionist was the key to their ability to achieve control over their fertility. Nearly every village of any size had such a specialist. And the stories about her were remarkably similar, no matter where recorded. Women expressed a mixture of revulsion and gratitude. With the help of abortionists, they were able to control their fertility—and thwart the intention of the government to turn them into baby machines while neglecting to supply their elementary material needs. Although they could not escape the folk aversion to those who performed such procedures, the women claimed to have always and everywhere protected the identities of village abortionists, and to have done so in the face of powerful police duress and even of death. This theme was repeated with extraordinary regularity and invariability. A comment by Efrosinia Ruleva was typical. She admired the courage of her abortionist, who was not afraid to do her work despite the many women being sent to prison for it. "I decided that even if I was going to die, I wouldn't say who did the abortion."[32] The formulaic nature of the testimonies suggests how women, in retelling stories of that era, could express their sense of being bound together in a community conspiracy against the party-state. This does not mean, of course, that they did not turn in their neighbors; we found cases of abortionists who were exposed and arrested. Yet the stories told by the women were hermetic.

The stories related so far came from women in western Russia. Informants from the villages in Moscow province likewise reported an upsurge in abortions in the second generation, just when the opportunities for legal abortion were closing down. Although most of the informants from this generation did not admit to having had abortions themselves, they noted that illegal abortions, either self-induced or performed with the help of village women, were frequent —and led to the death of many women.[33] The stories suggest that although the women were prepared to have abortions to limit their fertility, they sometimes met with resistance from their mothers and husbands. Elizaveta Smirnova (born about 1917) reported that after having two children, she was not sure that she wanted another. When she again became pregnant, she hesitated: "I thought and thought about it. Should I have it or not? But I finally decided that I had to give birth anyway. And my husband was categorically opposed to doing anything about it [ending the pregnancy] . . . really very opposed. . . . And my mother was a believer and such that she would start dancing around in front of my husband saying, 'Tell me, is it really possible to do such a thing! Is it really possible to go and kill children!' And that was it."[34]

The two Tambov women interviewed from this generation both had abortions, despite feeling the moral sting of it. Anna Mikhaleva (born in 1923) considered abortion a sin, and she first tried to limit her births by contraception. Since neither her mother nor her mother-in-law had used contraception, she had to learn about it from her girlfriends. But, again, contraception proved far from effective. "My husband used contraception, but he drank, so anything could happen." She was right about his lack of attention. In twelve years of marriage (before her husband died of war injuries and drink), the couple had five children, even though Anna did abortions between each birth. "The way it went was that I would have one child, be overwhelmed and think, That's enough. The next one I'd abort. But that is dangerous, too; so, the next time I'd give birth again, then again do an abortion, and so it went in each instance." Although Anna Mikhaleva knew of babki-abortionists in the village (they were pursued by the authorities, and a few apparently were prosecuted), she did the abortions herself with a syringe. "Using a syringe can be dangerous. If the water lands in your bladder, you die." Once, she had an especially scary time when the fetus lodged in the birth canal, and she nearly died before a medical midwife arrived to treat the problem.[35] Another woman from the same village also had to protect herself from having a large family with a drunkard who was unlikely to be around to support the children. Getting effective contraception was difficult, she said. "Abortion is a sin, but what was I do to? I had two abortions. My husband was opposed, but I was in an impossible situation. . . . If he had not been a drunkard, who knows? I might not have done the abortions."[36] As she expected, her husband did not last long, dying after only ten years of marriage, thereby solving her fertility problems.

Many women in this second generation placed the blame for their abortions on their husbands. The women presented themselves as victims of their husband's drunkenness and, therefore, unreliability in regard to contraceptive control. This served as a mitigating factor in their decision to have abortions. I have already included several such cases. In the Urals village, too, a woman complained that contraception proved pointless because her husband was a drunkard who "paid no attention and cared about nothing." The one thing he did care about was having a son, and he kept impregnating her until after five girls he finally got his wish. (The wife, Tamara Privalova, said that after the third girl he threatened to strangle the next child if it was also female!) Through it all, this poor, illiterate woman, supported only by the prayers and magical spells of her mother, sought to gain control of her fertility by abortions, some in the hospital but most at home on her own because she feared the hospital treatment. At home, she had no fear and just flushed out her womb with an enema. The boy this couple finally got, Privalova sighed, turned out to be a drunkard just like his father.[37]

Husbands also function in the stories as opponents (along with mothers and mothers-in-law) of abortion; so they represent traditional, if eroding, patriarchal power and the normative mores of the previous generation. The case of Galina Mamina (born in 1918) in the Urals village is illustrative. She had ten children between 1936 and 1957, an impressive fertility record considering that her husband was away serving in the military during the war. The only contraception she applied was prolonged nursing (her children were already talking and saying, "Mama, give me your teat," before she weaned them), but it offered little protection. She very much wanted to abort her final child. Her husband was ill and dying (indeed, he died before the child was born), yet he categorically refused to countenance abortion. "Take a big knife," he said, "go out to the highway and murder someone else, but don't touch an innocent child!" The interviewer: "Couldn't you go against your husband's wishes?" Galina: "No. A husband's word was law. . . . [If you resisted,] he'd say, 'Now, you'll catch it' (she laughs)."[38] Another woman from the same region, Anna Panacheva, also spoke of her husband's opposition to abortion. The couple lived in a remote village where no doctor or hospital was available. Anna had some friends who aborted themselves, but she said, "It was terrible if you did something to yourself without medical facilities [to intervene]. Many perished, and my husband would not permit it. . . . He said: We'll just raise them all, even if there are a lot."[39]

The explanations given by the women of this second generation for why they decided to have fewer children were terse: "Times were hard"; "I couldn't live the way my mother did." It is not easy to know exactly what they meant. Their memories of those times were shaped by the subsequent years of growing prosperity and completion of the fertility transition, a process accompanied by a radical change in attitudes toward children. The women of this middle generation were initiating that change. Though taught not to mourn dead children, they resisted this admonition. "When children died, we were not allowed to cry, but we cried all the same," reported Efrosinia Ruleva.[40] "You don't need to cry for dead babies," said another woman, "but it [was] hard not to."[41] The women of this generation had changed. They refused to accept the death of small children stoically. They also had adopted a new model of what it meant to be a woman, a wife, and a mother, a model bound up with the new demands on them as part of a collective farm work force or even as workers in nearby factories. This new model likewise included aspirations for a higher living standard. Their job demands and aspirations to a better life required control of their fertility.

Anna Varfolomeeva of Smolensk province is a good example. Born in 1928, she was thirteen years of age when she lost her father to death in the war. The oldest child, she had to bring up her six surviving siblings while her mother went to work in the fields or at a nearby mill. In her stories she continually compared her own life to the misery of her mother, who had nine births and seven surviving children to rear on her own. When Anna married, she was determined to limit her births. She said that neither she nor her friends knew about contraception, and so she had several hospital abortions:

> It was a sin, of course. But I didn't exactly believe in God. I mean, can you really believe in God after living the life we had? Women had to lug around seventy-kilo sacks; what kind of life is that? Well, how can you believe in God in that case? Besides, the idea that the unborn have a soul, I can't believe in that.[42]

Anna was proud of how she helped to bring up her siblings, but she felt sorry for her mother and the other women of the older generation, and could not imagine repeating their experience. The religious norms of her childhood still affected her, as her rationalizations for abortion reveal. But she was content that she was able to feed and clothe her three children better than her mother had been able to do for hers.

While many women claimed not to know about or have access to contraception, this means of limiting family size was spreading, especially after the war. We asked women how, apart from abortion, they accomplished this reduction in fertility and whether it was a family decision. "Well, you know the way," responded a woman in Moscow province, "at that time, you know, our men themselves, they learned from one another. They went to the pharmacy and bought [rubbers]." Question: So, you made a conscious decision, together, that you did not need any more children? "Yes, everyone here, altogether, it was like it was the fashion of the time. . . . In our years only [one family] had ten children." The proudest accomplishment of this woman was that both her daughters had a good education and were able to escape the poverty of village life.[43]

It is difficult to pinpoint the source of this aspiration for a different life, which varied by place and by individual, but the stimulus came, as one would expect, from the city. Some women had worked in towns before starting a family, often as a nanny for the children of a white-collar-class family. Others learned from teachers in local schools; whether of the prerevolutionary intelligentsia or the Soviet variety, these teachers had rejected traditional authority. Ultimately, the source was Western scientific thought, in either its pre-Soviet or Soviet version, brands of modernism that encouraged people to believe in their ability to remake their lives and world. For example, Anna Zueva, the medic from Novgorod province, told me that she was brought up in the old way, believing in devils, unclean powers, witches on brooms sent to cause harm. But she was fortunate to have schoolteachers from the prerevolutionary nobility: "They were not our Soviet types; they had breeding and wide knowledge, not like us." A favorite teacher showed the pupils a better way to live by teaching them cleanliness and grooming. "She also advised my mother about the coming changes, such as the collectivization of agriculture, and told her that children who were not educated would end up on farms forever, working with cows and pigs or in the field." It was too dangerous to say these things in school, Anna pointed out, but the teacher quietly gave good advice to her mother, and Anna was able to go on to professional training.[44]

The "pull" factors were this contact and the allure of a different way of life. The "push" came from the collapse of the traditional support structures for child rearing under the impact of collectivization and war, which together destroyed the patriarchal family as a unit of production. In other words, the women of this second generation had their children in a period when the protection that patriarchal families had earlier afforded women in their childbearing had broken down, but a new system of state paternalism had not yet been put in place. Tatiana Varfolomeeva (born in 1911) made this point, saying that collective-farm life was much harder on birthing women than was life on the independent farmstead (khutor). Likely this was the case, certainly so in the pre-war years before services reached the state and collective farms. This generation's women were doubly exploited. They were deprived of farm-family work units that could extend them assistance in their maternal contributions, were driven into working on the collective farms or for wages in nearby factories, and, finally, were deprived of legal abortion and expected to produce more children for the state. Courageously, the women resisted, taking control as best they could of their fertility, even though their resistance exacted a high price in physical and moral pain.

I cannot end the discussion of this generation without mentioning another difficult fertility choice that many of the women made after World War II: the decision to have children without husbands. The cohort of women who had been in their early twenties during the war were only half as likely as women in other cohorts to get married, because so many of the men their age had been lost in the war.[45] This issue came up in my conversation with Anna Zueva, and I said to her, "In Solzhenitsyn's Cancer Ward, he describes these women, their lives, how they suffered in having to live without husbands. They remained loyal to their boyfriends who had died in the war." Anna responded, "Well, not all remained loyal, of course, not all." I replied, "At that time, I have heard, they had many illegitimate children." Anna continued to elaborate:

> Yes, there were many widows here who had children. They grew up. Some of the women gave birth without fathers. Well, these were decent women and they did this consciously. They didn't want to have to go through life alone, and that meant they had to have a child, or even two, or even three without fathers. Now they have all grown up, they have gotten educated and are working. And their mothers are respected. No one here treated them with contempt, we didn't shun them or reproach them. After all, what was one to do?[46]

The government assisted these women for reasons of its own. Party leaders recognized the need to replenish the population quickly and provided subsidies to unwed mothers, an encouragement for them to create families for themselves and also sons and daughters for the nation.

Third Generation

Women of the third generation, born between the late 1920s and the late 1950s, made fertility choices that continued the sharp decline initiated by their elders. The means of control remained much the same: condoms, coitus interruptus, and especially abortion were employed until very late when some village women of this cohort began to gain access to birth-control pills and intrauterine devices.

Before relating the typical experiences, I should mention that while most women of this third generation accepted abortion (and others were less likely than their predecessors to condemn it), not everyone had dropped the religious and moral scruples against it. For example, one of our informants, Tatiana Vorob'eva (born in 1954) believed that a fetus was a living being, and she would not think of having an abortion. Besides, she loved children and wanted a large family. Although her first marriage at age nineteen fell apart after one child because of her husband's alcoholism, she married a second time at age twenty-seven, gave birth to four more children, and took in two foster children. Vorob'eva was modern in that she used contraception to halt childbearing after her fifth birth, but she rejected abortion on moral grounds.[47]

Tatiana Vorob'eva's attitude was unusual. Most informants from this generation spoke little of family resistance to birth limitation and were less likely than their elders to believe that abortion was an unforgivable sin. They sometimes felt, as did Antonina Ptichnikova (born in 1937), that abortion was a sin to be expiated. But this could be done by going to church and having prayers said.[48] Valentina Lopatkina (born in 1931) was altogether unapologetic about her three abortions. Two of them she did herself with a syringe. The third was performed by her husband's aunt, who lived in a nearby village.[49]

Lopatkina also spoke of the village abortionist with empathy. Instead of the aversion toward abortionists that women of the older generation expressed, she felt pride about Klavdia's skill and renown. "All of Moscow province used to go to her . . . yes, literally the whole province. Well, she did abortions by injecting soap, vodka, and baking soda. . . . and it was rare that a woman would land in the hospital as a result of her work. Yes, she had a nearly perfect record." As Lopatkina continued the story, telling of a time when things did go wrong, she offered a glimpse of how the authorities attempted to uncover and arrest abortionists—and the penalties they imposed on them.

> There was one time, of course, that she damaged the womb, and the woman landed [in the hospital]. She was doing an abortion for Nadia, a woman who

worked at the factory. The abortion was performed, but it somehow did not take effect. And Nadia had to go to the hospital. When she got there, she was hemorrhaging. . . . And [the doctors] there demanded to know "Who did this to you"? And she refused to say who did it. . . . Well, then, you know, they say, "Either you tell us or we won't cleanse your womb!" [i.e., perform curettage to complete the abortion and halt the bleeding].

The two doctors we had then were Lidia I. and a gynecologist, Natalia F., and they said, "If you don't tell us, we won't perform the cleansing. We'll reestablish the pregnancy." And [Nadia] says, "But you will arrest her and put her in jail." "No, we won't [do such a thing]. . . . " Well, you know, Nadia after all went ahead and told who did the abortion on her. And Lidia I. and Natalia F. immediately called up the police. The police went right out to the house and found all the abortion instruments at Klavdia's and arrested her. . . . She got four years' "vacation." . . . But, oh, how many women went to her and from everywhere—from just everywhere they would go to her.[50]

This story cuts against the frequently repeated assurance that women never betrayed their village abortionist, but it was also the case that this happened in the late 1950s when abortion was once again legal and the persecution of abortionists less ferocious than in Stalin's time.

In all the villages we studied we found that other women of the youngest generation had abortions regularly and, seemingly, with little sense of guilt. Raisa Semenovna, born in 1935 and the mother of two, explained without hesitation that she went to hospitals for "medical abortions" to control her fertility.[51] Valentina Shapovalova, born in 1933 and likewise the mother of two, endured sixteen abortions, many of them with a village abortionist. She described the woman's method of scraping out the womb with two fingers and told of how one of the abortions was bungled and landed her in the hospital. Shapovalova also took potions and pills (evidently not birth-control pills as such) to prevent pregnancy. She was not only poor but also the target of abuse from her mother-in-law and her drunkard husband. Determined not to build a family with these people, she was able to achieve this goal through the help of other women, such as her mother and the village abortionist. The role of the husband in this instance is invoked to justify the decision to have abortions, but we also see something new that was more typical of men in this generation: Shapovalova's husband left the decision entirely to her. "Do whatever you yourself wish [about the pregnancy]," he would tell her.[52]

Even in the Tambov province villages, where religion remained strong, the norms against abortion were softening. Antonina Abramova (born in 1931) still worried a bit about the possible sinfulness of her abortions: "I am a sinner and probably will never be done with praying about it." Her first husband was a drunkard and a brawler who died young, and she had an abortion to avoid a large family with him. Her second husband was a kind man, and her abortions in that marriage were solely to limit family size after two children. She knew women in her village on whom the pressure was much greater. Some had had frightening dreams that convinced them not to go through with planned abortions. The women were from families in which the old folks were very religious. In one woman's dream, she was walking through the village when another women approached and handed her a doughnut that had little arms and legs protruding. The woman said: "Give this to your neighbor; it's her [aborted] children." Another woman considering abortion dreamed that she saw her neighbor's aborted child trying to jump out of a deep hole full of such children, and this changed her mind about the abortion. Abramova herself was not unhappy with her choices, but wished she had known about and used contraception—and she had advised her daughter to do so, even though she still considered such issues indecent and difficult to talk about in 1994.[53]

The three other Tambov women interviewed from this generation, more accepting of the need for abortions, were not troubled by dream stories. In addition to having abortions, all of them also used contraception. Lia Brykina (born in 1932), a village school teacher, even went on the pill after three children and two abortions. Her sister worked in a local pharmacy and was able to keep her supplied. For Brykina, as for several other women of this cohort, a drunkard husband provided an excuse. But it is also clear from their descriptions of child care and their aspirations for their children that these women had an entirely new, modern notion of mothering, taking pride in providing store-bought clothes, toys, and buggies for their children. And the husbands had also changed. They were willing to leave decisions about family size and the means of achieving it to their wives and did not demand to have their way, as had many men of the previous generations.[54]

Anna Kasiakina's comments nicely illustrate these changes:

> I did several abortions and used contraception; that is, my husband used contraception, but not all the time. He considered it my responsibility to decide whether to give birth or get an abortion. But in our time people didn't want to have a lot of children anymore. Anyway, we were already looking after children better and dressing them better. We finally had enough diapers, even if we still had to economize by dressing them in diapers during the day and then, at night, when no one would see, we used an old shirt.

Kasiakina obviously wished to fit in with the changes taking place in her age group in regard to fertility control and child care, but at the same time she was still under the influence of the older generations' condemnation of abortion and felt some ambivalence. It should be kept in mind that the interview took place in 1994, when religious ideas and practices were reemerging and gaining renewed authority. In summarizing her life at the end of the interview, Kasiakina said, "Of course, it wasn't good that I had abortions. It's a sin, the old folks say, and you'll go to Hell for it. But women of my age had them, how many I don't know exactly because it wasn't something people liked to talk about. . . . If I could have stayed home with the children or if a reliable grandmother had been there to baby-sit, maybe I would have had more children. The children were good, and the births easy, but to work outside the home, plus do housekeeping and farming, and also raise children is hard. Maybe, if other people had not had abortions, I wouldn't have had them either; it would have been simpler that way. Now, as I grow older, it gnaws at my heart."[55]

Tatars and Fertility Choice

When I visited Tatarskii Kalmaiur in the summer of 1990, the village was celebrating the holiday of *Kurban bairam*. It was the end of Ramadan, a time for slaughtering sheep, feasting on the meat, and distributing portions to the needy families of the community. In honor of the holiday, everyone was dressed in the best clothes, and the style choices of the women marked the generations clearly. The different generations, as I soon learned, likewise represented different approaches to fertility control. The mullah first sent me the impressive matriarch of the village, Khatima Nizamova, a woman then eighty-seven years of age. She and her elderly female friends wore brightly colored, flowing traditional gowns and kept their hair well covered. The women of the middle generation also leaned toward the traditional in their dress but with some concessions to modernity. The third generation, the mothers of the current teenagers, sported modern, if plain, dresses; on their heads they wore small kerchiefs tied in the back that left most of their hair exposed. The teenage girls, who wore blouses, straight skirts, and nylons, were indistinguishable from their counterparts in Simbirsk and Moscow.

Even this picture of dress rightly suggests that the changes in these Muslims' lives conformed closely to the pattern of the Russian women. The oldest generation knew no means of contraception except lengthy nursing (which was in any case a strong Muslim injunction), and abortion was rarely an option because of severe norms against it. The oldest woman, Khatima Nizamova, had had nine pregnancies, of which two ended in miscarriages. Her other children survived childhood. She intentionally applied lengthy nursing to prevent pregnancy, a practice she learned from the village midwife and her girlfriends.[56] Otherwise, she exercised no fertility control. Abortion was considered a sin, Khatima affirmed, although she did report that she knew about four abortions done by acquaintances (of what age she was speaking, however, is unclear). Garifabanu Abdullina, born in 1908, had eight pregnancies; five of her children survived. She, too, reported no abortions. When she was asked whether her friends had had abortions, she replied that she doubted they had, but did not know because the sin of it was so great that no one would have admitted to an abortion.[57] Zubarzhat Rezvanova, a few years younger than these other women, could not consider abortion because of her husband's unwavering opposition to it. "We will have as many children as Allah gives us," he insisted.[58] She had ten children, of which eight survived early childhood.

The one Muslim woman of this generation who used abortion for fertility control was not from Tatarskii Kalmaiur. This was Sharifa Ialisheva, a Tatar from Mordovia who as a young woman in the 1930s had been able to escape to Leningrad and work for a time in a hospital. Her father then ordered her home and forced her into a marriage with a widower who had four children of his own. In addition to caring for his children, Sharifa gave birth to seven children of her own (of which four survived). Between her second and third surviving child, she had several abortions secretly: this was in the late 1940s when abortion was outlawed. She also had to conceal the abortions from her husband, who was a strict Muslim and absolutely opposed to abortion. Even so, her husband learned of one abortion when it was bungled and landed Sharifa in the hospital. Luckily for the family, her husband discovered that a doctor at the hospital was a friend of a friend, and he was able to persuade this doctor to report the abortion as medically required.[59] In contrast to most Muslim village women of her generation, Sharifa Ialisheva had enjoyed a taste of freedom, worked in an urban hospital at the time abortion was legal, and was only then forced into marriage with a man she did not love, who kept her "having children like a cat," she said. It is not surprising that she was determined to abort unwanted pregnancies and knew how to do it. Sharifa stood out in another way, as we shall see later: she was a respected folk healer in her village.[60]

The Tatar women of the second generation (whose birth dates ranged from 1917 to 1925) likewise differed little from the Russian women of this same generation of change. About the only departure involved contraception. Some Russian women reported using condoms and coitus interruptus. The Tatar villagers claimed ignorance of any contraception other than the effects of prolonged nursing. One particularly embittered informant complained "We lived like animals, not knowing anything about it [reproduction]." Even her mother failed to give her advice, she said, and it would have been too shameful and embarrassing to raise the question herself.[61]

Like the Russian women of this generation, the Tatars began to resort to abortion on a large scale. Interestingly, every Tatar informant of this generation was emphatic that no women of the older generation in their village had had an abortion. If abortions were done earlier, they were obviously well concealed, because the women of the second generation who obtained abortions understood what they were doing as a sharp break with the past. They also recognized abortion as a sin. According to the matriarch Nizamova, the break came after the famines of the 1930s. The older women readily admitted that they wanted fewer children even before this, but only after the famine did they consciously start to restrict fertility.[62] Her report fits well with what we learned from the women of this second generation. Each one recounted that she herself or friends of hers had sought abortions. One woman, Mariam Gimadeeva, was a medically trained midwife and able to give detailed information. During the period of her practice in Kalmaiur from 1941 to 1971, she recorded 72 legal abortions. She also knew of many women who went to Simbirsk to obtain illegal abortions. A local nurse likewise did underground abortions closer to home.[63]

For the third generation, education and the decriminalization of abortion, plus the choices already made by the previous generation, liberated the women from much of the guilt and fear of fertility control. The oldest informant in this third generation, Fakhiza Suleimanova, was born in 1930 in a Tatar village and moved to Simbirsk before her teen years. Even though she was living in the city and working as a typist at the time she wed in 1954, she told me that except for advice from her mother on female hygiene as a teenager, she entered marriage wholly ignorant. The subject was still considered shameful. Condoms were available in the pharmacy, and she bought them, but it was such an embarrassment even for a married woman that she waited until the store cleared:

> You know it was such a shameful thing to buy [condoms] at the pharmacy then, though nowadays it's of no account—young people go into a pharmacy and freely ask for things in front of everyone. But in our time, it wasn't like that. You'd go into the pharmacy and if you needed that product, you'd wait until everyone was gone and only then ask for it.[64]

Besides using contraception, Fakhiza had two hospital abortions, something that she did not consider a sin because of her understanding of the Quran. Fakhiza took enormous pride in her Tatar ethnicity and Muslim religion, and would not lightly have gone against religious injunctions. And, indeed, Islam is flexible on the matter of abortion. It is allowable if it contributes to the overall health of the family and community. The conditions that govern the decision vary from place to place and time to time. Fakhiza understood them in a way that no doubt reflected the views of her community as it adjusted to the new conditions of Soviet life. She explained:

> According to our religion, it is a great sin to have an abortion. But depending on her living conditions, of course, a woman is not going to have an extra child. They say that if the husband lets her get an abortion, the sin does not stay on the woman, but if she does it without permission, then she has to bear the sin.[65]

We can hope that this is the case because all the Muslim informants of this third generation either had abortions themselves or told of friends who had obtained, in some cases, a large number of abortions. These women commonly sought abortions after the third or fourth live birth. Nurania Badrieva related that two friends had had ten and fifteen abortions respectively. She, too, resorted to abortion.[66] Another woman, even though she feared her husband's wrath should he learn of it, twice obtained abortions after her sixth child.[67] An

unusually well-educated village woman of this generation, Roza Fakhrutdinova, had gone for a time to a teachers college and then worked in the village
nursery as a Pioneer leader. She had three well-spaced births (1955, 1960,
1964), and succeeded in controlling her fertility without abortion. Roza explained that a medical midwife in the village and her Russian language instructor had taught her about contraceptive methods, including condoms, pills, and
quinine. Yet the techniques she applied were either little employed or ineffec-
tually employed by other women in her circle. She counted sixty-three abortions among women acquaintances of her generation; one woman alone endured twenty-three abortions.[68]

The difficulty for most of these women, as was true for the Russian women
as well, was the refusal of the men to concede any comfort for the sake of
fertility control. The women, and in most cases the men, too, were unwilling to
"have as many children as Allah gives." Yet the burden of exercising control fell
almost entirely on the women. Even Mariam Gimadeeva, a medically trained
midwife married to a military doctor, could not persuade her husband to use
condoms, which were readily available.[69] A Bashkir woman married to an educated Muslim man complained that "in our ethnic group, the men nevertheless
think only of themselves, especially in the villages," and do not help in fertility
control.[70] In answering questions about other matters, several women of the
village admitted fearing their men. When asked about possible couvade practices, for example, Khatima and her friends said that "we were afraid of our
husbands and did not dare to wish such things on them."[71] Minzifa Mustafina
told of her dread of her husband when she went against his wishes and her
concern that he could have thrown her out.[72] In view of this continuing fear of
male power, it is doubtful that many women would have been able to limit their
husbands' sexual privileges.

For both Russians and Tatars the changes experienced by the three cohorts
were similar and sharply defined. The first generation claimed to know almost
nothing about contraceptive methods. As for abortion, only three women of
this generation acknowledged having them (5 percent of the sample), although
in view of the desire of women even then to have smaller families, many more
than admitted to it probably had tried the folk-method abortifacients such as
powders and herbs (that Pelagea Sharav'eva, for example, said she used to halt
her pregnancies after her husband started running around with other women).

The second generation produced a profound change. Collectivization of
agriculture, "dekulakization," and famine had destroyed the world of family-
based farming in which these women grew up. The government then forced
them into wage labor without relieving them of household responsibilities. At
the same time, they were deprived of the legal means of regulating their fertility
and admonished to produce a large harvest of children for the fatherland. The
women resisted and, in opposition to the state and to the established religious
norms, wrested some degree of control through risky underground abortions,

the numbers of which swelled to unprecedented levels in this period. Virtually every village had a specialist in this trade. This experience of resistance seemed to form a bond between the women of the second generation, for in their retellings of those difficult times, they spoke of their shared fears and risks and of their absolute refusal to turn their abortionists or their neighbors in to the authorities.

The lives and choices of the third generation were easier than those of their mothers and grandmothers. The state, under its paternalist and pronatalist policies, allowed the women time off before and after their deliveries and furnished medical services for them and their children. The end of war and of domestic turmoil brought a relative prosperity that permitted villagers to realize some of their aspirations for consumerism, including the purchase of buggies, toys, and manufactured diapers and clothes for their children. Women still labored under the double and triple burden of farm or factory labor, childbearing, and housework. And abortion, which became legal again and widely available, continued to play a major role in control of their fertility. But small families made the lives of the younger women more bearable, and the religious norms against abortion weakened, freeing the women from much of the physical and moral agony endured by their mothers.

Giving Birth

Maxim Gorky wrote a story called "Birth" in which the narrator tells of encountering a Russian peasant woman in labor while he was walking along a Black Sea road. When he tried to assist the woman, she beat him off and withdrew into the woods to escape his view. The narrator understood her behavior as motivated by "shame," a response that would make sense in an urban context (in which Gorky himself grew up). A Russian peasant woman might just as likely have instead feared the gaze of an outsider at this time because of her special vulnerability to spiritual forces, a gaze that could easily afflict her or her newborn with the "evil eye." Later in Gorky's story, the woman's concern about the harm that could arise from improper disposal of the afterbirth again points to the importance to her of spiritual matters.[1]

Gorky's story tells of the resourcefulness, resilience, and independence of the common women of Russia, and also of their fears and the associated practices by which they kept those fears in check to maintain control over their world. Such images of the rural woman in childbirth are repeated in the stories told by our informants about preparing for and giving birth. The women assert their strength against pain and adversity, sometimes even loneliness and desperation. They speak of the dangers that they learned from their mothers and other older women and also about the knowledge and practices that these same women taught them so that they might control their fears and fulfill their duties as mothers and wives.

One of the most salient sources of danger was the "evil eye." Until very recently women in rural Russia feared their susceptibility to the evil eye at times of change, such as birthing, and understood that the fewer people who knew about the onset of labor the safer it was for them. Folklorist Olga Semenova Tian-Shanskaia reported that at the turn of the century women in southern Riazan province spoke only indirectly in summoning the village midwife in order to conceal the errand from outsiders.[2] They might say, "What's this, old woman, you promised to look at my cow and you aren't coming?"[3] Although I did not encounter examples of speaking by indirection in my interviews, I did find concern about the evil eye. Olga Mal'tseva of Novgorod province told me that, yes, they kept the time of birth a secret. When she was going home to be delivered by her mother, her mother-in-law said, "Don't go through the village. Cross over the river on the planks so that no one will see you." Olga continued, "In those days everyone understood that the pain would be greater. The more people who knew about it, the more the mother would suffer."[4] Many other women explained that they had had the same concerns, which were aroused by the advice of mothers and mothers-in-law whose word they accepted implicitly.[5] Well into this century, despite a rapidly changing political and educational environment, the transmission of women's knowledge between generations in rural Russia sustained traditional ideas and practices.

For most women of the first generation, regardless of where they lived, birthing differed little from the experience of prerevolutionary times. They gave birth many times and lost a number of their children to early death. They worked right up to the onset of labor, had no prenatal visits to medical facilities, and delivered their babies at home with the assistance of a village midwife or a relative; in some cases, they delivered entirely on their own. Although conditions for the subsequent generations varied somewhat depending on the degree of remoteness from urban centers, birthing practices in almost all locations rapidly moved toward medicalization.

In this chapter, in contrast to the last, I will examine each region through all three generations. The changes in each region occurred in a slightly different sequence, and this organization will allows a mapping of the changes in each area without the confusion of shifting back and forth between regions.

Northern Russia

In the northern reaches of Novgorod province, birthing was remarkably unaffected by any modern notions right up to World War II. Anna Zueva, a medic from central Novgorod province, was given her first assignment in the north in the late 1930s. She told me that the people there were altogether illiterate and had little contact with the rest of the country. They had never seen a car or a train, and the only music they knew was ditties (*chastushki*). It was a life almost entirely cut off. "They scarcely paid any taxes or relinquished crops. Their autonomy was such that the national government hardly existed. If the *raion* center sent some instructor out—and this actually happened—he could vanish in the forest and swamps never to be heard from again. He might have been eaten by a bear or such like." As for limiting the number of births, the women had learned from their mothers about the effects of prolonged breast-feeding. But "they didn't know [contraception], and, frankly, neither did I. They didn't teach us about this. In my medical training there was no such course."

When I asked Anna Zueva about birthing and whether the women in the north had their own midwives, she could not recall exactly. "I remember only that they were all midwives. Every woman was able to assist at birth, but assistance wasn't really necessary. The majority of Russian women gave birth without assistance, even without midwives. . . . They would be sitting around over supper, so I was told, and would feel a pain in the abdomen. The woman would grab some rags and go out to the barn—and then come back with a baby." Anna Zueva thought that she had made some progress in educating the people of the northern villages before she was recalled home at the outbreak of the war, but she did not return there to find out. The husband she met and married in the north died in the Finnish war, and when the German invasion reached Novgorod province she joined the partisans as a medic.[6]

Stories from the Vologda region give a sense of the resourcefulness of these northern women. Natalia Skovorodina (born in 1902) told about giving birth in a hay field at mowing time. To all appearances, the baby was born dead, but she washed it in her birch-bark bucket, shook it to life, and carried it home. "I cut the umbilicus with my finger nail and pinched it closed. This is how the midwives do it here to prevent *gryzh* [umbilical hernia]."[7] As this comment makes clear, in the Vologda region special midwives were active. Skovorodina mentioned that the midwives washed the newborn babies and cleaned up the house, which for traditional Russian midwives (but not for Tatar—see later discussion) seemed to be a common practice.[8] They did not get paid but were given gifts. The mother, too, received gifts of pirogi from other women while she rested up in the steam-bath cabin for several days following delivery.[9]

Tambov Province

Women in the Tambov villages were less isolated than the women of the far north, and they had maternity beds available at the local zemstvo hospital early in the century and again later at a collective farm hospital. Still, they kept to their traditional birthing practices until after World War II.[10] In most cases these practices included hiding from outsiders knowledge of the onset of labor, saying farewells to close family members (just as a dying person would), and birthing with the help of a village midwife.[11] The women of this older generation worked right up to the onset of labor (often at less heavy chores than usual), and, as a result, occasionally had to give birth in the field or on the road home from work. Prenatal check-ups and maternity leaves were not part of their experience unless their childbearing continued into the postwar period.

Anna Reutova listed the taboos her mother had warned her about during pregnancy. She was not to touch a corpse or a casket (which could lead to the death of her child). Dogs, too, were off limits; they could cause her baby to die of "a dog's old age" (a common withering condition of infants, a form of rickets). If she touched her face during a fire, her child would have a birthmark on that spot. Even christenings were considered dangerous; if a pregnant woman attended one, either her own or the baptized child might die.[12] Another woman resolutely advised against sex in the second half of pregnancy because it could cause physical defects in the child. "Wise husbands observe this rule; fools demand sex right up to the end."[13]

Reutova went on to describe birth in the 1930s, the decade during which she had her three children at home with the help of a traditional midwife (*povitush-ka*[14]). "I did it lying in bed, but some women lie on the floor. Sometimes the birth is difficult either because the baby is lying the wrong way or because of the 'evil eye.'" She quickly added that the evil eye could, however, be treated. An old woman in the village was able to cure the eye by lighting matches, placing them in water, and using water infused with prayers as a curative. A difficult birth could also provide a role for the husband. In what was a residue of a couvade practice, by which birth pains were transferred to the husband, Reutova mentioned "that if the birth was difficult, the husband was supposed to pull on his forelock. This would make things go better." This custom was rarely mentioned. Although a wide variety of couvade practices appear in the ethnographic literature about Russians, they must have been extinguished in the twentieth century; we did not run across anything more in this regard, despite asking about it.[15]

Birthing in this region was followed by certain common therapies executed by the attending midwife over the next few days. The midwife also took responsibility for putting the home back in order.

> Right after the birth, the midwife puts you on a warm oven and pats [your stomach] lightly. The second day, she pours hot water in a basin and places it on the oven, covering the area with a blanket to steam your abdomen. Then you lie down and she massages the abdomen from the bottom upward. Bad blood drains out, and the stomach goes back into place. Occasionally, they would oversteam someone [she would die from heat and hemorrhaging], but that was rare. In the past they placed women on a heated oven, but in my time I did not lie on the oven after giving birth, even though they still washed on the oven, and I heard that they even gave birth on the oven earlier on. The midwife also washed all the clothes that had become soiled during birth. The midwife came back for three days and each time bathed me and the baby. At the end of three days, we "washed hands" [a ceremony ending the midwife's responsibilities]. She once more patted me, checked me and the baby, and washed her hands. I gave her a towel and a small bit of money.[16]

The oven played a central role in the birthing process for most of the women of this region and generation. Like the oven, the memories that the older women had of birth were warm and radiated feelings of security and control. Marfa Malikova had nine children, the first in the field before her husband could drive her home and summon the midwife. Her last birth (in 1951) took place in a hospital. But all the rest were at home with her mother serving as midwife. "After delivery, mother would set me on a warm oven and massage my stomach. She washed the baby right away and put it there too, and we lay together on the warm oven." Midwives like Malikova's mother would begin their work by invoking the Almighty: "'God bless me,' they'd say, and then with God's help, they'd get to their work."[17] After delivery, they not only massaged and ministered to the mother to help restore her abdomen to the right shape; they also "corrected" the head of the baby, giving it a rounded appearance. Again, in the case of Marfa Malikova and all other informants from this region, the ceremony of "washing the hands" and paying the midwife took place on the third day. These well-established customs and invocations of God's help, together with the control that the village midwife and members of the family exercised, free of the influence of outsiders, endowed the birthing process with a protective intimacy.

While some women like Marfa Malikova had their mothers serve as midwives, most did not have a specialist in the family and relied on the services of an experienced village woman, at least while these specialists were allowed to practice. The crackdown on village practitioners was under way after the new family law of 1936, and it can be followed in the birthing record of Praskovia Krivolapova. She had her first three children with a village woman, and her descriptions of her and other traditional midwives again conveyed a positive stance. "We had a woman named Masha Prokhovka. She was very old but a skillful midwife [povitushka]. She would straighten out your stomach afterward and also shape the baby as needed." Krivolapova's births took place at home on a bed, except for the third, which was done on the oven. "This third one was delivered by a povitukha but a different one, as Masha Prokhovka had died by that time. In those days [the birth was in 1938], it seems they had already begun to outlaw deliveries by village midwives, but it was the wintertime and difficult to get to the hospital. Thank goodness there were still village midwives who could help us. My fourth child [in 1939] was born in the hospital. We had to get there because by then you couldn't find babki anymore. They were being persecuted."[18]

Contrast these positive memories to those of another informant, who was treated by a medical doctor. Maria Malikova told particularly vivid tales about her hard life in a family ruled by a tyrannical mother-in-law who lived as a "nun."[19] Her birthing history was difficult, and she described it poignantly. She had seven children, three before the war and four afterward. Six survived. The first two were delivered by village midwives, but later births were attended by doctors in the period when village practitioners were outlawed. Maria was given no respite from heavy tasks, however, and had to haul firewood and spread manure right up to the onset of labor. A problem she experienced repeatedly was the failure of the placenta to be naturally expelled. In 1941 she gave birth to her third child. Because of the ban on village midwives, Maria recounted,

> they brought me a doctor, a Jewish woman. I gave birth but the afterbirth did not come out, and [the doctor] said, "I am not going to stay sitting here beside

you," and she rode off. Three days went by and I was swelling up all over. So I went outside to the barn, grabbed hold of a rafter and hung from it, saying, "Lord, if you want me to live, help me; if not, let me die here." Then everything came out of me in a stinking mess. So, you see how I was tormented, but God helped.[20]

Hanging from the rafters was a time-honored method for coping with difficult births. Women usually hung straps over the rafters of the house and slipped their arms through the straps, suspending themselves in the air.[21] Maria mentioned God's help, but this went only so far. The daughter she bore soon died because Maria's milk did not come in, a fact she blamed on her "hunger and exhaustion." After the war, the placenta twice again stuck inside her, and she had to be transferred from the collective farm's maternity ward to a city hospital because she was losing blood. Transfusions pulled her through until the placenta was separated manually.

So long as births were at home, disposal of the placenta was an issue of importance for the women. But, judging from the reports of the women we interviewed, no fixed notion survived about where the placenta was to be preserved. We heard three different versions, for example, from the women in the Tambov sample. Maria Malikova said that the afterbirth was buried in a hole in the yard or by a fence where no one worked.[22] Anna Reutova reported that it was placed under the floorboards of the house.[23] Praskovia Krivolapova differentiated between the placenta of boys and girls, which had separate and symbolically significant resting places associated with gendered work roles: the girls' under the floorboards next to the oven, and the boys' under the horse manure piles.[24] Peasants regarded the placenta as a part of the newborn baby, and they believed that if dogs ate it or ill-disposed persons found it, harm could come to the child. As the link to the mother, the placenta might also provide an avenue to her and, if handled improperly, could affect her future fertility. So they reasoned that the placenta had to be treated with something like the respect accorded to the dead.[25]

Another activity associated with birthing was a visit by friends of the new mother. The visit, known as "*zubki,*" took place a day or two after the birth, and usually included just women relatives and friends, who brought favorite foods for the new mother. Marfa Malikova remembered receiving bliny, kasha, and thick *oladia* pancakes. "Once in a time of famine, I recall, one sister-in-law brought only bread, and I was glad to have that!"[26] Praskovia Krivolapova noted that men, too, might be involved. "Usually, my husband's sisters came and had their husbands with them. They brought various foods: bliny, eggs. Someone might even bring a chicken. And my relatives would come, too, sisters and brothers. I would go around serving sweets to those who came."[27] So, again, this custom reinforced the positive memories that the older generation had of traditional birthing.

The next, or transitional, generation in the Tambov villages made the shift to medical births. The experience of Anna Mikhaleva (born in 1923) can be contrasted with that of her mother (born about 1895). Anna's mother had all her nine children at home with a midwife who steamed her on the oven. She lost four of her children to death in the period of war and famine from 1916 to 1922 (two children were thought to have died from the evil eye). Anna herself had five children starting in 1947. The first was born at home with a *povitushka*, but the next two were delivered at a hospital. "Probably the first would also have been done at the hospital," she reported, "but we lived far from the hospital." Her last two births took place at home again, but not as a matter of preference; the weather had made the roads impassable. She had to deliver with the help of a neighbor who had eight children of her own and knew what needed to be done. Afterwards a doctor arrived to give a check-up and see how mother and child were doing.[28] Another woman, a few years younger, from the same village had a similar experience. One of her births took place at the hospital, but her other two children had to be born at home because fierce snowstorms blocked the route to the hospital. But in these cases, which occurred in the late 1960s, an obstetrician arrived in time to assist at the births.[29]

The birthing environment for the women of the second generation had changed significantly. Although a small zemstvo medical facility with three maternity beds had served the region since prerevolutionary times, peasant women rarely used it, even after an inter-collective-farm maternity ward was added about 1936. According to Dr. Vasilii Dobrynin, who began working there in 1951 and whose father had long run the facility, a visiting nurse-midwife was active as early as the 1940s. She certified pregnancies and encouraged women to go for prenatal check-ups, but the women often failed to appear and sent for help only at the onset of labor, sometimes too late to get them to the maternity ward. The actual shift in practice came only in the 1950s. The maternity ward grew to twenty beds and handled 110 to 115 deliveries per year. Medical outreach also began in the 1950s, including conversations with village women and distribution of brochures that told about caring for themselves and their children. Early in the next decade, as transportation improved, authorities closed the collective farm's maternity ward and sent birthing mothers to the nearby city of Kirsanov.[30]

The women of the transitional generation, by their own accounts, preferred hospital births. Education also seems to have been having an effect, since these women rejected folk taboos related to pregnancy or the evil eye. But if modern ideas had broken through, modern benefits such as paid maternity leaves were slower in arriving. This boon remained limited to workers in state-owned enterprises. The only improvement for the collective farm women, in comparison with prewar and wartime mothers, was freedom from the requirement to work on the farm during pregnancy and in the period following birth. They could choose to stay at home with their small children but without compensation or support from their workplace or the government. Even when they made this choice, their families expected them to continue working in the house and garden, work that sometimes involved heavy lifting and led to the common affliction of Russian mothers, a prolapsed uterus.[31]

The third generation of Tambov village women completed the transition. They had all their children in medical facilities and also benefited from having maternity leave, which was finally extended to collective-farm women in 1965. Contrast the experience of Antonina Abramova (born in 1931) with that of her mother, who had given birth to ten children, all with village midwives, and lost eight of them in early childhood (mostly to measles and whooping cough). Antonina had just two children, the first in 1957 in a nearby inter-collective-farm maternity ward and the second in 1970 in a city hospital. She was able to take advantage of prenatal check-ups and two-and-a-half months' paid leave for the first baby, with even more time off for the second.[32] Other women of this area had similar experiences.[33]

Something altogether new appears in the stories of these third-generation women: nostalgia for the earlier way of birthing. Lia Brykina mentioned the opinion of old women that birthing was no worse when the *povitukhi* did it. The only difference was hygiene. "This even the old women acknowledge; it was hard to keep things clean because the house was crowded, and [looking after] all their many children left little time." But the younger women recalled, and possibly idealized, the amount of personal attention the older generations had enjoyed, contrasting it with the impersonal or lax care at the hospital. Antonina Abramova stressed this point, which a tragic incident had fixed in her memory.

> We had a [neighbor named] Niura who gave birth in the hospital. Her baby boy was large, and the birthing was very hard. But no one checked up on her regularly. So she died from bleeding, and the infant died too, and they were buried together. . . . The village midwives [babki] were more attentive. . . . My mom had all her children at home.[34]

It is difficult to say if this nostalgia would have been expressed had the interviewer not been probing for information about the past, for example, asking about the mothers of the informants as well as about the informants themselves. Nostalgia is often a reaction to an unpleasant present, and at the time of the interview Abramova was discouraged and angry about the changes taking place in post-Soviet Russia. But, as will be shown later, conditions at maternity wards had been deteriorating in Soviet times, enough so that some women were choosing to return to home births. The nostalgia for the old ways, heavily colored though the memory surely was, may also have included an astute assessment of risks and benefits.

Smolensk Province

The three women of the oldest generation from the Smolensk sample had much the same experience as the oldest of the Tambov mothers. Even though a medical station was available in the region, the women did not make use of it for prenatal check-ups until after the war. They gave birth either with the help

Steam-bath cabin, central Russia, 1990

of family members or, more typically, with a village midwife. Just as in the Tambov region, concern about the evil eye and the need for healers to treat it continued to be evident. Daria Fedosenkova told about her first birth in 1930.

> I gave birth at home in the hay, just as everyone did in those days. Only after the war did they begin to take women to the hospital, usually to Terino [fifteen kilometers distant]. Pregnant women did not go to have any kind of prenatal check-ups. Our midwife [babka-povitukha] was very experienced. She knew how to effect cures. I was given the evil eye after birthing, fell ill, and was altogether unable to sleep. They brought cow's milk to that babka, and she whispered on it. I drank it and everything got better. [35]

Though she survived this crisis, the unfortunate woman lost her next three children to death. One of them, she was certain, had been given the evil eye. She made the mistake of taking him to field work before she had been able to baptize him, and the eye was thought to have caused him to die of scarlet fever.

What distinguished the experience of the women in the Smolensk province sample was the use of the steam bath (banya) following birth. This was equivalent to the steaming on the oven that was common in the Tambov region in the southern plains region, which lacked the forests needed to build steam-bath cabins. In the forested regions farther north, steam-bath cabins were found in abundance and played a central role in peasant life. Symbolically, the banya had an ambiguous status, and it would be a mistake to read it, in modern Western terms, as associated with the cleanliness desirable for birthing. The banya harbored evil influences as well as good ones. In birthing, it was used to separate or protect the mother and baby from any harm that could be inflicted, even inadvertently, by the evil eye or other afflictions induced by the presence of outsiders; the mother was particularly susceptible to these in her "unclean" state.[36] It also gave the midwife a work space in which to perform her particular magic, as Tatiana Varfolomeeva proudly explained about her village midwife:

> Right after I gave birth, the banya was heated, and the babka steamed me and the baby. Our babka was a specialist who knew just how to steam and pat the mother and baby, and she somehow got everything back to normal, while she also whispered certain [spells], and the stomach stopped hurting. The next day I felt as if I had not even given birth. She delivered both my babies. No matter how many times she served as midwife in our village and even in neighboring villages where she was sometimes summoned, never did any of the women hemorrhage, and all the children were born normal.

The evil eye nevertheless continued to be an issue. "After my first birth, my mother-in-law wouldn't let me get up for a week, not because I felt bad but for fear of the eye. 'Stay in bed,' she would say, 'otherwise people will afflict you with the eye. Don't fear birth but fear the evil eye.'"[37]

Tatiana also told about another practice that was still in use in her time: the opening of the gates in the church icon wall in order to assist the delivery in difficult, prolonged labors. The opening of these "tsarist gates," as they were known, was usually a final resort after family members had opened cabinet doors, gates in the yard, and even loosened their clothes.[38] If the baby still did not come, the midwife would send someone to the priest to ask that the tsarist gates be opened. Although Tatiana's own births were not difficult, she knew of other women who had needed such assistance, and she was quite confident that it had saved the day. "It happened to my neighbor. She was giving birth back then, and there didn't seem to be any way that she was going to be able to get it done. The baby was very large. But then they asked that the tsarist gates be opened in the church, and right after that she gave birth."

As Tatiana's stories confirm, she and her peers, this first generation of women, operated within the older mental world that continued to furnish them a coherent understanding of birth, of its dangers and the means to control them.

The second generation of women in the Smolensk province villages moved away from traditional birthing to medical deliveries, but they did so more slowly than the Tambov women. By the 1950s female "medics" (*medichki*) began to be available to attend births, and women from the Smolensk villages accepted their assistance for home births. But they resisted the switch to hospital birthing. These Smolensk women had to bear the brunt of the war directly and lost many of their family members, especially their men. Their memories of birthing were colored by the horrors of the war and its aftermath. For the women whose husbands died in the war, childbearing years were brief. As Elena Sorokoumova judged, perhaps it was for the best because life had been so difficult there. She had one child before her husband went off to the war, never to return. The birth was traditional, and she worked until the end. "In the morning I was hauling manure and in the evening gave birth. We peasants give birth easily," she said, "the baby just jumps out and no special assistance is needed." The collective farm did not provide maternity leave, nor did she or others seek out medical assistance. "There was a kind of unwritten rule [zavet] that you didn't get medical help for birthing." She gave birth on the floor with an old village midwife in attendance. The midwife received a scarf for her work and was also invited to the christening where, in accord with custom, she and the new mother were given coins.[39]

Although Elena took pride in the strength of village women and her memory of birth could be seen as positive, most of the women from this area and generation told of more difficult birthing experiences. Efronsinia Ruleva, a literate and intelligent woman who was living comfortably at the time of the interview, did not willingly recall the painful years of her earlier life. She had had six children and lost two, one of which she believed she had poisoned with her breast milk when, during the war, she was reduced to eating flat cakes made from buckwheat grasses. The demands of family and farm, she complained, made matters little better at other times. The collective farm did not release pregnant women from heavy work, and if she took leave without pay, she had to work hard at home until the onset of labor.

> My first birth [in 1939] was difficult. I gave birth standing up, and everything tore open. A babka came, but there wasn't much she could do to help. I didn't go to the hospital, and gradually things healed up.

Many years later when her second surviving child was born (in 1950), she again did heavy work right up to the time of delivery. On the day she gave birth, she had to go to the field and rake hay. She still recalled with bitterness that when she complained about feeling sick, her mother called her a loafer. The context for birthing had, however, changed. By the 1950s, a medic was available to attend home births, and when Efrosinia gave birth that evening, a medic assisted her. Her succeeding births, except for the last, were likewise done at home with a medically trained woman. Efrosinia probably would have had the final birth there as well, except that her medic had dreamt about her death in childbirth and convinced her to go to the hospital in town.[40]

The experience of three other women from this region who had their children in the 1940s and 1950s provides a map of the shift from traditional to medically supervised birthing. Elena Bobkova (born in 1919) had her first baby in 1940 lying on the stove at home with only a babka in attendance. The second was also born at home a year later, but this time a medic attended. Tragically, both these children died during the war, as did Elena's husband. When she married her first husband's brother in 1948 and returned to childbearing (interspersed with several expensive underground abortions), she again birthed at home in 1950 but had her last two children in the hospital at Terino because "babki-povitukhi were no longer available at that time."[41]

Anna Kirsanova (born in 1920), like many women of her generation, still thought it best for the mother if no one knew about her pregnancy; she also avoided doing darning or patching during pregnancy for fear that birthmarks would result. She had all four of her babies at home in the years from 1952 to 1960. At the first birth, only the traditional babka midwife assisted. The rest of the babies, starting in 1954, were delivered with a medic in attendance. Even so, the traditional midwife came along, too, and the medic did not chase her away. Since Stalin's death the year before, persecution of these village practitioners had eased. The traditional midwife was allowed to perform her valued services of reciting prayers and spells and straightening the mother's stomach.

It is worth noting that Anna gave much credit to her husband for his compassion and help to her during childbearing, the kind of tribute that appeared only rarely in our interviews:

> My husband was wonderful. He felt sorry for me when I was pregnant and wouldn't let me lift heavy pails, and for two to three weeks after my confinement he did all the hard chores. He wouldn't let me outside so that no one would be able to afflict me with the evil eye. I didn't even go out in the yard.

She added that when the children were growing up, her husband "even let me go off to dances while he stayed home to watch the children." He took a lot of teasing about this, but he explained to his critics that Anna needed a break from all the demands of the children. Another help to Anna was frequent visits by the medic in the first month after birth to check on mother and child. All of her children thrived.[42] The regular medical attention and her husband's attentiveness contributed, she was sure, to her success as a mother.

Praskovia Korotchenkova (born in 1920) observed the usual pregnancy taboos known in this region and believed it best to keep the fact of pregnancy quiet so as not to invite the evil eye. She had her first and second babies in traditional ways, the first in 1941:

> I had [it] at home on the stove with a babka. . . . My sister-in-law also came to help out. Even before they arrived, I crammed my hair into my mouth [to bite down] against the labor pains. Our babki-povitukhi were generally good, they immediately saw how the baby was coming out and if something was wrong, they'd wash their fingers and insert them in the vagina to get the child to go the right way. In those days, we didn't have medics, only babki to help out.

Her second birth, this one in 1950, also took place at home and by herself, as her husband was at work in the field and not available to summon a midwife or medic. This was a new, younger husband she had wed after the death of her first husband in the war. The new husband neglected her and went around with other women, and loneliness is a recurring theme in her narrative. Without at first thinking of the consequences when alone, she went to the age-old method of dealing with difficult births.

> The birth was hard and, all alone, I hung myself from a big hook by wrapping a towel under my arms, and I didn't even think about how the baby would pop out and might smash itself. . . . And that's how it happened. Good thing that my neighbor came over. I had asked her to look for me, and if I wasn't in the yard, it meant that labor had started. She came in and saw me hanging from the hook while the umbilical cord was dangling down. She laid me down and sent for the babka. The babka came and cut the cord. Right after that, they heated the banya, and the babka washed me and the baby there and shaped up the baby's head and legs—that was it, no further help.

The next day her son ran the three kilometers to the village of Korobets to summon a medic, who was available at a medical station there. The medic disinfected the baby's navel and checked to see if everything was fine with the child. "After that she came on occasion, but not often, for there were lots of births in those days, and she didn't have time to come often." Although a hospital fifteen kilometers away in Terino was now available to women in Praskovia's village, she only went there for her last birth in 1960—and only at the insistence of her medic after twenty-four hours of labor and fears that it was a breech birth. Her reasons for staying at home were the lack of anyone to replace her there or to take her to the hospital; she was terrified of going there alone.

One reason Praskovia could choose not to go to the hospital was the continued presence of skilled granny midwives in her village. These traditional healers and helpers gave the women of this generation an option of using the old therapies, even if, during Stalin's time, doing so could be risky. Elena Tsygankova was happy that a skilled babka midwife was able to intervene when she gave birth in 1939:

> I didn't go anywhere for prenatal check-ups, and then when labor started, the babka showed up first. Later a medic came from Korobets and chased out the babka. Babki were forbidden to do deliveries in those days, though I felt more comfortable with the babka somehow. Our babka was old and very experienced. The birth seemed to go normally, and the afterbirth came out, but the pain wouldn't stop. When the medic rubbed my stomach, the pain became horrifying. So, the third day we called back the babka, she shaped my stomach, and the pain went away.[43]

After Stalin's death, if babki were still available, they were sometimes the preferred option. By the 1950s, as just noted, although Praskovia Korotchenkova had a choice of going to the Terino hospital, she preferred to stay home and use the services of her village midwife. Efronsinia Ruleva made a similar choice in the case of a postnatal complication. Her second birth was followed by inflammation of her breasts (mastitis), for which she was offered a machine to relieve the pain by drawing off milk. But the machine's suction was so rough and unpleasant that Ruleva resorted to the traditional method of having an old village woman suck on her breasts. In short, the second generation of women in the Smolensk villages resisted the shift to hospital birthing and some other forms of modern care right through their childbearing years.

The third generation of the Smolensk village women completed the transition to medical births. They also continued the downward trend in the number of births. Instead of the four or five children many women of the second generation had, they had only two or three, using abortion again and again to keep their fertility under control. Anna Varfolomeeva (born in 1928) was the oldest of seven surviving children. When her father died early in the war and her mother worked long hours at a grain mill to scrape together a living, Anna had to become mother to her siblings. After the war, when the collective farm was neither paying wages nor giving women documents to leave for work in town, she and her mother secretly went to the town of El'nia to earn enough to buy clothes for the family. After marrying at age twenty-five, Anna had three children, all under medical care. The first and last were born in the hospital in Terino. She stayed at home for the second child so that she could continue to look after her eldest, but this home birth was attended by a trained medic. Her abortions, too, done after the ban was lifted, all took place legally in the hospital.[44]

Another woman from this generation, Valentina Shapovalova, at first reverted to traditional birthing—but soon regretted the choice. The return to traditional ways resulted from an unhappy marriage that threw her into continued dependence on her mother and her mother's way of doing things. Valentina felt so abused by her husband and mother-in-law that she moved back in with her mother early in her marriage. Her dependence on her mother's support, she said, as late as 1957 caused her to follow her mother's advice and give birth in the old way, even though Valentina said that she had a secondary education and should have known better:

> I gave birth to my elder daughter, Lena, at home. When the labor pains started, mother called the babka. Why not the medic woman? Because I was a fool, and mother thought that the babka understood things better. But the babka was of no help at all. She forced me to ride around on a poker, like on horseback, as if that was going to speed up the birth, fool that she was! What it led to was that the labor stopped. Then they had to run and get the medic.

> She gave me a shot to induce labor and a girl was born, a blue baby—but she started crying right away.

The old ideas about birthing that made sense to her mother had no hold on Valentina. Her generation had been to school and looked on the babka's methods as silly, even harmful.

This experience cured Valentina of leaning on her mother's counsel and, indeed, of ever wanting another child. Her second birth was done after some abortions only because a doctor persuaded her, this one time, not to continue with abortions. But after this second birth, she went back to abortions, having a total of sixteen in resistance to her drunken, abusive husband, who, according to Valentina, could not provide a decent life and was egged on by his mother in his abusive behavior. Their cows died, and money was lacking to purchase others. "When the last cow died, I had to be screaming 'What am I going to feed the girls with?' Well, how was anyone supposed to give birth in these conditions?" she said in justification of her many abortions. She was modern and typical of her generation of women in rejecting ideas of the evil eye and traditional taboos. Yet although she worked her whole life as an orderly (*sanitarka*) at the Korobets medical station, she was not well informed (as her two daughters were) of methods of contraception that would have enabled her to avoid her many abortions, some of which were done by babki under unsanitary conditions.[45]

Urals

In our Urals venue, too, the older generation, like those elsewhere, recalled fears of the evil eye and kept their world under control through their knowledge of methods to deal with it and other potential difficulties associated with birthing. Here too the banya was an essential accompaniment to the birthing process. Every woman went there right after delivery so that the baby and she could be washed and rest in seclusion. But the banya offered no guarantee; someone might thoughtlessly praise the mother or child even there, as happened to Pelagea Sharav'eva.

> It was in the banya, it was, the first time I gave birth. I was ripe [*polnaia*], and they took me to the banya. My sister-in-law brought me. So, she came up and looked at me, and I was spotless and lovely [*baskaia*]. She went and said, "Oh, what a baby you have born!" According to her, it was so unblemished and beautiful, chubby, and [my] breasts were so large, clear, and nice.[46] Then she left and went to the old woman Efimikha and repeated all that to her. The old woman spat and said: "Fie, you probably went and inflicted the evil eye [*izurochila*] on the woman, ravaged her. Don't you know you can't talk that way about someone who is raw?"

This inadvertent inflicting of the eye on someone who is "raw," that is, vulnerable and naked after having just given birth, was regarded as a serious matter.

The consequences for Sharav'eva were, in her view, quite severe; she fell ill, nearly died, and spent twelve weeks on her back. Childbirth, she stressed, "is not a good time to be joyous."[47]

The other Urals villager from the oldest generation had six of her seven children at home. She shared the belief that it was best to hide knowledge of pregnancy from everyone but family and immediate neighbors. But her own fortunate experiences with her children told her that the evil eye was nothing to be concerned about, for none of her children (or, she added, calves!) suffered umbilical hernias. The ability of people to inflict the evil eye, she implied, had died out.[48]

In contrast to women at other interview sites, the second generation of informants from the Urals showed little decline in the numbers of their children. Perhaps the fact that this area escaped the direct impact of the war allowed changes in fertility to occur there more gradually, despite a change in the setting for childbirth in the late 1930s when a maternity home opened to serve the region.[49] Iulia Ortikova (born in 1917) followed her mother's example of giving birth to a child every other year. Her mother had produced eight children before losing her husband in the famine of 1921. Iulia's pattern of fertility would have given her even more children, except that she lost her first husband in the war and did not remarry for several years. She ended up with six children, all of whom were born in a maternity home.

Although the setting of childbirth had shifted, other types of support for birthing mothers had not yet arrived. Iulia Ortikova worked right up to the time of delivery. She once went into labor when she was raking hay and had to return in a rick pulled by an ox, arriving just in time at the maternity home. After delivery she was allowed to rest for a few days at the facility, but never longer than five days because her husband, she said, expected her to be home hauling water by then. "I rested for only five days and then said, 'For God's sake, let me go home.' I wrapped the baby up and came home. I looked around—here a mess there a mess, but, after all, I hadn't been at home."[50] So, while women of this second generation had given up some traditional beliefs about birthing and were having their children in a maternity home, these changes did not influence their workload or choice of family size.

A story similar to Ortikova's was told by another Urals woman of the same age, Galina Mamina, who had ten births and nine surviving children, despite a break in childbearing of nearly ten years while her husband was in military service (her first birth was in 1939, the others in the late 1940s and 1950s). All her births were in a hospital, but this access to modern medical care was not accompanied by other changes. She claimed to have received no respite from heavy work until 1953, when she was able to get a week's leave before giving birth. Her responses to the interviewer were heavy with implied contrasts to the easy life of women today. She asked, "Do you mean did I get privileges? . . . Who would you leave your child with? No one was interested. . . . And who was going to give you permission [not to lift heavy loads]? If something needed doing, you did it."[51] Aleksandra Gibert (born in 1921) likewise had all her five births in the hospital (whereas her mother's had all been at home), but she received no time off from the state farm where she worked. She received neither prenatal care nor any special postnatal medical service, except that a visiting nurse administered vaccinations to her children.[52]

Even informants born as late as 1928 continued to have as many or more children than their mothers. Tamara Privalova had seven children (compared to her mother's four), plus abortions.[53] She said that her abusive, alcoholic husband simply had his way with her and gave no thought to the consequences. Privalova was illiterate, without a job, too dependent to resist directly. Her births were all at the local hospital, but in other respects her experience remained traditional. She did not go for prenatal check-ups, despite scoldings from medical personnel for not doing so. For solace and protection, she relied entirely on prayer and her mother. She believed that prayer had shielded her developing fetuses from the effect of her husband's bad seed. When asked about the belief that a drunkard, such as her husband, produces sick or defective children, she responded:

> People were somehow surprised that . . . our children were normal and healthy. Well, how to tell you—just don't record it and I will tell you—it seems that Our Lord, again, helped us out. My mother would pray. While I went around pregnant, mom would all the time be praying, "God grant us this child, and grant to it, Oh God, brains." For me and mom, that was the main thing, and the right thing, that the children would be smart. . . . I, too, walked about saying, "Lord give the child inside me brains, so that it won't be insane."

She nevertheless suspected that her husband's alcoholism may have influenced the makeup of her last child, a boy who also became a drunkard when grown up.[54]

The last generation interviewed, women born in the early 1950s whose childbearing years fell in the 1970s and 1980s, reported scarcely any traditional beliefs associated with birthing. Antonida Popova, who had two children and several abortions, all in hospitals, said she learned more about childbearing and child care from medical authorities than from her mother or mother-in-law. By her time, she said, the old women were learning about these things from the young women. Even so, Popova did half-believe in afflictions of infants being caused by the evil eye, and was careful to take the usual countermeasures when her babies became colicky. Although this villager, who had spent some of her working life in the city and had risen to a white-collar job of insurance agent, adopted a skeptical stance toward traditional ideas, she was still close enough to the mental world of the village to share some of its beliefs. Indeed, this sharing of some beliefs doubtlessly helped her and others like her to continue to exchange experiences and information with the other village women and therefore to change that older mental world with their new learning.[55]

Valentina Tripapina (Aunt
Valia) and her daughter,
Moscow province, 1990

Moscow Province

For the women of Moscow province, conditions were a bit different. This
region, close to the ancient capital, had long been dotted with medical stations
supported by the zemstvo local governing boards, the imperial foundling home,
or private businesses and charities. Although many facilities closed following
the revolution, others continued to operate and provided access to medical
births for village women who lived nearby. For example, one of our oldest
interviewees, Aunt Valia from Laikovo village, west of Moscow, married in 1923
and had twelve children. While village women her age in other parts of the
country had most or all of their births at home with village midwives, Aunt
Valia had only her first child at home. The rest were born in a hospital about
eight kilometers from her village. In her second birth, the labor pains started at
night, and she and her husband had to run the distance to the hospital, fearing
that at any moment the baby would be born. They grabbed thread and scissors
as they left the house so that they would be able to tie off the umbilical cord if
need be. "A babka was active in my village," Aunt Valia said, "but the woman's
daughter-in-law was also giving birth and so you couldn't count on her. That's
why [we] grabbed the scissors and thread and made a run for it." The reason

Aunt Valia eagerly sought out the hospital for this and all her succeeding births was her delight at the regimen there. "In the hospital, they required you to stay for five days—and that was a godsend for women."[56]

However welcome, this blessing was brief and infrequent. The hospital seemed unconnected to life in the surrounding region. Evidently, it sponsored no educational outreach of the kind recommended by the Soviet press. Even though Aunt Valia had been able to use the maternity ward, her life in other ways remained similar to that of women of her generation in remote locales. She continued through her childbearing years to work up to the onset of labor, and as soon as she returned from birthing, she was back hauling manure and doing other heavy tasks. "There were no indulgences," she remarked. The much-touted campaigns of the 1920s and 1930s to improve birthing and child care in the villages, at the very time that Aunt Valia was building a family, had little impact on her life. She was emphatic about the absence of visiting nurses or party workers who might have provided information to women. Nor did her village ever see any summer nurseries or other child-care facilities (though she knew about such facilities in larger settlements). Despite having a hospital near-by, Aunt Valia lost six of her twelve children to death in their early childhood.

For the women of northeastern Moscow province, much depended on their proximity to the large factory in the town of Krasnoarmeisk. Those who worked at the factory were able to obtain child care and medical births in the 1930s. Anastasia Shishanova married into a family of independent farmers who did smithy work in a village close to the factory. Her first two children were born (in 1930 and 1931) at home before the family was forced into a collective farm. She then went to work in the factory at Krasnoarmeisk. The job gave her access to a nursery for her two young children, but with tragic results; both children soon died from accident and disease at the nursery. Her next three births, how-ever, benefited from her factory job, which provided prenatal check-ups, plus two months' leave before and after delivery, boons that were not available to women who worked on the collective farm. The three children born at the fac-tory hospital survived, perhaps because Anastasia did not make the mistake this time of sending them to the nursery but kept them at home with whatever supervision she could muster.[57]

Villages just a few kilometers farther from Krasnoarmeisk did not have the same access. Praskovia Kurkova and Olimpiada Bakhmesterova lived in the twin villages of Staroe Selo and Zhukovka, which lay some distance from the larger centers of Krasnoarmeisk and Pushkino. They continued to give birth at home, usually with the assistance of a village midwife by the name of Evdokia Slesareva. This woman, who had long served these small communities, was known affectionately as Aunt Dunia or, with time, Granny Dunia (Baba Dunia). Even so, in one instance Praskovia Kurkova tried to reach a medical facility. In the summer of 1931, she was harvesting rye when her labor pains started. Her father-in-law hitched the horse to a wagon, and they set out for a hospital sev-en kilometers away in the village of Talitsy. But after passing just two houses,

Kurkova asked to turn back. The baby was descending fast. The midwife, Aunt Dunia, was out gathering berries or mushrooms, and Kurkova's first two children were sent racing around to locate her; a neighbor heated water in a samovar. At the last minute, Aunt Dunia appeared. "She guided the baby out by stroking my sides and then straightened out the baby," Kurkova explained. "It was all done by hand." The birth turned out fine, except (said Kurkova's daughter) that on seeing the baby, the father-in-law moaned, "Oh, my Lord, it's another girl!"[58] It was the third girl in a row.

Olimpiada Bakhmesterova from the neighboring village had six children between 1925 and 1941, all with village midwives, some with Aunt Dunia and some with another women named Natalia, "also a well-made woman, very clean." For Bakhmesterova, birth came naturally and easily, and she took great pride in the strength and ability of the women of her time. "In those days, women were giving birth every day." When we asked about what the midwife did to help, she responded: "What? Nowadays that's a thing, but earlier on, you know, women were robust. Why the baby just popped out like a cork! . . . That's the kind of women we were then; we were strong . . . popped out like a cork; all my births were easy."[59] These women of the oldest generation often portrayed themselves as strong and self-reliant, able to handle crises fearlessly and with only the help of other women. Several of them implied, and in some cases made explicit, contrasts with what they regarded as the softness of young women today.

This community received its first maternity home in 1937. More will be said about this later in the section "The Midwife of Zhukovka." But even though birthing facilities became available here and elsewhere close to Moscow about this time, some women of the oldest generation who used them were not persuaded that medical birthing was the best method. Aunt Valia's opinion that birthing in a maternity home or hospital was a blessing for women was not shared by several of the other Moscow region women of her generation.

Anastasia Spiridonova was herself born in a maternity home in the village of Putilovo (just west of Voznesensk, the later Krasnoarmeisk) in 1907. She was one of six surviving children of her mother's ten births. After marrying in 1928, she had five children of her own starting in 1932; her last two births occurred after the war. Although her first children were born at the hospital in Krasnoarmeisk, she decided to have her last child at home with the help of an old woman, a village midwife. The reversion to home birthing was not inspired by nostalgia, as in the case of the women from the Tambov villages, or by an attachment to traditional ideas about birth; Spiridonova was more modern in her attitudes than most rural women her age. She did not use a rag pacifier or swaddle her children, and was proud of it. Our questions about magical ideas in connection with birthing actually angered her. "Don't insult me," she shot back when we asked about the "evil eye" and other folk notions.[60] Her return to home birthing appeared to be more of a practical decision, inspired by a woman friend who had done it. Conditions at maternity homes were far from ideal.

Not only did many women have the problem of care for their older children who were at home, but women often had to supply their own food—and, as the next story reveals, they might even have to share their food with undernourished workers at the maternity home.

This story comes from Lina Buldakova, a woman from the same region near Krasnoarmeisk. She complained that during her hospital stays, the staff fed her only lentils.

> Lentils in the morning, lentils at noon, lentils in the evening. You eat them one time, and you don't go for them again; you crawl away from them. My husband once brought me some bread when he visited, 'cause I had nothing to eat. So did my sister, a big white loaf that cost ten rubles. And I was thinking, thank goodness, now I can at least eat a bit. But then a nanny came in, sat on my bed, and said, "So, you're going to eat, and I'm not going to get to eat. Just you get to eat." I was going to cut off a piece for her, and then I, I just gave her the whole loaf, the whole thing. . . . When mama came to bring me home . . . she had some potatoes for me. I gobbled them down like crazy. [Mom says] "Lina, that's no way to eat potatoes, you on an empty stomach and potatoes after all." But I was just famished like never before and gorged myself —no way to stop myself. Without butter or anything, I just gobbled up those potatoes.[61]

Lina was having her children at a particularly difficult time for the country: the first baby in 1930, the year of the first collectivization drive, and the second in 1933, when famine gripped large regions. Yet, except for a time after World War II (see later discussion), conditions in maternity wards were far from ideal. Ekaterina Danilishina, a researcher at the Semashko Institute of Public Health in Moscow, confirmed that although many factories established birthing facilities, women did not like to use them because most lacked adequate food and linens. Rather than take food from home and deprive their youngsters there, Danilishina confided, they had their births at home in unsanitary circumstances, and the result was many unnecessary illnesses and deaths.[62]

Other conditions led to the return to home birthing, as Vera Belikova articulated. She was born in 1909 into a family that lost two of its six children in the famine following World War I (the children died from eating weeds, she reported). Belikova herself had seven children between 1928 and 1944 and lost two to death in the early 1930s. Her first child was born in the hospital at Krasnoarmeisk. The second she had to deliver on the road. She delayed leaving for the hospital to the last minute out of concern about leaving her firstborn at home (he was fifteen months old), and, as a result, she barely reached the next village where the baby had to be delivered en route. After that, she said,

> [I decided that] I would be birthing at home. I'm thinking: I'm not going to go [to the hospital]. Where will I put my little children in the meantime. I didn't go [but instead stayed] at home with a babka. Oh, Lord.

She engaged the service of her neighbor Auntie Avdotia, who was "not a regular village midwife [*babka-povitukha*], the kind who still practiced in some other villages. We didn't have those. But she did it out of neighborliness. You'd just send for her, send your little boy to call her, [tell him] go down to Auntie Avdotia and say that mama is feeling bad. . . . She wasn't available for everyone. No, no. She'd only come on request. Well, you see, that's the way things were."[63]

The village of Fedorovskoe had an illiterate granny midwife whom it valued and supported through charitable offerings as long as it could. A zemstvo hospital still functioned not far away in the hamlet of Mogilitsy, but, according to Vasilii Shumkov, who grew up in Fedorovskoe, the women did not go there for birthing. He continued to explain:

> [Instead, we had] babka Nadezhda. She had her daughter Nastasia, Aunt Nastasia, living with her, and Aunt Nastasia had her own daughter, Katia. Well, this one [Katia] was, as the villagers thought of her, defective [*ubogaia*]. She lived there up to the war and then died of hunger. Well, she never went outside, was naked all the time and kept in a fenced-off part of the house, sort of like a room. A pail stood there for her. The grandmother, Nadezhda, was, you know, she was a *povitukha*, a babka-povitukha, and attended the births of all the women in the village. . . . She was like a village doctor, and yet utterly illiterate.[64]

When Vasilii was old enough, his mother would send him to cut firewood for the midwife and her family. She had delivered all of his mother's ten children, including Vasilii himself. She also delivered women from the nearby villages of Nikol'skoe and Vasiukovo, who came over to Fedorovskoe when it was time to give birth. The people thereabouts pitched in to help the midwife's family survive. She took nothing much for her services, living poorly on whatever the villagers furnished.

> Someone would give her eggs, another milk. People gave what they could spare. The women neither sowed nor reaped. And then well, their house, I recall, had a straw roof, it was little. Earlier on, around here most houses had been covered with straw. The peasants could see that the house had got to the point that [the women] couldn't live in it anymore. . . . They took account of the woman's services. Decided at the village council [*na skhode*] to build her a new home. To build it in return for her services. . . . They cut the timber and built it . . . and the women lived in it right up to the war. Then during the war they all died.[65]

Here, just a few miles outside of Moscow, the old methods continued for many of the women, the traditional midwife worked and received the support of her neighbors, right into the 1940s.

But not all women stayed with the old ways this long. Although Vasilii

Shumkov thought that women from his village did not start birthing in medical facilities until the war, his opinion is contradicted by a woman from the same village who gave birth at medical facilities a few years before the war. The woman was Zinaida Shumkova. Vasilii may not have known about her because he seems to have been away at various jobs and in military training in the years before the war. Zinaida declared, "I was already Soviet." All three of her children were born in a maternity home in Krasnoarmeisk between 1935 and 1941 (her husband died in the war and she had no more). Her family history provides a good yardstick of the changes in birthing options for this village, located close to a factory town in the Moscow region. Zinaida's mother had seven children in the 1910s and 1920s at a time when the family still owned its own farm. In those days, Zinaida said, people believed that knowledge of the birth by outsiders would bring greater pain and possibly harm to the mother and child, but Zinaida herself did not share such beliefs. Then she described other differences. "When my mother was having a difficult birth, they moved the table to the middle of the room, placed lighted marriage candles on the table, and led her around the table. They did such things then." But in my time, Zinaida continued, "we were Soviets," explaining that they began to give birth in the hospital. For her first birth in 1935, she received no prenatal check-ups or maternity leave (and she soon lost her first child to dysentery). But by the time her second baby was born in 1938, the pronatalist laws had come into effect, and more health services were available. Zinaida was able to take advantage of prenatal check-ups and four months of maternity leave in this and her subsequent birth.

She also recalled, with pride, the ample supplies and good order of the maternity home in Krasnoarmeisk in her time. Compared with the deterioration that has since set in, she remarked, "How clean the maternity home was! Nothing like it is today, oh my!" How have things changed? we inquired. "Oh now it's far from what it was. It was so clean then, you know. They didn't let outsiders into the place, no one at all. . . . But now it's like a den of thieves [*sharashka*]." She went on to explain that since the 1960s when her daughter-in-law was there for a cesarean, the place had been going downhill. Before, they furnished free diapers and linens, and even gave out extra ones when needed. "You'd go in and they'd put you right in a bath and then dress you in state-provided gowns, slippers, and bed linen. . . . Now everything is filthy. . . . Women have to bring their own linen. . . . It doesn't matter whether it is the hospital or the maternity home. It's the same. A den of thieves."[66]

The birthing experience of other women of northeast Moscow province was similar, except that as time went on, the government extended the term of maternity leave. Like Zinaida, Varvara Baranova and Nina Gracheva of Lepeshki, Nina Novozhilova and Antonina Grafova of Nazarovo, and Anastasia Kuzina of Vvedenskoe gave birth at the Krasnoarmeisk maternity home. They went in for the prenatal check-ups that were required to obtain the allotted maternity leave of from two to four months, and eventually, in the more recent generations, of up to one year.

Women from villages more distant from Krasnoarmeisk were not able to benefit immediately from the provisions of the new law. In the mid- to late 1930s, however, many such villages did gain access to a medical station or maternity home that the government opened from assets acquired in the collectivization drive and its aftermath. Antonina Larshina (born in 1923) lived all her life in the village of Orlovo. Her birth family was poor and one of the first to join the collective farm. As part of collectivization in this area, the Viskov family, owners of a factory in the hamlet of Trubino, five kilometers south of Orlovo, was "dekulakized." The state confiscated the Viskovs' two-story home and turned it into a hospital. In this facility, Antonina gave birth to her two children in 1949 and 1951. When we asked about village midwives, she did not recall any at that time (traditional caregivers were then being persecuted), but said that women simply helped one another if someone went into labor at work in the fields or elsewhere and could not reach the hospital in time. She did not get prenatal check-ups or benefit from maternity leave.[67]

The women of northern Moscow province who gave birth in the 1960s also reported the beginnings of instruction in modern maternal and child care. Antonina Grafova, who had ten children between 1948 and 1969, said that for her first eight births (up to 1964) she went each time for a single prenatal check-up, at which the doctors merely determined the approximate date of birth and arranged for her to receive her two-month maternity leave. No training in birthing or child care was offered. Only at her next pregnancy in 1967 did medical workers start to show her how to dress and care for a baby, using a doll as a tool of instruction. Not surprisingly, Antonina found this patronizing.

> You had to show up for [this training]. If you didn't, they wouldn't list you in the "bulletin" [permission for maternity leave]. Well, why on earth should I have to do that? Here I am. . . . I had reared eight children, and I'm not going to know how to dress the ninth?![68]

If the training classes were not needed by Antonina Grafova, they proved more useful to younger women. Mothers who had their first babies in the 1960s reported going to prenatal check-ups and lectures every two or three weeks. The instruction included information on the birth process, care of the breasts, early child care, and the like. One of our informants had even bought child- and medical-care manuals such as *Mother and Baby,* the *Medical Encyclopedia,* and the *Encyclopedia of Homemaking.*[69] Modern managed birthing, backed up by prenatal instruction and "how to" guidebooks, the very things that reformers of the 1920s had hoped to install quickly, had finally reached Russian villages in the 1960s, at least villages that lay within the penumbra of the national capital.

Former village maternity home, Zhukovka, Moscow province, 1993

The Midwife of Zhukovka

The village maternity home was an institution serving as a transition from traditional to hospital birthing. We came across such a home in the village of Zhukovka in northeast Moscow province. The rustic, one-story log building had begun as a village school about 1927; ten years later, following the pro-natalist law of 1936, it was refurnished as a maternity home. Elizaveta Smirnova of the nearby village of Staroe Selo pointed the facility out to us; it was in this home that Smirnova gave birth to her three children in 1940, 1946, and 1951. Each time, she walked the two kilometers to Zhukovka accompanied by her husband. She remembered the maternity home as comfortable. "They had stoves that we could lie on, . . . and they fed us." The home served a dozen small villages until 1965, when improved communications could ensure speedy delivery of mothers to more distant hospitals. "Ambulances and telephones became available," Smirnova said, "and they began to take women to Krasnoarmeisk for birthing. Sometimes also to Pushkino but, in any case, to Krasnoarmeisk."[70]

Olga Glazunova and I walked over to Zhukovka and found the building still standing, now a peasant home. Next door lived the former midwife, Anna Konobievskaia, who had served there for 21 years. Anna was a very precise woman who maintained a spotless home surrounded by a large and well-organized garden. She was none too pleased to be coaxed outside to talk with us, as she was working on a dinner for her son, who was coming for a visit. But she gradually relented and agreed to answer our questions about her life and work. We began the conversation by asking about the situation of Russian women—and quickly felt the resentment of a woman who had worked hard all her life and was now, in 1993, coping with the declining standard of living that was the lot of most retired people and of aging single women in particular.

> What kind of position can women have when we are all slaves who work from morning to night? What can the position of women be today?! All we have is our pensions. It's good that I at least have some little bit of onions and beets [here in the garden]. And how do they get to be mine? Look here, all done with these hands of mine.[71]

Although Anna's life had not been marked by the terrible personal losses of husband and children that were experienced by many others we interviewed, it was far from easy. Born in 1922, she was the eldest of three children and had lost her father to death before she was seven years old. She completed seven years of basic schooling and then went to the medical technicum in the town of Pushkino where she studied from 1939 to 1941. Just before she was to receive her diploma, the Germans invaded, and she and her classmates were sent off to serve as military medics. Four years later, as the war was ending, Anna became pregnant and gave birth in Krasnoarmeisk. Her husband continued in the military, and though Anna was alone with a four-month-old baby, an official of the Ministry of Health ordered her to find work. Indeed, she needed to work, she admitted, to feed and clothe herself and her baby; she had nothing for her feet but canvas boots. So, Anna became midwife at the Zhukovka maternity home near where she grew up.

As a girl, she had gone to school in the building that now became her place of work and where she spent the next twenty-one years in service. The village maternity home had three rooms, one for delivery and the other two for labor and recovery, plus a small anteroom for undressing. Anna was assisted by two women who worked in shifts and doubled as cleaning women and nannies. Anna herself was the sole midwife and was on call day and night. Apart from deliveries, her duties took her on regular tours of her service district to learn who was pregnant and to examine these women to determine the approximate dates of delivery. She then scheduled the times to expect the women at her facility. Her rounds also included check-ups on the infants she had delivered. In other words, she served as a visiting obstetrical and pediatric nurse as well as a midwife. This travel was done entirely on foot to a dozen separate villages in an area that stretched four or five kilometers in every direction from Zhukovka. When she was on these rounds, her own children had to be alert to her whereabouts and ready to search her out if someone appeared at the maternity home in need of care.

Predicting times of birth was not an exact science, despite Anna's boasts that she became very good at it as time went on. She often had to cope with unexpected arrivals. Most difficult were the delayed or complicated births, especially extended labor, which exhausted both the mother and the midwife. She had to attend such pregnancies, she said, sometimes for several days in a row without leaving the room. She feared that a crisis might occur in her absence. How would she explain it? The authorities would accuse her of abandoning her post. "They would convict me and say, 'Where did you go?' And if I said I went home for dinner, no one would believe me, and they'd say, 'You went to do something else [i.e., a personal errand].'"

If a crisis occurred, she had to get the patient to a hospital for treatment, a difficult assignment before the mid-1950s, for it meant putting together a horse and driver team from a nearby collective farm. "Well, they would give me a horse all right when I needed it, no discussion about that. But I still had to find a driver. And the driver would be drunk. So, what am I supposed to do? Haul the patient on my bent-over back? We didn't have any ambulance service until about ten years after the war. . . . In those days, they didn't even know where Zhukovka was, nobody knew."

The midwife of Zhukovka found it annoying that women not from her service area would show up ready to give birth without any warning. She recalled a number of times when women, going against what they should have learned at prenatal visits, traveled to her region at the very end of their pregnancy and had to be treated in her facility. One woman from Pushkino came to visit her father on New Year's Eve when she was about to deliver twins. She turned up on the midwife's front steps in labor, brought in by her husband. Although Anna hated to deal with outsiders, she could not refuse someone in labor. Another woman, this time from Krasnoarmeisk, came to Anna's area with her husband to buy food in her last week of pregnancy. Anna was astounded at the irresponsibility shown by these women. She thought of herself as a controlled, neat, and punctual person. And here she had to deal with people who did not have the sense to stay close to home when they were about to give birth.

Anna claimed never to have lost a patient in her twenty-one years at the maternity home. This record, if accurate, was achieved in part by her referring the difficult or unexpected cases to Krasnoarmeisk or elsewhere—referrals that were proper, as she was not trained to handle abnormal cases. She told about a woman who appeared at the maternity home just one day prior to term in a state of utter physical and emotional exhaustion and presenting with very high blood pressure. The woman, earlier a resident of the area, had moved away and married. Now she turned up at the last minute, not registered to the district Anna served, and in a poor state to be treated in a village maternity home. Anna insisted that the woman's relatives take her to Krasnoarmeisk. She also wrote on the referral in Latin (for fear the patient would open the envelope and read the referral) that the patient should be watched closely. The next day she learned that the woman, who had reached Krasnoarmeisk and been placed in a room with a dozen other patients, broke a water bottle during the night and cut through her abdomen, killing herself and her child. Anna obviously felt some guilt about having turned the woman away but also recognized that she might not have been able to deliver the woman successfully in her inadequate facility.

Anna seemed to have taken the normal, expected aspects of her work in stride, even though the job kept her from enjoying common diversions. When she attended parties or went to the movies with her husband, she was likely to be called out to provide services. What made her job especially "hellish," she said, were the unexpected deliveries and the non-maternity medical services she was asked to perform.

The midwife's work was not limited to maternity services. The community also expected Anna to be an all-purpose healer and a kind of arbitrator of family conflict, and to provide first aid as well. Just as with birthing, she was called out at all hours for these other services. "Day and night, day and night, they would be knocking at my door. 'Come quick,' they would say, ' . . . my Vitka is sick. I don't know what it is; he is vomiting.'" Many cases were accident victims. A man crashed through a glass door and nearly bled to death before she could bind him up and get him to the hospital. A fisherman embedded a hook in his face, and Anna had to tear through his cheek to remove it. A man ripped all the flesh from his hands when he seized a cable to prevent a pump from falling into a well. Though offered hospital care, he went to Anna and asked her to treat him. On another occasion, she extracted glass from a patient's eye.

Often she had to patch up women who had been beaten bloody by drunken husbands. "Lenka Chernysheva from across the way would run here [urging] . . . 'Come, let's go, mama [is hurt], papa broke a glass over her head.'" Anna went on:

> So, here it is, the middle of the night, drunkards fighting at one A.M. But what are you going to do? I take my black bag, take it and go. Mama is covered in blood. Papa sits there, completely gone. He's already passed out on the table. And what can you do? You have to help out.

On another occasion, a woman eight months pregnant went into crisis with tachycardia when her husband came home drunk and provoked her. Anna had to ride out and treat the woman, giving her a shot to calm her. No sooner had she arrived home and gone to bed when again, "They are drumming on my door." Now the woman, feeling better, had started in on the husband, who rose from his stupor and fell to the floor injuring himself. "And then we have the Mishurovs across the road," Anna continued. "Their daughter runs over and says, 'Oh, Auntie, come quick. Papa's making an uproar, and it looks like he is going to knife mama!' So, I go over [and intervene]: 'Tolia, aren't you ashamed of yourself! Have you no shame! What are you trying to do?' Well, say it. I had to be like a police officer, an investigator."

Indeed, Anna asked more than once in our interview about what her real role in the life of her community had been. "I don't actually know what I am; am I a police officer or am I an aid-giver?" Whatever it was, "This was the hard life for which I was destined by God." But she also believed that God had been merciful and after twenty-one years of this unrelieved work, she was offered a job as a nurse at a kindergarten that was opening on a local collective farm. Despite efforts by her supervisor to prevent this move, the collective farm prevailed, and Anna was able to spend the next twenty years at this less-taxing work. The village maternity home was closed, and ambulances provided to take birthing women to the hospital at Krasnoarmeisk. So, by 1966, the transition to hospital birthing had been completed for the women of this region.

The personal values expressed by the midwife of Zhukovka were permeated with a sense of individual and community responsibility. She spoke critically of the chaotic lives of many of her neighbors and especially of the lack of responsibility shown by the younger generation, which she attributed to poor upbringing. "You can't even compare what it is today to how we reared our children. We reared the children in work. Yes, in toil, so that they worked, so that they built this house here; they helped. But nowadays upbringing scarcely occurs. That's how it is." She complained about the children in the neighborhood who stole from her garden and about the young people who "smoke, spit, and drink" and spend their time in buying and selling (under the recently introduced market system) but take no responsibility for their community. She also criticized the local doctor who refuses to go out on night calls (as Anna did) and summons an ambulance to have ill or injured persons delivered to a hospital. She compared Russian life to what she had seen when on vacation in the Baltic provinces.

> There, the children go neatly to school with their backpacks. . . . I saw one girl call to another to come over to her house. . . . It would have been easy for her to run across the grass, but she went on the walkway . . . even though it was three times farther to walk. . . . There, the children, you know, it seems to me the husbands, too, and the children work. And it is beautiful there, things are clean.

Anna then underlined the importance of personal responsibility and good upbringing if her community was to be improved.

> And how does this happen [in the Baltic]? Do you think someone just came down from heaven? God or Yeltsin came and caused it? No, comrades. All this depends on us. How we behave at home will determine if our house is in good order. If I never once in my life enter my home with shoes on and my children, too, don't do so . . . , then you won't have filth.

She was proud that her children had learned to behave properly, that her son, when about thirteen years old, even removed his galoshes before entering a bank. Anna spoke in very concrete images, and the point was always the same. Russians should not look to Yeltsin or anyone else to solve their problems. If people just educated their children to work and be responsible, things would be better. But, unfortunately, in Anna's view, Russians were no longer doing so, and to her that explained much of what she saw as the chaos and unfairness of post-Perestroika life. Anna was an expression of the best of the Russian rural work ethic, of her family roots and the Soviet values of equity and sacrifice for the greater good of the community. Despite her lack of humor and her carping, I could not help admiring the beautiful and well-ordered life she had created in her small private sphere and her devotion to work and community. Her strength and self-reliance were characteristic of many of the women we interviewed. Anna Konobievskaia was an example of what Russian and Soviet reformers had long sought: a combination of personal responsibility and attachment to the values of work and good order.

Anna's life was typical in another respect. Like many other women we interviewed, she had learned to mediate between the normative values of her elders, the needs of her family, and the demands of the state. Because of her special position as healer and representative of the state administration in her village, she had the additional responsibility of mediating between individual members of her community and between the community and the government.

Tatar Birthing

Tatar women seemed to have been more secure about birthing, perhaps even better cared for than Russian women. Most of the Tatar women we interviewed reported fewer fears and taboos associated with birthing than did Russian women. These more secure feelings may have stemmed from the cohesive communities in which we found most of our Tatar informants. At any rate, some practices and beliefs were significantly distinct and may help explain some of the different memories of birthing the two ethnic groups reported.

Like many Russian village women of the same age, Tatar mothers of the oldest generation birthed at home with traditional midwives, had large families, and lost up to a third of their children to stillbirths and early childhood death.[72] In contrast to a number of rosy ethnographic accounts about how Tatar women either did no field work or were relieved from such work during late months of pregnancy,[73] our Tatar informants of the oldest generation uniformly reported that they worked right up to the onset of labor, just as did Russian women of the same era. A typical example was Garifabanu Abdullina (born in 1908), the mother of eight children, who gave birth once in the field and again on the road, in both cases having waited too long to start home after her labor pains began.[74] The village matriarch, Khatima Nizamova (born in 1903), told of losing her first two babies to miscarriages because she was working at heavy labor in the field, mowing and binding hay in early summer. Khatima said that her neighbors reassured her with words that "there would be more children" for

Tatar women interviewed in the village mosque, Tatarskii Kalmaiur, 1990

her. The neighbor women were probably familiar with this common experience of women losing first children more often than later ones. And the reassurances were justified. Khatima gave birth seven more times, and all these later children survived.[75]

Despite many similarities, however, several differences also turn up in Tatar and Russian ideas about birthing. Take the notion, often found among Russian women, that it was dangerous to announce the onset of labor pains because the more people who knew about it, the more painful and prolonged the birth would be. Tatar women, too, sometimes kept silent about the onset of labor pains but for different reasons. The Russian notions about the need to hide the knowledge of labor to prevent prolonged and painful birthing were completely foreign to the Tatar women. None of them reported this concern nor seemed to know it when asked directly about it. The Tatar women who resisted saying anything about the onset of labor (something that seemed to occur most often during the field-work season) reported that they did so for three reasons: embarrassment, a stoical attitude toward pain, and the need to work. "You didn't speak about it," Khatima and her age cohorts told me. "Even though labor had started, a woman went out to do field work." "Why?" I asked. "Because we were embarrassed, and you had to work."[76] At other times, when work duties were not so pressing, women reported no reluctance to announce the start of birthing, although they might, again out of embarrassment, keep quiet until the pains were intense. Mariam Gimadeeva, for example, said that women in her village held back the news for this reason, and then told only their mothers-in-law so that a mother-in-law could tell the husband and spare the woman the humiliation.[77]

Despite embarrassment about their condition, pregnant Tatar women had little or no feeling that pregnancy and birthing made them "unclean" and therefore a danger to others or vulnerable themselves to harm from spiritual sources. Although the older women spoke of ritual cleansing for themselves following birth, they did not think of the place where the birth occurred as being unclean or even that they were particularly vulnerable to spiritual powers (visitors were welcome within two days of birth). Nevertheless, they did need to perform a ritual before they could return to regular prayer. "Women are cleansed at different times, between ten and forty days, depending on their organism," the older women told me at our first interview. "After cleansing, they can fulfill the *namaz,* that is they can pray." For the midwife, there was also a cleansing ritual that had to be performed before she could return to other activities and to praying. "This was called *kamgan,*" Khatima explained. "I'll show you [and she gestured with her hands]; water is poured, everything is done in the proper order and a prayer is said."[78]

Another difference between Tatars and Russians was the apparent lack among the Tatar women of any frightening taboos in connection with pregnancy. To our questions about food or behavior that should be avoided by pregnant women, the responses were uniformly negative. Pregnant women were evidently free to do their normal duties and eat and drink as usual. According to Khatima Nizamova, pregnant women could even break the standard rules. "If a pregnant woman wanted to eat even things that were forbidden," she told me, "then she was supposed to do so, because if she didn't get what she craved, the child might be born a freak." She gave an example. "One very religious woman had a desire to eat pork and yet didn't do it. When she gave birth, the boy was missing four fingers on each hand."[79] At first, I thought this story was less a real event than a moral tale about the importance of family and community satisfying the needs and desires of pregnant women; Khatima answered my question about when this happened with a vague "long ago." But when I again asked her and the other women at the interview about whether this unfortunate child was actually born in their lifetimes, they replied emphatically that it was a real event of "their time."

Among the Tatars, an interesting change could be detected between the oldest generation and the younger women in regard to isolation at the time of birth. The older women remembered birth as something a woman did alone or with the help of a village midwife (babka, *povitukha*). They insisted that only the midwife could be present, even if the birth were prolonged. "The woman would be lying in a barn or steam-bath cabin to give birth. It was good if a babka was there, but none of her relatives would approach her." As our conversation continued, it became clear that other people could be involved in special situations. When I asked if the women had remedies for a difficult birth, medicines or actions such as opening gates and cabinets, as Russians did, the older women responded that no medicines as such were given but that prayers and other actions could help.

> They drew triangles [triangular pieces of paper with prayers written on them. Or] the mullah would write prayers with strong tea on either a cup or a saucer and then pour a little water on it, which rinsed [the prayer] into the water and the woman drank it. This was considered a way to ease the pain.[80]

Khatima added in a follow-up interview that if the birth was prolonged (two days), "they called in the mullah. He would write a prayer on a piece of paper, place it in tea, and they gave the tea to the birthing mother to drink." When Khatima herself was giving birth to twins, the wife of the mullah helped out by rubbing her stomach in a clockwise motion, and the effect was that Khatima "immediately gave birth."[81]

In contrast to older women, the women of the younger generations, those born from 1918 onward, described birthing as more social. Mariam Gimadeeva (born in 1918), for example, said that a number of people besides the midwife could be present at the birth, including a woman's mother, mother-in-law, neighbor women, and girl friends.[82] Rkia Kamaletdinova (born in 1922) likewise reported that "any adult woman could be present at the birth, especially female relatives."[83] All the other women born in the 1920s and later expressed the same view. They reported that visitors, including men, were welcome soon after the birth. The women seemed to have little fear for themselves or their babies as a result of relatives, close friends, and neighbors being in proximity. This attitude conformed to their views about keeping the onset of labor quiet, which arose not out of fear of invasion by harmful personal or spiritual agents but out of embarrassment or concerns about frightening their young children. Once the baby was born, these embarrassments and fears could be dismissed and trusted relatives and friends brought in to celebrate the mother and baby.

Apart from the prayers of the mullah in difficult births, men had no role in birthing. The oldest Tatar women were very firm about this matter. It was a sin for the husband to be present, Khatima and the others emphasized. Besides, she said at another point, "the husband is at work. He has no idea of what is happening." Another woman added, "In the past, men didn't pay attention to their children; they didn't play any part in their upbringing and simply did not care." The Tatar men were so remote from this aspect of women's lives that we could find no trace even of couvade, a practice that symbolically transfers some of the mother's birthing pains onto the father. Couvade practices had shown up among Russian villagers in a variety of forms in ethnographic sources, and we encountered them in one case among our informants, but they seemed to be entirely unknown to the Tatars. In a revealing admission of the continuing power of village patriarchy, when pressed on this point, the oldest Tatar women said not only that they had not heard of couvade practices but also that they so feared their husbands that they did not dare to wish unpleasant things on them.[84] Only one women in the village of Tatarskii Kalmaiur, the very youngest and most educated of our informants, allowed as how a husband could be present at a birth, but this view cut against the categorical opposition expressed by all the other women.[85]

We heard of a couple of instances of men being called in to help at Muslim births, but both cases were emergencies for which women thought that the strength of a man was required. Zeinab Gimatdinova said that at the first birth of her husband's first wife in the 1940s, he had to help extract the baby when a medical midwife was unable to manage on her own.[86] Sofia Teleshova reported a similar situation in her Bashkir family. "Mother told me that when she was having her third baby, which died, she asked father to press down on her stomach. A huge baby was born, but she didn't live long. She died right away."[87]

Sexual separation was strict among the Muslims of the Volga. In the nineteenth century, visitors to Tatar homes noted that the women and men occupied separate sections of the house. Even if the home was only one room, trunks would stand atop one another forming a wall between the women's and men's sections.[88] While our Muslim informants said that this type of physical barrier no longer existed, boys and girls were long kept separate, and until recently women were not allowed to go to the mosque to pray. Now women do go to the mosque, but separately. They do not enter until the men have finished praying and have left.[89] Women were not supposed to allow men other than their husbands to view them unclothed even for medical treatment. Sofia Teleshova said that many women in her village, including her mother, suffered from a prolapsed uterus. "Earlier, they didn't go to doctors following a birth. . . . They didn't get sewn up; maybe there would be rips [in the perineum]. The *povitukha* obviously didn't sew them up but only pushed things back into place."[90]

"I saw how this happened to my own mother when we had gone to the steam-bath cabin together. . . . You could see it." But, she continued, her mother never thought of getting medical help because it was considered a great sin. The doctor might be a man. Sofia herself, though a modern woman who birthed in the city, was reproached for having a male obstetrician. "When I told people that a male gynecologist delivered my babies, they would say, 'Well, did you really have to? A male doctor, how shameful of you!' That's how things are supposed to be. That says it all."[91]

The change to institutional birthing in the village of Tatarskii Kalmaiur can be dated precisely to 1953, when a village maternity home opened there. Before that time, all the births were done at home in the winter or in a barn in the summer. If a steam-bath cabin was available, it would be used. Usually, the mother lay on the floor or on the oven in a space strewn with hay and then covered by clean cloths or an old blanket. In an interesting variation, Garifabanu Abdullina explained that she gave birth on a trestle bed in which a birthing hole was made by removing some of the boards. A pan was then placed under the hole and cloths spread around to catch and contain fluids.[92] There was also one report of a hanging birth of the kind known from some older generations of Russian and Belorussian women. Nurania Badrieva said that her mother gave birth at home on hay while hanging from a rope tied to the ceiling.[93]

The traditional midwife in the Tatar village had to be an older woman, experienced in childbirth herself and having served an apprenticeship with a practicing midwife. Midwives did not have to be widows, as was the case in some other cultures. Tatar midwives worked for free and did not refuse services when summoned. Unlike some Russian birth attendants, midwives in Tatarskii Kalmaiur were not expected to help out with household chores or to return regularly to check on the progress of mother and child, unless a new mother was bereft of other assistance. Nor did midwives in this village use medicines to ease the pain of birth, although they might serve tea or sour milk.[94] Normally, the midwife's services were limited to attending the birth and disposing of the placenta. During the birthing, her principal acts were to offer reassurance and prayers and to massage the mother's stomach when labor pains became intense.[95] When the baby arrived, the midwife severed the umbilical cord and then had the mother bite on her hair to expel the placenta. The midwife bathed the mother and child and tidied up the birthing area. She washed the placenta, wrapped it in several layers of rags, and gave it to the family for burial. In some cases, the midwife herself might bury the placenta in a "clean place."[96]

After the midwife completed her work, the family heated a steam bath for her so that she could wash up and relax. Before her departure (or a few days later when the mother was on her feet), the midwife received small gifts, such as food, a scarf, or toilet soap. Our Bashkir informants said that their village midwife was respected, and the children she delivered brought her gifts on religious holidays, much as happened in some Russian villages where a midwife might be regarded by the children she delivered as an extra grandparent or aunt. But the women in Tatarskii Kalmaiur reported that the midwife had no continuing relationship with the children she delivered. Tatar women may nevertheless have been concerned about the intelligence of their midwife. According to Fakhiza, a village-born Tatar women who lived in the city of Simbirsk, a belief circulated that a baby inherited the wits of the person who cut its umbilical cord.[97]

It was important that the person who delivered a Muslim baby was herself a Muslim and had mastered the appropriate prayers for assisting at birth. When I asked Fina Iurenieva how a woman became a midwife, how she received instruction, she replied:

> They are taught. The *babushki* teach others. They have to know the prayers, because without the prayers it won't work. They summon someone who knows the prayers. The very oldest women teach how to deliver the babies. Take my mother. When she was giving birth, an old woman was delivering it while a younger woman stood alongside. The old woman was teaching her

what she had to do. At the time mother was giving birth, that older woman who was doing the deliveries was already ninety years old. She couldn't deliver difficult births and brought along a younger woman, but stood next to her and told her what to do. Later, they started bringing in a medical nurse. But at first this nurse also wasn't able to do things right. They had to teach her. They sometimes would trust the nurse.

[I asked:] If the nurse knew the prayers, could she do the deliveries?

Well, whoever participated [including the nurse] would try to learn at least the most elementary prayers. And usually the nurse was also a village woman from that place, a Muslim. When [home birthing] was forbidden, religious women also tried to learn the [birthing] prayers. But when they put a final ban on it, no one any longer knew the prayers.[98]

Other women likewise explained the importance of an apprenticeship for village midwives, in which the novices mastered the prayers specific to assisting at birth.[99]

Although Muslim midwives had to know the special prayers for easing the birth pains and invoking God's assistance, the prayers of the birthing mothers themselves were much simpler. All the women reported saying prayers during labor and birth but prayers of the most ordinary kind, simple requests for help from Allah or the common religious expression "El'kham" (literally, "Help me, Oh my God").[100]

A custom often found in Russian birthing, the final farewell to family and friends (a practice otherwise associated with the process of dying and final rites), was not common among the Tatars we interviewed. Only the oldest woman, Khatima, remembered saying farewells before all of her births. She gave her farewells to her husband, a neighbor woman, sister-in-law and others close to her, asking them, "Don't forget me."[101] Except for two other women, Zatia Bagautdinova (born in 1925), who said farewells to her relatives at only the first of her seven births, and Nurania Badrieva, who told her children to be good to one another in case she died, none of the women could recall having said farewells to family or friends.[102] The expectation that one might die in childbirth and therefore should set things right with family and friends had evidently faded in this village well before mid-century.

Women of the oldest generation did not receive the government-mandated maternity leaves introduced in connection with the pronatalist legislation of the late 1930s. The older women in Tatarskii Kalmaiur reported almost no break between birth and resumption of the usual household and farming tasks for women. When I asked how long they were allowed to rest after birthing, they responded, "On the third day, or even on the second, [we went] to the field."[103] Their babies were brought along to the field to be breast-fed during work.[104] Muslim women from other parts of the country reported the same early return to work, their words sometimes tinged with both pride in their strength and resentment at the benefits enjoyed by younger women. Zukhra Pozdniakova, a

Tatar woman from Mordovia, said that a birthing mother's resumption of work depended on her health. "If she was healthy, then within five days she had to be firing the stove [i.e., doing all the normal household and garden tasks]." "Just five days?" I asked. "Yes. Do you think they got to lie around for months the way they do nowadays?"[105] Another Tatar woman from Mordovia, Sharifa Ialisheva, was able to give birth in a medical facility near her village, but even so she enjoyed no more rest than other women of her age. After four days, she told me, her husband appeared at the facility and demanded that she return home and start working again.[106] When I asked Fina Iurenieva, a Bashkir woman, how many days women of her village rested after birthing, she countered "[You mean] how many hours!" Fina was an older child who had observed her mother's hard life and who had had no easy time of it herself; she was expected to look after her younger siblings and help with the household tasks. When speaking of the work that women did soon after giving birth, she also stressed the contributions of older siblings like herself. "[Mothers right after birth] didn't do [heavy] work. The older children helped out. [New mothers] didn't haul water, but mother did everything else except for the laundry, which the older children did."[107]

Even though the women in Tatarskii Kalmaiur were eligible for a fifty-six-day maternity leave at the end of the 1930s, only two of our informants actually took advantage of this boon during the prenatal period; most women kept working because they needed the money and felt healthy enough to continue at the job.[108] After the birth, they took some time off from farm labor but not from household work, which they were expected to perform as soon as they were on their feet. Prenatal check-ups were not available to the village women until some years after the war. A visiting nurse at first conducted these and also gave the women instruction in care of the breasts, massaging the nipples, and child care.[109] But not until 1953 was there a regular medical station with maternity beds available for the women of Tatarskii Kalmaiur.

The transition to modern birthing and birth control in this Muslim community was completed by our two youngest informants, both born in 1933. Minzifa Mustafina, a milkmaid with a seventh-grade education, had six children between 1959 and 1967, all but one in the village maternity beds and attended by paramedics and a medical midwife. Prenatal check-ups were done at the village medical station by a visiting nurse from the regional hospital, who measured blood pressure and cervical dilation and gave advice about cutting back on heavy work. The nurse even offered to arrange a hospital abortion if the pregnancy was unwanted. The one birth by Minzifa that did not take place in the maternity beds happened unexpectedly outdoors at night. Right afterward, she was brought to the district hospital and given "a week-long course of injections" (presumably antibiotics).[110] Minzifa's age-cohort, Roza Fakhrutdinova, had three years of higher education at a teacher's college and produced three neatly spaced children between 1955 and 1964. Although she worked at some

Roza Fakhrutdinova with her husband, daughter, and grandsons, 1999

heavy tasks during her first pregnancy, such as stacking hay, she took leave from work two months before and two months after birthing. She resumed house-work within a week to nine days after a birth. Roza said that she went regularly for prenatal check-ups and to a service staffed by a medical midwife, whose responsibilities included educational work with the husbands. The midwife provided literature and counsel about proper nourishment for pregnant women and children, plus child care.[111]

Although each woman's birthing experience was personal and remembered for specific joys and pains, the generations shared common practices and memories as well. The oldest informants gave birth in much the same way as village women had a century earlier, either alone or, more often, attended by a granny midwife and other older women who supported the birthing mother by whispering prayers and spells, walking her about the room, even suspending her from a rafter (if required by a difficult birth). Maternal mortality in rural Russia before the twentieth century was high. Women of the first generation we interviewed understood the dangers of childbirth and, in many cases, said their "last farewells" to those closest to them. They observed pregnancy taboos and took steps to avoid the evil eye so as to prevent harm to themselves or their babies, matters they had learned about from their mothers, grandmothers, and mothers-in-law, the keepers of a large repository of female knowledge about the most fundamental issues of life and death. Birth attendees drew on this same reservoir of knowledge to ward off the dangers of birthing and to "correct" the mother's and baby's bodies after the birth was completed. Toward the end of the childbearing period of the oldest informants, the opportunities for traditional home birthing narrowed. Collectivization of agriculture and, soon after, state persecution of midwives and traditional healers brought about these changes. Even so, many of the women completed their families in home births attended by the same care and practices they remembered from their mothers' time, that is, amid familiar surroundings and reassured that harmful forces were well under control. Despite the rapid political changes taking place, many women of the oldest generation remembered their birthing as a positive experience; they took pride in the strength and self-reliance of women of their time, the ease with which they gave and managed birth, and their rapid return to work. The women of this generation likewise valued the services of their granny midwives, protecting and supporting them.

The second generation encountered major changes in birthing practices and expressed ambivalence about them. They gave birth in the period when medical services were arriving in the Soviet villages. This period saw the spread of the small village maternity home or, as in the Smolensk villages, provision of trained female doctors (*medichki*) to manage home births. For women who lived close to a town, hospital birthing, too, became available. All these services met with acceptance at first. Women recalled that during Stalin's time and for some years thereafter the medical facilities were tightly disciplined, well ordered, and well supplied. The women of this second generation were still not able or willing to take time from their heavy burden of household and farm labor to go for prenatal check-ups, at least no more than the one time required to be registered for maternity leave following birth. Some of them also missed the warmth and reassurance of village midwives—and insisted on having them present at the birth when it was again permitted to do so. But most of the mothers of this generation appreciated the changes, the break from household and farm tasks that birth in a medical facility ensured because of the obligatory four- or five-day stay after delivery and, as time went on, the increased options for paid maternity leave.

The third generation was "Soviet," as some of them expressed it. They enjoyed the advantages of full elementary education at least, and a few had even acquired post-secondary technical training as medics or teachers. Few of these younger women shared concerns about the evil eye or taboos connected with pregnancy. Among this generation, dependence of the younger women on their elders for information about birthing was broken. The young women no longer asked for or needed the help of the elders. Indeed, they instead became the teachers of the older women, bringing the modern ideas of maternal and child care to their mothers and grandmothers. What some of the younger women adopted from their elders, however, was their nostalgia for the old ways of birthing. The positive memories the older women had of home birthing—the care provided by traditional midwives, family, and friends—offered an appealing contrast with what they saw as the increasingly impersonal and poorly supplied hospital facilities of the Soviet health services. So, a revival of home birthing was taking place in some communities, though during the 1960s and early 1970s home birthing was not organized as a medical service but rather was assisted, as often as not, by neighbors or friends.

Baptism and Equivalent Muslim Rites

Baptism is a rite of passage, a public recognition of a person's entry into the Christian community. In the peasant culture of Russia, that religious community was a fundamental part of identity, as the language itself reveals: the Russian word for peasant (*krest'ianin*) is a modified pronunciation of the word for Christian (*khristianin*). Although the Bolsheviks mounted a campaign in the 1920s to replace Christian rituals with newly fabricated secular rites, including one for baptism called the *Oktiabriny* (after the October, or Bolshevik, Revolution), the message evidently met with indifference. Some letters arrived at the offices of the Party journals telling of the authors' decisions to observe the Oktiabriny rite rather than baptism. The writers referred to their hopes for a better world through Oktiabriny: "to make my child less dark than I am," "to live in a new way and lift the fog of religion," or to show the priests that they are no longer needed.[1] But nothing about this substitute ritual was recalled by our informants from the villages, even those whose families were headed by members of the Communist Party. For families in this position, some difficulties and conflicts arose in regard to continuing baptism, but informants confirmed that they nevertheless did not neglect baptism. Indeed, virtually all of our informants, right down to the present, continued to baptize their children and grandchildren. In the few cases in which baptism had not been performed, the individuals and families were seeking at the time of our interviews (which coincided with the revival of organized religion in Russia) to remedy the matter. The persistence of this rite throughout the period under investigation, despite the government's attempt to eradicate it, confirms that baptism was a conspicuous site of resistance to the values of the regime in power.

The assault on religious institutions, clergy, and active laity began with the advent of the Communist regime, and subsequently intensified in violent pulses associated with major shifts in policy or political shake-ups in the ruling regime. Because of the Communist Party's initial weakness, its first moves against religion were confined to the legal secularization of society, including a thorough overhaul of family law and the arrest and punishment of clerics who preached resistance to the regime. Clergy were deprived of citizenship rights, were not allowed to stand for election or to vote, suffered limits on rations and housing, and were required to pay high taxes.[2] After the Civil War the Party launched a concerted attack on the goods of the Orthodox Church. The campaign to confiscate church goods was mounted under the pretext of collecting valuables for use in combating the famine of 1921–1922. When clerics refused to turn over sacred vessels (after having contributed other assets), the government unleashed a reign of terror.[3] Altogether 8,100 priests, monks, and nuns were executed in 1922.[4]

In the same year, the Party assisted in the establishment of an alternative Orthodox Christian institution, the "Living Church," a creation of clergy willing to cooperate with the Communists. For a while thereafter pressure on the church eased, even though the leading hierarch of the regular Orthodox Church did not end his resistance to the regime until 1927, when he finally issued a declaration of loyalty and sought to make peace with the government. The declaration did not, however, slow a mounting assault on the church that had begun in earnest after the founding of the League of Militant Atheists in the mid-1920s. This attack reached a crescendo during the first Five-Year Plan and the drive to collectivize agriculture in the early 1930s. By 1939 Russian Orthodoxy had lost 90 percent of the churches and priests it had commanded in 1917; the number of bishops had fallen from 130 to 28.[5] It was no doubt of little consolation that the (suppressed) 1937 census showed that 57 percent of the population still described themselves as believers. Without places of worship and priests, the prospects for the Orthodox Church were not hopeful.

During World War II, religious institutions sprang into life in the regions occupied by the Axis forces. To counter this revival and capture the support of religious nationalism, the Stalin regime allowed the church to expand its activities elsewhere in Russia and to elect a patriarch (the patriarchal throne had been empty since the arrest of Patriarch Tikhon in the early 1920s). The price for this recovery was support of the government in its prosecution of the war and its foreign relations. The more relaxed stance toward the church continued into the mid-1950s.

The next great assault on religion came during the reign of Nikita Khrushchev (1955–1964). Scholars have offered no satisfactory explanation for this ferocious, if short-lived, attack. Indeed, few scholars even mention this episode in their treatments of the Khrushchev era.[6] As in the era of the first Five-Year Plan (1928–1932), this new assault coincided with a period of rapid change in

Party programs; it may have been intended as an emblem of ideological purity in a time when the regime was calling for renewed idealism in other spheres. One observer of the Khrushchev anti-religion campaign compiled a list of forty-four trials of Orthodox bishops, priests, monks, and nuns. Some of the trials had several defendants.[7] The number of monasteries and convents was cut in this period from 69 to 10, the number of seminaries from 8 to 3. Orthodox parishes in the postwar era, which had rebounded to more than twenty thousand, suffered another catastrophic decline from the Khrushchev reforms, falling to between one-half and one-third of that number.[8] This purge, though vicious and costly, came to an end with the ouster of Khrushchev, and thereafter the regime limited its persecution of the religious chiefly to individuals who directly challenged its authority or who sought help from sympathetic patrons outside the USSR. By the late 1960s and early 1970s, the Orthodox Church enjoyed a revival as young people, alienated from an increasingly corrupt and hypocritical regime, looked to religion for spiritual guidance and the restoration of their national culture.[9]

Despite their unleashing some savage assaults on organized religion, the Bolsheviks were less committed to attacking popular religious belief. They adopted this stance because of the strength of anti-Communist sentiment among the peasantry and the initial weakness of the Party's presence in the countryside. Not only were few activists available for anti-religious agitation in the villages, but before World War II many of the communists in small towns and villages continued to practice religion. Members of local parishes, they rationalized their participation to their Party superiors as necessary to maintain the trust of the local populace.[10] The effectiveness of anti-religious work likewise suffered because of the low quality of the people leading it. The League of Militant Atheists, whose job was to spread the anti-religion gospel, offered one of the least reliable routes to personal advancement and was consequently unable to recruit and retain first-rate activists. Moreover, the League's leaders were gradualists in their approach to reform. Perhaps even more, they were self-seekers who devoted most of their energies not to transforming popular belief but rather to bureaucratic infighting. They lobbied for their small share of financial resources from the Party—and reined in the overly enthusiastic and destructive anti-religious assaults occasionally mounted by Komsomol hotheads during important religious holidays.[11] Ultimately, the Party's primary approach to the eradication of popular belief was the inculcation of scientific values through the regular system of education.[12]

In turning now to the interview material, I again group the testimonies by regions, and within a region by generation, treating the Moscow and Smolensk province sites separately from the Tambov villages. The Muslims, as usual, are considered alone. The depredations suffered by organized religion—and the greater expectation of children's survival as time went on—affected the timing of baptism and equivalent Muslim rites among the three generations. The timing, however, varied somewhat from place to place.

Moscow and Smolensk Provinces

In the oldest generation (women born in the first decade of this century or earlier), baptism was not only universal, it was also performed within a few days of the birth of the child. "Earlier we baptized the babies—we had churches then—we did it right away, within two days," reported Anastasia Vakhromeeva, born in 1907. To the question, Why so soon? she replied simply, "Well, in the past many of the babies died."[13] Another woman, Ekaterina Gerasimova, born in 1909 (who like Anastasia and virtually all those in her generation gave birth at home with a village midwife), said that her children were washed down with holy water the first day. "Then, on the second day, we had them baptized. It was not like nowadays, when you see people getting baptized after they are grown up. . . . In those days, we took them the day after birth to be baptized. Infants. It didn't matter if there was mowing or harvesting to do—you had to take care of this matter."[14] Both these women came from large families that had lost many children to disease and accidents. Ekaterina's mother, for example, gave birth to eleven children, of which only five survived.

The practice of early baptism was confirmed as well by women slightly younger, women born in the teens of the century. These villagers had either observed the birthing of their younger siblings or carried on their family's practice of early baptism in the case of their own children, born in an era when, because of the persecution of priests, this standard was more difficult to maintain. Zinaida Shumkova, born in 1915, watched as her mother gave birth at home in 1925 with the help of a village midwife. They baptized the baby within a week.[15] Evdokia Sevriukova, born in 1911 into a family of six children of which only half survived childhood, gave birth to her first (and only) child in the mid-1930s and had it baptized within a week.[16] Nina Novozhilova, born in 1916 into a family of ten children of which two died in infancy, did not start having her own children until after World War II. But she followed her family's practice of having an early baptism:

> [For example, my daughter] was born in June and by the Feast of St. Peter was baptized. She was born on the third of June and was brought to church on the twelfth. We baptized them all [as infants]. . . . I didn't want any unbaptized kids around. Faith is after all faith. . . . You have to get them baptized. Who knows [what could happen].

"Did people," we asked, "think that an unbaptized child could be harmed by unclean powers?" "Yes. . . . Quite a lot was said."[17]

The status of a particular child's health influenced the timing of baptism. Tatiana Varfolomeeva, a woman (born in 1911) from the oldest generation whose parents had twelve children of whom seven survived, reported that in her day "We baptized children on the next day after birth, especially if the infant was weak, but in every case within a week. We feared that the child might die unbaptized, and that would be such a sin for the parents."[18] Praskovia Kurkova, a woman born in 1899 whose first child was born in 1924, related that she baptized the children after a few days, but she did not take a sick child to the church right away. She waited for the baby to get better before risking a trip to church with it. "If the child had no feeling, people got it baptized early, but if it was sick . . . they, of course, waited until the baby improved." But what, we asked, if while you waited for it to get well, it suddenly died unbaptized? "Well, what do you mean? Unbaptized, what to do then? You use holy water, holy water. You baptize the baby with it, wash it with holy water. That's if it is dead."[19]

If the oldest generation of women in the sample still followed the traditional practice of baptism in the first days after birth, the next generation was much more likely to delay this ceremony. Women who had their children at the period of high Stalinism from the mid-1930s onward faced the difficulty of finding a priest. Many churches had been closed, their priests either arrested or driven underground. The integration of some rural families into the ruling class, through Communist Party membership following collectivization, also imposed constraints on open participation in Christian ritual. No doubt, too, from the late 1930s onward baptism could be delayed in part because women were having fewer children and, due to the advent of improved hygiene and public health services in the villages, more of the children were surviving. The reduced risk of infant death accompanied by the increased risk of an open religious commitment made delay a logical option. Better to wait for a safe and opportune moment than to risk the well-being of the family by insisting on traditional practice. Even so, the women of the generation born in the 1910s and 1920s continued to see that their children were baptized.

Elena Sorokoumova, who, due to the loss of her husband in the war, had only one child (in 1939), delayed christening her baby for two months because the "local" church in a town three kilometers away had been closed down. Her family had to locate a reader (d'iachok) from that parish and get him to come to their home and perform the baptism in a large bowl. Elena admitted to knowing no prayers, even though she considered herself a Christian and reported going to confession and communion together with her mother-in-law when it was possible to do so. She knew that baptism was absolutely required: "It is the custom, and to be unbaptized is a sin."[20] Efrosinia Ruleva, a woman born into a typically large, prerevolutionary peasant family (her mother had eleven children, of which six survived), had her own children in the late 1930s through the mid-1950s. Of her six children (though one was stillborn and another died in infancy), all were baptized—but three of them only after delays of two, four, and six years. "I am a believer and wished to baptize the children sooner, but there was no place to do it. It is a sin for the parents if a child dies unbaptized. Even all my grandchildren are baptized."[21]

Not merely inconvenience but also fear was involved. Elena Tsygankova related that, while all her children and grandchildren were baptized, she had delayed these baptisms. "Earlier, the littlest tads were baptized, but I had mine baptized when they were about a year old; I was somehow afraid for the very little one. . . . And in those times it was forbidden to have your children baptized, especially in the case of those who were communists." But she underlined that "baptism is an absolute requirement; it was here long before us and will be here long after us," confirming the character of this rite in the thinking of peasant women as something as natural and unavoidable as the weather and the seasons.[22]

When clergy could not be found to perform the service, others stepped in to fill this role. Olimpiada Bakhmesterova, a woman of the oldest generation in the sample, told of what happened to a woman who did this. Earlier, she related, "people rode to the church to have the children baptized; everyone did it. There were priests in those days. Afterward, I'll tell you what happened, an unmarried woman took up the work, one of our peasant gals, and the authorities [arrested her and] gave her twenty years." Olimpiada added that the woman in question was not careful about how she did this job, and infected the babies she handled with severe skin rashes.[23] Given the salience of this memory, it may well have been that the woman's "Typhoid Mary" reputation was the key to overcoming the peasants' usual reluctance to turn in one of their own to the authorities. Other women also spoke of the important role that lay baptizers sometimes played in meeting emergencies caused by the early or unexpected death of infants.[24]

Once the Party took over the villages in the 1930s, a new authority was everywhere—even in the same house and same bed with women who wanted their children to be baptized. Praskovia Korotchenkova, a woman who had four children between 1941 and 1960, explained that she had to arrange for baptisms so that her husband, who was a communist, would not get into trouble. "[Communists] were not allowed to have their children baptized, but we managed nevertheless to get them baptized on the quiet. . . ." "I baptized all my children, absolutely. The first was baptized in 1942 at the time of the war."[25] (This was during the German occupation, when priests were able to become more active for a time.) She took two other children to a priest in a town twelve kilometers from their collective farm. Her last child was baptized at home, the priest being brought there for the ceremony. Praskovia noted that it was not only communists who could get into trouble if the Party activists learned they had baptized their children. Others were punished as well. "My daughter was a secretary of the village council and a deputy, though not herself a member of the Party. When she had her son baptized at age thirteen, they fired her from her job."[26] The time, though not specified in the interview, can be calculated from the age of the child to have been in the mid-1980s. This woman was proud to point out that all her grandchildren had received baptism. Other informants likewise mentioned the impediments faced by families of Party members. Nina Novozhilova told about her daughter, a Party member, who was unable to risk having Nina's granddaughter baptized. Nina herself finally took the girl to get baptized in 1989, when the threat to her daughter's career appeared to have lessened.[27]

For Russian villagers, it was not contradictory both to hold a firm belief in Lenin, who hated and persecuted the religious, and possess an equally firm determination to have children baptized. Vera Belikova was of the oldest generation (born in 1909), a woman whose childbirth experience followed the pattern of traditional families: she had seven children, of which four survived. Though far from happy about government social policy after the onset of perestroika (especially the inequities in pensions and other benefits), she thought the tsar was accursed, and Lenin a good man. Even so, she made certain that all her children (born between 1928 and 1944) were baptized within a month or two of birth, despite the difficulties she must have encountered in carrying out such a commitment in that era.[28] Vera lived poorly and perhaps had little to lose if her actions on behalf of her children became known. But even women with ordinary jobs on a collective farm could suffer unwanted consequences if it became known that they baptized their children, as the next story reveals.

According to two sisters-in-law, Antonina Ptichnikova and Zoia Vovoshkina, both born in 1937, the mothers and mothers-in-law in their village had continually pressured the women of their generation to get babies baptized, despite the obstacles and dangers of doing so. Having a more understanding family, Antonina felt able to delay baptism until her child was ten years old. She feared the repercussions at work. "We were afraid to baptize," she declared, "that's how it was. And at work they would send for you, you know how it was . . . they would investigate. . . . You had to go when they called you out, and they had some kind of books and would copy things down there. . . . And [if we baptized our children,] they would send us out on special work details. We were really afraid of this." Antonina explained how, without asking for a travel document, she had to sneak off to another village in order to arrange a baptism. Zoia chimed in, "My daughter, too, had her son Sergei christened in the same way— secretly." Antonina elaborated on Zoia's remark, "Yes, in secret. . . . Yet, well, even so, we also wanted to get the children baptized, you know how it is!"[29] If it was so risky, we asked, why did you want to take the chance? Did someone tell you why you had to have your children baptized?

> Zoia: Because it was a sin.
> Antonina: Grandmother would tell us about this.
> Zoia: If your child was not baptized. . . .
> Antonina: It was a sin.
> Zoia: Yes.
> Antonina: It wasn't a matter of shame, but they feared the sin of it.
> Zoia: And the other children outside would tease him, calling him a "heathen" and that sort of thing. . . .
> Antonina: Yes.[30]

The church of St. Nicholas, built 1812–15 in pseudo-gothic style by the architect I. V. Egotov, in the central hamlet of Tsarevo in northeastern Moscow province. Photo from 1993

These women seemed to be saying that for their grandmothers the central issue was the sin of having an unbaptized child. For them, on the other hand, shame was in some measure a key. In their own less religious idiom, they saw themselves as performing a customary, expected sign of allegiance to their community and at the same time protecting their children from embarrassment and rejection.

The tension between the generations over this issue appears in several accounts. Valentina Lopatkina, a woman born in 1931 who gave birth to twins (a boy and girl) in 1958, reported that she delayed having them baptized for about a half year, though she did not remember why. The twins were born in January and baptized in the summer, and Valentina recalled that weather could have played a role. But possibly she also had to be careful because of the Khrushchev regime's tough campaign against religion. When it came to her daughter's child, Valentina told us that she was very upset at the delay in christening him. She kept after her daughter about this, fearing for the boy should he fall ill. Finally, after about a year, the baptism took place. The tension was even worse between Valentina and her son's family, because her daughter-in-law had not been baptized. "You know," said Valentina, "I have a daughter-in-law who only recently got baptized. . . . The whole time I was scolding her, 'What's the matter with you? Have you lost your mind?' I didn't know, maybe she had not even had Irina [Valentina's granddaughter] baptized. And if . . . if I should let that happen! We were all baptized people [in this family]. And . . . and then suddenly we have a child who is unbaptized. So, the first thing is you have to get your baby baptized."[31]

The consequences for the unbaptized children were multiple. First and most important, they could not be counted members of the Christian community. If they died, they would find no place to rest. So declared Anna Varfolomeeva, a woman who claimed not to be a Christian, born in 1928 into a large family and herself a mother of three. Anna was altogether convinced of the dire consequences for unbaptized children.

> You absolutely have to baptize. Though I am not a believer, there's no way that you could not baptize your children. It's a sin. What if suddenly one should die? The kid won't get in anywhere, either in heaven or in hell. He won't be welcome anywhere. That's the way it is here. Everyone gets baptized, even the communists. They do it secretly, but they baptize their own, like everyone else.[32]

Ekaterina Gerasimova, also of the oldest generation, pointed out that in the old days such an unbaptized baby would not even be given a funeral.[33] Just like Anna Varfolomeeva, she was recognizing the rule that unchristened people cannot receive Christian rites and be buried in sacred ground.[34] But another woman from the same village as Gerasimova remembered things somewhat differently. She thought that unbaptized children probably would have been buried along with the others. However, she could not recall having ever heard of such a case, perhaps because all her relatives and neighbors did as she did: "I gave birth, got my children baptized, and had everything in proper order."[35] Possibly, she was projecting current practice onto the past; her fellow villager Ekaterina Gerasimova acknowledged that the rule against burying unbaptized children in sacred ground was no longer followed. "Nowadays it is all the same. They bury an unbaptized person just like the others." "You mean in the cemetery?" we asked. "Well, of course. Not just any old place. In the cemetery."[36]

But these traditional religious concerns were not the only ones village women expressed. Their mental world included many spiritual agents and dangers. They believed that unbaptized children were vulnerable to conscious and inadvertent assaults from "unclean powers." One cause of this vulnerability, they explained, was the incomplete nature of such a child, which was not yet a full person (krest'ianin) because not yet a Christian (khristianin). Antonina Grafova (born in 1922) explained that she had all her children baptized within six months, in part because her mother-in-law refused to baby-sit an unbaptized child. "And why was that?" we asked. "Well, unbaptized children, they are, she said, not fully human. Once they enter the faith, then they are as they're supposed to be. A Christian. Without that, they aren't yet real persons."[37] Their incomplete state, believed women of the oldest generation in particular, often explained the deaths of children before baptism. Daria Fedosenkova, for example, had three children who died before being baptized. One was a son born during the war when her husband was away at the front. "He was a very good boy, but after about a half year he died of scarlet fever. I think that someone afflicted him with the evil eye. After all, he was unbaptized, and I was especially careful not to show him to anyone for fear that they might visit unclean powers on him. But then I went out to pick flax and took him along with me—not wanting to leave him with anyone else—and [the women] all started saying, 'Oh, how nice he looks, how large!' Right after that he got sick and died."[38]

Even for conditions less threatening than scarlet fever, the lack of baptism could rob the usual peasant medical treatments of their expected effects. When Valentina Lopatkina's daughter delayed having her baby baptized, the grandmother panicked:

> I told her again and again, you have to get him baptized, you must, must, must—do it now! You have to do it quickly. Anything can happen. And then, then, I was telling her what if he should suffer a ruptured belly button . . . the spells wouldn't take. If a child is not baptized. Yes, the spells do not work on him. An old woman will come to whisper these spells, and if the child is unbaptized, can her [work have effect]?[39]

By the same token, the baptism of a sick child might have positive, curative power. Another woman of the oldest generation, Anastasia Vakhromeeva, told a story about how, in her granddaughter's family, they had long delayed having their baby girl baptized. The father of the girl was a communist, and he did not want the child christened. As she grew up, the girl became sickly and nervous. "She would go around bumping into things; if they said something to her, it was as if she didn't think it was to her. Well, then they got her baptized, and she became altogether changed . . . completely. . . . And she grew up and was entirely different."[40]

Tambov Province

A look at the villages of Tambov province in the south reveals the same generational shift as occurred in the Moscow and Smolensk villages but with a much stronger retention of earlier religious norms. Because the women in the Tambov villages held more firmly to earlier ideas about baptism—including a fuller explanation of how to remedy crisis situations—they seemed less confused and less anxious about this aspect of their lives.

Like the women of the first generation interviewed elsewhere, the Tambov women grew up with a keen sense of the fragility of infant life. Their mothers' childbearing years fell in the last period of high fertility and teeming infant death.[41] The Tambov women were aware that nearly half their siblings and their neighbors' children had died in infancy. And although their success in keeping their own children alive was greater than that of their mothers, every informant from this first generation had lost at least one child, and the average was 35 percent. They understood the importance of early baptism. All of the women explained that baptism was done on the second or third day after delivery. The only woman of this cohort who broke this rule (and then only for her last births) met with shaming from a neighbor. The woman in question had her first two children baptized within three days, but at the time of her next birth the local church had been closed, and she waited some months until she could go to the region's capital city where a church still operated. "Once I went to a neighbor," she explained, "and, while there, his father called my son 'a heathen' [*nekhrist*]. Oh, how this seized my heart!"[42]

Most of the women of this generation mentioned the important role of midwives, whom local priests authorized to immediately baptize premature or weak babies in a bowl of water. This evidently happened quite often and therefore obviated the need for the lay baptizers mentioned earlier in connection with the Moscow and Smolensk villages. The women referred to this type of stopgap christening as only "half a baptism," which for a surviving child had to be followed up by a regular church christening. If the child died, this half baptism by the midwife was sufficient for it to receive Christian burial, but a problem remained of how to say prayers for a child with no name. Unlike the women interviewed in Moscow and Smolensk provinces, who said nothing about this dilemma yet seemed dissatisfied with the decision to make no distinction between baptized and unbaptized babies who had died, the Tambov women recognized the importance of this distinction and knew that a remedy was available. If the baby died without formal baptism, the mother was instructed to go to church and have special prayers said. In this connection, she also had to purchase forty baptismal crosses and distribute them to people in the community, saying "Remember, O Lord, Your unnamed child." In the case of one very poor woman, the priest told her that instead of buying crosses, she could distribute forty eggs and achieve the same effect.[43]

The consequences for a child who died without being baptized were serious: the child would forever "sit in darkness." And the blame for this outcome fell squarely on the mother, according to the women who spoke of this matter in the Tambov villages.[44] In the Moscow and Smolensk regions, parents were said to be guilty for this sin of omission, but in the Tambov villages mothers were evidently understood to bear full responsibility for the spiritual well-being of their babies and could not shift it to or share it with their men. Yet because of the active intervention of midwives as emergency baptizers in these southern villages, the problem of babies dying unchristened scarcely existed. Not a single case was mentioned by the women in the interview sample.

Just how midwives acted in a crisis situation can be seen in the following story, an instance of a horrifying birth experience occasioned in part by the special religious needs of the birthing woman's mother-in-law (and what some would regard as a callous disregard of her son and daughter-in-law).

Maria Malikova (on left), Inakovka, Tambov province, 1994
(Photo courtesy of Svetlana Inikova)

The mother-in-law had planned to lead the religious life of the *chernitsy*, peasant women who choose not to marry and who usually live apart from their families (sometimes together with other religious women) and play an active role in the religious life of the village. In the absence of a priest, they perform some priestly functions. In this region, such women are referred to as "nuns." The mother-in-law in question was, however, orphaned before she came of age, and her uncle forced her into a marriage in which she had four children before the death of her husband. (After ten years of marriage the husband was found outdoors one winter day, drunk and frozen to death.) Widowhood allowed her to pursue her original vocation. Though continuing to live with a daughter (whom she refused to allow to marry), and a son and his wife, the widow was referred to as a "nun" and took exceptional measures in the performance of her religious duties. Her daughter, who led the unsullied, celibate life denied to her mother, shared in the complicated ablutions of her mother and was excused from the heavy farm work that was assigned to the daughter-in-law, our informant.

> I recall how when I was pregnant my mother-in-law sent me into the forest for firewood. . . . I lifted a load of wood, and blood started to gush out of me. That is when I was pregnant with my second son [summer 1938]. I was scared that I was going to give birth, right there, but I calmed myself with the thought

that "it will be as God wills." At the time, I was with my sister-in-law [wife of the husband's brother]. We went to the village midwife. She started to scold me: "You know that you're not supposed to be lifting heavy things." And I replied that "my mother-in-law knows this, too, and yet she sent me [to do the work]." I was up all that night, pacing around and feeling labor pains, tortured by pain the whole night.

And in the morning, mother-in-law again sent me out after firewood, not saying a word but merely handing me a sash so that the load would not cut my shoulders. My husband said nothing, and I said that I did not want to offend his mother. So, I decided to go. My husband's brother took pity on me; he had seen how I had been crying all night and even went out to the sunflower patch so I wouldn't be heard and disturb the others. He intervened: "There's nothing to be said. Let her stay home and have Liza [the unwed daughter] go to the woods." My mother-in-law didn't want Liza to have to go. Well, he just pulled Liza off the stove then and she had to go. Mother-in-law got angry with me. And my sister-in-law now even tried to shame my husband: "What's the matter with you that you won't stick up for your wife?" Then those two left.

After that, mother-in-law handed me a huge basket and demanded that I collect manure in it. I tried to refuse but finally had to give in. I was walking along and weeping, "Heavenly Mother, help me." The children of my sister-in-law helped me fill up the manure basket. After that, mother-in-law ordered me to sweep out the threshing barn, which I did. Then she sent me to pick sunflowers. By now, I was barely alive, and she tells me, "You'll survive." I took the produce basket and left.

I saw my relatives coming from the woods. My sister-in-law ran to get the midwife and brought her back. My mother-in-law then threw all of us out of the house and heated up water for herself. The next day was the Feast of the Assumption, and she says that she has to be clean, and because [she is] a nun, no one is supposed to see [her] body. My husband, who had been at the mill, returned and sees that I am in a bad way, and he starts to plead with his mother to let us in. But she won't let anyone in. Now I go into a faint. My husband grabs the handle of the locked door [and yells], "Please, mom, let us in, Masha is dying!"

The midwife tells my sister-in-law, "Quick, heat up some water, make the stove hotter." She heated water and took hot cloths from the water to put on me. My water had already broken, after all, and that is dangerous. The midwife took a warm shawl off of her and laid it over me and then again placed the cloths in the hot water and back onto me, for I had completely cooled off. And so, several times the cloths cooled, and she kept putting them in the water and then onto me. I was lying on the floor. Early in the morning, my mother-in-law and Liza left the house to go to mass. Just about 10 o'clock in the morning I gave birth. The midwife squeezed the baby right out of me. It was bluish and barely alive. "Come on, let's revive it" [she says], and the midwife put it now into hot water and now into cold. Then they laid the baby on a sheet and rocked it to this side and that, shouting "Ours!" That meant that the baby belonged to our faith, and if you don't shout this, then the evil spirit [nedobryi] will take it. After all, he wasn't baptized.[45]

The "well" where baptismal water is disposed of in Inakovka, Tambov province, 1994 (Photo courtesy of Svetlana Inikova)

The story paints a vivid picture of power relations within a large, joint family. The authority of the mother-in-law over the other women of the household was complete, an authority in this case augmented by her status as a widow and "nun." Although she exercised her power carelessly, the younger members of the family would not resist her until a life was in danger. Even then, the mother-in-law's will prevailed.

The important point here is the intervention of the midwife and others in attendance as emergency baptizers. "[They] rocked it to this side and that, shouting 'Ours!' This meant that the baby belonged to our faith." Russian ethnographers, even in post-Soviet accounts, interpret baptism as primarily an expression of national and ethnic particularism.[46] But in a moment of crisis, the fundamental purpose emerges clearly: it is religious. If the women did not shout "Ours!" then "the evil spirit" would take it. Because Russian ethnographers usually exclude non-canonical folk beliefs from the classification "religious," they misread this behavior as something other than baptism—and baptism, in turn, as something other than this decisive claim of a child for the faith. Although it is true that "Orthodox Christian" can in some contexts substitute for "Russian," middle-class scholars too easily impose on peasants their own notions of national identity. Peasant baptism expressed spiritual needs and claimed a child for a local community and a faith; it did not invoke some larger national identity.

In addition to the timing of baptism and emergency intervention, another aspect of interest is the naming of children. The Russian ethnologist G. A. Nosova writes that the tradition of naming children after the saints whose days fell on or close to the birth of a child was waning in the nineteenth century. Peasants, she contends, began to choose names of their own liking.[47] Under the old practices the choice of a name might usually have been left to the priest. The ethnographer Olga Semenova Tian-Shanskaia mentions that at the turn of the century in the villages she studied, only the wealthiest peasants were able to have their choice for a name prevail over the priest's.[48] The custom of naming children after saints' days continued in some of the families of our Tambov province villages through the first of the generations interviewed, women who were having children in the 1930s and 1940s. Anna Reutova, who had three children between 1930 and 1937, reported that "the names were chosen according to saints' days that fell on the day of birth, but I named our younger son Valentin just because I liked the name and not after a saint's day."[49] One woman in the Smolensk province interviews also mentioned that she named her child (born in 1936) Nikolai after the saint's day. She also implied that this was a common practice, though exercised with some leeway for drawing on names of nearby saints' days. "We did not choose names based exactly on the saint of the child's day of birth or day of baptism, but we could take a name from a day close by."[50] The children of the daughter-in-law of the "nun," born between 1935 and 1957, all received names based on saints' days.[51] The "nun" saw to that. But the survival of this custom into the late postwar years was apparently unusual. Women of the younger generations mentioned that in the past the custom was to name children after a saint's day (again, as in the Smolensk interview, either the saint of the day of birth or one whose day closely adjoined it) but that they now selected names that appealed to them.[52]

The second generation of women in the Tambov villages, women born in the 1920s and early 1930s, all gave birth for the first time after World War II. Although two of the women interviewed from this cohort were school teachers with an obligation to fight against religious practices, they and all other women of this age group (and younger ones as well) had their children baptized. Again, as in the other regions studied, baptism in this generation was occasionally delayed. Anna Mikhaleva, for example, believed that babies were supposed to be baptized within six weeks. She explained that she sometimes waited longer but that all her five children were baptized about that time. At the same time as the baptism, she received her "churching," the ceremony that announced the end of a woman's confinement, danger, and "unclean" state and proclaimed her reincorporation into community life.[53] Delays were caused for this generation by the closing of the local church and the need to go to a village fifteen kilometers away or to the district capital of Kirsanov, where churches were still operating. Alternatively, they had to arrange for a priest to come to their home village.[54] A pattern seems to have developed in this locale and continued into the 1960s for women to delay baptism of their children for a few weeks and combine it with their own churching.[55]

In the Tambov villages, virtually every child was baptized right through the entire period of Communist rule. Conflict occurred not over baptism, which everyone understood as necessary, but over two related practices: churching and wearing of the baptismal cross.

Unlike baptism, which was often arranged and managed by someone other than the mother, churching was a personal act on the part of women that exposed them to penalties if they occupied an official position.[56] So, while nearly every woman in the Tambov communities underwent churching (after miscarriages as well as live births), the practice clearly presented a danger for two of the women interviewed who worked as teachers in the local school.[57] Both were from the second generation and had their children in the period 1955–1965, during or close to the reign of Nikita Khrushchev. The older of the two reported: "I did not get churched. For doing that, I could have lost my job and might never have been allowed to work in a school again."[58] She added that her mother-in-law understood the situation and did not force the issue. This teacher had no regrets about her failure to be churched; she harbored doubts, in any case, about the truth of religion. The other teacher expressed some regret over the matter. She reported that in her childbearing years, her mother-in-law had told her and the other daughter-in-law (also a teacher) sharing their joint household that birthing women should not leave the house for six weeks after delivery, until they go for churching. Otherwise, they could be afflicted with the evil eye. But our informant said that she and the other daughter-in-law rejected this idea and went outdoors, and that she did not get churched (presumably because of her teaching job), although she now thinks that maybe she should have risked this public religious act.[59]

These same two teachers had to negotiate another conflict between community values and Communist Party requirements, this time concerning the wearing of baptismal crosses. At baptism, every child received a small cross to be worn throughout life. At first, parents usually affixed the cross to the baby's crib as protection against evil spirits. When the child started to walk, the cross was placed around its neck. Conflict occurred when the children started to attend school. We heard about such conflict only in the Tambov villages, where local authorities were likely to subject anyone wearing a cross to ostracism and vilification. In the other locales informants said less about this matter, apparently because parents had succumbed to the power of the Party and removed the crosses from their school-age children.[60] But parents in the Tambov villages resisted this violation of their religious practices and forced a compromise. The teachers in the Tambov villages offered insight into the process of negotiation.

The conflict centered on the participation of the school children in the Pioneer youth movement (similar to scouting elsewhere). The principal symbolic expression of participation was a red scarf explicitly intended to supplant the neck cross worn by Christians. The Party insisted on 100 percent mobilization of schoolchildren into the Pioneers. The older of the two teachers reported that before World War II, when she was a child in the local schools, there were no Pioneers. Even when she came back as a teacher in the late 1950s, hardly any children belonged to the Pioneers because the parents still would not permit it. "They insisted that their children wear baptismal crosses, and the families regularly attended church services. I was criticized [by my superiors] for doing a poor job of anti-religious propaganda. But then gradually during the 1960s and 1970s, [the children] began to join the Pioneers and the Komsomol."[61] Her fellow teacher told much the same story. In the early 1960s, few were Pioneers:

> The mothers were opposed, though the children wanted to join—there were interesting things to do in the Pioneers: camping, games. Pioneers were not supposed to wear a cross but instead to have a neckerchief. There was no way you could wear them both. I had to try to persuade the mothers to give in. [Finally], they said all right, in school you can do as you like, but let them come home from school without the neckerchiefs. When in school they can take off the crosses and put them out of sight but at home they'll wear their crosses.[62]

In other words, the women of the village and the teachers negotiated a compromise, a kind of charade that would satisfy Party authorities and allow the children opportunities to participate in scouting (and unavoidably also in Party indoctrination, but that was already in the schools) while giving the mothers a sense of continuing control at home and continued supervision of their children's spiritual well-being.[63]

Tatars

The equivalent Muslim rite of initial community incorporation likewise continued throughout the Soviet period among the Tatars we interviewed. The rite included a visit from the mullah soon after the birth for prayers and declaration of the child's name into its ears (a rite known as *azan,* which is a recitation of the Muslim call to prayer), plus, in the case of boys, circumcision.

Just as with the Russians, the women of the first generation sensed the urgency of proclaiming the newborn child as theirs. The old women of the village explained that they did not wait for the visit of the mullah but immediately after delivery said prayers into the baby's ears, first the right ear and then the left. If the mother was unable to do this, the midwife (who had to be trained in religion) did it for her. "What words did you use?" I asked. "We said 'God is great' [*Allah akbar*] four times." "But that is no longer done [now that births take place] in maternity wards."[64] Not only concern about death but worries about the action of evil spirits prompted the quick arrangement of a visit from the mullah. "Mama told me that just as soon as the new baby was brought home, you had to give it a name, because according to the Quran, an 'unclean power' might give the child a name. For this reason, you had rush to invite the mullah and give the name right away." "If not, the child could be afflicted with the eye?" I asked. "Yes, they can inflict the evil eye, make the child sick, or cause it to act up. The child should not remain without a name for long."[65] This naming rite often included dinner for relatives.[66]

Circumcision was more complicated because of the need for a specialist and also the requirement, apparently unique to Volga Muslims, that it be done in an odd-numbered month or year. According to the oldest women of the village, circumcision could take place as early as the third day after birth.[67] But early circumcision became difficult for women of the second generation because of the infrequency of visits by the specialist (known as *babai*) in this trade, who lived some distance away in Tatarstan. The women reported a wide variation in the timing of circumcision; some boys were done as early as two weeks, others as late as two or three years (even seven years was mentioned in one case).[68] The babai available to this village was in great demand throughout the region. Evidently, collectivization and religious persecution had reduced the number of specialists. Interestingly, the women of this village stressed the hygienic benefits of circumcision. This seems to be a result of modern medicine reaching the village, for the women made reference to a surgeon of their acquaintance who had made this point.[69]

Among the Turkic women who had moved to the city, circumcision became a matter left to trained medical personnel. Fakhiza Suleimanova, who lived most of her life in Simbirsk, said that surgeons now did circumcisions for the Tatars in her city, which was preferable because they were able to perform the act in hygienic circumstances.[70] A Bashkir informant who gave birth to her sons in Leningrad explained that she returned to Bashkiria to have them circumcised and that the rite was performed by a veterinarian. This well-educated urban woman held strictly to odd-numbered years, having one boy circumcised at age one and the other at age three, for fear that otherwise the act would not have the proper effects.[71] This testimony suggests the powerful hold that these religious- and community-bonding practices continued to have on Soviet Muslims, despite the broad-based and sometimes ferocious measures to end them.

Baptism as the basic ritual of incorporation was common in Russian villages right through the Soviet era. Our Tatar and Bashkir informants likewise continued to perform the equivalent Muslim rites. Despite the assaults of the 1930s and beyond that caused the loss of 90 percent of their places of worship and clergy and despite the risks to their own livelihood and safety, peasants contrived to provide their children with protection against the spiritual and temporal dangers of this life and the hope of salvation in the next. The question of how this practice functioned in the culture, and therefore endured when so much else was lost, might be answered, at least partially, by looking more closely at the ways women in these communities maintained social bonds and defended arenas over which they still had some control. So much had been taken from them. Collectivization robbed them of their property and destroyed the autonomy of their villages, enslaving their families to the state. Their churches and mosques were closed, their clergy and even their village folk healers were persecuted and driven underground. Their husbands and sons were called out to defend the country, many of them never to return home. In these matters, the women could only suffer and submit. But the care and protection of their children was a sphere in which they could continue to exercise some authority, deploy a respected knowledge, and build a sense of control through their defense of their families' health, bodily and spiritual. Their insistence that baptism (and equivalent Muslim rites) be performed, no matter the risks, and their ability in most cases to achieve this strengthened both the families and the women themselves by according them the power to act effectively, beneficially, and in defiance of the ideological state.

Coping with Infant Death

The oldest of our informants were the last generation of Russian and Tatar women to experience the demographic regime of high fertility accompanied by high mortality. To the extent that their fertility was limited, the cause was likely to have been the long absence of their mates as a result of wars, revolution, migration, and other disruptions of family life rather than a conscious decision to curtail births through the use of contraception or abortion. Accompanying the high fertility of this and preceding generations were extraordinary rates of infant and child mortality, among the highest ever recorded anywhere. It would be interesting to know how women were able to cope emotionally with the expected death of many of their children and still preserve the energy and will required to care for their remaining children and do all the other demanding tasks of housekeeping, farming, cottage industry, and community responsibilities. Our interview study may shed some light on this matter.

High fertility and high infant mortality are linked. Historians and social scientists have mapped the physical and social connections between them, showing that women who lose children in infancy more quickly regain the capacity to conceive because they are less protected by the physical and social effects of breast-feeding. Likewise, where a large completed family size is normative, parents are motivated to produce another child soon after the death of the previous one. What is less certain is a possible emotional link between high fertility and high mortality. This issue was raised by the pioneering French historian of childhood Philippe Ariès, who suggested that the loss of many children induced a "callousness" or fatalism that led mothers to give minimal attention to their young children in order to shield themselves from the emotional trauma of loss.[1] Presumably, this low level of attention and care would in turn help to explain the high number of deaths among the children, for a greater investment of the mother's time and concern might have saved infant lives.

This view seems to fit well with what Russian doctors and administrators had long been saying about peasant families. They complained about the "in-difference" with which peasants greeted the death of a small child and criticized what they saw as the "neglect" of children by their peasant mothers. They la-mented as well the failure of the mothers to bring sick children to a doctor until the children were so ill that it was impossible to save them. Somewhat con-tradictorily, the doctors also railed against mothers' "superstitious remedies" for ailing children, their use of folk healers, herbal medicine, spells and other forms of magic. "Indifference" and "neglect," when pronounced by doctors, evi-dently referred to indifference (at least initially) toward the advice of urban-based medical specialists. Otherwise, the doctors might have thought to ask why, if mothers were truly neglectful, they were resorting to so many folk meth-ods to save their children? The response of these doctors is simply one more illustration of the distance between the mental worlds of urban-based medical workers and village women. If we are to understand the world of the village women, we cannot rely solely on medical workers' interpretations of their be-havior.

In thinking about this issue, I have found it helpful to look at sociological studies of villages of the developing world. The people in these villages face the same problems of high fertility on a limited resource base that Russian villagers contended with until recent times. Many villagers in the developing world have more children than they can feed, and they live by the commonsense notion that not all members of a household are of equal value. Accordingly, no one has an automatic entitlement to an equal, or even a comparable age or sex-graded, share. In the case of infants, village women make assessments of their desirabil-ity and viability, and they make choices about which of their babies they should invest their energies and material resources in and which they should not. The children identified as ineligible for normal care are labeled with a verbal for-mula that relegates them to a special category, and they are left to their own devices. If they survive, it is the will of God or some other power, and, once having shown that they could endure, these children are loved just as much, in some cases even more, than the others to whom more care was initially allotted. People have always had to make choices about investments of time and re-sources, and in a subsistence economy with high rates of fertility, some choices they make are likely to have life and death consequences. In these communities of the developing world, outright infanticide is not acceptable, but differential nurturing of small children is not only condoned but expected. In some cases, the decision is based on sex (girls are less nurtured) or on birth order. In north-eastern Brazil, the standard is the apparent viability of the child. If a child looks and behaves in ways that offer little prospect of its survival, it is not nurtured as the more robust infants are.[2] Ethnographic evidence from the prerevolution-ary period and information garnered in our interview study suggest that village women in Russia may have been making similar calculations about investments in their infants; that is, calculations based on the apparent viability of their children. The evidence also suggests some mental categories that the women used in making the choices they did.

Before turning to this evidence and an examination of the mental world of peasant mothers in Russia, I want to review two other circumstances, mentioned earlier in this book, that led to a difference in the care of small children. These circumstances require no special analysis, for their link to behavior can be understood in straightforward economic and social terms.

The first has to do with seasonal requirements of women's labor and seasonal fluctuations in the risk of illness and death. When mothers were busy with summer work in the fields, their small children received less maternal attention than during the off-season. And this, combined with the greater prevalence of pathogenic organisms in the summer, produced a higher infant morbidity and mortality than at other times of the year. Children born in the summer received less attention not because of some calculation about their individual viability (even if that was possibly also a consideration) but because their mothers had responsibilities to the household economy as a whole, that is, to the other members of the household and especially to those who were producers or potential producers. Because of the special requirements of Russian agriculture these responsibilities could not be neglected or postponed. Russia's short growing season and inadequate capital and labor inputs meant that every able-bodied person, including mothers with small children, had to work intensively. A time-budget study done in the 1920s revealed that Russian farm women spent nearly as many hours at agricultural labor (as distinct from household tasks) as did the men.[3] In other words, Russian peasant mothers had obligations to the collective welfare of their families that surpassed their responsibility to any one member.

This obligation to ensure the survival of the family as a unit was also the basis of the second circumstance. Earlier I referred to the many accounts in which urbanized middle-class observers accused peasant mothers of neglecting their children and being indifferent to their deaths. In this connection, doctors sometimes remarked that peasants cared more for their cow than for their children.[4] Such comments were based on observation but little understanding of the emotional world of the peasant mother and the circumstances with which she had to contend. Middle-class observers with their material resources and notions of the individual value of each infant failed to take account of situations in which the responsibilities of village mothers required them to devote more attention to a cow than to an individual child. A case of this sort was actually described by one of our informants from her own experience. Praskovia Korot-chenkova was a seventy-three-year-old woman from the El'ninsk region of Smolensk province. Typical of women of her age and place, she had given birth four times, the last in 1960. All but the final birth took place at home with the help of a granny midwife. In discussing the need to have milk to keep her children alive and growing, she told the following story.

The main thing was that the children would get enough food to eat, especially enough milk, so that they would be satisfied. One time my younger son Mikhail got sick. I had been working on the spinning wheel. Well, it spins around and causes a draft, and he was lying next to it. His temperature went up and he started to cough. The local medic sent us to the hospital in El'nia for treatment. There they examined him and said that the boy had double pneumonia and I'd need to stay at the hospital with him. Well, I told them that I couldn't do it; my cow was just about to calve. The doctors started to chew me out: "What's more important to you, your son or a cow?" And I told them, "The cow is a second mother to me; she feeds everyone." And so I took my son and went home. . . . After all, how was I going to manage without the cow? What was I going to feed the children with?[5]

Who could think that she made a poor choice in devoting her attention first to her cow and then to her son? Under the circumstances, it was clearly better that she risk her youngest child than place her remaining older children in jeopardy. She had already invested much in them, her husband was unreliable and often absent, and her older children would the sooner be able to assist her in managing the household. Fortunately, her young son Mikhail eventually got well. Saving the cow was, of course, important to his survival as well.

In sum, the pressure of seasonal work obligations and the recognition that no individual, especially no small, unproductive individual whose survival was far from certain, could be allowed to put the rest of the family in jeopardy were important considerations in the amount of attention children received. In addition to these matters, the apparent viability of small children may also have led to some differentiation in nurture.

Differential Care

The idea that some children were labeled soon after birth as being unlikely to survive can be found in the reports of Russian ethnographers and doctors from the prerevolutionary era. According to these accounts, certain signs allowed the women to gauge which babies were viable and which were not. If an infant looked odd, if it was too heavy, too pudgy, or too delicate, "the earth pulls it back to itself," they said, and they assumed the child would die soon. If a baby developed too fast, was too quiet, or stared too much at its surroundings, it was "a goner" or "not long for this world" (*ne zhilets* or *ne zhilets na belom svete*).[6] Presumably, like babies similarly labeled in northeastern Brazil and elsewhere today, these children were treated differently than were the babies considered to be normal, robust, and likely to survive.

Although this labeling practice and other means for coping with infant death faded as the high rates of infant mortality declined in the twentieth century, our oldest informants remembered examples from their youth of this way of thinking about and treating babies. Several women from northeastern Moscow province mentioned labeling of the kind reported in prerevolutionary sources. Pras-kovia and Tatiana Kurkova recalled that the midwife from their time, Aunt Dunia, and some other women, were able to identify a child as a goner (*ne zhilets*). "How did they do that?" we asked. "They could tell by the eyes," Tatiana responded. "How exactly?" we wondered. "I can't say. They knew from the eyes, but it was their secret. They did not divulge it to anyone. They just somehow could look into the child's eyes and know that it wasn't going to live very long. . . . They would see that there was no life there, but how they knew I cannot say." The Kurkovas added that some of the children so designated survived all the same, a finding consistent with what we know from other parts of the world. It is also an indication, as the Kurkovas further noted, that care was not altogether withdrawn from children labeled as *goners*.[7] Elizaveta Nikolaeva likewise knew the traditional label for *goner* (*ne zhilets*) and had heard it applied in an updated form to her own daughter Dina, who died at four months of age in the 1930s of an inflamed cranial membrane. One night the child stopped suckling. The next day Elizaveta went to work as usual at the cattle yard and, finding no one willing to watch her sick baby, she left Dina with her five-year-old daughter, Tamara. And on her return from work that evening, Elizaveta took the still ailing child to a clinic at a nearby factory. The doctor there told her that the child was "hopeless" (*beznadezhnyi*).

> Oh, how I was crying. And she said: "Mother . . . , little mother, you shouldn't weep. Your child is hopeless. It is not going to live. It has an inflammation . . . of the cranial membrane," or such like that, he [*sic*] told me. Yes. "This baby of yours is hopeless, it is going to die." And that evening she died at home.

When I asked Elizaveta later in the interview if she knew the traditional label *ne zhilets,* she responded that, yes, it was the same kind of marker that people had attached to her baby Dina. "The baby stopped suckling at my breast, and they said, 'Now you know, the baby is going to die.'"[8]

The responses to our questions about how babies were treated once they were designated as goners or clearly defective in some other way were mixed. Most of our informants recalled that such children were treated with a variety of remedies in hopes that they would revive. Only in a few cases did we receive indications that care was withdrawn altogether. If a removal of care had been occurring more widely, reports of it would not likely have shown up in episodic interviews of the kind we were doing. Women are reluctant to acknowledge such behavior nowadays. In other parts of the world where researchers have come across it, they spent much time living among the people and earning the trust of mothers before this manner of dealing with children became visible. Elizaveta Nikolaeva responded that women "took measures" if a child had signs of death; they would massage it, steam it in the oven, butter its chest, and the like. However, a neighbor of her own age (both were born in 1905), Anastasia Shishanova, said that old women of her time would advise those of her own generation not to do anything with a child who was born sickly. "Don't give it anything to drink and don't do anything to it," they would say. But then she added: "In those days they also had some old women who did all kinds of things. They would steam them. Yes, that's the sort of thing they did. And we did it too."[9] Another woman of the same generation and locale, Anastasia Spiridonova, was very feisty and unusually modern in her outlook compared with other women her age. When she was told that she had a "hopeless" child, she simply refused to accept this label and to give up. She went to nearby Moscow and bought an herbal remedy, mixed it into a tincture, and spoon-fed it to the child until it started to improve. She said proudly that the doctors could not figure out how she did it.[10]

Many of our Tatar informants were likewise aware of the signs of death on small children. They most often used the term "soft" for such children. Minzifa Mustafina said that such a "soft" child could be known from the large size of its fontanel, which caves inward, and the baby's being weak and not taking the breast. She had such a baby and did not stop caring for it—indeed, placed it in a doctor's care—because she feared her husband's wrath, that he would throw her out if the baby died.[11] Nurania Badrieva also had a goner, her first child, which lived only a month and a half. It had the usual signs; it was "weak, slept all the time, and suckled poorly."[12] Several other Tatar and Bashkir women in our interviews acknowledged that the women of their time could read the signs of a child not fated to survive and recognized quite naturally the marks of defective babies. As for their treatment, people reacted differently. Most women said that the parents felt sorry for such children and did what they could for them. Garifabanu Abdullina, however, reported that while some Tatar parents loved and cared for defective children, others said it was best that they died.[13] Zeinab Gimatdinova gave birth to her first child prematurely. "It was weak, and the women said that he is 'soft' and is not going to live." But there was one old woman in the village who had a different opinion. She slapped the baby on the back and declared it healthy but counseled that "it was necessary to feed it well, especially important was the mother's breast milk."[14] With this encouragement, Zeinab decided to make every effort for her baby and pulled it through.

The action or inaction prompted by village women's insight into the viability of infants can perhaps best be seen in the story of a Russian informant, Aunt Valia, a woman nearly ninety years old when I interviewed her in the summer of 1990. She had given birth to twelve children, half of whom died in early childhood. She had the rough-and-ready measure of this world of chance that was so typical of Russia one hundred years ago. And that attitude in the countryside lasted right up into the 1920s and 1930s, when Aunt Valia was having her children in a small village just west of Moscow. She said that people really did not give a lot of thought to whether children died; "If they survived," she told me, "it meant they were born strong." She added that she had looked after the other children, the six who died; she did not abandon them utterly. But the impression she conveyed was that it was up to the children to prove that they could make it. Then she told me of one of her sons (eventually a survivor) on whom she had given up hope. This is a wonderful story because it illuminates at once the treatment of infants regarded as "goners" and also the powerful and beneficial effects of folk medicine in reversing a decision to give up on the care of a child.

Aunt Valia related that one spring her eight-month-old son fell ill and was dying on her. A neighbor woman had visited and said that her boy was going to die, "Yes, right away he'll die; he's completely hopeless." Aunt Valia nevertheless took him for medical care. "I personally carried him, wrapped in a felt blanket, to the hospital [eight kilometers away]. The doctors there told me that he would not even last the trip home; the boy was hopeless. So, I carried him back home in the blanket. The neighbor came over and asked what had happened, and I told her, 'Well, right, he's altogether hopeless,' and so I put him on a pillow and just let him lie there." Here she gave a gesture of dismissal, the sense being that she had not planned to do anything more with him. A while later, an old woman of the village visited her, looked at the child, and told her that she should leave the baby there and go to see Aunt Akulina. The woman said that Akulina "will give you some special water [for the child], and if he is going to live, he will, and if he is going to die, he will do it the sooner." Aunt Valia continued, "I went there, the woman found the water for me, I returned home, roused the child, and made him drink the water, and that evening he began [again] to suckle at the breast." As I learned later in the conversation, the water had been infused with magical powers by spells, which Aunt Valia had overheard.[15]

The story reveals two characteristic features of the boundary between the living and those who will soon be gone. Valia at first exerted what efforts she could to save her child, but when told by the doctors and her neighbor that the case was hopeless, she put the child aside and awaited the inevitable. But the story also illustrates the power of folk medicine to shift the boundary of hope and despair, and in this sense, interestingly, to confront a definition imposed by modern clinical medicine, a cultural system outside the village but still recognized by villagers as having great power. Nevertheless, the old woman Akulina and her magical water possessed their own power, the power to restore Valia's hopes, and to convince her to shift her baby from the mental category of "goner" back into the world of the living, and therefore to begin again to care for the child, to rouse it and to feed it. The markers of viability constructed to allow people to cope with the swarming death that surrounded them could be stretched by the powers of folk healers who were sensitive to the signs of death and survival and could persuade a mother not to give up hope when hope was still justified.

Death without Weeping[16]

In chapter four we saw some examples of what doctors or officials might have interpreted as indifference toward the death of small children. Women from Smolensk province spoke about how they were instructed by older women not to cry about the death of their children. Elena Bobkova lost her first two children and was told that she should not weep for them. "God knows better than we what He is doing. The children will go directly to heaven," she was assured.[17] Anna Kirsanova likewise reported that people believed "you should not cry over the death of children, or even of adults, or else in the afterlife they will remain in water," but she added that whether this was true or not only God knew.[18] Other women also explained that they were not permitted to weep over the death of their children but found it hard not to do so.[19]

Women of the older generations in other locales communicated much the same message. The death of children was a normal, expected part of life. More important matters had to be kept in mind, especially the survival and health of the mother. The Tatar woman Rkia Kamaletdinova from Kalmaiur village, for example, grew up with three siblings in a family that lost fifteen other children. She saw her mother go through several difficult births, some lasting three days. She said that while sad, the deaths were accepted stoically. The attitude was "God giveth and God taketh away." They were most of all happy that their mother survived these ordeals.[20]

Evidently, the mental health of the mother was part of this calculation, judging from the admonitions not to be overly concerned about and not to dwell on the death of children. Marfa Malikova (born in 1910) from the Tambov site was one of only four surviving children from her mother's nine births. Marfa also gave birth nine times and lost four of her small children. Inured to such losses, she spoke about the deaths with a kind of calm indifference. As her daughter confirmed, using an expression employed by women in this area, "Marfa Ivanovna doesn't agonize [ubivaetsia] over the family."[21] The same expression was used in connection with another woman of the same age, Pelagea Nikulina. Her mother had given birth to seventeen children, only eight of whom survived early childhood. Pelagea had even less success than her mother. Her first two children died in infancy. Then she divorced, remarried, and endured five more pregnancies. The first ended in a miscarriage, the second produced stillborn twins (the result, she believed, of a collision with a cow), and of the three subsequent live births, a boy died at one year of age, a girl "dried up" at eight months, and just one remaining daughter survived. This seemingly tragic family history did not cause Pelagea to feel bad about her life. As an older daughter, she had done much of the upbringing of her siblings and knew from her mother's experience that many children could be expected to die and that too many survivors would impose an unbearable burden. She felt bad about the death of her own children and wished she could have brought more of them to adulthood, but she did not agonize about losing them and, indeed, explained that "though I appear unlucky, I cannot say that I am. . . . Only one daughter survived, yet, if you look at it another way, the people who had a lot of children had a very difficult life." The interviewer added a note that Pelagea had been accustomed since early childhood to the hard life of a rural woman, and she had a very sober view of the relationship between the number of children a woman had and the heavy burden of work she endured. Her positive feelings about her life show through in her other stories, a reflection of her characteristic resilience and the fact that she was not isolated in old age but visited often by her grandchildren and great grandchildren.[22] This growing and loving progeny may indeed have been the key to her acceptance of the loss of her other children.

Several women also expressed the view that babies sorted out their own life chances; they had a way of demonstrating whether or not they had the strength to endure the difficult life for which they were destined. Aunt Valia, mentioned earlier, was quite clear about this: if they did not survive, they probably were not strong enough. Aleksandra Guseva (born in 1907) from the Urals site came from a family of six children. One of her brothers died of "a dog's old age" (sobach'ia starost'), technically a form of rickets but applied more generally to babies who dehydrated and shriveled up. It was one of the most common causes of death of small children, according to peasants. In this case, the women tried to revive him by the traditional remedy of baking him in a flat cake—they sandwiched the baby in dough and placed it in a warm oven—but to no avail. Aleksandra also lost two of her own seven children in early childhood, even though she followed her mother's advice to carry the sick children to church and take communion three times. There was no hospital within reach in those days, Aleksandra sighed, and "what would be, would be; children were either healthy or not."[23] Lia Brynkina, looking back on her mother's generation, likewise suggested that children had to survive on their own resources and prove that they were strong enough. The women of that time were too busy working for their men and for themselves to be able to devote much attention to children. "Infant mortality was high, but the ones who survived were strong; they hardly ever got even a cold."[24]

Possibly, the common Russian ways of thinking about "old" and "young" may have helped women release their sick and dying children into another realm. As in other cultures, one of the central oppositions in Russian thought is old/young (star/molod). These classifications are descriptive of biological age, of course, but in Russian usage they likewise embrace many other states of being. Among the most readily recognizable are those in which old and young stand for rank, as in the Kievan Russian "younger retinue" (mladshaia druzhina), whose members were not younger but of lesser rank than those designated "boyars" or "prince's men." In this same way, "boyar children" were not younger but lesser in rank than other Muscovite servicemen. In another sphere, molod and its extensions in Russian bear the meaning not so much of age as of ability;

"young" has the specific meaning of "capable of conceiving offspring," as we see in the use of *molodoi* among peasants as synonymous with bridegroom and new husband.[25]

"Old" has even more numerous applications beyond its designation of biological age. Again, rank is a major category. "Those older in rank sit in front" (*Starshie chinom v peredi sidiat*). The chosen leader of a social unit or military group was often called "elder" (*starosta*). The term *starshina,* whether designating an individual administrator or a Cossack council, revealed a level of authority—and not a biological age. Examples of this kind are numerous. It is less often noted that the male and female leaders of youth games were also known as *starik* and *starka.* More important for our analysis is the religious realm, where the term *starets* denoted a learned or pious man, and not necessarily an old man, as is clear from the use of the term *riadovoi starets* for an ordinary monk. A woman who renounced marriage to save her soul could be known as *starka.*[26] In these usages, we also see the opposition played out with *molodoi* in the meaning of capable of conceiving a child (although in the case of the clerics personal choice, rather than age as such, was the cause of infertility). The clerical "old" people were not necessarily old biologically but were in some sense outside this world, or at least on its margin, its edge toward heaven. Another category of persons who occupied a margin—a margin that shared certain religious elements with the clerics, persons who were not wholly part of this life and were thus designated as "old"—were beggars (known as *stariki* or *startsy*). As the famous folklorist and lexicographer Vladimir Dal' tells us, they were no more necessarily old in years than they were unable to see, however much they often presented themselves and were accepted as blind.[27] Accordingly, when not used for biological age or superior rank, "old" was a classification of impairment with certain sacred connotations, a category for persons who were marginal to this life and perhaps closer than ordinary folk to God.

Peasant women may have placed infants not expected to survive into a similar (perhaps, even the same) mental category, viewing them as closer to God. As noted earlier, the formula often mentioned in ethnographic accounts of these fragile, impaired infants is of someone "not long for this world" (*ne zhilets na belom svete*). The label "old" was nevertheless often used directly, as in the commonly fatal condition known by the peasants as "a dog's old age." Children labeled as "old" in this sense of being on the downhill side of life, on the margin toward eternity, were thought of as the concern of God more than of their families. When they stopped suckling or showed other signs of weakness, they were no longer ministered to while nature took its course—unless, as in the case of the Russian woman Aunt Valia and of the Tatar mother Zeinab Gimatdinova, a wise woman of the village understood that the child might be saved with further effort.

This practice of placing an infant in a mental category outside of one's direct responsibility could be interpreted in Freudian terms as a form of denial. It is probably more helpful, however, to analyze this behavior in symbolic terms.

In our experience, for example, the physical death of a person almost always occurs before we consign them to death in the symbolic order through a funeral and other rituals. In the case of village women, we see the reverse process. The women who labeled children with signs such as *ne zhilets*, "soft," or "hopeless," and thus placed them in a mental category that lifted from the mother's shoulders responsibility for what ensued, were consigning the children to death in the symbolic order before they died their actual physical death. The children were consciously placed in a reserve space closer to God. And, as the women's stories confirm, this was a community decision. Female neighbors, relatives, even doctors are always mentioned as participants in the identification of a child not fated to live. Mothers were evidently not expected to have to make such determinations on their own.

Villages also contained persons of formal or informal religious authority who helped mothers in easing the dying children into this area of God's responsibility and then through it into the afterlife. Anastasia Vakhromeeva told us how this happened in the death of her son when she was a young mother living in Saratov province. She had been out working in the fields all day and threshing all night, only to be called home in the morning to find her boy terribly ill. She had left him with a rag pacifier filled with kasha and cookies, and now he was vomiting and convulsing. The hospital was far away, and she could not get organized to go there right away.

> In the meantime, I was cleaning myself up, then going back and forth. . . . Then on the second day I was ready to go, but he had already gotten worse; it was kind of like he was beginning [to die]. So, I summoned this granny. She was something like a nun . . . there. Well, a kind of a nun, yes, yes. I called for her to come. And she says, "What do you have on you?" At first, I didn't really catch on to what was meant. "Don't you have a wedding ring or such?" And I say, "What could I have?!" We lived badly. I tell her: "All I have left is a kerchief." A kerchief.
>
> It was a big one. . . .With tassels.
>
> I tell her: "There's only this kerchief." I got married in the wintertime, you see. Yes. And so, there was only a kerchief that remained. She took the kerchief and said some words over it, covered the [little boy] with it, made the sign of the cross, and then he began to be quiet. And that's how he died.[28]

Priests also helped out in this way. Zinaida Shumkova told us that children born defective or sickly were not really ever seen by people outside the family except by chance. But she did happen into church once when her neighbor Sasha Makeeva had brought her dying baby for a blessing.

> I was in the church and she came in with him, with her child. Oh! I said, "Sash, what's wrong there with the. . . .?" The boy was with her. "What's with that boy, what kind of kid is he?" And she says, "They say that he has some

kind of old age [*starost'*], a dog's old age." You could see that there was only this face . . . there were just bones, and skin stretched over them. His eyes were huge. He was all scrawny. And she went into the church and ordered, I don't know exactly what there, a prayer perhaps it was. And they opened up the tsarist doors . . . the big ones. They are called tsarist doors. They opened up those doors. And she stood there bent down, and the priest read something over her. Well, then, her boy, very quickly after that, he died.[29]

These women well understood how to deliver their children into the area of God's responsibility and to lighten the weight of sorrow that they inevitably felt at the loss of their little ones.

A final consolation could be found in the role the dead children played in the world beyond as intercessors for their parents. In old Russian religious thought, children who died before the age of seven were said to become angels.[30] In recent times, this idea has been attributed more specifically to Old Believers, those Russian Orthodox Christians who refused to accept the church reforms of the seventeenth century. A writer who traveled among the old believers in the 1920s claimed that they still held to the idea that children who die before age one become angels and are able to absolve half of the sins of their parents.[31] This belief could also be found among standard Orthodox believers. The ethnologist A. V. Balov recorded it in the central province of Iaroslav in the late nineteenth century, where children who died soon after birth were thought to turn into angels—and children who suffered in dying were said to be doing so for the sins of their parents.[32]

I, too, ran across this way of thinking in my discussions with the medic in Novgorod province, Anna Zueva. We were in the midst of a conversation about science and religion, and I asked her how the ordinary people with whom she had worked every day in her medical practice explained the death of their small children. "Well," she responded, "it was considered normal that not all of them could stay alive. Life is hard, and if an innocent child should die, it is because God has called it to Him. So, they did not weep for these children." I interjected, "So, they believed that these children who were dying. . . . " "They went to God," she finished my thought. "There is a belief," I continued, "that dead children can pray for their parents because [these children] are closer to God and do not have sins on their souls." "Yes, yes," Anna jumped in. "That's right, very much so, [they believe] that all those who die young, that they are all transformed into angels, and they are close to God in heaven and they also serve him well. That is how they were always reassuring one another and what they were saying to one another."[33]

These stories make clear that the common expression used by villagers faced with very ill or dying children, "It is God's will," was not, as doctors and officials lamented, a sign of peasant indifference and neglect. It was a positive statement about their own care for their child, their decision to place it nearer to God and to pass responsibility for it to a power greater than their own. This was different from neglect (or abandonment or exposure) because it left open the possibility that the child could be moved from this interim space either farther toward God, in the case of its death, or back toward the living, as happened in the case of Aunt Valia's child and others. Folk medicine and folk categories of thought would be more likely than city medicine to understand and accommodate this interim status, even in its therapeutics.

These stories also make clear that more was going on in peasant thinking than Philippe Ariès' simple notion of emotional distancing. Women did not respond mechanically and unemotionally to all children, even if care was minimal at times because of the other tasks mothers had to perform. They made distinctions about which children were blessed with life powers and which were not likely to survive—those who, like holy people and beggars, were "old" in the sense of being closer to God. The older women instructed the young mothers not to weep over their dead children, for God knows better than we. And the children whom God calls to Himself serve as intercessors for their families before the throne of heaven. Could such assistance to parents be expected from children who were simply "neglected," as outside observers liked to believe? Or would it make better sense that such intercession could be understood as effective only in the case of children whose mothers had in their thoughts placed them nearer to God when the mothers could no longer do anything to save them?

Child Care

Nineteenth-century village child care in Russia had three characteristic features: long breast-feeding accompanied by chaws and the rag soska, swaddling accompanied by a suspended swing crib (*liul'ka*), and home remedies for childhood illnesses accompanied by the intervention of folk healers. The modernization of village mothering involved the elimination of the beliefs that sustained these practices and the transformation of the practices into new methods sanctioned by urban-based medical authorities. These changes can be mapped in the testimony of our informants, even if some of the old practices continue to this day as supplements to the newer methods.

Feeding

Russians

Ever since doctors began observing Russian child care in the eighteenth century, they had denounced the feeding practices, in particular the use of the rag soska and the early introduction of solid foods. They regarded the soska as a primary vector of pathogens that sickened and killed babies. The early introduction of foods that infants could not yet digest was seen as the principal cause of diarrheas that brought rapid dehydration and death. The soska combined both disadvantages, since this ubiquitous instrument of Russian child care was not only a "pacifier" intended to give the baby some oral gratification between feedings. Just like the "chaw" of chewed bread that was sometimes placed in an infant's mouth, the soska was also a food-delivery vehicle meant to provide some measure of nourishment to the child in its mother's absence. Moreover, peasant women often began the soska before anything else, before even the mother's milk. The most vivid description of this act comes from a British writer who was serving as a country doctor for a Quaker mission in Russia during

World War I. He described the scene shortly after he delivered a baby in a village home.

> Then in came the proud grandmother, chewing a rag in which was pocketed bacon rind and baked flour; this she was about to pop into the child's mouth to be the first intruding touch from the outside world when I stopped her, and asked her to consider whether it was as nice and clean a comforter as the mother's breast; and besides, had she not got pyorrhoea (her gums were awash with pus). . . . It was an ill-judged if not unkind interruption, because in any case the cosy rag would be thrust in the moment our backs were turned and by giving the babe something she had herself chewed she was in an animal sort of way binding her love to it as best she knew how.[1]

These remarks reveal both the city person's view of villagers as primitives and a failure to understand the grandmother's gesture as an assertion of her place (temporarily usurped by the doctor) in the birthing process. The doctor was a foreigner, but this in itself was not significant. His views coincided with those of Russian physicians, who, if anything, protested this practice even more loudly; they were embarrassed for their own people and determined to eradicate what they regarded as a characteristic sign of backwardness in Russian mothering.

Several of our informants confirmed that practices long continued to occur similar to what the British doctor described. Despite the campaigns against the soska and changes that had intervened in infant feeding, these women recalled the use of the soska and chaws positively, and stated that in their time it was important to give the baby a soska shortly after its birth and only later should the breast be offered. Maria Somova, whose mother was a skilled village midwife and healer, said that women instantly gave the babies a soska with bread and did not put them to the breast because the milk did not start up for a while.[2] Marfa Malikova noted the same thing, saying that "if, for example, you gave birth in the morning, you would give [the baby] a soska with bread, and in the evening you'd put it to the breast since by then something would be coming there."[3] Anisia Gureeva likewise reported the immediate introduction of a soska of chewed bread with sugar to newborns in her village.[4]

Not surprisingly, a few of the women in the oldest generation expressed opposition to the soska and claimed that they did not use it, even if their neighbors did. It is hard to know whether they were reporting accurately or denying a practice that they knew was no longer approved. But it is not hard to believe that after decades of condemnation of the soska, some village families had decided not to use this form of nurture. The practice could be dangerous in ways much more obvious than as a vector for pathogens, and these more obvious dangers would be seen and understood by many villagers. For example, doctors reported that babies left all day with the soska for comfort sometimes choked to death on them. Indeed, one of our informants told of such a case

Informant from Moscow
province standing in her
doorway, 1993

from her own experience. Her playmate, a neighbor boy, was responsible for
watching his infant sister while his mother was at work. Like other older siblings in the same position, he chewed bread and mixed it with sugar in a rag
soska for his sister and went off with his friends. Once, our informant recounted, while she was playing with this neighbor, his sister choked on a soska and
died.[5] But if some of the women in the oldest generation had learned from such
tragedies and ceased to use the soska, they were not typical. The overwhelming
majority reported the continued use of this method of supplementing the diet
of their babies and providing them with comfort and nourishment while the
mothers were away from the home.

   Breast milk was, of course, the main source of nourishment for the babies.
Ethnographic accounts from the prerevolutionary period state that Russian
women breast-fed their infants for three fasts (counting only the major ones) or
about one and a half years. The women of the oldest generation conformed to
this practice; nearly all of them claimed to have nursed their children for from
one to one and a half years. A few reported breast-feeding even longer, up to two
and three years, primarily in hopes of delaying a subsequent pregnancy. These

Informant from Moscow province with her grandchildren, 1993

women recalled that some children continued suckling long after they were running about and speaking, and they would pause from play and ask their mothers to "give me the teat" or "let me suck for a bit."[6] When Russian women spoke of breast-feeding, however long it may have persisted, they did not mean to say that breast milk was the sole form of nourishment for their babies. Apart from the nearly ubiquitous soska, other forms of supplementary feeding were begun while breast-feeding continued. Much depended on the woman's ability to produce milk, whether or not the family had a cow, and the apparent needs of the baby. Russian village mothers fed on demand (despite efforts of doctors to convince them to feed on a schedule), and if a baby seemed unsatisfied with its diet of mother's milk, the women added cow's milk and solid food. Solid food usually began at about six months with semolina kasha; cow's milk could begin even earlier. Possession of a cow was a great asset to women of this first or old-est generation, for milk was not yet available for sale in many places and families were large. Women whose families had a cow or cows announced this fact proudly and confirmed its importance. One woman reported having fed cow's milk in the age-old way, through a horn bottle with a cow's teat nipple.[7]

The next generation of Russian women scarcely changed the feeding practices of their predecessors. These women were born between about 1912 and 1928 and were building their families in the difficult years of the 1930s through the 1950s. Almost the only difference in their practices was that the younger women of this cohort, the women who were having babies after the war when work discipline in the countryside became even stricter than it had been in the 1930s, shortened the duration of breast-feeding. These mothers in many cases were not allowed to stay at home with their babies, even if they were willing to do so without compensation. If they wanted to continue breast-feeding for as long as their mothers had, they needed to express milk from their breasts before leaving for work or find some means of having their infants delivered to them at work for daytime feedings. Natalia Mikhaleva used both methods. "I breast-fed for a year and a half and longer," she said. "But I also started supplementing very early. After two weeks, I'd leave the babies with my mother-in-law, squeeze out milk and go off for the entire day. We would make semolina kasha for them. . . . I'd also take nursing infants to the field with me, right in a sack, and placed them on the edge of the field. I'd be digging potatoes, and if the baby cried, I shook the dirt off my hands and breast-fed it. Some women actually took their hanging cribs with them into the field. We didn't feed on schedule, but whenever the baby cried."[8]

In Natalia's final sentence can be glimpsed the defiance that many women of this generation expressed against the admonitions of authorities about how to care for infants. We have seen this defiance already in this generation's frequent use of abortion to control family size and thwart the plans of the state to turn the women simultaneously into exploited farm workers and bounteous baby producers. In their feeding practices, they likewise refused the dictates of medical workers and continued their own familiar methods. Antonina Abramova recalled that "the doctors advised us about the right way to feed the babies, to do it on schedule, but I nursed in the old way. As soon as they cried, I gave them the breast. Feed them quickly and then back to work. There wasn't any time to be keeping track of schedules, and I doubt that it is really necessary." To a question about the use of child-care books, she responded that no one had such manuals, and she herself had no interest in reading them. "We asked one another about such things and listened to what the older women had to say."[9] And the same defiance can be seen in reports about the use of the soska. Praskovia Korotchenkova recalled that the doctor (*medichka*) "gave us some instruction in the care of infants, but she pretty well understood that we were going to do things in our own way anyhow. For example, she would tell us that we shouldn't be giving a child chewed up black bread wrapped in a rag like a soska because you could get an infection from it, but we did it anyway, and my sons, especially the second one, grew like a bull (*bugai*)." Her mother-in-law taught her how to care for children, and that was all she needed to know, she asserted. Besides, they had to use solid food and other supplements, because "the mother's milk often was not sufficient. The amount of milk a nursing mother has," Praskovia continued, "depends after all on how well she is nourished, and food was in short supply. Lard couldn't be eaten every day but just on Sundays, and during fasts nursing mothers weren't given any milk. And they worked like horses."[10]

An interesting behavior reported by some women from this second generation was shared nursing of one another's babies. I had not run across this in medical or ethnographic accounts about Russian women. My earlier research on abandoned children in Russia included many reports of infant fosterlings from the foundling homes being passed around from their registered foster mothers to other women, but it is far from clear that the women who took them were able to breast-feed them. Among our informants for this current study, Maria Mikhaleva related that she and her sister-in-law resided in the same large household and gave birth about the same time. Since they worked at different hours, they traded off nursing one another's children when they were home.[11] A neighbor, Natalia Mikhaleva, recalled nursing another woman's baby for two days when the woman's milk was slow to get started.[12] At an interview site in another province, women likewise reported being called on to help out with nursing when a new mother took a few days to get her milk in. Elena Tsygankova explained that in all three of her births, the milk started late, and one time they asked a village woman to do the breast-feeding, another time the doctor herself took on the job of nursing the infant.[13] Since our questionnaire did not contain a reference to this type of shared feeding, comments about it were spontaneous. It is impossible therefore to judge from our materials whether the practice was more widespread. Wet nursing had been a common enough practice on Russian country estates in the past, and extensive rural wet-nursing operations had been managed by Russian foundling homes from the early nineteenth century up to the 1917 revolution. In other words, the practice was familiar to many villagers and may have been continued or taken a new direction as a consequence of the strict work requirements imposed on village women after collectivization, at least until modern baby formula reached the countryside.

The Russian women of the third generation reported somewhat shorter breast-feeding periods and earlier transfers of babies exclusively to solid food than was done in the previous generations, although it is hard to generalize in view of the small number of interviews and considerable variation in behavior. Most often, the women of the third generation counted their breast-feeding in months (two, up to seven or eight), as distinguished from the year and more their predecessors had continued the practice. The younger women also reported starting solid foods as early as two months. The soska was less in evidence or had been replaced by a rubber pacifier of the same name. These changes appeared gradually. Among the Russians, it is not until interviews with those women having children in the 1970s and 1980s that we hear of feeding regimes that were fully medically directed. These women have finally broken the chain of intergenerational knowledge transfers and begun to view the practices of their mothers and grandmothers as quaint or dangerous. One woman, after breast-feeding for a few months, even switched to "Similac" to bottle-feed her children born in the 1970s and 1980s. However, she claimed to have used this product only because at the time her family had no cow. Like many Russians, she privileged the natural; she preferred the fresh products of her locale, including the use of cow's milk. She returned to feeding cow's milk to the last three of her seven children, after the family finally acquired its own cow.[14]

Tatars

The feeding practices of the Muslim women differed significantly. Recall the debates referenced in chapter 2 about infant mortality during the prerevolutionary period. The participants contrasted child care among the Tatars (and other Muslims of the empire) with that of the Orthodox peoples and praised the Muslims for their much greater success in bringing their children through the dangerous early months of life. Researchers attributed this success to the Muslims' prolonged breast-feeding, late introduction of solid foods, avoidance of soskas, and greater attention to the cleanliness of their homes and bodies. Our interviews with Tatar and Bashkir women confirmed that important differences of this kind continued well into the Soviet era, indeed almost to the present day.

The most striking difference was prolonged breast-feeding. The oldest Tatar women reported that they nursed their children for a minimum of two years but usually longer, and some of them continued to suckle their children for four and even five years. They also told of mothers, aunts, and neighbors who nursed from three to five years, or to the next pregnancy. Garifabanu Abdullina, one of the long breast-feeders, explained that she did so in part because there was not enough other food to share with the children, and so she continued nursing them until they were old enough to be looking after themselves. She offered an example. "I gave my daughter the breast in the morning before I went to work in the field and again in the evening, after returning. She would be waiting for me on the road." But, Garifabanu added, the two of them would first get cleaned up, have tea, and then Garifabanu would begin to nurse this growing girl. Mariam Gimadeeva said that her mother told her of how women in the previous generation would be sitting outdoors and children ages five and six would take a break, suckle at the breast, and return to their play. Zakia Zagidullina, a Muslim from our Urals village, remembered that in her natal family all the children nursed and ate nothing else until they could hold a spoon and feed themselves from the common table. She nursed her own daughter for five years. "Well, she must have also been eating other things besides breast-feeding?" our interviewer asked. "Yes, she was eating other things," Zakia answered. "When I was at work, she ate food. But as soon as I returned, she was all the time asking for the breast. Then after a time she got embarrassed. She would sit and wait. Then if someone came, she would take off (laughs)."[15] Like her mother, Zakia did not start her children on a solid food regimen but simply waited until they started feeding themselves with what was offered at table.

In nursing their children over an extended period, these women reported that they were consciously following a Quranic injunction. It will be recalled that doctors working among the Muslims before the revolution also recorded women's testimony that they nursed in accordance with the Quran. Indeed, the Quran does contain a verse (2:233) to the effect that mothers should nurse children for two years, but the passage in question also mentions a number of loopholes that permit early weaning or the use of wet nurses. The women we interviewed had another reason for lengthy nursing. Many of them acknowledged that they understood the contraceptive effects of breast-feeding and hoped to be able to delay the onset of the next pregnancy for as long as possible. So, the women's choices often signaled their own efforts to take control of their fertility.

Another local belief with no direct support in the Quran concerned the length of breast-feeding for boys and girls. The oldest women in the village of Tatarskii Kalmaiur disclosed that they had very precise rules that dictated different durations for boys and for girls. The women formulated a gender-related interpretation of the babies' nursing needs. They said that boys had to be nursed for two years and ten months and girls for a longer time, "because boys are stronger, and girls weaker."[16] Though not a Quranic injunction, this rule may reflect the powerful sex-role differentiation in Muslim teaching. It also reveals the ideological power of patriarchy among these women, since it cuts against what must have been their observed experience. Girl babies are demonstrably more robust and more likely to survive early childhood than boys, unless the girls are intentionally abused or deprived of nourishment. So, in this case, the power of patriarchy may have worked to the benefit of the girls.

The second generation of women in Tatarskii Kalmaiur also nursed their children for the prescribed two years and more, and indeed a woman born as late as 1933 and having her children between 1955 and 1964 continued nursing for four and five years.[17] Another woman from this cohort related that she continued nursing one child after a second one was born.[18] It was only starting with births in the 1960s that the length of breast-feeding began to fall into line with the Russian practice of nursing for about a year (but by that time many Russian rural women were nursing less than a year).

The use of the soska by the Tatars likewise proved to be very different from Russian practice. Accounts by doctors in the nineteenth and early twentieth centuries had noted that the soska was rare among the Tatars, and when the al'va, as it was known to Tatars, was used at all, it was heated and wrapped in clean cloth.[19] Although the reports of our informants were not as categorical as this description, they generally confirmed its accuracy. Six of the seventeen Muslim informants mentioned the use of a soska by their mothers or themselves, but only two of these women recalled having introduced the soska early in the feeding regime.[20] In the other four cases, the soska was associated with the introduction of solid foods at about six months of age. The rest of the Muslim women were quite certain about the soska's not being used; some were emphatically against its use. Amina Teleshova remembered a story about her mother becoming very angry with Amina's aunt when the woman gave a soska to her against her mother's wishes.[21]

Apart from the bread soska and mother's milk, most Tatar children received little other nourishment before age one, when their diet began to include a shell pasta (*salma*) followed by small portions of what everyone else was eating: semolina kasha, noodles, potatoes, tea. This regimen seemed to be standard, and it was passed down from one generation of women to the next—until very recently.

A few younger Muslim women informants had moved to cities before building their families, and their practices were converging toward a generalized Soviet, urban model advocated by medical authorities. Although they were moving closer in their behavior to the Russians of their age, these urban Muslim women nursed longer than did the youngest of our Russian informants who had stayed in the village: a year or more of nursing in the case of the urbanized Muslims as compared with a few months for the Russian village women of the same age.[22] In other words, feeding practices continued almost to the present day to be a prominent marker between the Russian and Muslim communities.

Swaddling, Crib, and First Clothes

Russians

Swaddling, or the binding of infants from shoulder to toe with strips of cloth to prevent free movement, was another characteristic feature of Russian child rearing that was under assault by Soviet social and medical authorities. So pervasive was swaddling in Russia that a team of Western researchers working on studies of national character in the late 1940s advanced the idea that swaddling, in combination with other reinforcing social and political institutions, could explain virtually the entire spectrum of Russian behavior. Put simply, the argument went that Russian babies were forced to endure long periods of immobility and neglect interrupted by brief bursts of free movement, petting, and feeding. When paralyzed by swaddling, infants were being bombarded by audio stimuli that they could not pull into their field of vision and, according to the swaddling hypothesis, must have experienced a sense of rage against poorly defined and potentially threatening external forces to which they could not react. This rage against a poorly defined object must, in turn, have induced an equally diffuse sense of guilt. It followed, so the argument goes, that persons in power could use the feelings produced by this early conditioning to mobilize Russians against poorly defined enemies or, alternatively, persuade them to confess to crimes they did not commit. The argument also suggests that Eastern Orthodox notions of communal togetherness and mutual responsibility evolved along with and were reinforced by this fundamental common experience of swaddling.[23]

The psychologist Erik Erikson picked up on this idea in his study of Russian personality. While skeptical of the most generous claims made for the swaddling hypothesis, Erikson credited it with pointing to "configurations of experience singularly alive in Russian behavior and imagination." He was thinking in particular of the effect of such preverbal indoctrination "according to which people, for their own good, must be rigidly restrained, while being offered, now and then, ways of discharging compressed emotion." Erikson's analysis was based principally on a movie version of Maxim Gorky's *Childhood,* but he also saw a broader reflection of the behavior associated with swaddling in his reading of Russian literature, which represents its characters as isolated and constrained and yet strangled with emotion that they are able to release only in alcoholic excess or spiritual exaltation. He read parallels to swaddling in the "sanctioned behavior of wooden endurance and apathetic serfdom on the one hand, and on the other, periodic emotional catharsis achieved by effusive soul-baring."[24]

These impressionistic observations about the influence of swaddling were not grounded in empirical research or even in a deep knowledge of Russian history and culture. Developed at the time of high Stalinism, they were obviously shaped by questions Western analysts had about important events in the Soviet politics of that era, such as the terror, purge trials, and dawning cold war. It also needs to be kept in mind that swaddling was practiced by many other peoples of Eurasia and the Americas who are not regarded by these analysts as sharing the same personality traits as Russians are thought to exhibit (although Geoffrey Gorer attempted to dismiss this apparent contradiction by emphasizing the peculiar nature and length of Russian swaddling). Those who like to investigate the influence of early child rearing on adult political and social attitudes might nevertheless find some scope for such speculations in comparative studies. It is interesting to observe that swaddling was a prominent feature of Anglo-American child rearing in the seventeenth century and then receded in the eighteenth century as democratic values rose.[25] The Russian efforts to construct democratic institutions in the 1990s were also preceded by a retreat in the practice of swaddling. Swaddling does not fit in the cluster of modern, liberal values—indeed, is directly rejected as unnatural and unhealthy—and its retreat can be seen as a victory for that set of ideas and for a new way of thinking about what children are.

Doctors in Russia had expressed opposition to swaddling since at least 1766 when Ivan Betskoi published a child-care manual for the imperial foundling homes and imported the most progressive ideas of west European medical authorities.[26] This book was intended for wider distribution than the foundling homes. Although its influence evidently did not extend very far at the time, it did set the tone of Russian medical advice into the future. Nineteenth-century child-rearing manuals as well as Soviet child-care guides and medical authorities followed the same enlightenment model, appropriately updated, and counseled women to wrap babies in a loose-fitting configuration. They also urged abandonment of the hanging crib because of its dangerous height, covering of heavy cloths, stifling heat, and constant swinging. They wanted it replaced by a stable, low bed in which the baby was free to exercise and develop its motor

Hanging crib

skills. Despite two hundred years of medical opinion and decades of Soviet propagandizing of these methods in connection with prenatal and pediatric care, swaddling continued in the villages of Russia until very recently. Indeed, it can be observed to this day not just in Russian villages but in the cities as well. However, a trend away from the old style of very rigid binding did get established during the period covered by our study.

The retreat of full-body and prolonged swaddling was timed a bit differently in the various interview sites. The villages within the penumbra of Moscow began the change earlier than the others. The first generation in Moscow province still adhered to the practice. Virtually all the women of this cohort swaddled their babies in the traditional way. Aunt Valia, from a village just west of the city, swaddled her many children with both large and small bands for up to seven or eight months.[27] The other women from this region did the same, "tied them up like criminals," one of them said.[28] The reasons they offered for doing so were consistent. Swaddling kept the babies warm, ensured that their legs would grow straight, prevented them from scratching their eyes and face, and kept them calm so that they would sleep better. The women reported that they learned how to swaddle from the older women of their own households and developed skill at it from caring for younger siblings or working in another home as a nanny. The swaddled babies were in most cases deposited in a hanging crib (*liul'ka*), which consisted of a box frame, often with a gunny-sack bottom, suspended from a rafter on a spring and fitted with a looped line used to swing it. Most of the women also covered the crib with a curtain, as they said, "to darken it." A dark crib seemed to be associated in their thinking with a calm setting for the baby's rest, but the curtain also had importance for minimizing external assaults from flies and from the evil eye.[29] The effect of leaving the babies in this condition for most of the day was that the mothers came home from work to find them swimming "in piss and shit," as Antonina Larshina explained. "It was a horrible mess."[30]

It is worth noting here parenthetically that the women's practices and observations evidently caught them in a vicious circle. Their concern about their babies' legs growing straight no doubt rested in part on observations of deformities arising from rickets. Rickets is a disease of vitamin D deficiency caused by a lack of exposure to sunlight. It was most commonly found at sun-poor latitudes (or among peoples in sunny climates who sequestered their women and children indoors or swaddled their babies).[31] Social and climatic conditions in Russia—northern location, swaddling, covering of cribs and keeping children indoors to avoid assaults of cold, flies, and the evil eye—deprived many children of ultraviolet radiation sufficient to synthesize in their skin the needed supplies of vitamin D. The resulting skeletal deformities must have reinforced ideas about the need for swaddling to keep limbs straight, ideas and practices that then perpetuated the problem. The women nevertheless had other strong reasons for swaddling, including the need to leave babies at home while they went to work, as we will see.

The next generation of Moscow province women varied in their behavior. A few continued swaddling just as their mothers had done. But at least half the women recalled wrapping the infants more loosely than had the previous generation, using diapers alone rather than the swaddling bands. Nina Novozhilova stated that in her natal family the children were tightly swaddled. "I remember how they did it. Swaddled us. They would bind us up into a tight roll and 'Good day to you!' Neither hands nor legs could budge. But I didn't swaddle my own. . . . Swaddling was bad for them. It was hot enough anyway, and then to roll them up like that. . . . No, I just folded the diaper around them."[32] She had her three children between 1948 and 1954. Other women diapered in the same way, although for some it presented challenges. Elizaveta Smirnova recalled that her loose form of swaddling did not prevent her baby from freeing his arms and scratching his eyes, and she had to make protective mittens of cheese cloth for him.[33] Another woman who had given up swaddling went back to it for one child (born in 1949) because his legs were weak.[34] So, to judge from this sample, swaddling was beginning to recede in the villages close to Moscow in the immediate postwar period, the time when the women of this second generation were building their families.

In the Smolensk villages, the change came a few years later. Not only the women of the oldest generation but most in the next also swaddled their children. Several claimed to have swaddled for a shorter span of time than their mothers had. Even so, most remembered having swaddled for from six months to a year. After the first few months, however, they tied the infants up really tight from shoulder to toe only at night. Just one of the older women had changed the pattern significantly, Efrosinia Ruleva, who was born in 1915 and was building her family between 1939 and 1955. "We bound them up like prisoners for the first six weeks," she reported. "They said you had to do that so that their legs would be straight, but that seems like nonsense to me. When you change the swaddling, you let the baby move about, lie there unbound. After six weeks you wrap the legs less tightly and leave the arms free."[35]

More generally, the move away from the customary rigid swaddling first appeared in the 1950s, when the women of these villages began to give birth in medical facilities. Elena Bobkova reported that she swaddled her first several children tightly with linen shirts for five or six months and thereafter only at night. But her last two children were born at the hospital in 1954 and 1956, and there she learned not to tie them up with swaddling bands. "Nowadays people usually don't swaddle. But earlier, after all, need forced us to swaddle children in that way. The mothers went off to work, and it was necessary so that the baby would lie there quietly." She added that mothers also gave their children a morphine solution, made from poppies, to keep them quiet. "This was only when the baby cried a lot. We didn't know it was harmful. This was used especially, of course, in families with many children. I didn't use it much with my own kids."[36] Praskovia Korotchenkova, too, mentioned that many women cooked poppies in milk and fed the drink to their children as a sleep potion. At least this way the mothers, who were too exhausted from work to nurse, could get enough rest to keep their breast milk flowing, she explained. As for swaddling, Praskovia followed her mother's practice of binding the babies tightly in old shirts for about six months. Only in the case of her final child, born in a hospital in 1960, did she make a change. At the hospital, they showed her how to use large diapers and to fold them over the baby without using the constricting bands (or shirt sleeves that often substituted for actual swaddling bands), and she then taught this method to her own daughter. "I think that it is better to diaper without the bands. All my grandchildren grew up without the bands, in creepers. We changed the diapers regularly so that the children did not lie there wet."[37]

The same change—made over the course of three generations—was described by another woman, Anna Varfolomeeva, who had her three children between 1953 and 1958.

> In comparison with how we lived as children with my mother, my own children lived, of course, better. I was a milkmaid, earned a bit of money and kept a cow. Food for the children was better. And the diapers were better. Our

mothers made diapers from old shirts. I remember my little sisters had only two or three diapers that were made from my mother's old clothes. They were forever hanging out to dry and, of course, were never enough. My own children had enough diapers, some made of old clothes, others store bought. And I purchased baby vests and little caps. Earlier they rolled up the babies tightly with their arms pressed to their sides like toy soldiers. Granny Tatiana's [her mother-in-law] and my own children were bound up tight with bands, at night for sure. But my children did not use the bands to diaper their babies. Only at night, for about the first three months, they would anyway bind them tightly and tuck in their arms so that they wouldn't startle themselves awake.[38]

Although Anna and her mother-in-law continued to swaddle tightly into the late 1950s, it was clear that change was coming rapidly. Anna was now buying diapers at the store in addition to using old shirts and rags. She had even entered the consumer economy by purchasing vests and caps for her babies.

The one woman from the younger generation who continued to swaddle her first baby for half a year claimed that she did so in large part because of her poverty. This was Valentina Shapovalova. Though expressed as a problem of poverty, the real issue was social acceptance in an environment being transformed by the introduction of consumer goods. It was no longer respectable to show a baby in old shirts and rags. As Valentina's story illustrates, children were now being displayed loosely diapered and outfitted in store-bought clothes. "My first girl [born 1957] I swaddled for up to six months and longer, basically because I had only tiny diapers made from torn-up old clothes, and it was impossible to buy the clothes required for nursing infants—that is, vests and creepers. Those weren't being sold here and, if they had been, there wasn't anything to buy them with, wasn't any money. But for my second girl [born 1961] I was able to buy some of the special clothing, and earlier on began to unbind first her arms and then her legs. I didn't notice any difference in their development."[39] Hospital birthing no doubt played a role in this case as well as in the others referenced here. Valentina, on the advice of her mother-in-law, had her first baby at home with a babka—and nearly lost it. For her second, a premature birth, she went to the hospital for a lengthy stay, time enough to learn new methods of care. Valentina had secondary school education, and aspired to the new standards of urban-based baby care and display, but an unfortunate domestic situation (she claimed to have suffered continued abuse from a drunkard husband, who was egged on by his mother) and poverty frustrated her hopes of improving her life. The key to her story is the aspiration itself, which reveals that an entirely new view of small children was emerging. The idea that they were highly vulnerable, easily deformed, and chaotic creatures that had to be bound tight and hidden away was being supplanted by a sense that infants possessed a stable form and could be given greater freedom. Furthermore, they could and should be dressed up and shown off to neighbors, provided the parents could afford to array them in appropriate clothes.

If the change in swaddling was occurring in the Smolensk villages in the mid-1950s to the early 1960s, the shift came a few years later in the more tradition-bound Tambov region. The two oldest generations there swaddled babies tightly for six months to a year and kept them in the hanging crib for from one to one and a half years and beyond. Tambov women gave the familiar reasons for swaddling: the need to keep the babies quiet and calm for sleep and to ensure that their legs grew straight. In every case, the women also explained that they did not have actual diapers or swaddling bands but simply used rags and old shirts, the sleeves of the shirts serving as the constricting bands. Sometimes the outer package of the swaddled child was further bound with string or rope. The babies lay most of the day in this condition. When changed, they were sprinkled with mushroom powder, tooth powder, or some other drying agent, and their dirty diapers rinsed or washed and hung out to dry. The babies themselves were bathed twice a week at first and then only once a week.

A few women mentioned that they never left a baby alone in the crib without first tying it to the crib. This safeguard was scarcely foolproof, however. Anna Mikhaleva explained that once when she used a towel to tie her baby daughter (born in 1949) into the crib while she went to fetch water, she returned to find the baby hanging from the crib nearly strangled to death by the towel wrapped around her neck.[40] The hanging crib was the only form of baby bed in use in the villages. Despite the longstanding opposition to this device by medical authorities and their urging that families put infants in stationary, low baskets or beds, every household we surveyed had used the hanging crib until very recently and had no intermediate sleeping arrangement between the crib and adult accommodations. When children were old enough to leave the hanging crib, they went onto the oven shelf with grandmother and the older children or onto hay spread on the floor. Likewise, it was common practice in all the areas not to take small children out of doors in the wintertime, and only occasionally in the good weather, until they were themselves able to get around on their own.

Here, too, as in villages elsewhere, children were clothed in shirts and sometimes long socks for crawling in the house at times of release from swaddling. Gender-coded clothing first appeared at age two or three, when boys were outfitted with pants and girls with loose dresses.[41] Once out of swaddling clothes, neither sex was diapered. The seam in the bottom of the boys' pants was left open and the girls wore nothing under their dresses, so that both sexes could simply do their business without any fuss, whether toilet trained or not. Anna Kosiakova from the Tambov region remembered that in her time girls went all the way to age seven without underpants.[42] This was also the case elsewhere. Elena Tsygankova from a Smolensk village recalled that her older sister had to learn how to wear underpants at the time she was to start school.[43]

Only in the third generation of women in the Tambov villages did change begin to appear. These were women born between 1929 and 1939 who were having children from the late 1950s into the 1970s. The oldest woman of this cohort, Natalia Mikhaleva, said that she swaddled her children tightly in the daytime for only two to three months; after that, only at night. Creepers were not yet available in the late 1950s and early 1960s when her children were born, and she and her neighbors were still sewing all the children's garments.[44] Other women of this generation followed the same pattern, a shift away from the long-term, tight swaddling of the previous cohorts. Actual store-bought diapers began to appear in this period, although to judge from Lia Brykina's story, they were still in short supply. Lia explained that she had just five such diapers and used them only for wiping spittle off her children. Her swaddling and diapering continued to be done with men's old shirts.[45]

By the time the youngest of the women in the third generation, Anna Kasia-kina, was having her children between 1963 and 1973, people were as much concerned about appearances in diapering their children as they had been earlier about the effects on the child's sleep and growth. Anna remarked that "in our time people weren't any longer having a lot of children but were giving more attention to the ones they had. They dressed them better. Diapers were available finally in sufficient number, but we economized all the same. In the daytime we'd dress them in real diapers, but at night, when no one could see, we'd wrap them in a man's old shirt. And as for the diapers, if we had no time, we wouldn't wash them but simply hang them by the oven to dry."

The same concern about appearances pertained to the crib. Anna said that the first two of her four children slept in the hanging crib for a year and managed without injury. Then someone gave her a buggy. At first, she did not see much need for it, because with these first children she had stuck to the old custom of not bringing them outdoors in the winter at all and seldom enough even in the summer. The last two children, in contrast, got taken out in the buggy. Anna added, "We also kept them in the buggy at home until we were able to purchase a baby bed, since it was already embarrassing if other people knew [you used the old hanging crib]."[46] In other words, by the 1970s homemade diaper substitutes and the traditional crib no longer enjoyed social acceptance. Whether one could afford the new manufactured baby-care products or not, one could not afford to let neighbors know that things were still being done in the old way.

Tatars

Early child care in the Tatar village was the same as in Russian villages in most respects. Nearly all of the Tatar mothers swaddled their babies tightly for an extended period. The reasons they gave were the same as those mentioned by the Russians: to keep the babies warm and to prevent scratching and crooked legs. The Tatars seemed especially anxious about the leg straightening of small children, a concern that continued until very recently. One of the youngest Tatar informants, an educated woman who studied at a teachers college for three years, described the method of baking legs straight, a procedure still used in the 1950s and which she applied to her own first child (born in 1955). The women tightly swaddled the baby, then lit the oven and baked bread in it. After the oven cooled a bit, they opened the oven door, placed the swaddled infant on the wooden shovel used to insert and remove bread, and pushed the child's legs into the heat chamber. The mother then shouted into the stovepipe: "I am roasting."[47]

Like the Russians, the Tatars made their own diapers and swaddling bands from old clothes, and they used powder to dry wet baby bottoms (though the Tatar women mentioned cosmetic powder, not the mushroom and tooth powder that the Russians had). The Tatars likewise put their toddlers in pants with an open seam and let them take care of their toilet needs in this way, being fairly relaxed about toilet training. One woman told me that some children were not toilet trained until age seven.[48] Though difficult to credit as strictly accurate, this observation does suggest that considerable delay could occur in this matter.

Despite a relaxed attitude toward toilet training, an expression of pride about their cleanliness is the one characteristic that sharply distinguished Tatar reports on their handling of babies at this stage. This emphasis on cleanliness continues to this day to serve as a powerful ethnic marker for Tatars. Nearly all the women stressed their frequent bathing of their infants, twice daily as a rule. Most informants likewise underlined that they bathed with soap. One woman even linked twice-a-day bathing to the successful development of children. "We washed them twice a day so that they would grow faster," Zatia Bagautdinova announced.[49] These reports indeed contrast with the testimony of Russian mothers, who usually mentioned bathing their children twice a week at first and then once a week. In many cases, the Russians also spoke of using ash as the cleansing agent because of the expense or unavailability of soap.

Supervision, Illness, and Healing

Russians

The supervision of small children was handled until very recently in the age-old ways. The nurseries and kindergartens promised by the revolutionaries and again by leaders in connection with collectivization did not appear in most of our interview sites until long after World War II. Before that, families looked after their small children with whatever resources they could spare for a task that was in most cases far down on their list of priorities; their first concerns had to be scratching out a meager living in the brutal conditions of Russian rural life in this century.

In surveying the interview testimony of Russian women, I focus here on just the Moscow, Smolensk, and Tambov sites.[50] What was interesting about the responses to our questions concerning child care and supervision was the lack of detail the informants offered in regard to their experience as mothers. They often had more to say about how they handled this task when they were supervising their younger siblings or working as nannies in other homes. This should probably not have been surprising: in most cases, mothers were working to support their families and were too busy to be able to care for their children. The task was sometimes left to others, and often to no one in particular or no one at all. Our oldest informants had survived to the 1990s, that is, into the era of smaller families, the advent of child-care facilities, and greater attention to the health and well-being of children. Not surprisingly, they sometimes expressed regret about conditions at the time they were building their own families, conditions that allowed them little time for their children. Yet most of these older women did not consider the lack of attention to children particularly harmful. Except in a few cases of preventable deaths from accidents when mothers were absent, few women expressed any sense of guilt about their mothering. Most of them thought that too much was made of children these days and that the children were being spoiled. In their time, children were thought of as responsible for their own upbringing. Mothers had to see that they were fed and kept warm, but children were otherwise pretty much on their own. Tatiana Kurkova from our Moscow province villages explained:

> In every home there were five or six children. In general, here in the village no one paid much mind . . . or gave the kind of attention to children as they do today. . . . Mother left for work and said, "You need to sweep the floor, put some water there, look after the chicks." That was it. Then she'd come home and feed us a meal and [returning to work] tell us not to leave the house.[51]

Apart from this visit for the midday meal, the parents were at work all day and the children left to their own devices.

Nearly every woman in the Moscow region whom we asked about child care answered in the same terms: "They stayed by themselves," said Olimpiada Bakhmesterova.[52] Vera Belikova, explaining why two of her young children died, pointed out that "the little ones had to stay alone with ones a little bigger. There wasn't any [grandma]. And it was too expensive to hire a nanny."[53] Another woman, speaking of her sibling's death, identified the cause as "lack of supervision."[54] Indeed, nearly all the informants from the first two generations either looked after their own siblings or nannied in another family. Several did both. This was a village's way of child care until the 1960s and 1970s, when nurseries and kindergartens first opened at some of the state and collective farms in the Moscow-province villages we surveyed. The memories that stayed with the women from their experiences as babysitters were mainly about such emotion-charged events as injuries or deaths that occurred to children left in their care. These nannies, scarcely out of early childhood themselves, frequently ran off to play with their friends, rather than be stuck at home with the babies, and accidents naturally happened. They might also recall a punishment for some childish breakage. For example, Lina Buldakova was left at home at age five to watch her younger sister while her parents went mushroom hunting, and she broke the family clock by pushing the hands ahead to hasten her parents' return.[55] Lina's story was intended to underline the tender age at which children were asked to take on adult responsibilities.

The women from the villages in Smolensk province told similar stories. Authorities allowed mothers no time off from work to care for children. The scarcity of working-age men everywhere in the countryside was acute, and in this region, which the war had blighted, the shortage was catastrophic. Every able-bodied woman had to work on the collective farm. Sometimes a relative who was too old to be fit for work would be available to watch the children. If not, siblings supervised the toddlers or the women took the small children to work with them. Inevitably, awful things happened. And the women, because of their role as primary caregivers and the way they thought about the action of disease and accidents, bore much of the blame and associated remorse. Praskovia Korotchenkova recounted her own and her mother's problems and lapses:

> Of course, when I went off to work, it was necessary to leave the children at home alone. But my work place was close enough that I could from time to time run home and check on the children. Mama, I recall, took very good care of us, but, even so, my little sister "gave up the ghost." Our parents rode off to the field, and we kiddies dashed off to play outside and left the door wide open. Little sister in the crib caught a cold from the draft and died. I remember that many women back when it was still private farming would take their nursing infants with them in their cribs and hang up the crib somewhere near the field where they were working. I can't recall if my mother did that, but I didn't any longer. When I went off to work, I put the crib with the baby on the floor so that even if it crawled out of the crib, nothing terrible would happen.[56]

Praskovia's mother had six children and lost two to early death. Praskovia built her family of four children between 1941 and 1960, and they all survived childhood. None of the women of this time and place had any government-sponsored options for baby care. No nurseries or other child-care facilities appeared in this area within the child-rearing years of even our youngest informant, whose last birth occurred in the early 1960s.

In the Tambov villages, conditions described by our oldest informants were very much akin to those reported by Russian country doctors in the period before World War I. Natalia Mikhaleva remembered that "mama left us at home alone, locked the door, and went off to work, and we older ones looked after the younger. I had to sit for my littler brother when I wasn't very big myself either." She was just six years old at the time. Natalia added, recalling some still vivid memories, that "I would swing him in the crib and he would sometimes fall out, or I would go off to play by the brook, and the little fellow would fall out of the crib and cry. When mom came home, she beat me with a switch."[57] In describing the deaths of four of her nine children (born between 1929 and 1951), Marfa Malikova listed "lack of supervision" as one cause, along with diarrhea and diphtheria, and also indicated that this was the cause of death of neighbor children as well.[58] Pelagea Nikulina's remarks confirmed this condition and alluded also to the great change that had intervened since her childbearing years when she lost four of her five children to early death. "I didn't get advice on child care from outsiders," she declared. "I had already learned everything from mama while I was caring for my younger siblings. Of course, there wasn't much by way of care, not like today when people have few children and look after them well. There are even nurseries nowadays, but in my time, you know, we just went off to work and left the children at home alone."[59]

In the Tambov villages, as was true in the others surveyed, the 1930s had actually afforded women more opportunity to stay home with their small children than did the postwar period, as long as the mothers of the 1930s were able and willing to forgo income from collective-farm work. Praskovia Krivolapova recounted that before the war she was not forced to work and could stay home with her four children, who were born between 1934 and 1939. Once the war started, the farm directors no longer allowed such indulgences, and Praskovia had to go to work and leave her children at home alone—with nearly tragic results. One time her daughter was terribly burned; another time all the children nearly died of gas poisoning when she closed the damper before departing for work for fear that, if left open, the children would freeze when the fire died out.[60] Maria Malikova remembered that conditions after the war became more difficult for mothers of young children, even when, as Maria Abramova reported, the collective farm did sometimes hire ten- to twelve-year-old girls during harvest time to baby-sit for mothers who had no other help.[61]

The first appearance of regular child-care facilities in this area was in the mid-1970s, too late for even the youngest of our informants, Anna Kasiakina, who was building her family of four children in the 1960s and early 1970s. The supervision she could provide for her children was little different from that of the previous generations. "It was hard to look after the children," she explained. "I'd go off to work and leave the younger ones in the care of the older, and I didn't know what I would find when I returned. I couldn't always even locate them right away, and in the house itself they had created an ungodly mess. There weren't any nurseries. When I gave birth to the last one [in 1973], it was just then that they started to build a nursery, but they didn't actually get it finished. Now they have finally built one, but there are no longer any children in the village." Then, in reflecting on the conditions at the time her children were small, she repeated a thought we had heard from several other women. "Truth to tell," Anna said, "we didn't provide much care for our children, but they grew up healthy all the same."[62]

It was clear from the interview with Antonina Abramova from the same set of villages that this phrase about the children growing up well anyway, despite a lack of attention, was simply a way that women had learned to talk about this matter and to shield themselves from the memory of their many losses. In responding to a question about how she learned to take care of small children, Antonina related this experience:

> No one really showed me how you should care for a newborn. I was the fourth of my mother's children and at age seven began to look after the little ones. Mama would take the infants to the field with her in the crib, and I would baby-sit them. We didn't have any grannies, and so everything was on the shoulders of the older children. But I wasn't the only one out in the field doing that. In all the families, the children did the same, and I would get to play there with the other girls my age. The babies would fall out of their cribs and crawl around. Again, we would gather them up. If the mothers didn't have time to feed them, we'd just shove a soska filled with bread and sugar into their mouths and no matter. They grew.[63]

They grew, but not for long. This last story was told by a woman whose mother lost six of her eight children! The belief that children could manage with only a minimum of supervision and care was beginning to lose its hold on the women of the youngest cohort, those who were building their families after Stalin's time. Their attitudes reflected a new understanding, a view that even the children who had proved they were tough enough to survive infancy remained vulnerable and in need of attention and guidance. Consider Natalia Mikhaleva, who grew up in the 1930s. Her mother had six surviving children from eight births, and having no one to care for them, she simply locked them in the house when she went off to work; the older children (including Natalia) had to look after the younger ones. Natalia resolved not to do that to her own three children, who were born between 1956 and 1962. She could not herself stay home with the children because only state workers at that time, not collective-farm laborers such as Natalia, received paid maternity leaves. At the end of the 1950s, her collective farm organized a summer nursery, but Natalia refused to send her children there because the staff had dropped her sister-in-law's baby and given him a humpback. She chose instead to take her nursing infants with her to the field and, after weaning them, to rely on the help of her devoted mother-in-law, who looked after Natalia's growing children and also lived in harmony with Natalia for 30 years: "May her kind bones never decay," declared Natalia. About the care of children, Natalia said emphatically, "You should never dump your children somewhere; not only nursing infants but even a five year old should not be left alone."[64]

When it came to illness and healing, the Russian women distinguished three different categories: serious or life-threatening diseases, ills that could usually be cured by home treatment, and conditions induced by the evil eye. Just what the women considered a life-threatening or serious classification shifted over time, as the communities under study became more influenced by the availability of medical help. The oldest women reported that in their youth, hospitals and medical stations were too far away to serve as a resource. When we asked Anastasia Kuzina about her childhood and whether her mother took her to the doctor, she replied: "What? Are you kidding? Where were you going to find doctors in those days? Back then, they had the field, horses, and that was it. There weren't any doctors then. Maybe there'd be someone who had something unfortunate and they would go. But God looked favorably on us [i.e., her own family]." She added that even to this day she did not go to doctors, and then she spit three times over her shoulder to ward off any consequences of making such a statement. "If I don't feel up to snuff, if my heart starts thumping, I just take a dear little aspirin. Or there is that dear little validol. And if validol doesn't help, I take some nitroglycerin."

Even Aunt Valia (born in 1902), who walked eight kilometers to give birth in the regional hospital, thought that it was too far to be carting sick children for most things, although she did take a dying son there once as a last resort.[65] Olimpiada Bakhmesterova (also born in 1902) had the same attitude. "People didn't go to hospitals," she affirmed, "there wasn't any time to go. [The children] recovered at home." She did recall that a doctor once came around to her house to check on her small children sometime in the early to mid-1930s. Someone came to give vaccinations, too, but that was the extent of it. Of the first generation of Moscow province women, those born before World War I, only the women who lived in the large central village of Tsarevo reported having taken children to a medical facility—and then only if they were gravely ill.[66] Mothers of that time in other villages were evidently on their own. Even in the case of the typhus epidemics of the Civil War era, villagers contrived their own methods to save themselves. Antonina Larshina recalled her mother's stories of how the better-off members of their community covered their windows with wet blankets to create a barrier between them and what they mistakenly understood as an airborne infection.[67]

The second cohort of village women of Moscow province, born during and after World War I, were building families in the late 1930s through the early 1950s, the decades when medical facilities were being established in connection with state farms and rural industrial enterprises. These women began to seek out medical assistance for illnesses that they considered serious, such as scarlet fever, pneumonia, and whooping cough, and the set of illnesses treated with home remedies accordingly diminished. The decision to seek medical help still usually involved a trip. Doctors did not normally make house calls. But medical stations were closer than before, and children were fewer and more valued as individuals. Sometime after the war, medical services began to be delivered more frequently to the villages themselves in the form of visiting nurses or doctors. These medical workers appeared from time to time to check up on children, administer vaccinations, and urge better hygiene.[68] Where a midwife was available, as in Zhukovka, she also visited the homes of sick children, took their temperatures, administered medicine, and applied the expected therapies of cupping and pepper plasters.[69]

A large number of illnesses, even in the second- and third-generation families, still were treated with home remedies, especially colds, diarrhea, and measles. Every family had its favorite cures for these and many other more minor ailments. These were the kind that the mothers believed most children easily survived if they were strong and fated to live. Among the most prominent remedies for colds and other respiratory maladies were boiled milk, lard of various sorts (the softest layers of pork and chicken fat were thought to be especially effective), and rest on, or even in, a warm oven.[70] A variety of herbal concoctions were given for stomach conditions. A tea made with Saint-John's-wort and drunk twice a day as a tonic was recommended as a preventative. If diarrhea nevertheless occurred, a tea of dried bilberry and increased doses of Saint-John's-wort could help. Many women valued lime-blossom preparations for general health. They also understood that herbs could be helpful against sore throats if sewn into a bag and worn around the neck. Ashes sewn into such a bag could likewise be effective.[71]

Serious injuries, too, were often treated with herbs. Lina Buldakova recounted how her sister cut her foot open with a sickle when she was harvesting; she was going barefoot, as all the children did in the warm season. Her mother immediately applied yarrow. Lina's daughter, Tatiana Kachalkina, jumped into the conversation to explain, "It stops bleeding; it's an astringent." Then Tatiana continued to list several more plants that were part of their regular pharmacopoeia:

> Plantain and coltsfoot. Those are—what do you call it?—good expectorates. They're good to use for a cough. There's a whole bunch of different kinds of herbs. You can make a cocktail of them. I remember an old woman here, real ancient, she used to collect trefoils . . . down by the bog. . . . Everyone did this; in every home, you'd go in, and there'd be bundles of herbs hanging there.[72]

Lina and her daughter also told about how Lina's brother was cured of a speech impediment by the application of fish fat. But the main antidote was herbs. Indeed, Tatiana Kachalkina remarked, people were back to collecting and preserving herbs again, gathering them from the fields and woods and drying them for use as tonics and medicines. We were not surprised to hear this news in view of the rapid deterioration in the early 1990s of both the value of villagers' pensions and the Russian public health system. Villagers were being thrown back on their own resources and were necessarily reviving trusted folk remedies to provide for their health.[73]

In the Smolensk villages the picture was similar. Virtually no medical services had been available to the oldest generation, apart from smallpox vaccination. One woman mentioned that in cases of serious illness, they would seek out a physician's assistant (*fel'dsher*); otherwise, they relied on their own resources. Women of the second generation, in contrast, usually took their very sick children to a hospital, although they did not always keep them there if a recommended stay interfered with essential farm work. We saw this in the case of Praskovia Korotchenkova, who checked her ailing son out of the hospital to return home and care for her cow.[74] For colds, rashes, measles, and chickenpox, the women had their own cures, including the standard warm milk and fats and steaming on the stove as well as herbal teas, extracts of bark, and other forest products.

Villagers at the Tambov province site began using medical facilities some-what later than women did in the other interview regions. Not only the first generation but also most Tambov women in the second generation avoided medical stations and hospitals. Dr. Vasilii Dobrynin from the local hospital confirmed that it was not until the 1960s, when more of the women had become literate, that they started turning to doctors. This is evident in the testimony of the women themselves. They had their own highly skilled healers and did not see the need to resort to hospitals. Maria Somova told about her mother, a woman renowned throughout the region as a talented midwife and gynecologist. Though completely self-taught, she was valued and consulted by women from far and near.[75] Aleksandra Krivolapova explained that her family did not suffer much from illness, and her mother handled whatever ailments occurred. "We got diarrhea, but probably less than other people because mama paid attention to the food and, the main thing, kept the place clean. Flies there were anyway, but not all that many, and mama hung dark cloths over all the windows so that the flies wouldn't bite." Her mother maintained the children's health, Aleksandra believed, by serving them an herbal tonic each day while forbidding coffee, tea, and alcoholic beverages. "She kept various dried herbs (Saint John's wort, mint, chamomile, and others) in barrels. She'd light the samovar, go right to brewing something for the whole family, and the house always smelled so good." Her mother, she continued, did not go to a hospital until she was ready to breathe her last. "Even my older sister, who lives in Moscow, did not take her children to the polyclinic. She cured them with herbs, both her own children and her grandchildren."[76] Another woman, born in 1929 and building her family as recently as between 1956 and 1962, was equally reluctant to take her children to a clinic or hospital. Comparing her own mothering with her daughter's, she observed that her grandchildren get a lot of attention to their health, whereas in her own day no one had time to devote to such concerns and it was altogether unacceptable to go to the doctor "for trifles."[77]

Measles was one of the most frequently mentioned childhood diseases at all interview sites. Scarcely any of the women considered it a serious illness requiring a doctor's call or a trip to the clinic. Indeed, doctors could do little against this endemic disease, and the fatality rate was low enough that people were not likely to panic.[78] The primary treatment was to cover the face of the sick child (or the windows) with red cloth and to keep the child in a quiet, dark corner of the house. Sensitivity to light, fever, and rash were the main concerns for what was sometimes a lingering but seldom a life-threatening disease. The tight quarters in which people lived also made it virtually impossible to isolate sick children from healthy ones to limit this and other highly contagious diseases. When asked about this problem of isolating a sick child, Antonina Abramova, who had lost siblings to measles and whooping cough, exclaimed, "In those days, they didn't really look after children's health very much. They couldn't even have discussed isolating them. There wasn't any place for that, you know. Everyone was living in the same hut."[79]

The third category of illnesses affecting children was associated with the evil eye. This affliction was taken very seriously. Most often conditions brought on by the evil eye were general restlessness, colic, and the like that could horribly disrupt the household but might not pose an immediate, acute medical crisis. It was nevertheless understood that children could die from these problems if not treated effectively and cured. Nearly all the women we interviewed believed in the evil eye and tried as best they could to avoid its miseries. Many of them had endured the personal experience of suffering the evil eye or, more commonly, witnessed their children suffer from it. The symptoms were varied but usually included prolonged restlessness and especially screaming and arching of the back. The standard procedure for determining whether a child was afflicted with the evil eye, according to an informant from the villages in Moscow province, was to "place a piece of coal in a water glass, pour in clear, fresh well water, and then light three matches over the glass and stick them into the water. If the matches sank, it meant that the child had been given the evil eye." If this happened, she continued, "you have to drink the water. You have to drink it three times, and also pour the water three times through the door handle. Besides that, you need to say the Creed and the Lord's Prayer." She added that people much feared the evil eye and made every effort to avoid showing their babies to outsiders. Outsiders "might praise an infant and thereby 'pollute' it, sometimes quite innocently. It is even possible for a mother herself to inflict the evil eye [on her child]."[80] Despite this reference to the mother, most commonly the evil eye was thought to come from a source outside the home, and the cures therefore involved door handles, door and window frames, and the like associated with entry from outdoors.

Valentina Lopatkina said that a mother could sense when her child had been afflicted, even before the tests to confirm it were done:

> VALENTINA: Something just wasn't right. The child would yell . . . and scream, sleep poorly, and the like. Yes . . . [to treat it] many times I had to wash through the door frame. Through the frame I washed.
> OLGA GLAZUNOVA: With what?
> VALENTINA: Holy water.
> OLGA: Umhum, only get it in church, eh?
> VALENTINA: Yes, right, and it cost a bit.
> DAVID RANSEL: Why did people inflict the evil eye?
> VALENTINA: I don't know. . . . They might even have been taking joy in the child. And affect it in that way. Someone might be praising the baby, saying

things like "What a fine, fine baby. A nice boy or girl." They just praise it
and that's all it takes. They leave, and the child gets sick.

Then Valentina went on to describe how she would take her teapot to the
church, purchase holy water, and pour it through the door handle ring, and
wash the baby with it.[81]

The symptoms, discovery, and cure of conditions brought on by the evil eye
were not entirely consistent in the retelling by our informants, but they ran
along the same lines everywhere. To continue with the Moscow villages, Antonina Ptichnikova learned from her mother that "you have to take fresh well
water, put it in a mug, and place coals in it. If the coals hissed, it means the child
was given the evil eye." Then a prayer was said over the coals and washing done
with the water after it was poured through the door handle.[82]

Women in some of the interview sites described how it was important
not only to specify the illness as the evil eye but also to identify precisely the
source of the affliction. This requirement was repeatedly mentioned by women
in the villages of Tambov province. Maria Abramova explained the treatment
she knew of for a child who had been given the evil eye: "It was necessary first
of all to determine who had done it. You had to fetch fresh water from the well
and light matches one after another, each match standing for a person who was
suspected of having inflicted the evil eye. You would throw the burning matches
into the water one by one, and when one sank to the bottom, it meant that the
person you were thinking of at that moment caused the evil eye." She added
that if matches were not available, needle leaves could be used in the same way.
Once the culprit was known, the child had to be sprayed with the water used
for identification, and this water also was poured under the door.[83] Pelagea
Nikulina and Marfa Malikova from neighboring villages likewise stressed the
importance of ascertaining who had caused the evil eye, for the water used in
figuring out the culprit was a key to the cure.[84]

This need to identify the source of the evil eye and to do so by working with
a list of suspect persons suggest that the illness served as a method of social
exclusion and control. It guarded against an improper distribution of praise
and consequent disruptive envy. Because even inadvertent praise could upset
the apparent balance of good fortune and respect in a community—and thus
engender envy and undermine the basis for cooperation—it had to be discouraged.[85] The affliction could also serve to exclude people who did not conform
to village norms, either because they had engaged in prohibited behavior, remained unmarried, were physically marked in some way, were unable to have
children of their own, or in some other way might be thought to be envious of
their neighbors. Such persons would presumably not be included in any occasion that could give them access to vulnerable women and children, and they
would have to be avoided when outdoors.[86]

We came across a number of cases in the Moscow villages in which adults
had been afflicted with the evil eye. It happened to Anastasia Vakhromeeva

when she was out harvesting rye with the other women of her village. They worked on opposite sides of a row, and a woman working across from Anastasia (a suspicious person in that she was unmarried though well beyond marrying age) said something to Anastasia about difficulty in harvesting and then quickly departed. Almost immediately Anastasia went limp and felt as if she was about to die. At home, her mother-in-law recognized what must have happened, fetched water from the well, coals from the oven, and determined that the woman had given Anastasia the evil eye. A sprinkling with the discovery water and a night's bed rest cured her quickly, and Anastasia returned to work the next day in good health. Something similar happened to Anastasia's daughter, who was then treated with the same cure.[87] Characteristically, these cases involved persons who were not following the normal life course of villagers and therefore represented a danger to the given order.

Spells could also play an important part in curing the effects of the evil eye and other afflictions. Although spells were no longer used as commonly in the villages close to Moscow as they were in the other places we studied, our Moscow informants remembered folk healers who had been active in their villages. Tatiana Kurkova recalled two respected healers in her village of Zhukovka. One was a church elder who evidently combined Christian practices and some powerful magic to effect cures on his fellow villagers; he tried to conceal the pagan aspects of his work so as not to get into trouble. Sometime after, Tatiana continued,

> an Aunt Masha came to us from Riazan. I don't know her last name—Vrikhina or the like, it seems to me. She cast spells. For example, we have a younger brother. He lives hereabouts, three kilometers away. When he was young, a rooster attacked him. He was frightened. Later a dog went after him. Again, he took fright. And then he started to stutter. He was about five years old. He couldn't get a single word out. He'd talk . . . you wouldn't understand a thing. And she did spells. Mama took him to her [Aunt Masha] at four in the morning, and she interpreted some kind of iron . . . and some coals in some kind of water. She said prayers. Then she told the prayer to mama, explained how to wash through the door handle with holy water or whatever, to say prayers, and not to carry the child around . . . and also not to wake him before sunrise. . . . She uttered this a few times and that was it. He got better.[88]

Aunt Masha, Tatiana recounted, likewise cured her sister's sore-ridden and rotting leg. Doctors had given up on it, but Aunt Masha was able to restore it to health with spells. She did the same for Tatiana's son, when Tatiana's mother-in-law gave him the evil eye out of what she later confessed must have been envy.

We asked Tatiana how people could protect themselves, and she explained that if you give birth to a nice-looking baby, you have to be careful to cover the crib and not to show the baby to anyone until it reaches a safe age. "Many people, still today, in the city will not show their babies. They don't uncover [the crib] for about two or possibly even three months." Livestock, she explained, might also have to be protected. They, too, can suffer from the evil eye. For example, Tatiana's sister was very concerned about this happening to her goats, and would not allow Tatiana into her yard for fear that she might inflict the evil eye on the goats. This worry must have been common enough, for we encountered a number of women who claimed to be able to effect cures if cows and goats were afflicted.[89]

In the Smolensk villages, concern about the evil eye persisted. Anna Kirsanova replied to questions about it:

> Yes, there were evil-eye afflictions. Suddenly a baby would start screaming and arching its back. The babka taught us to take fresh water from the well, pour it through the door handle [kliamka]—a lot of people can affect you through a door handle, you see—and you say, "From gray eyes, from black, from blue, . . . " and wash the child all over, arms, legs, face. And right away it will fall asleep. My oldest son often had the evil eye.[90]

Anna's husband was a caring and helpful spouse, and he much feared the possibility that someone might afflict Anna herself when she was pregnant. Not only did he relieve her of heavy work during pregnancy: "He did not let me go out into the street so that no one might pollute me. I only went into our yard."

Ethnographic studies from the pre-Soviet period often mentioned the practice of carrying colicky children affected by the evil eye out to the hen house. Although women from the Moscow villages did not refer to this practice, it was still an important element of cures in the minds of our informants from the Smolensk region. The procession to the hen house, they explained, was associated with a specific childhood affliction referred to as "the howls" [kriksi]. Anna Kirsanova described it for us:

> To stop the howls, we carried him in a procession around the hen house. At midnight you carry the child there, put it down and say: "Rooster-singer, take little Sasha's cries beyond the blue sea, beyond the steep mountains." Say this three times. . . . Something that helps a lot is holy water. You add some clear well water to it. My grandson was recently treated this way for the howls, and they went away.

While Anna did not believe that the evil eye caused the howls, other women thought of the howls and the evil eye as closely related. The symptoms and treatment of both illnesses were much the same. Anna Varfolomeeva was one of those who mentioned the connection to the eye: "It happened that people inflicted the evil eye on children, and the eye caused the howls." The cure for the howls, according to her, was to carry the child to the hen house and declare: "Take away the howls." This worked well, she emphasized. "I actually observed

Children at the holy spring, Inakovka, Tambov province, 1994 (Photo courtesy of Svetlana Inikova)

how my mother did this and cured the smaller children by herself. And against the evil eye she poured water through the door handle three times and washed the baby with it." Anna's mother-in-law, Tatiana Varfolomeeva, reminded her that in these cases it was also necessary to simultaneously say the "Our Father" three times.[91] Younger women had forgotten this Christian aspect of some cures, perhaps a sign of the weakening hold of formal religion, if not magic, on more recent generations of women from the Smolensk villages.

By contrast, the stronger religious orientation of the Tambov villagers was accompanied by greater emphasis in all the generations on sacred elements in the cures for childhood ills thought to be caused by the evil eye. One of the oldest informants, Anna Reutova, who had her children in the 1930s, mentioned that people warned mothers, if they wished to escape the evil eye, to keep their babies covered for forty days and show them to no one. Indeed, as an extra precaution many families washed their babies in water taken from a nearby sacred spring. This spring also played a part in the cure of those who became afflicted. Pelagea Nikulina explained that when children suffered from the evil eye, people gave them water to drink that had been touched by stones from the holy spring. They would collect stones from the spring, "carry them home, and store them there. When necessary, they placed them in water and then washed the ailing children in that water." They also took the children themselves to the sacred spring to be bathed directly in the water; in fact, this practice continues to this day.[92] A few informants mentioned the use of special healers in these cases. One woman even found it necessary to travel to the near-by city of Kirsanov to have the spells done by an expert healer.[93] This respected village healer had migrated to the city, and her clientele apparently was now having to follow her into town for treatment.

The methods for identifying the evil eye in the Tambov villages resembled in most respects what was done elsewhere, but with some additional twists. Pelagea Nikulina told about taking fresh well water and scattering salt on it in the form of a cross, again using a religious element not mentioned at other sites. Marfa Malikova mentioned the importance of using holy water in the cure or, if holy water was not available, of saying prayers to the Holy Mother twelve times over ordinary water and then washing both the baby and the mother with the water. Another religiously inspired variant was offered by Maria Abramova: "It was also good in cases of the evil eye," she advised, "to wash the baby in water that had been used to wash an icon." In the case of the howls, as in the Smolensk villages, people here recommended both taking the child to the hen house and the reading of prayers.[94] In short, religious elements were always included in the practices of the Tambov villagers.

I have been presenting these observations mostly in the past tense. It is nevertheless worth keeping in mind that some of the informants continue to see the evil eye as a danger and to treat cases of it in the customary ways.

Tatars

Tatars had their own means of handling supervision, illness, and healing, which were similar in some respects to the Russian methods but different in others. The village of Tatarskii Kalmaiur was ahead of many others in organizing summer day care to help supervise young children. In the late 1930s the village's collective farmers identified homes on each street as care centers for small children during the times their parents were working in the fields. Two or three women with infant children worked as caregivers (one of them serving as cook), and for this contribution they received payment in farm "work days."[95] Before the organization of this seasonal care, and even afterward at other times of the year, mothers in this village, like the Russian mothers interviewed elsewhere, had to rely on grandmothers, neighbors, or older children to look after the infants and toddlers. The lengthy breast-feeding mandated by the Quran nevertheless obliged Tatar mothers to stay close to their children in the first year or two of life, whether by working close to home or bringing the children with them to work.

Not only these temporary summer child-care operations came relatively early to Tatarskii Kalmaiur. Year-round nursery care was also established there earlier than in most other interview sites, though not until 1958.[96] No doubt the proximity of Tatarskii Kalmaiur to the provincial capital of Simbirsk/Ul'ianovsk and the village's comparative prosperity were important in this early start on developing child-care facilities.

Muslim informants from other areas of the country said that their home villages did not get such facilities until very recently, if they got them at all. To some degree, this tardiness may have been a result of Muslims' resistance to the imposition of Party-inspired institutions, which propagandized Soviet values threatening to the Muslims' way of life. Soviet agitational literature includes references to this type of resistance on the part of Muslim communities. One of our informants from Bashkiria recounted that after the war, the governing council (selsovet) in her village tried to get a child-care facility started to free more of the women for work, but the women boycotted it and took the children with them to work instead.[97]

As regards illness, the oldest Tatar women, like their Russian counterparts, had very little—if any—contact with modern medical services during their youth and at the time they were building their families. At best, the contact amounted to visits from a medical officer who gave smallpox vaccines. The primary cure for all serious illnesses in the 1920s and early 1930s were prayers by the mullah and his wife. Beyond this, the women applied the customary methods of care that they had learned from their mothers and mothers-in-law. Treatments for some of the common illnesses included application of breast milk for eye problems and sniffles, rubs with butter for crying, and "green stone" (alumroot?) for cuts and fevers. Bouts of diarrhea called for strong tea, egg yolk, black bread, and wheat kasha. Lice were attacked with a rub of sour milk on the scalp and a wash in the steam bath. Similar folk remedies had to be used even for very serious illnesses. Khatima Nizamova, a victim of typhus during the terrible epidemic following World War I, remembered being treated with teas of black currants and apple leaves.[98]

Women of the subsequent generations had greater access to medical services, yet, like their Russian counterparts, they distinguished between three types of illness: acute conditions requiring hospital care, ailments treatable at home, and disorders caused by the evil eye. And like Russian mothers, the Muslim women usually prefaced responses to our questions about childhood illnesses with assurances that their children did not get sick often. The children, they asserted, went around in light clothes, barefoot from early spring into the fall, and were consequently hardened against the environmental conditions that might cause illness. Zatia Bagautdinova added that diet contributed importantly to the health of the children. They consumed a hardy menu of pumpkins, turnips, and edible wild grasses that they collected by the river, berries, potatoes, sunflower stalks, and other nutritious and medicinal foods.[99] Again, we see the strong privileging of natural conditions and natural foods as healthful and protective.

When children became ill, mothers took them to doctors for typhus, mumps, pneumonia, and high fevers. Otherwise, they relied on home treatments. These might begin with a gendered ritual slaughter to set a positive tone for healing. Sex roles being highly marked in Muslim life, it is perhaps not surprising that they emerged in the rules for coping with illness. When children first took sick, Nurania Badrieva explained, people advised her "to slaughter a red hen if a girl was ill and a rooster if the sick child was a boy." She continued, "Then, you were to cook kasha from grain or flour, place butter in the middle of it, and pray to Allah."[100] This procedure could precede treatment for measles and even malaria, which mothers until recently did not consider illnesses serious enough to warrant a trip to the hospital (even though at least three children in the immediate families of informants from Tatarskii Kalmaiur died from measles). Like the Russians, Tatars treated measles primarily by darkening the room and placing a red cloth over the sick child's face. Prayers and restorative foods accompanied the treatment. Sometimes skilled healers from outside the family would be brought in as well. They offered herbal remedies and prayers. Familiar ailments like coughs and colds received the usual home remedies of warm milk with sugar. The herb marjoram, apple leaves, and various pumpkin preparations were all much valued by our Muslim informants as cures for common ills. As already mentioned, Tatar women also prided themselves on their cleanliness and high frequency of bathing. This likewise included regular steam bathing of their children as a preventative; steam baths were given at least once a week in winter and twice weekly in the summer. "The steam-bath cabin is a second hospital," declared Nurania Badrieva. "You wash up and sleep soundly."

A frequent problem for newborns was umbilical hernia and related complications, all of which were grouped by villagers under the general heading of *gryz* or *gryzha*. The cure in Tatarskii Kalmaiur included squeezing oil from dried hemp and giving it to the child to drink. Women also made a hemp cake in the shape of a phallus and offered it to both the mother and child.[101] But to cure gryz, more than medicine was required. Prayers and spells were also key elements. Certain women specialized in this aspect of the cure. Khatima Nizamova professed a talent for this work and claimed that the local doctor recognized her gifts and regularly sent patients suffering from gryz to her. Khatima's observations indicated that it was mainly an affliction of boys; she only once saw it in a girl. Her explanation of its action was also coded in a male form. "Something like a thread grows inside the groin," she believed. Her cure involved thrice intoning a certain magical prayer or spell.[102]

I should add that phallic symbols operated not just as curatives but also as important and powerful cleansing agents for Tatar women. After each trip to the toilet or sexual encounter, they washed their genital region with a pitcher called a *kumgan,* whose spout represented a phallus. Fakhiza Suleimanova explained to me that if the kumgan did not have the phallic spout, it could not do its job

Two *kumgan* used by Tatar women for cleansing themselves

of cleansing women and keeping them healthy.[103] Ayse Rorlich, a specialist on Muslim women of the former Soviet Union, told me that in less rustic settings the ritual bath after sex might consist of a full washing from head to toe, or at least a sponge bath.[104] Neither Rorlich nor I could, however, find the phallic symbolism of these Tatars discussed in the literature on them by prerevolutionary or Soviet scholars or determine its relationship, if any, to other cleansing rites such as the ablutions preceding the five daily prayers.

The powers of village healers continued to play a vital part in the recovery process of Russian and Tatar villagers well into the postwar period in many places (indeed the healers continue to be important in some areas to this day). These powers brought recognition to the women who could claim them and allowed the women and the community at large to preserve an alternative, spiritual vision that cut against the purely materialist doctrines of the Soviet state. One of the most interesting Tatar informants was just such a healer. Sharifa Ialisheva was from a Tatar village in Modovia. When I started our interview, I had no idea she was a healer. This fact came out only when I began to question her about the nature of disease. Her understanding was different from what I had encountered in medical ethnographic writings about Russians and other peoples, which usually order folk and modern urban therapies in a hierarchy of resort. People try their own remedies first, and if those fail, they then go to the trouble and expense of seeking help at hospitals and clinics. Sharifa saw the issue more as a division of labor. She had worked for a time in a Leningrad hospital before being ordered home by her father and married off against her will to a widower. She respected hospital medicine but also knew that it was powerless before certain conditions, and she had somehow learned to treat such conditions. The magic she used was powerful enough, in her judgment, that she worried about relating some of the cases she handled, fearing that the mere retelling of these stories might bring harm to me. One of them concerned a woman in her village who once sang all night at a party and the next day found that her legs were too weak to support her. For three days she lay in the hospital, but the doctors could find no effective treatment for her condition and sent her home with the suggestion that she look to her own people for a cure. Sharifa was called in. She blessed some water and rubbed the woman's legs thoroughly with it while whispering spells and prayers, a treatment that quickly restored the woman's strength.[105] The apparent psychosomatic collapse of the woman, possibly a response of embarrassment at her party performance, could indeed only be cured by procedures that spiritually reintegrated and reconciled her with her community.[106]

Tatar women considered the evil eye just as much a danger as did the Russian women. As the women understood the matter, if not treated properly, this affliction could and did lead to the death of small children. The cause, just as in the Russian case, was usually praise of a newborn. Visitors could exclaim, "Oh, what a lovely baby," or Russians might innocently blurt out on seeing a Tatar newborn, "What a beautiful black-eyed child."[107] For this reason, many people believed that it was safest to keep outsiders from viewing babies. One woman recalled that her husband asked her not to show the children in public before age two or three.[108]

Every woman knew the symptoms of the evil eye and measures to ward it off. Symptoms included restlessness, crying, fever, fear, blue on the bridge of the nose, and refusal to take the breast. Prevention started with written prayers (a mother could obtain them from the mullah) that were sewn into the baby's pillow or cap or into a separate triangular pad that could be hung from the baby's crib as an amulet.[109] Another recommended measure was to take a first hair of the child and sew it into an amulet.[110] Placing a bright-colored bow on the baby's cap was also helpful in drawing an outsider's gaze away from the baby's eyes, and thereby minimizing the chance of an inadvertent evil eye.[111] Some women likewise suggested rubbing soot on the child's forehead; should someone happen to praise the child anyway, they recommended spitting several times over your left shoulder.[112] In the women's view, it was well worth taking precautions, not just to avoid unpredictable praise, however innocent, but also because there was a woman in the village well known to have "bad eyes."[113] Here again is a belief that might be used for excluding a particular villager regarded as deviant on some grounds—therefore potentially envious and someone inclined to wish harm on others.

The essential ingredient of any cure for the evil eye was a special prayer read by an older, knowledgeable woman. But women employed a number of other remedies as well. Zubarzhat Rezvanova's mother-in-law washed the door handle and windowpanes and rubbed water on the sick child's cheeks and forehead. The washing of possible entryways of the evil eye to the home was reminiscent of Russian methods for treating the ailment, and may indeed have been borrowed from them. The Muslim women we interviewed put much less stock in such magical washes and more in prayers and, in the case of the Bashkir informants, written prayers that could be attached to the body of the child. The women from Tatarskii Kalmaiur told about another treatment that, as in the case of the Russian cures, required identifying the source of the affliction, the person who caused the evil eye through envy or inadvertent praise. The procedure was to obtain a piece of material from the clothing of the person responsible, for example, tassels from a shawl. The material was then burned and the child fumigated with the smoke. Zeinab Gimatdinova knew of a case in which this method had worked well.[114] Families also supplemented prayer with medicinal treatments. A neighbor advised Zeinab, for example, to dissolve blue vitriol in water and feed it to the child. When Zatia Bagautdinova's daughter (born in 1949) was given the evil eye by a neighbor's thoughtless praise, Zatia's mother-in-law used "golden leaf" (ragwort?) in an effort to cure it. The child's situation was nevertheless serious enough that the family also took the little girl to Simbirsk to seek additional advice and cures.[115]

Although even some of the youngest Muslim women continued to believe in the evil eye and to recommend precautions to avoid it, the use of modern medicine and child-care manuals had become common by the third generation of mothers in Tatarskii Kalmaiur. An important source of information for this younger generation was their neighbor and medically trained midwife Mariam Gimadeeva. She kept a library of child-health manuals and advised women on proper care of themselves and their children. Others drew on basic manuals in the school library, such as the Soviet standard, *Mother and Child*. New knowledge was entering the village, but it did so without entirely displacing the customary understanding of illness and, in particular, the important spiritual dimension of healing.

How mothers supervise and handle their children mirrors their understanding of the nature and needs of children. It also includes a calculation of the mothers' other responsibilities and commitments. The testimony of our informants makes clear that the mothers of the first and, for the most part, the second generations did not regard child rearing as one of their primary tasks. Their principal responsibilities included childbearing, care of the household and its working members, plus farm work on their families' private operations and on the collective or state farms organized in the 1930s. Early child care, such as it was, had to be left to others.

The first two generations of mothers learned about children and caring for them from their grandmothers, mothers, and mothers-in-law, and not from the urban-based medical authorities who sought to inculcate modern, profession-ally directed, scientific ideas of child care and development. The oldest women interviewed for this study had continued to think of small children as their mothers had taught them to, namely, as highly malleable beings in need of physical molding and restraint if they were to turn out normal. Just as the vil-lage midwife had to shape a newborn baby's head into a rounded form and straighten and shape its limbs, children had to be tightly swaddled for several months to ensure that their limbs would grow properly and that they would not injure their eyes or face. In other words, they thought of babies as an unformed mass of impulses that, without rigid restraint, could easily become deformed or impaired. The hanging crib with its high-sided box form and heavy cloth cover was another device for containing the impulses toward deformation and muti-lation.

Small children were also regarded as highly vulnerable to harm introduced from external sources. They had to be bundled and covered up against the cold, as drafts were believed to cause illness and even death. The importance ac-corded to cold as a cause of illness can be seen not only in direct comments about it but also in a principal antidote to disease and disfigurement: an in-creased application of heat, including, in severe cases, the baking of children in a warm oven. The fear of cold was likewise one reason small children were never taken outdoors in the wintertime and seldom enough even in the sum-mer. Another reason for the confinement of children in the home under heavy crib covers was their vulnerability to the evil eye and other afflictions that outsiders might intentionally or unintentionally visit upon them.

The tight swaddling of infants; the use of soskas, chaws, opiates, and rocking to keep them quiet; and their sequestration for hours on end in covered cribs obviously responded to practical needs as well. Since the care of babies was turned over to physically incapacitated older family members or to siblings too young for such a responsibility, the infants had to be packaged in a convenient form. The swaddling roll, in which "we bound them up like prisoners," kept the baby relatively secure with a minimum of supervision and allowed its easy transport to the mother for nursing, if need be.

It is scarcely surprising that the mothers of our first two generations shared their elders' understandings about the fragility of small children. Their mothers and grandmothers had lost from a third to a half and more of their babies. In other words, our informants directly experienced the loss of several of their own siblings, and nearly every informant from the first two generations suffered losses of her own children. A few of them lost a half or more of their children. What is interesting but also not surprising is that the women expressed admi-ration and confidence in the children who had survived the ordeals of early childhood. These children, they believed, had demonstrated an exceptional toughness; they were well formed, inured to the harsh conditions of rural life in Russia, and therefore expected to thrive.

In short, mothers understood their responsibilities, beyond bearing and feeding children, to extend to shaping and confining their babies so that they would grow straight and enjoy some protection against their own chaotic impulses, the cold, and outside sources of harm. But, as Aunt Valia and others suggested, it was up to the children themselves to demonstrate that they were capable of overcoming the rigors of village life into which they were born. If they did so, they were considered exceptionally strong and resistant to the hazards of rural life.

Change in the attitudes and, accordingly, the caring for children first came to the villages in the 1950s and 1960s, when the third generation of informants were building families. By this time the majority of rural women were receiving schooling. When they reached their child-bearing years, they were going for prenatal check-ups and, in that connection, having to accept instruction in new methods of child care. With rare exceptions, the women were limiting their fertility through contraception and abortion. They had smaller families, often only two or three children, nearly all of whom were surviving. Because of their small numbers and expectation of their survival, these children were commanding more of their mothers' attention and emotional investment. By the 1970s and 1980s the developing Soviet welfare state and budding consumer culture had reached the villages, and mothers enjoyed maternity leaves that allowed them to spend more time with their babies and form powerful attachments. Welfare guarantees, maternal images projected through the popular culture, and the growing consumer ethic allowed rural women to adopt an entirely different attitude toward their children. Mothers were becoming as anxious about the clothing and presentation of their small children as they had been previously about their confinement and survival. Rural children were becoming, as children in the towns earlier had, objects of psychic satisfaction for their mothers. In the past, children had been more like "producer goods," a sufficient number of which had to be created and brought to maturity in order to continue the family's farming production and provide support for aging parents. Now they represented not a production investment but an emotional investment.

This shift can be discerned in the life of Marfa Malikova's family. Marfa was born in 1910 and gave birth to nine children between 1929 and 1951. Five of her children died in early childhood. She remembered that the working members of the household were the primary concern and that her grandmother had even advised her to eat the "best pieces of food herself and not leave them for the children, who would manage on their own." Marfa took the birth and death of children in stride and was not apparently deeply attached to any of her children. Indeed, she was unable immediately to recall all of them. Her daughter Natalia, who lived with her, remarked that when she moved away to Central Asia at age 17, her mother was not especially concerned about her departure. This interview was being conducted by my collaborator, Tatiana Listova, and she jotted down that "it was not the case that [Marfa] did not love her children but that she had accustomed herself beforehand to the notion that anything could happen to them and it was necessary even so to go on with one's life." By contrast, the emotional connection of Marfa's daughter to her children was entirely different. Natalia was born after World War II and reared her two sons in Central Asia in a time of relative Soviet prosperity. Listova observed that "her whole life was invested in them just as in the typical modern family." One son had recently completed military service, the other was just beginning his, and Natalia "literally lived from one letter to the next from her sons."[116]

Conclusion: Life and Loyalty in Hard Times

Although each woman's life was different and each experienced individual joys and sorrows, the members of a particular generation, religion, or locale inevitably shared certain experiences as a group. The great upheavals of the twentieth century—the World Wars, Civil War, collectivization, terror—touched the women of each generation at a particular time in their life cycle, shaping their perceptions and limiting or expanding their choices in some common ways. Confessional differences likewise played a part. Some of the variation in the practices of Russians and Tatars recorded by ethnographers and doctors of the nineteenth century persisted into the mid-twentieth century, even if these differences changed with the changing generations—and in some respects narrowed under the influence of common Soviet educational and institutional policies. This concluding chapter discusses the women by generation and religion, as they considered their lives and choices from the perspective of the early 1990s.

First Generation

The women of the first generation grew up and came into consciousness at the time of World War I and the Revolution and Civil War of 1917–1920. They began working at home from age seven or younger, assisting their mothers in the barnyard and garden and looking after their younger siblings. Their paid working lives began in their early to mid-teens, when they took jobs as nannies or farm workers in the 1920s. They lived on family farms, including, in some cases, the large joint families of co-resident married brothers and their children under the overall authority of a patriarchal father. This was the time when fathers still ruled their families and controlled family-based farming operations, whether they were part of a communally managed land system or a separate, privately owned farmstead. The girls of this first generation had little if any formal schooling, but the Russians and even more so the Tatars were thoroughly tutored in the religious norms of their communities. They were taught to fear God, obey their parents unquestioningly, and remain chaste until marriage. They also learned the necessity and value of hard work through the example of their parents and the demands their parents placed on the girls themselves. The paid employment of their teenage years gave them the opportunity to contribute financially to their families and to build a trousseau for their later marriage. It also provided an introduction to a different way of life in the case of the girls who worked for families in towns.

A few of the women lived in families of adequate means, but most were not well off and, indeed, by any standard would be considered poor. The Tatar woman from Mordovia, Zukhra Pozdniakova, recalled a childhood without white bread. She claimed that when she first saw it during the Civil War at the beginning of the 1920s, she rejected it, not knowing what to make of it. "The city wasn't far away. One day, father brought me a white roll. Up to that time, we had been baking only potato pancakes. When my father gave me the white roll, I threw it aside and asked for the usual [potato pancakes]." Her diet consisted largely of potatoes supplemented by carrots, radishes, and cabbage, plus apples and cherries when available.[1] Another measure of the poverty in which some of the informants had grown up can be seen in the lively retelling by Ekaterina Gerasimova of a discovery she made in her teenage years when she went to work as a nanny. She was delighted to find that her employer had a butter churn and was able to cook pirogi in butter. "This was truly the good life," she declared.[2]

In choosing mates, the young women of this first generation enjoyed greater freedom than has been reported for peasant women of the mid-nineteenth century. The abolition of serfdom, reduction of household size, and increased contact with the city had by the early twentieth century expanded a young woman's opportunities to exercise choice in this matter. In most cases, the women of our first generation found their mates either at work or by attending parties, dances, and other sites of youth socializing. Even so, their dependence on and ultimate loyalty to their natal families meant that if their fathers insisted, they would have had to allow themselves to be married off at his command, as indeed happened to some of the women, both Russian and Tatar, who we interviewed from this generation.[3]

At the time the women of this generation were getting married and starting families, their lives were shaken by the upheaval of collectivization. Even though we did not ask questions specifically about this event, one-third of the informants in this generation volunteered stories about how their families had been "dekulakized" and their fathers exiled or killed. These women remembered this loss with bitterness. For those who had married before the change and settled into the life of private farming, collectivization disrupted and in some cases tore apart their families and ruined their lives. Women slightly younger who had not yet married explained how collectivization and the subsequent famine wrecked their chances of assembling an attractive trousseau and of getting properly established in life.

Yet the attitude of women in this generation toward collectivization was far from uniform. Those who had very little to lose or who felt isolated in a patriarchal household found that the collective farm offered an opportunity to get out from under the exclusive power of the household head and to work in groups together with women of the same age from other households. Although most women conceded that the earlier farm families had provided more support for women in their mothering role, some believed that the work of the collective farm was easier than under private farming. Tatiana Varfolomeeva encapsulated much of this feeling in speaking of life in her village in the years after she married in 1928: "We lived in private farming. Here, in Nikitino, the collective farm was established late because the people did not want to join under any circumstances, and they just stuck to their own farming until the authorities finally drove us into it by a combination of taxes and threats. The young people then got together and decided to create a collective farm. Then, after a time when things settled down, it wasn't bad living on the collective farm. We got along working together, and our farm administration was good."[4]

It is important in evaluating such statements to keep in mind that in the memory of the informants, events in the long history of collectivization sometimes became collapsed. And, of course, they were likewise inflected by the concern over the deteriorating conditions of post-Soviet life at the time most of the interviews were conducted. Tatiana Varfolomeeva's comment, just cited, was particularly clear (probably the more so because it was recorded as a field note and not in a tape-recorded conversation) in separating the disruptive onset of collectivization and the subsequent period of normalization. The testimony of Vera Belikova, which I recorded directly on tape, captured the same ideas in a set of signs that reveals some of the confusion of events and policies. She urged on me the task of telling the story of the suffering that Stalin had inflicted on her people. "Under Stalin we had nothing, no chickens, no eggs. There's an assignment for you. There wasn't any milk, the cow got sick from something, I sold her, and no milk! There, you see what we had to endure." Lenin was her man. He "reestablished life for everyone," she stressed, whereas the tsar took men into the army, maimed them, and sent them home without a pension, as happened to her father, who died young as a result of his wounds from World War I. In Vera's opinion, "the tsar was accursed," Lenin a good man, and Stalin a destroyer. This formula repeats a general evaluation we know from the post–World War II Harvard study of refugees from the Soviet Union that peasants thought of the 1920s as the best time of their lives, the time when they were the freest and most prosperous. But Vera also spoke of her collective farm with pride, noting that it usually produced a good supply of vegetables so that she could keep her children healthy and that new families had joined the collective to share in its prosperity.[5] In these jumbled recollections we can see Vera's effort to distinguish between the brutality of the initial collectivization blamed on Stalin, a later period of improved food supply in the late 1930s and from the 1950s onward, and an implied criticism of the new conditions of the 1990s.

Whatever the stance toward collectivization, what most strongly characterized the women of this first generation was their adherence to religious norms and devotion to hard work, family, and pre-collectivization community values of mutual support and charity. These were women who in most cases married as virgins and rejected abortion as sinful and odious. Several spoke proudly of their natal families' faithfulness to the obligations of villagers to their neighbors and passing strangers. They praised their mothers for taking in pilgrims, feeding and lodging them, caring for neighbors in illness and pregnancy—in short, meeting their traditional community responsibilities.[6] They understood their primary obligations as the care of their families, and accepted these responsibilities even when they were exceptionally onerous. Ekaterina Gerasimova, who had to bring up her three children on her own when her husband died in the war, also took on the support of the three children and an infirm old woman whom her sister left when she died in 1942. "The old woman was not from our family, but I fed them all. . . . She died [after a short time] and everything was entirely on my shoulders. . . . I brought them all up, all three . . . , plus my own three."[7] Similarly, Sharifa Ialisheva, Lina Buldakova, and Anastasia Vakhromeeva recounted how they stuck to their duties in those hard times. Sharifa had found satisfying work in the city, but at her father's insistence had to give it up and return home to marry a village widower and bring up his children; in addition, she gave birth to and reared several of her own children. She felt she had no choice but to obey her father. Lina Buldakova, too, accepted her father's decision that she be married off to someone she did not know in order to quiet rumors harmful to her family. As for Anastasia, some years after losing her first husband and one of her two children in the early 1930s, she married a widower with four children of his own and had to bring up all five children by herself when this second husband died in the war. She took comfort in the praise of one of her stepchildren, who told her: "Mom, you're not a bad woman anyway. During the war we were little and left without our father, and you didn't abandon us, didn't walk away."[8]

The contributions that these women regarded as most important involved this loyalty to family, including respect for their elders and constancy in caring for their children and doing their work. Anastasia Shishanova sighed that her family was forced onto the collective farm and made to work without pay, and then the war came along and killed the men, so that the women were left alone with the children and nothing to eat. It was a terrible life. But she did her duty: she worked constantly to support and bring up her children, whom she hardly got to see for the amount of work she had to do. Still, most important, "I gave birth to them, baptized them, and did everything in proper order." Marfa Malikova strove to be no worse than others, to lead a proper life by the standards of her community.

> I lived like the others here. I feared God, worked hard for the children, and respected my elders. My husband thought that however many children came, that's how many we would have. We would, he said, bring up all of them [*vsekh spokoim*]. But times were so harsh. There was collectivization, then war, and as a result we lost many [children]. My husband and I were saddened by this—such a good, wise husband and yet he had a bad life.

And she continued, "It was hard then for everyone to rear children. After all, there were no nurseries or kindergartens. It was just good if someone had a grandma. And the older kids looked after the younger."[9]

Comments by her neighbor, Maria Malikova, reflected two attitudes common to women of this generation: an acceptance of their difficult lot and at the same time pride in what they were able to accomplish against long odds. "My life has been sorrowful. Not only has it been hard, but I also suffered many abuses. A dream told me that it would be this way, that my life would be filled with sorrow but that it was necessary always to submit to the will of our Holy Mother. St. Nicholas told me this in a dream, and I was able to converse with him in this way. When things got really terrible, I would say, 'Well, whatever God brings, that's how it will have to be,' and then things got to feeling better. But however harsh the times were, anyway I brought up all my children and got them an education. Two of them live in Moscow, and now they bring the grandchildren to me, and I teach them their prayers and how to behave properly."[10]

In short, the women of the first generation presented themselves as sustained by religious belief and an abiding loyalty to family and the idea of work and home as the proper spheres for a peasant woman. They had had to mediate between these values and the changing demands of the time, including especially the move to collectivized farming. This change had stripped their families of independent means of production, weakening the power of the household head and forcing the women to take on greater individual responsibilities. In some cases it took away their men altogether and left the women to care for their families on their own. Even so, they continued to identify with the ideas and values of their youth. Their comments expressed an ethics of duty. Like their birthing and child care practices, their ethics were grounded in an earlier time, in the pre-Soviet collectivist values of the village order of the nineteenth century.

Second Generation

The women of the second generation came to maturity in the new world of collectivized agriculture and the beginnings of Soviet education and indoctrination. Unlike their predecessors, who entered adulthood before the upheavals of the 1930s and brought to this difficult time a set of loyalties and established rules of morality, the values and allegiances of the women of the second generation were less fixed. The radical shifts in government policy, terror, and personal loss left many of them without much faith in anyone or anything. These women were getting married and starting families from the late 1930s through and until just after the war years. They were therefore expected to do the work of the men of their generation who had been eliminated as kulaks or taken away to fight and die in the wars—starting in the mid-1930s against Japan and continuing through World War II. At the same time, the government deprived women of the right to control their fertility and exhorted them to produce a bounty of children for the state. Though they were promised prenatal care, maternity homes, maternity leave, pediatric services, and child-care facilities, these boons did not arrive in most villages until well after World War II, and in many places not until the 1960s and 1970s.

The women of this second generation lived through a period of profound change in moral and social values. The power of patriarchal family heads had decayed and been replaced by the less personal forces of Party leader and collective farm chairman. Religious values were likewise under challenge from Soviet propaganda and schooling that encouraged young people to believe in their ability to transform their lives. The women responded to these messages. They were determined not to live as their mothers and grandmothers had: that is, in subordination to a household head, continuously pregnant through their childbearing years, and producing a dozen or more children, many of whom would die in early childhood. When the government robbed them of the legal right to control their fertility, they defied the law and obtained underground abortions. This choice inflicted a high cost both physically and emotionally. Many women died from botched abortions. The survivors suffered physical pain from the unregulated procedures. They also witnessed the deaths of friends and neighbors and imprisonments of the women who provided the services. Finally, they had to deal with the moral sting of abortion because they were not entirely free of the religious scruples of earlier generations about this choice.

Not surprisingly, this generation, which was asked to make enormous sacrifices with no reciprocity from the government or society, was also an angry generation. Most of them regarded their lives as not only hard but as unfair and unfulfilled. Their predecessors, the women of the first generation, also saw their lives as hard and the times as difficult, but they had a set of standards against which they could measure their sacrifices and draw meaning from them. They understood the value of their lives to lie in service to their families and their neighbors, respect for their elders, and faithfulness to the moral codes of their youth. The goals of the second generation were more personal and their ethics more utilitarian than duty-bound. They wanted a better life for themselves and their children, but work demands on the collective farms were punishing and poorly remunerated. The women had little time left over for their children and no means of fulfilling their aspirations for a better life. Nearly every woman in this cohort complained about the toll that work took on them and their children—and about the failure to receive anything in return for their efforts. Zinaida Shumkova said, "I lived like a slave. They [the family she married into] were doing things, and I was at their beck and call. And I didn't see my own children. They reared them. My lot was to work. In the winter, I worked in the stables, in the summer in the fields. I didn't see [my children]." She went on to explain how her children, too, were exploited by her father-in-law, who crippled her son by forcing him to do work beyond his strength. Nina Novozhilova told a similar tale of constant work and separation from her children: "We got up at half past three in the morning and worked through until half past eleven at night. Sometimes even longer. That's how it was earlier. We had to tend to the livestock. And what kind of pay did I get? A pittance. . . . There was a whole stable to look after. . . . And I also worked in the factory. . . . We worked and that was that. Not like they work today." Or take Antonina Larshina who, when she heard that I was writing about the life of mothers, described the trials of work and motherhood and then declared: "It wasn't any kind of a life. It was penal servitude. . . . That's what you have to write down. That's what it was; tell it in that spirit."

The women of the second generation were inclined to be bitter about the lack of respect and appreciation for their sacrifices. They observed that their children and grandchildren enjoyed easier lives, at least until the recent collapse of the economy after perestroika and the fall of the Soviet Union. They spoke of how the younger generation received shorter hours of work, privileges, and the benefits of state-supported medical, welfare, and transportation services. Most women, of course, did not begrudge their own offspring these boons. Indeed, they derived some consolation from the fact that their children had the time to visit them and to help them in small ways. Yet the women were critical of young people in general for what they regarded as their easy lives and especially the loose morals of the young women. It was shocking that they could see on television or read in magazines information about things these older women had not learned until they were married.[11]

Even more galling were the economic issues. The women of this second generation had suffered much and had to sacrifice their own aspirations for a better life. Finally, when they entered late middle-age in the 1970s and 1980s, conditions began to improve. It was too late for these improvements to change their lives significantly, but they at least promised some security in old age. Then, suddenly, this comfort was also denied them by the reform and fall of the Soviet Union. Anna Varfolomeeva (born in 1928) captured much of the experience of this generation in her testimony. She praised her mother for bringing the family through the war after the death of Anna's father at the front, and Anna extended this praise to others of that time. "In general, people earlier were better. If they had been the way people are now, they wouldn't have survived." Reflecting on the life of her mother, who had given birth to nine children and lost two in early childhood, Anna conceded that "of course, it wasn't as hard for me as for mama. In the stores you could buy everything, and I had only three children so that it was easier for me." At another point she observed that "our parents had really hard lives, and I, too, was somehow constantly plagued by something. It's true that in recent years [1970s and 1980s] things got a bit better. But now, again, we are not able to live but just to survive. And this is the legacy that's being given to my children. My middle son has four children, and his wife can't find work. It's difficult, of course. . . . Again, the young people don't have enough to survive on, and in the stores everything has vanished so that they have lost interest in having children."[12] Others said much the same. "Life was really hard back then," Nina Novozhilova sighed. "And now again it is barely possible to live; here I am facing old age, and again there's nothing much good. Thank God that my children are decent. They don't treat me badly and even bring me some things."[13]

The most striking characteristic of women of this generation is their lack of attachment to any institutions large or small. While some harbored nostalgia for the Brezhnev years when conditions briefly improved, the time before that was remembered as one of continuous suffering, enforced labor, separation from their children, and destruction of their families. And they rightly understood the new world of perestroika and capitalism to be a return to difficult economic conditions and a threat to their security in old age.

Only a few women, those who ended up reasonably well, were able to look back on their lives with any sense of satisfaction. Anna Kirsanova was one of the lucky ones. Though orphaned and illiterate in youth, she married a good man who helped her in her own tasks and even did baby-sitting so that she could go to dances. Their children turned out well and got educated. At the time of the interview, Anna lived on her son's sizable farm and was visited by children and grandchildren from the city. She could feel that despite the terrible times in which she lived, she had done all that was in her power to do and had fulfilled the most important duties in life, namely, to work hard and bring up her children.[14] Praskovia Korotchenkova, like others of this generation, had suffered many blows, including losing her father to "dekulakization," four difficult births, abortions, dire poverty, and the betrayals of her second husband. But she was able to accept calmly the things she did not have the power to change, and derived satisfaction from her adherence to the traditional expectations that a peasant woman should work hard and care for her family. Despite her tribulations, the interviewer explained, "she persevered, reared her children, and inculcated in them industry and respect for the family."

But most women of this second generation remained bitter. They had broken from the old ways of their mothers and grandmothers and expected to forge new, more comfortable, and individually fulfilling lives for themselves and their children. Their hopes were continually frustrated, first by a government policy denying them control of their fertility and then by war and reconstruction, which left them to rear their children alone under a harsh labor discipline and few, if any, government services. Their sacrifices and sufferings went unacknowledged and uncompensated. It is hardly surprising that they felt little allegiance to anything, whether Party, government, workplace, or local community. Except for personal ties to their children and neighbor women of their own age, many of them spoke of themselves as people cut loose from the surrounding world, forgotten and abandoned. They felt victimized by a cruel age that had not allowed them to form wider social bonds or develop a sense of believing in and belonging to something greater than their personal struggles for survival. The slogans and purposes of the government rang hollow for them.

Antonina Larshina, a member of this generation, told a story that could serve as a parable for her age mates. She grew up under the influence of her mother's traditional religious devotion. A corner of the house was filled from top to bottom with icons. But then Antonina's father joined the Communist Party in the 1930s, became "an inveterate communist," and decided he was going to remove all the icons. Antonina's mother protested furiously. "She nearly got into blows with him. But no matter; he cleaned out all of the icons anyway, and to this day we don't know what he did with them." Her father later died in the war, and the family was never able to restore the symbols of their mother's faith. Antonina was to all appearances not especially interested in religion. Like other women of her age, she still insisted on the importance of baptism, but religion did not seem to be an important part of her life. She also acknowledged some contributions made by the Communist regime. Recalling the famines and poverty into which she was born, she said: "How could we be developed people? Still and all, Soviet power brought us along a little bit. We at least started to know some geography. Where before we didn't know what was north and what was south."[15] In short, Antonina felt some nostalgia for the religious symbols of her youth and her mother's devotion to them. She also recognized some contributions of the Communist regime embraced by her father. But she registered no allegiance to either set of beliefs.

Anna Zueva, the medic from Novgorod province and a woman about the same age as Antonina Larshina, expressed the same cynicism about the belief systems of her time. Her family was religious and mingled in its faith many of the Christian and pre-Christian figures common to Russian popular belief. The following story she related contains elements of the basic conversion tale told by many initiates in the Communist Party and by village correspondents.[16] Anna undoubtedly borrowed from such formulations while also revealing why she saw herself as emancipated from all belief systems. "In the 1930s," she said, "I was uneducated. Until age ten, I was brought up to believe in devils, unclean powers, witches, and such. Well, there were soothsayers and, it goes without saying, they could do anything. All kinds of old women. Old women could do whatever: inflict the evil eye, carry away livestock, and destroy the harvest. And, they'd say, they would fly around on brooms in the night, fly down the chimney, and harm your neighbor. . . . But then at some point I began to think through these things, and came to the conclusion that it was all made up. So, since then I have lived my whole life believing in nothing." Anna told another story from about the same time of how the communist school system helped free her from religious ideas and how she used a student newspaper to mount a small rebellion. "Our mama prayed to God, and we all had get down on our knees every night before bed and say our prayers. This was before the 1930s. Well, it was also required that once a year we went to confession. So, we had to miss school for two days. In Gorodno there was a church, and we'd go there to say confession. We stayed overnight with an aunt, and on the next day we would take communion and then go home cleansed. One time I did this, I guess it was when I was in the fourth grade; mama sent me. When I got back, I got a 'D' on my exam. So, I wrote a comment on this for the wall newspaper and then they released it. I wrote it all down how I went [to the church]. And the title they placed on the article was 'God Is No Help.' They hung out the newspaper before the school parents' assembly, read it, and said, 'Now, you're going to catch it, when your mom comes to the meeting and reads this comment.'" I asked some questions about how this all was done, but Anna got me back to the main point. "The fact was that I got a 'D' on the arithmetic exam, and out of resentment I wrote this comment about how God is no help. . . . Already at that time I had started to protest in my soul. I was about ten years old at the time, probably only about ten, and I came to the conclusion that God was no help, and what you had to do was use your own head."[17] Anna Zueva's sense of identity and purpose came as much as anything from her service as a medic with the partisans behind German lines in World War II and her subsequent career as a medical officer in her village. She had been married to the collective farm chairman and expressed some appreciation for the positive achievements of the Stalin regime, more than most people were willing to admit at the time I was conducting the interview. This was not surprising, since the technical schools promoted by that regime provided the education for Anna. She was the first person in her family to get more than village schooling, and was able to achieve professional status in one generation. Her daughter made it to the next step up by becoming a doctor in a nearby city. Even so, Anna was not a spokesperson for the Communist system; she acknowledged its costs and kept her own counsel and view of the world. To the extent it was systematic, this view was consonant, it is true, with the secular, scientific view advanced by Marxism. But Anna, as she often emphasized, was not a believer in any systems.

The women of this generation had to mediate between the strict norms of their parents' generation and their own schooling that rejected much of what their parents believed. They also accepted ideas of the new regime about transforming their lives and acted on them in defiance of that same regime's pronatalist policies. So, while their identities were shaped in part by their uncompensated sacrifices and their rejection of both the old and the new, it cannot be said that they portrayed themselves solely as victims. Some women derived satisfaction from their ability to negotiate the demands of both the old world and the new, to form their own counsel and independently make the agonizing and perilous decisions that allowed them a measure of control over their lives. Although they did not describe their defiance of the law as political, their actions had political effect. The women forced repeal of the law against abortion and an increase in social benefits for rural women. In this sense, these women who felt alienated and abandoned by government were actually more engaged with it than were their predecessors. They were engaged in a struggle to assert their individual needs against preferences defined by the state.

Third Generation

Women of the third generation were born in the 1930s and afterward and did not start building their families until after the death of Stalin. By this time, conditions in the countryside had begun to improve, girls were receiving full elementary education, and some government services were reaching the village. The ban on abortion was lifted in 1955. Provided there was a hospital within reach, village women of the third generation had the opportunity to restrict their fertility safely through hospital abortions, and they felt more comfortable emotionally and morally about this option than had their predecessors. Maternity benefits accorded state workers were extended in the mid-1960s to collective-farm women. Work discipline on the collective farms and in rural factories was also becoming less punishing. These improvements gave mothers the option of spending more time with their children. The government was at last acknowledging the contributions that farm women made and providing some reciprocity in terms of benefits. The women of the third generation had become in some measure "sovietized," that is included in the social contract that offered workers social assistance and security in return for acceptance of the system.

Valentina Lopatkina from the Moscow province village of Tsarevo gave birth to twins, Lena and Sergei, in 1958 in a hospital in the town of Pushkino. She had to manage them on her own. Her mother-in-law was not able to help, her husband worked jobs far from home, and hiring a nanny for twins would have cost Valentina's entire paycheck. Valentina's problem was that Lena was colicky for several months, screaming and upsetting the in-laws, until Valentina in utter exhaustion was driven to the brink of madness. "I didn't know what I was going to do, didn't know," she told me. "I didn't know what I could do [to stop the screaming]. Should I smother them both or smother just the one? Or should I just go hang myself instead? Oi! Oi! I grabbed [Lena] so hard . . . I took her and I threw her. And she knows about this. How many times I've told her. 'Lenka, I nearly smothered you to death.' I was utterly exhausted. I threw her down so hard. I pressed a pillow onto her and was thinking, 'Well, go ahead and choke to death.' Because I had had it." But Valentina stopped herself in time and decided to leave Lena with a neighbor while she traveled with Sergei to her husband. She recounted how she carried Sergei through a snowstorm many miles to where her husband was working. The workers thought that she had lost her mind, but they took pity; the work council released her husband and allowed him thereafter to work close to home where he could help with the children when needed. Valentina was able to stay at home with the children for three and

a half years until they were old enough to be placed in a weeklong kindergarten at a state farm far from her village.[18] Her story makes clear that personal
needs were at last being given consideration by the authorities and that some
child-care services—if not yet nurseries for the very young and if not yet close
to home—were beginning by the early 1960s to make an appearance in the
countryside.

Antonina Abramova from the Tambov villages was the same age as Valentina.
Antonina had her first child in 1957; she was widowed, remarried, and then
gave birth a second time in 1970. Both children were born in medical facilities,
the first in a village maternity home, the second in a city hospital. She received
two-and-a-half months' maternity leave for the first child and more time for the
second. The collective farm offered pregnant women lighter work, but Antonina
claimed not to have spared herself; she performed heavy labor right to the end
of pregnancy. Like Valentina, she benefited from the new medical services and
job-related assistance that were beginning to ease the reproductive lives of rural
women. Though she had some complaints about the impersonal treatment in
maternity wards, still Antonina looked back on this period appreciatively and
compared it favorably to the post-Soviet regime, which she disliked intensely
and wished to see destroyed. "Earlier, people treated one another better, whereas in recent times they have become embittered and mean. Village life is very
hard now and doesn't offer a ray of hope. Under the communists, things were
a whole lot better. We had a lot of people on the collective farm, and the farms
generally were quite strong. You knew that if you worked hard, you'd get a
living wage. But now no one is certain of anything."[19]

As a final example, Antonina Ptichnikova, one of the youngest of our informants, was born in 1940 and reared her children in the 1960s and 1970s, when
conditions had improved substantially. Compared to the lives of the women in
the first and second generations, hers seems much more manageable and was
certainly not touched by tragedy and privation. Even so, Antonina described it
as grueling. She worked in a rural factory and took her two children each day
to a kindergarten on the way to work. "It was very hard," she recounted, "that
a woman had to work for eight hours. . . . You couldn't leave even for an hour.
That's how it was. And at work it was hard. I worked in the shop as a technician.
Then I'd go home, and there were two kids and my husband and that. This is
how life went by for me, so that . . . well, I think it was hard, very hard." The
comparison here is clearly not to her predecessors, who worked twelve- and
fourteen-hour days at heavy farm labor and had to leave their children unsupervised, but to the younger people of recent years who had more freedom to
skip work, longer maternity leaves, and other benefits. It should also be kept in
mind that, according to Nancy Ries, this type of lament was a standard conver-
sational element during this time of change, its purpose being to stake a claim
on the sympathy of the listener and validate rights to compensation that the
speaker now had some doubts would be honored by the government.[20]

After reciting this lament, Antonina continued on a different note, one that contrasted a number of positive sides of the Brezhnev era, which had been at the center of her life, with the situation at the time of the interview. "One thing was good then, which nowadays I don't like; for example, how it is here. That is, at least I knew that my children [were] . . . always, so to say, at some appointed place whether in the kindergarten or at camp." She continued, "Second, I always had work, and no one could ever . . . lay me off. Never. That's not the way it is now. Things are running in an entirely different direction now. . . . Now they can let you go and they can do anything they want to you. But when we were living, that's under socialism, the thing that we felt good about was that I knew that I would always have a salary, . . . on which I could, so to say, live. That is, well, in the sense of getting food. We had a normal situation. . . . Of course, it wasn't luxurious, not at all. But housing, food, and work you had for sure. And the children were taken care of. That is, we never worried that you wouldn't have a place to live. So, on that level, things were good. And now what's going to happen no one knows."

Antonina Ptichnikova likewise praised the equality of those times. Everyone lived about the same, she remarked. Workers and engineers, the difference was not great. She had heard some of the recent revelations about how well the top people lived, but the local Party people were not like that, she asserted. "Before, we all lived about the same," and "in any case, we ate much better than we do now." She also expressed concern about the change in health care, something they had never worried about before. They had their free clinics, she related, and "If you needed a complicated operation, they would send you to a special institute in Moscow." But now medical services cost the users. "We don't have money for medical care," she complained. "We weren't accustomed to needing it. . . we didn't save up."[21]

For the cohort of Valentina Lopatkina, Antonina Abramovna, and Antonina Ptichnikova, the primary historical reference was the one period of comparative prosperity in Soviet rural life, the last Khrushchev years and especially the Brezhnev era. They suffered some privation in their childhood and knew something of the misery and losses that touched women of earlier generations, but their own experience of courtship, marriage, childbearing, and child rearing fell into better times. They felt allegiance to the regime that had provided a life of job security, social benefits, and a comfortable retirement, and they resented the loss of this security just as they were entering their declining years.

To sum up the experience and stance of the three generations, the first built their lives around the value of hard work and loyalty to family and to the religious institutions and ideas of their childhood. Allegiance to these institutions and ideas remained and guided them through the terrible ordeals and losses that inevitably touched rural women in twentieth-century Russia. Despite their losses, they retained a coherent sense of what made their lives worthwhile. The second generation is the most confused, angry, and bitter. And not surprisingly, as these women had greater aspirations than the older women, were continuously frustrated in their hopes, were required to sweat and slave on factories and farms, to sacrifice everything, and received very little in return. Now they face the privations of post-Soviet life. What saved some of them from despair was their identity as independent actors who had been able to merge the old and the new, defy the authorities in their reproductive decisions, protect the secret practice of their persecuted abortionists and healers, in short, to form a bond with their female age-mates in opposition to the unreasonable demands of the authorities. The third generation shared in some of the boons of Soviet society. Medical and some social services reached the countryside in time to assist them in their childbearing and child rearing. Their work lives, while arduous, were considerably easier than those of their mothers and grandmothers. They naturally felt allegiance to the Soviet system, which acknowledged and compensated their work contributions. Now that it is gone, they face an anxious and uncertain future. At the time of the interviews, they had not fully confronted the difficulties of the new, leaner times. It is difficult to say how well they will negotiate the tension between their self-identity as "sovietized" rural women entitled to some reciprocity from the government and the government's retreat from such obligations.

Tatars

Although the Tatar women had many points in common with the Russians, certain differences stood out in their choices and self-representation. The courtship of the older Tatar women was more closely regulated than that of the Russians, and, on average, the Tatar women of the first generation married men much older than themselves, in several cases older by more than ten years, whereas Russian spouses were close in age. The Tatar women of this generation likewise reported cases of polygamy, a practice permitted by Muslim law but not allowed in Russian families. In the next two generations, the modernizing and homogenizing forces of Soviet education induced changes in the practices of both groups, bringing about some convergence.

Tatar women of the middle generation, for example, were very close to the Russians in their acceptance of abortion for fertility control—and, in this regard, their defiance of Soviet law. What distinguished the Tatar informants of this generation from their Russian counterparts was their declared ignorance of any methods of contraception other than prolonged nursing. The Russian women of this cohort reported having knowledge of condoms, and they used them. It is unlikely that the Tatar women were as ignorant of condoms as they claimed, since at least one of their number, Mariam Gimadeeva, had received medical training in Kazan and reported trying in vain to convince her husband to use condoms. Later she worked among the women of the village. Mariam's experience with her husband may nevertheless be a clue to why most Tatar women of her generation professed ignorance of condoms. They portrayed themselves as unable to oppose the wishes of their men. They may therefore have assumed the futility of persuading the men to obtain and use condoms and so put this option out of mind.

Tatar women differed from Russians in regard to experiencing anxiety about birthing. They claimed not to fear letting others know about an impending birth, and concerns about the evil eye harming them or their newborn children were less apparent than among the Russians. Tatar women kept quiet about a birth, they recalled, out of embarrassment and stoicism rather than out of fears of contamination. Neighbors were welcome to visit them and their babies soon after delivery. This positive stance may have owed something to the supportive conditions that seemed generally to surround Muslim women in their reproductive roles. This environment attended the strong patriarchal norms of Tatar village life. Strict sex-role differentiation and subordination of the women implied reciprocity on the part of the men in protecting the women and easing the burden of the reproductive duties. And Tatar women indeed appeared to feel more confident and protected than did the Russians in this aspect of their lives.

Related to this were child care and, especially, breast-feeding. Even though most Tatar women, like their Russian counterparts, were expected to participate in farm work, including field work, the burden was modified in the case of Tatars by the powerful Quranic injunction to breast-feed for at least two years. Lactating women were naturally allowed some latitude in work obligations. Because they fed on demand, this practice afforded frequent breaks from heavy tasks, opportunities to rest and deepen their bond with their children. The advantage of this practice for easing work burdens should not be underestimated, since women in the first two generations did indeed nurse their children two years and longer.

What was most impressive about the Tatar women of every generation and locale was their pride in being Tatar and their allegiance to their wider community. Their pride rested first of all in their religious identity and tradition of education for all children, boys and girls, however humble. All the women had mastered the rudiments of reading and writing, knew the most common prayers in Arabic, and were aware that Russian and other Christian neighbors could not boast a similar reading ability. Secondly, they took pride in the cleanliness and orderliness of Tatar life as compared with the non-Tatars around them. The Tatars of Kalmaiur shared their village with Chuvash peasants. Although Tatar informants confessed to avoiding contact with the Chuvash and not knowing much about them, nearly all the women believed or claimed to know that until very recently the Chuvash lived in filthy conditions, their children were dirty, and as a result the Chuvash suffered much from trachoma. One woman declared that the Chuvash were simply in every respect "a vile people, prone to knife fighting." But most disturbing was that the Chuvash, like other Christians, ate pork. This caused one Tatar woman who did have contact with the Chuvash to be "very squeamish about eating with them." For another woman, any kind of meat butchered by a Chuvash was inedible, whereas she would accept meat, other than pork, from a Russian butcher.[22] Probably the combination of filth and pork, attributed to their Chuvash neighbors, made foods from them doubly unwelcome. Abstaining from pork indeed remains to this day a powerful ethnic marker for Tatars. For many of them the very thought of contact with it prompts revulsion. Fakhiza Suleimanova told me that "if someone came to my home with pork, I would boil the pot it was in a thousand times. In my family, that is a very strict rule."[23]

I am sometimes asked whether this assertiveness and pride in Tatar identity has translated, in the disintegrating Russian Federation, into support for Tatar autonomy or even independence. Here I must go mainly on impressions, because this specific issue was not part of our research program. Not surprisingly, differences were apparent in the stances of villagers and urbanites. The Tatars of the village, informants and others I met, while proud of their difference from the Chuvash, Russians, and other Christians, did not express a larger view of ethnic relations. As early as 1989, they had brought a mullah from Kazan and constructed an impressive timber mosque in the center of the village, and they have since improved and tended the mosque lovingly. Today they appear secure in their place, and their concerns revolve around the village economy, family-survival strategies, and personal rivalries within the village itself. On a return visit to Kalmaiur in the spring of 1999, I noticed that discussions of national issues settled mostly on identifying scapegoats for the current economic difficulties. Talk of separate development under Tatar leadership would not have been realistic for these people, in any case, since they live beyond the borders of the Tatar Republic. Nor is it likely that the older people who make up my informant pool would be eager to risk a major shift in the political landscape. Indeed, many of them clearly would have been happy to return to the security and predictability of the last two decades of Soviet rule.

Tatars living in town were different. My first encounters with urban Tatars at the start of the 1990s revealed a minority people who had felt the sting of discrimination. More of them than I would have expected, given their achievements in education and employment, nursed ambitions for Tatar autonomy, in some cases even full independence for Tatarstan. They told stories of how their children were teased in schools with filthy appellations rhymed to their Muslim names. Some believed that the chaotic language policies of the schools and the requirement to take post-secondary entrance exams in a foreign tongue had deprived them of opportunities for advancement. Others, in contrast, saw their bilingual abilities as an asset and acknowledged that, at least in principle, Soviet life had included them on an equal basis with Russians and other ethnic groups. Like many others, Russians and non-Russians, who had been lifted socially by Soviet educational institutions and professional opportunities, they were not unhappy with the Soviet system as such. Now, however, following perestroika and the breakup of the Soviet Union, questions of identity and community were becoming acute. Russians were forging new identities on the basis of religion and culture rather than the more inclusive secular, professional, and institutional Soviet categories. Tatars, too, expressed a strong need and desire to cultivate and assert their own ethnic and religious heritage. Of the people I met in the early 1990s at the time of the initial interviews, only a few nationalist radicals actually believed in and were campaigning for an independent Tatar national state. Many more people nevertheless spoke wistfully of this possibility, even if they did not believe it was a realistic option. On a recent visit to Tatarstan, I found that Tatar cultural assertiveness had strengthened. Tatar Republic flags flew everywhere, street signs were in Tatar, mosques were appearing like mushrooms (as were renovated Orthodox churches), and people of both major religions were exploring their cultural roots and freely nurturing their religious and ethnic identity in what for now appeared to be cooperation and peace.[24]

Tatars have lived under Russian domination and as islands in a sea of Russian settlement since the sixteenth century without relinquishing any of their cultural and religious distinctiveness, including an unmistakable sense of the superiority of their beliefs and practices. Although the women we have met in this book, like their Russian counterparts, modernized their reproductive practices by selecting new methods and benefits that eased the burden of childbirth and child care, they retained their cultural particularity and pride in their inherited practices of feeding, bathing, caring for, and educating their children. The women who stayed in the village never lost their sense of community, security, and identity. Those who grew up in the village and moved to town, however much they wished to fit in and sought to enter the Soviet professional class, were not willing to shed their Tatar identity. Nor were they permitted to do so, as Russian prejudice reminded them of their differences. They are now seeking to create a new, post-Soviet, urban Tatar identity.

This book is a study of the entry into Russia of Western medical discourse on reproductive health and early child care and of its reception by Russian and Tatar women in the twentieth century. The study began in the eighteenth century, with the era when Enlightenment thinking convinced Russian rulers and medical authorities that something could and should be done about the country's extraordinary rates of infant and childhood death. They had some ideas about what was wrong. Most children were being delivered by women with no medical training who were guided by folk practices and magical ideas about the birth process. Russian mothers were not breast-feeding consistently, and they were introducing very early in their babies' lives solid food and bottled substitutes for mother's milk. Child care was poor or non-existent. Many children were being abandoned in the streets and the woodlands by unwed mothers or married women too burdened with offspring to care for more. Yet the government had few means of correcting these problems. It published some tractates and handbooks on the best methods of birthing and care, but these reached few people. The greatest effort went into institutions for abandoned children. Here the government could quickly achieve two important goals; it ended the pub-lic scandal of tiny corpses littering the streets and gave evidence through the attractive foundling homes of tsarist beneficence toward the common people. Sadly, children brought to the foundling homes had even less chance of survival than those left with their families.

When demographic and public-health surveys in the nineteenth century revealed the social and especially the cultural determinants of child death, the Russian authorities were embarrassed to discover that several of the despised minority peoples of the empire did far better than the Russians themselves in bringing their children through the dangerous years of early childhood. Public-health officials and leaders of charitable foundations felt a new sense of urgency and believed they now knew what was required: a cultural transformation of village life. But the resources and personnel for such a task were inadequate. For the tsarist government, the priorities were the army, police, and infrastruc-tural development. Public health was left largely to poorly funded local govern-ment boards and private charities, which were able to do little more than mount a few summer-nursery programs as possible models for contacting and educat-ing village mothers.

The Soviet regime was far more committed than its predecessor to trans-forming village life and creating a new type of woman, free of religion and su-perstition, and whose life would be guided from cradle to grave by the light of scientific knowledge. Yet Soviet programs in the 1920s to educate village wom-en through lecture tours, mobile medical units, and summer nurseries were too understaffed to reach any but a tiny proportion of rural women. Moreover, the preferred approach—working with mothers while ignoring or criticizing the old women on whom they relied for birthing and child-care services—proved shortsighted. It failed to take into account the three-generational order of vil-lage mothering, in which grandmothers and girls provided most of the child care. This order and the powerful bond that it fostered between the generations reinforced inherited ideas of birthing and child care. Changing the village ways required a much larger investment than the government was initially willing to make, including basic education for the girls and especially provision of mod-ern maternity and child-care services to the village women. Education began to arrive in the 1930s, and the new schooling nurtured women's ambitions for a different way of building a family. These women of the middle generation achieved their ambitions, however, only to the extent that they were able to re-sist the state's laws on abortion and elude the normal work discipline. Not until the decades following the war, in most places as late as the 1960s and 1970s, did sufficient maternity and child-care services reach village women to enable them to safely control their fertility, spend time with their small children, and place them in day care while they were at work.

Village women were not opposed to learning new ways of managing fertility, giving birth, and caring for children, and indeed many were quick to take advantage of whatever assistance proved convenient and did not ask them to sacrifice what little autonomy they enjoyed in making life-shaping decisions for themselves and their families. They were flexible and willing to merge the old and the new, to incorporate modern methods into their mothering repertory when the superiority of such methods could be demonstrated. But they resisted attempts to deprive them of cooperative bonds with women of the older generation. They also refused to alter practices that were fundamental to their religious faith. They continued to baptize their children and to share with them their religious knowledge and the inherited magical practices that gave them a feeling of control over a world that too often was ravaged by war and the exactions of their own government. In recent years they have faced new threats, economic distress and the withdrawal of government services, which have prompted a revival of inherited practices, including home births and the use of herbal medicines and magical spells.

The lives of these women do not lend themselves to the simple narrative, familiar from Soviet public-health writings, of linear progress in the modernization of mothering. Nor does a story of resistance and accommodation seem adequate. Women expressed great willingness to accept some changes. But they were selective. They eagerly incorporated changes that promised to ease their burdens, yet fiercely resisted government efforts to exploit their full potential as both workers and vessels of reproduction. They retained fundamental religious beliefs and practices as well as control over decisions about their children's physical and spiritual health, despite government efforts to usurp these sites of authority. The women placed their ultimate reliance on one another and on their religious faith. They were able to merge the old and the new, to mediate between the needs of their families and the demands of the workplace, to draw as needed on a combination of inherited knowledge and modern services—to survive and endure.

Appendix A: List of Informants

For convenience of reference, informants are listed alphabetically by religious affiliation. The interviewers are Ol'ga Glazunova, Tat'iana Listova, Inna Peshkova, David Ransel, Galina Shapovalova, and Guzel' Shugaeva.

Russian Informants Listed by Last Name

Abramova, Antonina Nikolaevna, born 1931, interview by Listova, Inakovka 2, Tambov province, summer 1994.

Abramova, Mariia Ivanovna, born 1911, interview by Listova, Inakovka 2, Tambov province, summer 1994.

Baranova, Varvara Ivanovna, born 1915, interview by Glazunova and Ransel, Lepeshki, Moscow province, June 7, 1993.

Bakhmesterova, Olimpiada Timofeevna, born 1902, interview by Glazunova and Ransel, Staroe Selo, Moscow province, June 7, 1993.

Belikova, Vera Nikiforovna, born 1909, interview by Glazunova and Ransel, Nazarovo, Moscow province, June 6, 1993.

Bobkova, Elena Pavlovna, born 1919, interview by Listova, El'ninsk raion, Smolensk province, summer 1993.

Brykina, Liia Nikolaevna, born 1932, interview by Listova, Inakovka 1, Tambov province, summer 1994.

Buldakova, Lina Ivanovna, born 1907, interview by Glazunova and Ransel, Vvedenskoe, Moscow province, June 5, 1993.

Danilishina, Ekaterina I., interview by Ransel, Semashko Institute, Moscow, July 1, 1993.

Dobrynin, Vasilii Egorovich, born 1923, interview by Listova, Inakovka villages, Tambov province, summer 1994.

Fateeva, Klavdiia Ivanovna, born 1920, interview by Listova, Kiiasovo, Stupinsk raion, Moscow province, spring 1994.

Fedosenkova, Dar'ia Emel'ianova, born 1909, interview by Listova, Suglitsa, El'ninsk raion, Smolensk province, summer 1993.

Gerasimova, Ekaterina Vasil'evna, born 1909, interview by Glazunova and Ransel, Tsarevo, Moscow province, June 6, 1993.

Gibert, Aleksandra Nikolaevna, born 1921, interview by Peshkova, Maminskoe, Sverdlovsk province, summer 1993.

Gracheva, Nina Mikhailovna, born 1926, interview by Glazunova and Ransel, Lepeshki, Moscow province, June 7, 1993.

Grafova, Antonina Nikolaevna, born 1927 (together with husband Pavel Ivanovich Grafov, born 1922), interview by Glazunova and Ransel, Nazarovo, Moscow province, June 6, 1993.

Gureeva, Anis'ia Kondrat'evna, born 1911, interview by Listova, Kiiasovo, Stupinsk raion, Moscow province, spring 1994.

Guseva, Aleksandra Ivanovna, born 1907, interview by Peshkova, Maminskoe, Sverdlovsk province, summer 1993.

Isafieva, Anna Fedorovna, born 1900 (?), interview by Glazunova and Ransel, Fedorovskoe, Moscow province, June 5, 1993.

Kasiakina, Anna Vasil'evna, born 1939, interview by Listova, Inakovka, Tambov province, summer 1994.

Kirsanova, Anna Vasil'evna, born 1920, interview by Listova, Vititni, El'ninsk raion, Smolensk province, summer 1993.

Konobievskaia, Anna Ivanovna, born 1922, interview by Glazunova and Ransel, Zhukovka, Moscow province, June 7, 1993.

Korotchenkova, Praskov'ia Petrovna, born 1920, interview by Listova, Elizavetino, El'ninsk raion, Smolensk province, summer 1993.

Kosiakina, Nina Ivanovna, born 1937, interview by Listova, Inakovka, Tambov province, summer 1994.

Kosiakova, Anna Iakovlevna, born 1927, interview by Listova, Inakovka 1, Tambov province, summer 1994.

Krivolapova, Aleksandra Nestratovna, born 1949, interview by Listova, Inakovka 2, Tambov province, summer 1994.

Krivolapova, Praskov'ia Egorovna, born 1912, interview by Listova, Inakovka 2, Tambov province, summer 1994.

Kurkova, Praskov'ia Alekseevna, born 1899, interview by Glazunova and Ransel, Zhukovka, Moscow province, June 6, 1993.

Kurkova, Tat'iana Vasil'evna, born 1925, interview by Glazunova and Ransel, Zhukovka, Moscow province, June 6, 1993.

Kuzina, Anastasiia Nikolaevna, born 1923, interview by Glazunova and Ransel, Vvedenskoe, Moscow province, June 6, 1993.

Larshina, Antonina Alekseevna, born 1923, interview by Glazunova and Ransel, Orlovo, Moscow province, June 8, 1993.

Lopatkina, Valentina Ivanovna, born 1931, interview by Glazunova and Ransel, Tsarevo, Moscow province, June 6, 1993.

Malikova, Mariia Vasil'evna, born 1913, interview by Listova, Inakovka 1, Tambov province, summer 1994.

Malikova, Marfa Ivanovna, born 1910, interview by Listova, Inakovka 1, Tambov province, summer 1994.

Mal'tseva, Ol'ga Timofeevna, born 1913, interview by Ransel, Chernaia, Batetskii raion, Novgorod province, May 25, 1990.

Mamina, Galina Ivanovna, born 1918, interview by Peshkova, Maminskoe, Sverdlovsk province, summer 1993.

Markova, Anna Dmitrievna, born 1914, interview by Listova, Inakovka, Tambov province, summer 1994.

Mikhaleva, Anna Aleksandrovna, born 1923, interview by Listova, Inakovka 2, Tambov province, summer 1994.

Mikhaleva, Natal'ia Pavlovna, born 1929, interview by Listova, Inakovka 2, Tambov province, summer 1994.

Nikolaeva, Elizaveta Ivanovna, born 1905, interview by Glazunova and Ransel, Tsarevo, Moscow province, June 6, 1993.

Nikulina, Pelageia Andreevna, born 1910, interview by Listova, Bulgakovka, Iuzhavinskii raion, Tambov province, summer 1994.

Novozhilova, Nina Pavlovna, born 1916, interview by Glazunova and Ransel, Nazarovo, Moscow province, June 6, 1993.

Ortikova, Iuliia Fedorovna, born 1917, interview by Peshkova, Maminskoe, Sverdlovsk province, summer 1993.

Panacheva, Anna Petrovna, born 1928, interview by Peshkova, Maminskoe, Sverdlovsk province, summer 1993.

P-va, Anna Ivanovna, born 1914, interview by Glazunova and Ransel, Vvedenskoe, Moscow province, June 6, 1993. (This woman asked us not to use her full name.)

Popova, Antonida Georgievna, born 1953, interview by Peshkova, Maminskoe, Sverdlovsk province, summer 1993.

Privalova, Tamara Aleksandrovna, born 1928, interview by Peshkova, Maminskoe, Sverdlovsk province, summer 1993.

Ptichnikova, Antonina Ivanovna, born 1937, interview by Glazunova and Ransel, Kablukovo, Moscow province, June 8, 1993.

Reutova, Anna Konstantinovna, born 1908, interview by Listova, Inakovka 2, Tambov province, summer 1994.

Ruleva, Efrosin'ia Filippovna, born 1915, interview by Listova, Korobets, El'ninsk raion, Smolensk province, summer 1993.

Sevriukova, Evdokiia Petrovna, born 1911, interview by Listova, Suglitsa, El'ninsk raion, Smolensk province, summer 1993.

Shapovalova, Valentina Vasil'evna, born 1933, interview by Listova, Korobets, El'ninsk raion, Smolensk province, summer 1993.

Sharav'eva, Pelageia Grigor'evna, born 1911, interview by Peshkova, Maminskoe, Sverdlovsk province, summer 1993.

Shishanova, Anastasiia Vasil'evna, born 1905, interview by Glazunova and Ransel, Tsarevo, Moscow province, June 6, 1993.

Shumkov, Vasilii Mikhailovich, born 1915, interview by Glazunova and Ransel, Fedo-rovskoe, Moscow province, June 5, 1993.

Shumkova, Zinaida Danilovna, born 1915, interview by Glazunova and Ransel, Fedo-rovskoe, Moscow province, June 5, 1993.

Skovorodina, Natal'ia Efimovna, born 1902, interview by Listova, Cherniakovo, Tar-nogskii raion, Vologda province, 1981.

Smirnova, Elizaveta Ivanovna, born 1917, interview by Glazunova and Ransel, Staroe Selo, Moscow province, June 7, 1993.

Somova, Mariia Andreevna, born 1905, interview by Listova, Pakhotnyi ugol, Bon-darskii raion, Tambov province, summer 1994.

Sorokoumova, Elena Anisimovna, born 1915, interview by Listova, Nikitino, El'ninsk raion, Smolensk province, summer 1993.

Spiridonova, Anastasiia Petrovna, born 1907, interview by Glazunova and Ransel, Lepeshki, Moscow province, June 7, 1993.

Sudakova, Anfisa Aver'ianovna, born 1923, interview by Listova, Barkanovskaia, Vo-shegodskii raion, Vologda province, 1981.

Tripapina, Valentina Vasil'evna, born 1902, interview by Ransel, Laikovo, Moscow province, July 8, 1990.

Tsygankova, Elena Nikitchna, born 1917, interview by Listova, Elizavetino, El'ninsk raion, Smolensk province, summer 1993.

Vakhromeeva, Anastasiia Artemovna, born 1907, interview by Glazunova and Ransel, Kablukovo, Moscow province, June 7, 1993.

Varfolomeeva, Anna Egorovna, born 1928, interview by Listova, Nikitino, El'ninsk raion, Smolensk province, summer 1993.

Varfolomeeva, Tat'iana Ivanovna, born 1911, interview by Listova, Nikitino, El'ninsk raion, Smolensk province, summer 1993.

Vorob'eva, Tat'iana Sergeevna, born 1954, interview by Peshkova, Maminskoe, Sverd-lovsk province, summer 1993.

Vovoshkina, Zoia Konstantinovna, born 1937, interview by Glazunova and Ransel, Kablukovo, Moscow province, June 8, 1993.

Zaitsev, V. I., born 1913 (together with wife), interview by Glazunova and Ransel, Fedorovskoe, Moscow province, June 5, 1993.

Zueva, Anna Vasil'evna, born 1919, interview by Ransel, Chernaia, Batetskii raion, Novgorod province, May 24–26, 1990.

Russian Informants Listed without Last Name

Mariia Ivanovna, born 1905, interview by Listova, Inakovka, Tambov province, summer 1994.

Nina Mikhailovna, born 1928, interview by Ransel, Repnino, Leningrad province, April 22, 1990.

Pilot interviews in Udel'nyi Park, designated as #1 and #2 in the tapes and transcripts, conducted by Shapovalova and Ransel with a number of women without asking for names, May 12, 1990.

Muslim Informants Listed Individually

Abdullina, Garifabanu Nasybulla kyzy, born 1908, interview by Shugaeva, Tatarskii Kalmaiur, Ul'ianovsk province, summer 1993.

Badrieva, Nuraniia Sheikh-Islam kyzy, born 1932, interview by Shugaeva, Tatarskii Kalmaiur, Ul'ianovsk province, summer 1993.

Bagautdinova, Zatiia Garifulla kyzy, born 1925, interview by Shugaeva, Tatarskii Kalmaiur, Ul'ianovsk province, summer 1993.

Fakhrutdinova, Roza Gabdrakhman kyzy, born 1933, interview by Shugaeva, Tatarskii Kalmaiur, Ul'ianovsk province, summer 1993.

Galeeva, Nafisa Nasybulovna, born 1910, interview by Ransel, Moscow, June 19, 1990.

Gimadeeva, Mar'iam Khaliulla kyzy, born 1918, interview by Shugaeva, Tatarskii Kalmaiur, Ul'ianovsk province, summer 1993.

Gimatdinova, Zeinab Abdurakhman kyzy, born 1923, interview by Shugaeva, Tatarskii Kalmaiur, Ul'ianovsk province, summer 1993.

Ialisheva, Sharifa Khusainovna, born 1912, interview by Ransel, Leningrad, April 21, 1990.

Iurenieva, Fina Asrorovna, born 1941, interview by Ransel, Ethnographic Institute, Leningrad, June 5, 1990.

Kamaletdinova, Rkiia Badretdin kyzy, born 1922, interview by Shugaeva, Tatarskii Kalmaiur, Ul'ianovsk province, summer 1993.

Mustafina, Minzifa Mukhammed kyzy, born 1933, interview by Shugaeva, Tatarskii Kalmaiur, Ul'ianovsk province, summer 1993.

Nizamova, Khatima Khairulla kyzy, born 1903, interview by Shugaeva, Tatarskii Kalmaiur, Ul'ianovsk province, summer 1993.

Pozdniakova, Zukhra, born 1917, interview by Ransel, Krasnoe Selo, Leningrad province, April 20, 1990.

Rezvanova, Zubarzhat Kerim kyzy, born 1917, interview by Shugaeva, Tatarskii Kalmaiur, Ul'ianovsk province, summer 1993.

Suleimanov, Rakhmet, interview by Ransel, Simbirsk, Ul'ianovsk province, July 15, 1990.

Suleimanova, Fakhiza, born 1930, interview by Ransel, Simbirsk, Ul'ianovsk province, July 15, 1990.

Teleshova, Amina, interview by Ransel, Leningrad, May 8, 1990.

Teleshova, Sof'ia Asrorovna, born 1950, interview by Ransel, Leningrad, May 31, 1990.

Zagidullina, Zakiia Gabitovna, born 1940, interview by Peshkova, Maminskoe, Sverdlovsk province, summer 1993.

Muslim Informants Listed as Group

Women in mosque (principal informant was Khatima Nizamova but also contributing were Emmegel'sem Aiukianova, Merfuga Kaiumova, and others), interview by Ransel, Tatarskii Kalmaiur, Ul'ianovsk province, July 16, 1990.

Jewish Informants

Krugman, Fira Abramovna, born 1915, interview by Ransel, Leningrad, May 12, 1990.

Rabinovich, Khana, born 1906, interview by Ransel, Philadelphia, PA, November 16, 1994.

Vulakh, Faina Samuilovna, born 1925, interview by Ransel, Philadelphia, PA, November 16, 1994.

Appendix B: Questionnaire

Name
Address
Year of birth   Place of birth
Occupation   Religion
Education
Year and place of birth of mother
Education   Occupation   Religion
Year and place of birth of father
Education   Occupation   Religion
Years and places of birth of brothers and sisters (their names)

Year of marriage   Matchmaker
Dowry   Bride-price
Second marriage

Year and place of birth of husband
Education   Occupation   Religion

Years and places of birth of children (their names)

1. When you were a child, how did your mother look after the family? (How did she care for the health and safety of the children; how did she maintain cleanliness?) How did she care for a newborn child? How long did she breast-feed? Why? (If she used artificial feeding, what kind? Cow's milk, dried or fortified milk?) Fight against flies, etc.? How were you fed later?

2. What kind of diseases did the children suffer from? How often were they ill? What methods of cure and what medicines were used? Were sick children isolated from healthy ones?

3. Where did you get medical care? At home, in a clinic, a medical station, or from a folk healer or wise woman? What care did you get from them: curatives, shots?

4. Did your mother look after you in ways different from how your relatives, neighbors, or friends cared for their children? What differences were there?

5. Did women in the family and neighbors help one another during birthing, in the care of young children, and at the illness or death of children? How so?

6. What is your most pleasant memory of childhood? Examples.

7. What is your most unpleasant memory of childhood? Examples.

8. How did you get to know your husband? Was there any mediation by matchmakers or relatives?

9. How much did you know about childbirth before you were married? From whom did you learn? School, mother, matchmaker, friends?

10. When did you give birth for the first time? How did you arrive at the decision? Did you plan ahead of time to have the child or not? Describe how you and your husband made decisions about having children, how much it was planned.

11. Did you know about contraceptive methods or devices? Which? Did you receive any advice from your mother, from friends, teachers, sisters, doctors or other medical workers? What was your opinion of abortion? What means existed for doing it? Were there special women who performed abortions?

12. What was the family's attitude toward a pregnant woman? Did pregnant women work along with everyone else right up to delivery or were they freed from work around the house, at the job? How soon after delivery did you return to work at home? At the job?

13. Were pregnant women forbidden to eat certain things, work at certain tasks, or engage in certain behavior? Was a pregnant woman considered "unclean"?

14. What medical care was there for a pregnant women? Were there prenatal check-ups? Did a nurse visit you at home? What advice did you get?

15. Were there special village midwives? Who could be such a midwife? Widows, old women, or could she be of any age?

16. At what time was the midwife summoned? Could a village midwife refuse for some reason to come and attend a birth?

17. What actions did the midwife take to relieve the discomforts of birthing? Medicines? Prayers? Spells?

18. During a woman's confinement did the midwife help her family in cleaning and managing the household? How long did she remain after delivery, and how often did she make return visits? What relationship did she have to the children she delivered?

19. Was the onset of labor kept a secret from outsiders? If so, why?

20. Where did delivery take place? At home, in the steam-bath cabin, at a medical station, or in some other place? Why?

21. Was there a notion that giving birth was unclean? Was the space in which the birth took place considered unclean? Were there taboos about visiting the house in which the delivery took place? If so, for whom (for girls, old people . . .) and for how long?

22. Did the birthing mother say last farewells to the members of the household?

23. Were there special prayers for easing the labor pains? Prayers to whom?

24. Who could be present at a delivery? Could the husband be present at the delivery?

25. Was there a belief that the labor pains could be transferred from the mother to her husband? How could this be done?

26. How many of your pregnancies failed to lead to a live birth? How were these pregnancies ended?

27. To the extent you know, approximately how many abortions did your acquaintances have? Where were the abortions done? Did they do more or fewer abortions than your mother's generation?

28. How many of your babies survived? What was the cause of their death?

29. What was the attitude toward the sex of a newborn? What caused you and your husband greater joy: the birth of a girl or a boy?

30. When did you begin to feed your babies? How long did you breast-feed? Did women know that lengthy breast-feeding reduced the risk of becoming pregnant? Did women consciously apply this method? When did you find out about it and from whom?

31. When did you begin solid food? What kind? Did you use a chaw or a rag pacifier? If so, what did it consist of? If you began solid food early, what were the reasons (insufficient breast milk; did women think that milk alone was insufficient to nourish a baby)?

32. How did you manage your home, keep things clean, care for the health and safety of the children? Did your methods differ from those of your mother, your neighbors, women of other nationalities?

33. What illnesses did your children suffer from most? How did you treat them; what medicines did you use? How did your treatments differ from those that were used by your mother, the family of your husband, or your friends?

34. In what cases did you go to the doctor, to a clinic, or to a rural medical station (for a check-up when a child was well? For shots? For any illness? Or only when a child had a high temperature or other severe illness?)?

35. What sources of information did you have about the care of children? When your children were small, did you have at hand any books, brochures, or magazines that gave necessary advice? How did this advice differ from that you received from your mother or from friends? Were there doctors, fel'dshers, nurses, or other medical workers among your relatives or friends?

36. Were there any prenatal facilities in your village, nurseries, supervised playgrounds, visiting nurses? Were there any state, factory, or collective-farm agencies for assisting birthing mothers? When did such facilities first appear in the places where you lived or worked?

37. What were your ideas about the soul? Was a child born with a soul? Did a child acquire a soul only after birth? How so?

38. Did women make judgments about the viability of newborns? Were there thought to be certain signs that told of the viability of a newborn? What were they? If women determined that a baby was a "goner," how did they treat it?

39. What was the attitude toward children who were born with physical defects? Did they receive the same care as healthy children?

40. How did a mother and father respond to the death of an infant? Was there a difference between the feelings of a mother and of a father?

41. What were the means of guarding against contamination from unclean powers, from the evil eye? Prayers? Spells? What illnesses were the most terrifying? Who did the cures? How?

42. Did people of another nationality live close to you? How did they differ from you in their attitudes toward birthing, children, household management, cleanliness, and food?

43. When did women of your acquaintance begin to make decisions to control their fertility? What means did they use?

44. Religious rituals in connection with birthing? Baptism (or equivalent Muslim and Jewish rites)? Churching of new mothers after delivery? Continuation of religious practices during state efforts at repression?

Notes

Note: The following abbreviations are used in the archival references: f. = *fond* (collection); op. = *opis'* (inventory); d. = *delo* (file); l. and ll. = *list, listy* (leaf, leaves); ob. = *oborot* (verso).

Introduction

1. See my "Mothering, Medicine, and Infant Mortality in Russia: Some Comparisons," *Occasional Paper,* Kennan Institute for Advanced Russian Studies, no. 236 (1990).

2. See the interesting analysis of this topic by Victoria E. Bonnell, "The Peasant Woman in Stalinist Art of the 1930s," *American Historical Review* 98:1 (February 1993), 55–82.

3. One of the latest examples of this view can be found in Christine D. Worobec, *Peasant Russia: Family and Community in the Post-Emancipation Period* (Princeton, 1991).

4. I want to thank Nanette Funk for some of this formulation.

5. In some cases, however, the work provided little more than room and board. One woman told me that she worked from Easter to November and received in payment one dress and 36 pounds of grain. Women in Udel'nyi Park, interview #2, Shapovalova and Ransel, May 12, 1990, Leningrad.

6. Anna P-va, interview by Glazunova and Ransel, Vvedenskoe, Moscow province, June 6, 1993.

7. Elizaveta Nikolaeva, interview by Glazunova and Ransel, Tsarevo, Moscow province, June 6, 1993.

8. Elisabeth Reuterswärd, *Kulturell intervention. Ett participatorisk experiment* (Lund, 1990); Donald A. Ritchie, *Doing Oral History* (New York: Twayne, 1995), 196–99.

9. Nancy Ries, *Russian Talk: Culture and Conversation during Perestroika* (Ithaca, 1997).

1. Child Welfare before the Revolution

1. There was one exception. Well into the eighteenth century a father's inadvertent killing of a child or even his wife in the course of disciplining them was treated as justifiable homicide—the need to bolster patriarchal power overriding all other considerations.

2. For specific decrees and the development of legislation and institutions, see Ransel, *Mothers of Misery: Child Abandonment in Russia* (Princeton, 1988), chapters 1 and 2.

3. Translation from Paul Dukes, ed., *Catherine the Great's Instruction (Nakaz) to the Legislative Commission, 1767,* vol. 2: *Russia under Catherine the Great* (Newtonville, Mass., 1977), 77 (I have modified spelling and syntax slightly).

4. *Kratkoe nastavlenie vybrannoe iz luchshikh avtorov s nekotorymi fizicheskimi primechaniiami o vospitanii detei ot rozhdeniia ikh do iunoshestva* (St. Petersburg, 1766). Ivan Betskoi, designer of the foundling homes, is credited with the compilation, but the principal work was done by Dr. Sanchez, chief doctor of the foundling homes.

5. These comments are from Semen Zybelin's *Slovo o sposobe, kak predupredit' mozhno nemalovazhnuiu mezhdu prochimi medlennogo umnozheniia naroda prichinu, sostoiashchuiu v neprilichnoi pishche, mladentsam davaemoi v pervye mesiatsy ikh zhizni* (Moscow, 1780), 13. See also his *Slovo o pravilnom vospitanii s mladenchestva v razsuzhdenii tela . . .* (Moscow, 1775).

6. On the European shift, see Londa Schiebinger, "Why Are Mammals Called Mammels?" *American Historical Review* 98:2 (April 1993), 382–411.

7. Zybelin, it should be noted, did not hold a chair in obstetrics. While this specialty was taught at St. Petersburg starting in the early 1770s, Moscow had only a midwifery school until 1790, when a department of obstetrics was installed at Moscow University. N. I. Rachinskii, "Glavnye momenty v istorii razvitiia akusherstva," *ZAZB* 15:3 (1901), 395–96.

8. This is from S. P. Ely's *Fiziko-medicheskie primechaniia o vrede proizkhodiashchem ot upotrebleniia rozhkov dlia kormleniia mladentsov, i o proistekaiushchikh ot togo chastiiu ves'ma zhestokikh, chastiiu zhe i smertonosnykh detskikh bolezniakh* (St. Petersburg, 1785), as cited in A. N. Antonov, *Okhrana materinstva i mladenchestva,* vol. 1, part 1 (Leningrad, 1929), 172–73.

9. Antonov, *Okhrana materinstva,* 173–74.

10. N. M. Maksimovich-Ambodik, *Iskusstvo povivaniia ili Nauka o babichiem dele . . . ,* 6 vols. (St. Petersburg, 1784–1786). .

11. *Kratkoe ispytanie mnogikh zakosnelykh mnenii i predrazsuzhdenii kasatel'no beremennykh zhen, rodil'nits i novorozhdennykh detei . . .* (St. Petersburg, 1786), a work that Maksimovich-Ambodik translated from the French original of one of his teachers.

12. F. Uden (probable author), "O pervykh estestvennykh prikliucheniiakh novorozhdennogo cheloveka," *Sanktpeterburgskie vrachebnye vedomosti* [1792–1794], cited in Antonov, *Okhrana materinstva,* 176–77.

13. German's study appeared in 1819; the second, by G. A. Attengofer, a year later. Both are cited in Antonov, *Okhrana materinstva,* 178.

14. The entire order from Arakcheev, "Kratkie pravila dlia materei-krest'ianok Grusinskoi otchiny" is reproduced in Antonov, *Okhrana materinstva,* 188–92. Grusinskaia otchina was a military settlement in Novgorod province.

15. Antonov, *Okhrana materinstva,* 180.

16. I. R. Likhtenshtedt, *O prichinakh bol'shoi smertnosti detei na pervom godu zhizni i merakh k ee otvrashcheniiu* (St. Petersburg, 1839), 70–89 (emphasis in the original).

17. On the situation in France, where this practice was widespread, see George D. Sussman, *Selling Mothers' Milk: The Wet-Nursing Business in France, 1715–1914* (Urbana, 1982).

18. Antonov, *Okhrana materinstva,* 184–86.

19. Or so it appears from the date and content of his publication "O nekotorykh pogreshnostiakh i predrassudkakh kasatel'no soderzhaniia detei, v pervoe vremia ikh

zhizni," in *Trudy sanktpeterburgskogo obshchestva russkikh vrachei,* part 1 (St. Petersburg, 1836), 160–66.

20. V. Snigirev, *O smertnosti detei na pervom godu zhizni. Opyt mediko-statisticheskogo issledovaniia v Stavropol'skoi gubernii s 1857 po 1862 god.* (St. Petersburg, 1863), 15–20.

21. See chapters 7 and 8 below.

22. Article is referenced in A. P. Zhuk, *Razvitie obshchestvenno-meditsinskoi mysli v Rossii v 60–70 gg. XIX veka* (Moscow, 1963), 303–307.

23. F. V. Giliarovskii, *Issledovaniia o rozhdenii i smertnosti detei v Novgorodskoi gubernii,* Zapiski imp. russkogo geograficheskogo obshchestva po otd. statistiki, vol. 1 (St. Petersburg, 1866), 235, 338, 495, 525.

24. Ibid., xliv.

25. Ibid., lxxii–lxxiii.

26. Ibid., xv.

27. M. Shmelev, *Opyt meditsinskoi topografii iaroslavskoi gubernii* (St. Petersburg, 1868), 41, 76–77.

28. Ibid., 41.

29. P. A. Peskov, *Opisanie Durykinskoi volosti moskovskogo uezda v sanitarnom otnoshenii* (Moscow, 1879), quote in 110n.

30. Ibid., 158–60.

31. P. Griaznov, *Opyt sravnitel'nogo izucheniia gigienicheskikh uslovii krest'ianskogo byta i mediko-topografiia cherepovetskogo uezda* (St. Petersburg, 1880), 153–54.

32. E. A. Pokrovskii, *Ob ukhode za malymi det'mi* (Moscow, 1889), 41–46. Also see field reports of foundling home officials in RGIAg SPg, f. 8, op. 1, d. 187ch2, ll. 242ob and d; 187ch4, ll. 140–41. Also see A. Balov, "Rozhdenie i vospitanie detei v Poshekhonskom uezde, Iaroslavskoi gubernii," *Etnograficheskoe obozrenie* 2:3 (1890): 94.

33. From a study of Saratov province in 1879–1888 by Dr. N. E. Kushev, cited in V. P. Nikitenko, *Detskaia smertnost' v evropeiskoi Rossii za 1893–1896 god* (St. Petersburg, 1901), 30.

34. V. I. Nikol'skii, *Tambovskii uezd. Statistika naseleniia i boleznennosti (s tablitsami i diagrammami)* (Tambov, 1885), quote on 108, also see 320–21.

35. Ibid., 158–59.

36. Ibid., 157–58.

37. Ibid., 157, 160. Some support could be found for this observation in a study appearing the same year, which cited the work of a doctor in Viatka province who recorded large differences in infant mortality in the fifty-two villages he surveyed in a small area. "Everywhere babies are left in the care of old women in the summertime," he wrote, "everywhere they are fed with 'chaws' and the like, and everywhere the care and feeding of them are uniformly bad." Yet the outcomes for the children were different, a finding that the researcher had no answer for other than to call for detailed studies of each village. Report by Dr. P. Krasovskii to the Third Congress of the Viatka Zemstvo Doctors (1876), quoted in the dissertation of P. N. Serebrennikov, *Opyt medikotopograficheskogo opisaniia g. Irbiti Permskoi gubernii s planom goroda i diagrammami* (St. Petersburg, 1885), 109–10.

38. Nikol'skii, *Tambovskii uezd,* 341.

39. See Carroll Smith-Rosenberg, "The Female World of Love and Ritual: Relations between Women in Nineteenth-Century America," *Signs* 1 (1975), 1–29; and Judith Walzer Leavitt, *Brought to Bed: Childbearing in America, 1750–1950* (New York, 1986).

40. See, among others, the recent studies by Irina Paperno, *Suicide as a Cultural Institution in Dostoevsky's Russia;* Laura Engelstein, *The Keys to Happiness: Sex and the Search for Modernity in Fin-de-Siècle Russia;* Cathy A. Frierson, *All Russia Is Burning: A Cultural History of Rural Fire and Arson in Late Imperial Russia* (forthcoming).

41. Antonov, *Okhrana materinstva,* 196.

42. See, for example, studies by L. N. Malinovskii, *K izucheniiu v mediko-topograficheskom i statisticheskom otnoshenii g. Revelia* (Revel, 1891), and I. Feitel'berg, *Opyt mediko-topograficheskogo opisaniia goroda Vindavy* (Iur'ev, 1894).

43. P. P. Chubinskii, *Trudy etnografichesko-statisticheskoi ekspeditsii v zapadno-russkii krai* (St. Petersburg, 1872); M. Berlin, *Ocherk etnografii evreiskogo narodonaseleniia v Rossii* (St. Petersburg, 1861).

44. L. Golynets, *K izucheniiu v mediko-topograficheskom i statisticheskom otnoshenii gubernskogo goroda Mogileva* (St. Petersburg, 1887); A. A. Bekarevich, *K izucheniiu v mediko-topograficheskom i statisticheskom otnoshenii gubernskogo goroda Minska* (St. Petersburg, 1890); V. V. Koshelev, *Mediko-topograficheskoe opisanie goroda Mogileva na Dnepre* (St. Petersburg, 1901). I have standardized their counts and then used them for analysis in my "Mothering, Medicine, and Infant Mortality in Russia: Some Comparisons," and in my "Culture, Childbirth, and Disease among Women in Belarus in the Late Imperial Period" (forthcoming in Belorussian).

45. The Jews lost 113 infants per 1,000 live births; Lutherans, 206; and Orthodox, 227. I. Feitel'berg, *Opyt,* 76.

46. See the detailed breakdown and analysis in V. I. Binshtok and S. A. Novosel'skii, *Materialy po estestvennomu dvizheniiu evreiskogo naseleniia v Evropeiskoi Rossii za 40 let (1867–1906)* (Petrograd, 1915).

47. Chubinskii, *Trudy,* 22; Golynets, *K izucheniiu,* 23.

48. M. G. Iakovenko, *Materialy k antropologii evreiskogo naseleniia Rogachevskogo uezda Mogilevskoi gubernii* (St. Petersburg, 1898), 15.

49. Koshelev, *Mediko-topograficheskoe opisanie,* 72.

50. Binshtok and Novosel'skii, *Materialy,* iii–iv. For more on Jews and Belorussians, see my "Culture, Childbirth, and Disease among Women in Belarus in the Late Imperial Period" (forthcoming).

51. S. A. Novosel'skii, *Smertnost' i prodolzhitel'nost' zhizni v Rossii* (Petrograd, 1916), 144. I use the standard term "live births" here and elsewhere, although what is reflected in some of the records is baptisms and equivalent Muslim registrations, with the consequence that the actual mortality is understated.

52. V. I. Nikol'skii, *Sanitarnoe issledovanie Penzenskoi gubernii. Statistika naseleniia gorodov i uezdov za 10 let (1880–89 gg.)* (Penza, 1893), 56.

53. Novosel'skii, *Smertnost',* 145–46.

54. Sergei Ershov, *Materialy dlia sanitarnoi statistiki sviiazhskogo uezda. Opyt sravnitel'noi demografii russkoi i tatarskoi narodnostei* (St. Petersburg, 1888), 113.

55. A. Dalinger, *Mediko-statisticheskoe issledovanie tatarskogo naseleniia Astrakhanskogo uezda* (St. Petersburg, 1887), 91; V. I. Nikol'skii, *Sanitarnoe issledovanie Penzenskoi gubernii,* iii.

56. N. Spasskii, *Ocherki po rodinovedeniiu. Kazanskaia guberniia,* 2nd ed. (Kazan, 1912), 67–80.

57. N. I. Teziakov, *Materialy po izucheniiu detskoi smertnosti v Saratovskoi gubernii s 1902 po 1904 gg.* (Saratov, 1908), 40.

58. A. A. Sukharev, *Kazanskie tatary (uezd Kazanskii). Opyt etnograficheskogo i mediko-antropologicheskogo issledovaniia* (St. Petersburg, 1904), 30–32, 39; A. O. Afinogenov, *Zhizn' zhenskogo naseleniia Riazanskogo uezda v period detorodnoi deiatel'nosti zhenshchiny i polozhenie dela akusherskoi pomoshchi etomu naseleniiu* (St. Petersburg, 1903), 76. For a similar report from the Simbirsk area, Mil'kovich, *Byt i verovaniia tatar Simbirskoi gubernii v 1783 g.*, ed. N. Vinogradov (Kazan, 1905), 7.

59. K. Fuks, *Kazanskie tatary v statisticheskom i etnograficheskom otnosheniiakh* (Kazan, 1844), 27.

60. A. E. Romanov, *O zabolevaemosti naseleniia kuznetskogo uezda, Saratovskoi gubernii v 1882 godu i ob ospoprivivanii za etot zhe god* (Penza, 1883), 9.

61. Ershov, *Materialy*, 112–13.

62. Ivan Blagovidov, *Materialy k izledovaniiu* [sic] *zdorov'ia inorodtsev simbirskoi gubernii, Buinskogo uezda (Chuvash, Mordvy i Tatar), sobrannye posredstvom izmereniia rosta, okruzhnosti grudi, emkosti legkikh i vesa* (St. Petersburg, 1886), 13–14.

63. Dalinger, *Mediko-statisticheskoe issledovanie*, 111–13.

64. Ershov, *Materialy*, 113–16. See similar observations by P. F. Kudriavtsev, *Derevenskie iasli-priiuty v Simbirskoi gubernii letom 1899g.* (Syzran, 1900), 20–21.

65. M. M. Kenigsberg, *Sanitarnoe sostoianie Orenburgskoi gubernii po dannym estestvennogo dvizheniia naseleniia za trekhletie 1897–1899 gg.* (Orenburg, 1901), 103–108.

66. Antonov, *Okhrana materinstva*, 196.

67. See, for example, reports on 3rd and 5th Saratov congresses (1887 and 1889) in Teziakov, *Materialy*, 25–26; D. P. Nikol'skii, *Obzor deiatel'nosti gubernskikh s"ezdov zemskikh vrachei*, vyp. 1 (St. Petersburg, 1888); K. I. Shidlovskii, *Svod postanovlenii i rabot I–VI vserossiiskikh s"ezdov vrachei* (Moscow, 1899).

68. Both quotes reprinted in Kudriatsev, *Derevenskie*, 27–28, 32.

69. V. I. Nikol'skii, *Sanitarnoe issledovanie*, 58. See also Popov, *Russkaia narodno-bytovaia meditsina*, 4; and Nikitenko, *Detskaia smertnost' 1893–1896*, 24–26, 36–37.

70. Kenigsberg, *Sanitarnoe*, 101–102 (italics in original).

71. P. I. Kurkin, *Detskaia smertnost' v moskovskoi gubernii i ee uezdakh v 1883–1897* (Moscow, 1902).

72. See, for example, on provision of a midwife from the foundling home school for an udel estate in Kostroma. TsGIA, f. 515, op. 7, d. 2505.

73. Or so a *fel'dsher* reported to a teacher at one of the midwifery schools. Quoted in V. Zhuk, "Shkola sel'skikh povival'nykh babok," *ZAZB* 4:7–8 (1890), 508.

74. The debates are detailed in Samuel C. Ramer, "Childbirth and Culture: Midwifery in the Nineteenth-Century Russian Countryside," *The Family in Imperial Russia*, ed. David L. Ransel (Urbana, 1978), 218–35.

75. G. E. Rein, *Rodovspomozhenie v Rossii. Sbornik dokladov na IX Pirogovskom s"ezde* (St. Petersburg, 1906), especially the report by V. K. Bokadorov, "Organizatsiia akusherskoi pomoshchi sel'skomu naseleniiu v zemskikh gub.," 34–56, and I. V. Sudakov, "Statisticheskie dannye po organizatsii rodovspomogatel'noi pomoshchi v Rossii," 57–88.

76. S. M. Iampol'skii, "'Kaplia moloka' i ee znachenie v bor'be s detskoi smertnost'iu i zabolevaemost'iu," *Vrachebnaia gazeta* 43 (1909), 1297.

77. TsGA SPb, f. 4301, op. 1, d. 2062, 88ob–89 (from report by A. N. Antonov to the Leningrad Province Health Ministry in 1924).

78. Konius, *Puti razvitiia sovetskoi okhrany materinstva i mladenchestva (1917–1940)* (Moscow, 1954), 51–52.

79. Antonov, *Okhrana materinstva,* 209–10; Konius, *Puti,* 72.

80. RGIA, f. 767, op. 1, d. 175. The work was expensive, amounting to more than 256,000 rubles, paid only in part by local donations. And after the tsarist regime had fallen, the Guardianship was having to appeal to the ministries of education, internal affairs, and agriculture for support. For 1924 figures, see GARF, f. 4591, op. 9, d. 61, l. 159.

81. RGIA, f. 767, op. 1, d. 37, 85.

82. Letter to M. M. Cherpomordik, ibid., d. 133, l. 40ob.

83. Ibid., d. 186.

84. Ibid., d. 37, ll. 1–2.

85. Quoted in Konius, *Puti,* 36.

86. Nina Berberova, *The Italics Are Mine,* trans. Philippe Radley (New York, 1969), 17.

2. Soviet Efforts to Transform Village Mothering

1. See especially Konius, *Puti,* and Elizabeth Waters, "The Modernization of Russian Motherhood," *Soviet Studies* 44:1 (1992), 123–35.

2. Konius, *Puti,* 96–110.

3. Report by Dr. A. Shuster, Oct. 2, 1920, TsGA SPb, f. 4301, op. 1, d. 402, ll. 40b–5.

4. Konius, *Puti,* 123.

5. TsGA SPb, f. 4301, op. 1, d. 402, ll. 5–6.

6. Formerly Tsarskoe Selo, later Pushkin.

7. Reports by Drs. Marshak and Mikhailov, Oct. 28, 1920. TsGA SPb, f. 4301, op. 1, d. 402, ll. 13–13ob.

8. Wet nurses complained, for example, of summoning the duty doctor in an emergency and finding him making love to a nurse and refusing to see the patient until morning. Complaints were by subordinate personnel but serious enough that Commissar of Health Semashko ordered an investigation. GARF, f. 482, op. 1, d. 156, ll. 25–26.

9. TsGA SPb, f. 4031, op. 1, d. 402, l. 13ob.

10. Ibid., d. 406, l. 77.

11. Ibid., d. 467, l. 56.

12. Depending on the locale, 30–80 percent of the children were anemic, 50–90 percent had swollen glands, and 60–80 percent had bad teeth; TsGA SPb, f. 4301, d. 34, ll. 18–23.

13. For more on this, see Elizabeth Wood, *The Baba and the Comrade* (Bloomington, Ind., 1997), esp. chapter 6.

14. See Rabkrin report on OMM work, 1926, GARF, f. 406, op. 1, d. 667, l. 19.

15. Theses on OMM "S perekhodom na mestnye sredstva," GARF, f. 482, op. 1, d. 156, ll. 33–33ob. Report by Dr. N. F. Shtiftar on developments in the early 1920s, TsGA SPb, f. 4301, op. 1, d. 3023, ll. 29–30.

16. TsGA SPb, f. 4301, op. 1, d. 2062, ll. 137–40; and d. 3048, ll. 3–6.

17. Nor was it even able to support many urban facilities, which were being rapidly liquidated. See report from Luga district, January 13, 1923, ibid., d. 1569, l. 17.

18. The figures have been added up by Elizabeth Waters in her "Teaching Mothercraft in Post-Revolutionary Russia," *Australian Slavonic and East European Studies* 1:2 (1987), 31–32.

19. *Sel'skie korrespondenty*, usually shortened to *selkory* (male) and *selkorki* (female).

20. There are so many of these that a separate study could easily be justified. A large number of peasant women's biographies appear not only in the bulky file, RGAE, f. 396, op. 2, d. 30, but in other related files as well.

21. When letters were not good enough to be published at all, the writer might nevertheless be used as a conduit to others who might be more helpful. A very wooden report sent in by a certain Shkuratov from Smolensk province, for example, received the uncomplimentary reply: "Dear Comrade. . . . Your comments are uninteresting and therefore we cannot place them in the journal." The secretary then added: "Connect us with activist peasant women from your township." In another case, the secretary responded to a woman correspondent that although they were not able to print the letters and essays she had sent, the editors would draw on material in them for articles and stories characterizing the mood in the villages. Her work was good enough that she was asked to fill out the questionnaire to become a correspondent. "Write about your life and work. If you write often, we will send you a correspondent's card." RGAE, f. 396, op. 2, d. 29, ll. 294, 297–99.

22. A few examples from many in *Krest'ianka* in the year 1926 include no. 8, "Pomogi otkryt' iasli"; no. 10, lead essay; no. 10 "Pervaia lastochka"; no. 14, "Gde eshche plokho"; no. 15, "Geroi-delegatka"; and no. 19, letters column, p. 4.

23. Among many examples, see RGAE, f. 396, op. 2, d. 31, ll. 9, 19, 43; op. 3, d. 8, ll. 92–112.

24. Ibid., op. 3, d. 8, ll. 85–85ob.

25. Ibid., l. 61.

26. Ibid., l. 27ob; for similar problems with the poor peasants, see also ibid., ll. 10–11ob.

27. See report from Kugushevo village in *Krest'ianka* no. 19 (1929), 16.

28. For example, RGAE, f. 396, op. 3, d. 8, ll. 37, 41.

29. Correspondent Nikitina, Oct. 8, 1924, ibid., op. 2, d. 30, ll. 217–18.

30. Correspondent M. Miniaeva, June 27, 1925, ibid., op. 3, d. 8, ll. 16–17ob.

31. Interview with archives publication editor, Tatiana Mironova, at GARF publications office, July 6, 1990. The first places I found examples of the letters were in Party and literary archives, which then led me to the collection belonging to the publications. This appeals function in regard to nurseries can be seen in a letter that I found in a provincial archive. The barely literate letter was sent in the spring of 1925 from Gdov district, then in the southwest of Leningrad province:

> Comrades, when I returned home from the congress, I told my peasants what I could about the opening of nurseries . . . and requested that a nursery be opened here. The peasant women were very happy with that initiative, but the joy of our poor peasant woman did not last long because you can't live on promises. Nurseries here bogged down, nothing more was heard about them. I went to ask the [township] organizer, and he told me, do as you please, go and open one yourself, we don't have any funds for it.
>
> I had to leave feeling so disgraced by this answer that I cried. Personally, I don't now need nurseries. My daughter can look after herself. But I wanted to see that unsupervised children were taken care of. . . . If the township is considered wealthy, then so is the chief and ought to help us at least open [nurseries]. . . . The children were feeling so good about getting a nursery

here, but now they say nothing, because we have to live on promises and bring up the children unsupervised as in the past.

In a word, our poor corner is forgotten by everyone.

Delegatka Ksenia Akimova
(TsGA SPb, f. 4301, op. 1, d. 2060, l. 586)

The chief secretary at the publishing house sent a copy of this letter to the head of the OMM provincial office, asking that she let the editorial office know "if they intended to open nurseries in that township and also send us a list of the places where in the near future (for the summer season) they will be organizing in the countryside dispensaries, nurseries, and midwife stations." The editorial office also asked for a copy of the guidelines used for organizing nurseries there. The head of the OMM office then sent this packet of materials on to the person in charge of nurseries in that area of the province. So, the publishing house served as an instigator of pressure on the township authorities from further up in the administrative hierarchy in response to calls from powerless local activists to get their needs met. For other examples see TsGA SPb, f. 4301, op. 1, d. 2066, l. 585; RGAE, f. 396, op. 2, d. 29, ll. 280–83ob; d. 31, ll. 445–47; op. 3, d. 497, ll. 20–23.

32. See, for example, report by Dr. N. F. Shtiftar, TsGA SPb, f. 4301, op. 1, d. 3023, l. 40.

33. TsGA SPb, f. 4301, op. 1, d. 2683, ll. 65–65ob, 70ob.

34. Ibid., l. 58.

35. Ibid., l. 58ob.

36. Ibid., ll. 75–76, 83.

37. A research specialist and historian of maternal and child welfare in Russia, A. N. Antonov, proposed this as a general approach, writing a small book based on surveys he did in Staraia Russa, Gdov, Pskov, and Petrograd in 1919 and 1920. *Podgotovka devochki k materinstvu* (Leningrad, 1929). To the extent the approach was tried in the villages, much of the knowledge implanted there would soon after have been transferred to the cities and industrial sites where many young women migrated in the 1930s.

38. TsGA SPb, f. 4301, op. 1, d. 2683, ll. 85ob–86.

39. Report dated received December 27, 1925, ibid., ll. 2–4ob.

40. Report by Dr. Gofmekler in *Krest'ianka,* 1926:3.

41. TsGA SPb, f. 4301, op. 1, d. 3023, ll. 41–42.

42. Ibid., ll. 122–23.

43. Ibid., ll. 47–51.

44. From director of Leningrad OMM; ibid., d. 2682, ll. 59–59ob.

45. However, there were other specific terms for midwives and healers as well.

46. For some examples, see *Krest'ianka* (1926) no. 2, 17; no. 5, 17; no. 6, 16–17; no. 14, 7; no. 19, 8–9.

47. *Krest'ianka* (1926) no. 3, 12–13.

48. The series began in the first March issue and continued through most of the year. Similar series followed under a variety of titles in subsequent years of the magazine.

49. District health officer Kuzman's report, TsGA SPb, f. 4301, op. 1, d. 3407, ll. 270–270ob.

50. Ibid., d. 3031, l. 64ob.

51. Ibid.

52. Ibid.

53. Ibid., ll. 64ob–65.

54. Ibid., l. 65ob.

55. Ibid., d. 3050, ll. 11–11ob.

56. Ibid., ll. 240–42.

57. RGAE, f. 396, op. 2, d. 26, ll. 21–22ob.

58. TsGA SPb, f. 4301, op. 1, d. 3401, l. 239, and d. 2682, l. 13.

59. Ibid., ll. 245–46, 270–270ob.

60. Antonov, *Okhrana*, 218; a somewhat higher number for 1926 (3,056) is given in V. M. Kurzon, *Okhrana materinstva i mladenchestva v SSSR* (Samara, 1928), 154.

61. Konius, *Puti*, 210–14.

62. See Bramson report, April 16, 1927, TsGA SPb, f. 4301, op. 1, d. 3031, l. 83. Also 1927 circular for Leningrad province, "Instruktsiia k deiatelnosti volostnykh i sel'skikh komissii po OMM," TsGA SPb, f. 4301, op. 1, d. 3407, l. 237.

63. TsGA SPb, f. 4301, op. 1, d. 3031, l. 34.

64. Ibid., d. 3050, l. 11.

65. Ibid., d. 3041, l. 7.

66. Ibid., d. 3023, l. 119.

67. Ibid., d. 3407, l. 237.

68. Lilian Liu, "The Development of the Soviet Rural Health Care System and the Role of the Feldshers, 1917–1941," 108.

69. A. M. Bol'shakov, *Derevnia 1917–1927* (Moscow, 1927), 291.

70. D. Glebov, "Okhrana zdorov'ia zhenshchin i rebenka v kolkhozakh i sovkhozakh," *ZAZB* 41:2 (March–April, 1930), 138.

71. Liu, "Development," 109.

72. The change can be followed in the two treatments with rather different emphases: Nancy Mandelker Frieden, *Russian Physicians in an Era of Reform and Revolution, 1856–1905* (Princeton, 1981), and John F. Hutchinson, *Politics and Public Health in Revolutionary Russia, 1890–1918* (Baltimore, 1990).

73. Konius, *Puti*, 233–34.

74. I. F. Makkaveev, "Osobennosti organizatsii okhrany materinstva v Leningrade i puti dal'neishego razvitiia v etoi oblasti," *ZAZB* 41:1 (January–February, 1930), 82–91.

75. "Protiv gnilogo liberalizma v meditsinskoi pechati," *ZAZB* 43:1 (1932), 2–6.

76. D. Glebov, "Okhrana zdorov'ia zhenshchiny," *ZAZB* 41:2 (March–April 1930), 135.

77. Konius, *Puti*, 240–44.

78. Ibid., 239, 253.

79. From report "O sostoianii rodovspomozheniia," April 5, 1933, GARF, f. 482, op. 24, d. 80, ll. 195–97.

80. Ibid., ll. 195–195ob.

81. Ibid., l. 196.

82. Some offices directly refused to implement the order, including in particular the distant regions of Eastern Siberia, Western Siberia, and Cossack Territory, but also the more central Gor'kii Territory. Others pretended to implement the program but in fact did nothing more than formally assign people to it who were busy with other work. Ibid., l. 2, 196.

83. Konius, *Puti*, 291.

84. Ibid., 291–92.

85. Ibid., 293.

86. On mobilization directed by Sergiev and others see GARF, f. 482, op. 1, d. 744, ll. 43–44, 98–101, 157–70. See B. Ts. Urlanis, "Dinamika urovnia rozhdaemosti v SSSR za gody sovetskoi vlasti," in A. G. Vishnevskii, ed. *Brachnost', rozhdaemost', smertnost' v Rossii i v SSSR,* 8–27, who uses an index of "effective fertility" to indicate the demographic result.

87. GARF, f. 482, op. 29, d. 7, ll. 24ob–25. The number of known abortions per 100 births in 1939 in Leningrad and Moscow ran to about 50, but this was down from the period before the ban, when the number of abortions in some large centers outpaced births.

88. My spot checks of hospitals indicate an 80 percent rise in incomplete (illegal) abortions in Borovichi from 1935 to 1939, and a 25 percent rise in Luga from 1937 to 1939. See GARF, f. 482, op. 29, d. 2, l. 2. A study by the abortion commission in Moscow province in this period reported that of the women rejected for an abortion, 55 percent carried the child to term. Not all the rest could be found and checked, but undoubtedly a large number found another way to obtain an abortion; ibid., d. 54, ll. 54–57.

89. Ibid., d. 2, l. 3.

90. Ibid., d. 56, passim. One of our informants had been a village medical worker in Novgorod province in this period and admitted that she tried to protect her patients from the authorities by not reporting obviously botched abortions as such (see also chapter 4).

91. Ibid., d. 2, l. 3.

92. Definitions of literacy varied from time to time in Russia. In this period, literacy was defined as merely the ability to read, and reports were not based on standard tests. While these statistics must accordingly be used with caution, authorities agree that female education grew rapidly in this era. See Susan Bridger, *Women in the Soviet Countryside* (Cambridge, 1987), 15; Barbara Evans Clements, *Daughters of Revolution: A History of Women in the U.S.S.R.* (Arlington Heights, Ill., 1994), 70–71; Gail Warshofsky Lapidus, *Women in Soviet Society: Equality, Development, and Social Change* (Berkeley, 1978), 136–37.

93. Ob organizatsii i sostoanii rodil'noi pomoshchi v RSFSR," *ZAZB* 44:3 (1933), 145–47.

94. GARF, f. 482, op. 29, d. 2, l. 8; d.7, l. 8; d. 33, ll. 1–2ob; d. 48, ll. 10–11.

95. Report from February 2, 1937, TsGA SPb, f. 3007, op. 3, d. 266, ll. 6, 15–16.

96. Apparently designed by Dr. Aleksandr Nikolaevich Rakhmanov (1861–1926), a research obstetrician and innovator.

97. Report signed by Inspector Vishnevskaia, August 22, 1940, GARF, f. 482, op. 29, d. 33, ll. 5–5ob.

98. Ibid., d. 63, ll. 63–64ob.

99. See chapter 5.

100. GARF, f. 482, op. 29, d. 2, l. 9. See also Zachepinskii's report, with similar concerns, to the Leningrad conference in January 1941, ibid., l. 41.

101. Konius, *Puti,* 304. Figures on total dispensaries from GARF, f. 482, op. 29, d. 1, ll. 78–79; for villages, ibid., d. 7, l. 21.

102. Polotskii wrote that "none of the four dispensaries fulfills its important obliga-

tion to link up with birthing facilities. They limit themselves to superficial exams of pregnant women and the allocation of documents for maternity leave, sending women for urine analysis, and, very rarely, a Wasserman test. . . .There is no link between the dispensaries and district hospitals and midwife stations. The dispensaries do not conduct any preventive work with the district institutions or check on what is being done in them. The buildings and equipment of the dispensaries are often altogether unsatisfactory. For example, at the Luga dispensary pregnant women are seen in a pediatric cubicle of 10–12 square meters, the entire instrumentation consists of a wooden trestle bed and a pelvimeter. No obstetrician has been on staff for a year, and exams are conducted by a 70-year-old midwife. Things are far worse in the outlying institutions, where in the overwhelming majority of cases no urine analysis is done, not to mention Wasserman tests, and outreach is nonexistent." GARF, f. 482, op. 29, d. 2, ll. 12–13.

103. Ibid., d. 7, ll. 1–2.

104. Ibid., ll. 48–51.

105. Calculated from figures in ibid., l. 21ob.

106. TsGA SPb, f. 3007, op. 3, d. 266, ll. 29–32.

107. Ibid., ll. 38–40; more such reports, ll. 31–74. For note on the similar efforts of Moscow doctors, see GARF, f. 482, op. 29, d. 54, ll. 50–51.

108. TsGA SPb, f. 3007, op. 3, d. 266, ll. 38–40.

109. See translation of full text of the law in Rudolf Schlesinger, ed. *The Family in the U.S.S.R.* (London, 1949), 269–79.

110. Konius, *Puti,* 303.

111. *Bol'shaia Sovetskaia Entsiklopediia,* 2nd ed. (1955), vol. 31, 476. Reports for the Russian republic indicate that there were 199,000 year-round nurseries in villages in 1940, rising to 204,000 in 1945, and 267,767 in 1954. N. N. Grigor'eva, "Sorok let okhrany materinstva i detstva v RSFSR," *Voprosy okhrany materinstva i detstva* 2:5 (1957), 9.

112. GARF, f. 482, op. 29, d. 2, l. 14. *Naselenie SSSR za 70 let,* ed. L. L. Rybakovskii (Moscow, 1988), 51.

113. GARF, f. 482, op. 29, d. 2, l. 15.

114. E. I. Danilishina and A. S. Fedoseev, "Deiatel'nost' organov zdravookhraneniia po okhrane zdorov'ia detei i podrostkov v gody velikoi otechestvennoi voiny," *Voprosy okhrany materinstva i detstva* no. 5 (1985), 13–18; E. I. Danilishina, "Okhrana zdorov'ia zhenshchiny-materi v gody velikoi otechestvennoi voiny," *Sovetskoe zdravookhranenie* no. 3 (1986), 40–42.

115. Bridger, *Women,* 17.

116. On the controversy surrounding this law, which sacrificed the rights to support and dignity of hundreds of thousands of women and children on the pretext of protecting the family, see Peter H. Juviler, "Family Reforms on the Road to Communism," in *Soviet Policy-Making: Studies of Communism in Transition,* ed. Peter H. Juviler and Henry W. Morton (New York, 1967), 29–60.

117. GARF, f. 482, op. 47, d. 5875, l. 95.

118. For reports from a variety of provinces in 1947 and 1948, see ibid., d. 5881, ll. 18–19, 62–64, 107–108; ibid., d. 5879, ll. 91–101; for reports from Moscow city and province in 1952 see ibid., op. 49, d. 4775, ll. 36–39, 77–88.

119. It is worth noting that the law against abortions did additional harm to women generally (besides the suffering from illegal abortions): the use of beds to care for

women with incomplete abortions deprived more than 14,000 women during this year (1952) in Moscow city and province of hospitalization for other ills. GARF, f. 482, op. 49, d. 4775, ll. 37, 86.

120. Bridger, *Women,* 129.

121. Ibid., 208–15.

3. Courtship and Marriage

1. Bride-show is the meeting at which the prospective groom is formally introduced to his proposed bride. She is dressed in her finery. He has the opportunity to view her and even to probe her body through her clothes to see that she comes as advertised. For a description of this phase of the marriage negotiation, see Olga Semyonova Tian-Shanskaia, *Village Life in Late Tsarist Russia,* chapter 6.

2. For background on this issue, see L. N. Semenova, *Ocherki istorii byta i kul'turnoi zhizni Rossii, pervaia polovina XVIII v.* (Leningrad, 1982), 15–34, esp. 22–23.

3. V. A. Aleksandrov, *Sel'skaia obshchina v Rossii* (Moscow, 1966), 303–308.

4. Valentina Tripapina, interview by Ransel, Laikovo, Moscow province, July 8, 1990.

5. Olga Mal'tseva, interview by Ransel, Chernaia, Novgorod province, May 25, 1990.

6. See the recent study of this problem by Alan M. Ball, *And Now My Soul Is Hardened: Abandoned Children in Soviet Russia, 1918–1930* (Berkeley, 1994).

7. Praskovia Kurkova, interview by Glazunova and Ransel, Zhukovka, Moscow province, June 6, 1993.

8. Ibid. "He forced her to marry," her daughter, who participated in the interview, reported.

9. The father's suspicion may have been aroused by the fact that the job for Lina was not arranged by him but by Lina's older sister, who was working for a relative of the family to which Lina was sent.

10. Lina Buldakova, interview by Glazunova and Ransel, Vvedenskoe, Moscow province, June 5, 1993.

11. Peter Czap, "Marriage and the Peasant Joint Family in the Era of Serfdom," in *The Family in Imperial Russia,* ed. David L. Ransel, esp. 108–18; Olga Semyonova Tian-Shanskaya, *Village Life in Late Tsarist Russia,* ed. David L. Ransel (Bloomington, Ind., 1993), chapter 5.

12. Olimpiada Bakhmesterova, interview by Glazunova and Ransel, Staroe Selo, Moscow province, June 7, 1993.

13. Anastasia Shishanova, interview by Glazunova and Ransel, Tsarevo, Moscow province, June 6, 1993.

14. Elizaveta Nikolaeva, interview by Glazunova and Ransel, Tsarevo, Moscow province, June 6, 1993.

15. The most thorough recent description is in D. M. Balashov et al., *Russkaia svad'ba: Svadebnyi obriad na Verkhnei i Srednei Kokshen'ge i na Uftiuge (Tarnogskii raion Vologodskoi oblasti)* (Moscow, 1985), though it details a specific northern form of wedding.

16. A turn-of-the-century version of this for Riazan province is described in Olga Semyonova Tian-Shanskaya, *Village Life,* chapter 6.

17. See, for example, reports by Maria Abramova and Anna Reutova, both interviews by Listova, Inakovka 2, Tambov province, summer 1994.

18. Maria Somova, interview by Listova, Pakhotnyi ugol, Tambov province, summer 1994.

19. Steven L. Hoch, *Serfdom and Social Control in Russia: Petrovskoe, a Village in Tambov* (Chicago, 1986), 95–106.

20. Anastasia Spiridonova, interview by Glazunova and Ransel, Lepeshki, Moscow province, June 7, 1993.

21. Zinaida Shumkova, interview by Glazunova and Ransel, Fedorovskoe, Moscow province, June 5, 1993.

22. Anisia Gureeva, interview by Listova, Kiiasovo, Moscow province, spring 1994.

23. Aleksandra Gibert, interview by Peshkova, Maminskoe, Sverdlovsk province, summer 1993.

24. Anna Panacheva, interview by Peshkova, Maminskoe, Sverdlovsk province, summer 1993.

25. Maria Somova, interview, summer 1994. See also interviews with informants Marfa Malikova, Maria Malikova, and Anna Markova from Tambov province.

26. Maria Abramova, interview, summer 1994.

27. A sazhen is usually thought of as a measure of length, but it can also be a measure of volume or of area. A sazhen of land was traditionally defined as the amount that could be sown with a chetverik of barley (a chetverik is a dry measure equal to 26.239 liters). See Vladimir Dal', *Tolkovyi slovar'*, vol. 4, 129.

28. Anna Reutova, interview, summer 1994.

29. Praskovia Krivolapova, interview by Listova, Inakovka 2, Tambov province, summer 1994.

30. See a description of this custom in Semyonova Tian-Shanskaya, *Village Life*, 86–90.

31. Praskovia Krivolapova, interview, summer 1994.

32. Pelagea Nikulina, interview by Listova, Bulgakovka, Tambov province, summer 1994. In a village some distance from the twin Inakovka villages, even the memory of this custom, had it ever been practiced, was gone. "Here they did not check on a bride's innocence, perhaps because all of them were honorable. It would also have been shameful for the people and for the husband," said Maria Somova, interview, summer 1994.

33. M. Kaplun, "Brachnost' naseleniia RSFSR," *Statisticheskoe obozrenie* no. 7 (1929), 91, nevertheless reports that about 10 percent of men and women in rural areas entering marriage were remarrying following a divorce. Cited in Wendy Z. Goldman, "Alimony and the Peasant Dvor: The Gap between Family Law and Rural Life" (paper delivered at AAASS National Convention, New Orleans, November, 1986).

34. V. I. Zaitsev, interview by Glazunova and Ransel, Fedorovskoe, Moscow province, June 5, 1933.

35. Nina Novozhilova, interview by Glazunova and Ransel, Nazarovo, Moscow province, June 6, 1993.

36. Anna Zueva, interview by Ransel, Chernaia, Batetskii raion, Novgorod province, May 24–26, 1990.

37. Antonina Larshina, interview by Glazunova and Ransel, Orlovo, Moscow province, June 8, 1993.

38. Her husband, unlike many others, did return from the war, and they had a family together. Anastasia Kuzina, interview by Glazunova and Ransel, Vvedenskoe, Moscow province, June 6, 1993.

39. Nina Gracheva, interview by Glazunova and Ransel, Lepeshki, Moscow province, June 7, 1993.

40. Elena Sorokoumova, interview by Listova, Nikitino, El'ninsk raion, Smolensk province, summer 1993.

41. A fifth informant did not, but she was a Muslim Bashkir who will be considered later together with other Turkic women.

42. Anna Panacheva, interview, summer 1993.

43. Anna Mikhaleva, interview by Listova, Inakovka 2, Tambov province, summer 1994.

44. Natalia Mikhaleva, interview by Listova, Inakovka 2, Tambov province, summer 1994.

45. Antonina Abramova, interview, summer 1994.

46. Anna Kasiakina, interview by Listova, Inakovka, Tambov province, summer 1994.

47. Aleksandra Krivolapova, interview by Listova, Inakovka 2, Tambov province, summer 1994.

48. Elena Sorokoumova, interview, summer 1993.

49. Elena Bobkova, interview by Listova, El'ninsk raion, Smolensk province, summer 1993.

50. Mil'kovich, *Byt i verovaniia tatar Simbirskoi gubernii v 1783 g.* (Kazan, 1905), 7–10; K. Fuks, *Kazanskie tatary,* 2–30. See also N. Spasskii, *Ocherki po rodinovedeniiu. Kazanskaia guberniia,* 80–81; and on Bashkirs: P. S. Nazarov, "K etnografii bashkir," *Etnograficheskoe obozrenie* 2:1 (1890), 189–90; S. I. Rudenko, *Bashkiry. Opyt etnologicheskoi monografii,* 2 vols. (Petrograd, 1916; Leningrad, 1925), 258–62.

51. Sukharev, *Kazanskie tatary,* 43.

52. E. P. Busygin et al., *Sel'skaia zhenshchina v semeinoi i obshchestvennoi zhizni* (Kazan, 1986), 20–21. Such a school was known as *mekteb* (Arabic: *maktab*).

53. Ibid., 22.

54. Khatima Nizamova, interview by Ransel. See women in mosque interview, Tatarskii Kalmaiur, Ul'ianovsk province, July 15, 1990.

55. N. A. Kisliakov noted, in regard to Central Asia, that in the peoples "among which one observes a tendency toward a diminution and gradual disappearance of *kalym* and increase in the relative weight of the dowry there appears still another marital regulation provided by the Shariat, namely, *makhr*. Makhr is a type of security given by the groom to his bride and is usually divided into two parts: a personal makhr . . . and a reserve makhr. The first is a certain sum of money or property given to the bride at the time of the wedding; the second is money or property previously agreed upon but which is only given to the wife in the case of the death of her husband or a divorce initiated by him." *Ocherki po istorii semi i braka,* 81–82, as cited in Busygin et al., *Sel'skaia zhenshchina,* 23.

56. Minzifa Mustafina, speaking of her mother's marriage and dowry, interview by Shugaeva, Tatarskii Kalmaiur, Ul'ianovsk province, summer 1993. Possibly, too, some defect of the bride could have made such a match a necessity.

57. Mariam Gimadeeva, interview by Shugaeva, Tatarskii Kalmaiur, Ul'ianovsk province, summer 1993.

58. Rakhmet Suleimanov, interview by Ransel, Simbirsk, Ul'ianovsk province, July 15, 1990.

59. Khatima Nizamova, interview by Ransel, women in mosque interview, Tatarskii Kalmaiur, Ul'ianovsk province, July 15, 1990.

60. According to my colleague Nazif Shahrani, much depended on the qualifications of the mullah's wife. Some of them were quite knowledgeable and could and did teach more than basic reading and reciting.

61. On schooling in Arabic, see also Roza Fakhrutdinova, interview by Shugaeva, Tatarskii Kalmaiur, Ul'ianovsk province, summer 1993; Zukhra Pozdniakova, interview by Ransel, Krasnoe Selo, Leningrad province, April 20, 1990; Sofia Teleshova, interview by Ransel, Leningrad, May 31, 1990; Fakhiza Suleimanova, interview by Ransel, Simbirsk, Ul'ianovsk province, July 15, 1990.

62. "Rabotala kak mullakh." Reported by Shugaeva from interview, summer 1993.

63. Khatima Nizamova, interview by Shugaeva, Tatarskii Kalmaiur, Ul'ianovsk province, summer 1993.

64. Ibid.; and Sharifa Ialisheva, interview by Ransel, Leningrad, April 21, 1990.

65. Garifabanu Abdullina, interview by Shugaeva, Tatarskii Kalmaiur, Ul'ianovsk province, summer 1993. On sex separation, see also Zukhra Pozdniakova, interview, April 20, 1990.

66. Garifabanu Abdullina, interview by Shugaeva, Tatarskii Kalmaiur, Ul'ianovsk province, summer 1993.

67. After the war, she did get back to the Leningrad area when her family relocated to Gatchina. Sharifa Ialisheva, interview, spring 1990. Follow-up interview with Sharifa's relative, Amina Teleshova, interview by Ransel, Leningrad, May 8, 1990.

68. Mariam Gimadeeva, interview by Shugaeva, Tatarskii Kalmaiur, summer 1993.

69. Zukhra Pozdniakova, interview, spring 1990.

70. Valentin Teleshov, as part of interview with Zukhra Pozdniakova, spring 1990.

71. Fina Iurenieva, interview by Ransel, Leningrad, June 5, 1990.

72. Roza Fakhrutdinova, interview, summer 1993.

73. Rkia Kamaletdinova, interview by Shugaeva, Tatarskii Kalmaiur, summer 1993.

74. The marriage may have been compelled by a pregnancy, for Zeinab's first child arrived within nine months of her official marriage (although possibly *nikiakh* had been performed earlier and opened the way for a religiously sanctioned sexual life). Zeinab Gimatdinova, interview by Shugaeva, Tatarskii Kalmaiur, summer 1993.

75. Zatia Bagautdinova, interview by Shugaeva, Tatarskii Kalmaiur, summer 1993.

76. Fakhiza Suleimanova, interview, summer 1990.

77. Nurania Badrieva, interview by Shugaeva, Tatarskii Kalmaiur, summer 1993.

78. Ibid.

79. Sofia Teleshova, interview, spring 1990.

4. Fertility Choices

1. But not abortion on demand (see later discussion). The evolution of law on abortion rights has recently been surveyed by Wendy Z. Goldman, *Women, the State and Revolution: Soviet Family Policy and Social Life, 1917–1936* (New York, 1993).

2. See chapter 5 on childbirth.

3. Maria Malikova, interview by Listova, Inakovka 1, Tambov province, summer 1994.

4. The mother in question was born about the same time, circa 1913, as Maria Malikova. Aleksandra Krivolapova, interview by Listova, Inakovka 2, Tambov province, summer 1994.

5. Elena Bobkova, interview by Listova, El'ninsk raion, Smolensk province, summer 1993. Pelagea Nikulina, interview by Listova, Bulgakovka, Inzhavinskii raion, Tambov province, summer 1994.

6. Anisia Gureeva, interview by Listova, Kiiasovo, Stupinsk raion, Moscow province, spring 1994. Klavdia Fateeva of same village affirmed her mother's rejection of abortion because it was sinful. Interview by Listova, Kiiasovo, Stupinsk raion, Moscow province, spring 1994.

7. Efrosinia Ruleva, interview by Listova, Korobets, El'ninsk raion, Smolensk province, summer 1993.

8. Elena Bobkova, interview, summer 1993.

9. Anna Varfolomeeva, interview by Listova, Nikitino, El'ninsk raion, Smolensk province, summer 1993.

10. Daria Fedosenkova, interview by Listova, Suglitsa, El'ninsk raion, Smolensk province, 1993.

11. Elizaveta Nikolaeva, interview by Glazunova and Ransel, Tsarevo, Moscow province, June 6, 1993.

12. See more on this story in chapter 3 about marriage. Lina Buldakova, interview by Glazunova and Ransel, Vvedenskoe, Moscow province, June 5, 1993.

13. Pelagea Sharaveva, interview by Peshkova, Maminskoe, Sverdlovsk province, summer 1993.

14. Anastasia Shishanova, interview by Glazunova and Ransel, Tsarevo, Moscow province, June 6, 1993.

15. Maria Somova, interview by Listova, Pakhotnyi ugol, Bondarskii raion, Tambov province, summer 1994.

16. Maria Abramova, interview by Listova, Inakovka 2, Tambov province, summer 1994. See similar comments about having not used contraception or abortion personally but knowing of some abortions being done on others: Pelagea Nikulina (born 1910), interview, summer 1994, and Praskovia Krivolapova, interview, summer 1994.

17. This informant added, in regard to shame, that one young woman in her village gave birth unmarried; although it was regarded as shameful, mores were such in those days that the man in question did marry her. Marfa Malikova, interview by Listova, Inakovka 1, Tambov province, summer 1994.

18. Maria Malikova, interview, summer 1994.

19. Recall, too, that Father Giliarovskii reported on village abortions in the mid-nineteenth century. See chapter 1.

20. Anastasia Spiridonova, interview by Glazunova and Ransel, Lepeshki, Moscow province, June 7, 1993.

21. Maria Malikova, interview, summer 1994.

22. See chapter 7 on infant death. I have worked out there and elsewhere an analysis of this labeling behavior; see my "'Starye mladentsy' v russkoi derevne," in *Mentalitet i agrarnoe razvitie Rossii (XIX–XX vv.)*, ed. V. P. Danilov and L. V. Milov (Moscow, 1996), 106–14, which is similar to the behavior described in the work of Nancy Scheper-Hughes, *Death without Weeping: The Violence of Everyday Life in Brazil* (Berkeley, 1992).

23. Some women returned to home birthing after having had a hospital birth.

24. M. M. Levin, "K kharakteristike prichin iskusstvennogo vykidysha," *ZAZB* 42:3 (1931), 377.

25. Anna Zueva, interview by Ransel, Chernaia, Batetskii raion, Novgorod province, May 24–26, 1990.

26. This doctor, Vasilii Dobrynin, went on to say that legal pressures eased on criminal abortions after the ban on abortions generally was lifted. Although his hospital did not do abortions even after they again became legal (the hospital lacked a specialist and proper facilities), one of his women doctors did abortions secretly, and, when caught, the worst she received was a reprimand. Vasilii Dobrynin, interview by Listova, Inakovka, Tambov province, summer 1994.

27. Anna Kirsanova, interview by Listova, Vititni, El'ninsk raion, Smolensk province, summer 1993.

28. She paid the village woman 36 pounds of oats for the abortion. The second abortion was performed in a hospital and cost 25 rubles. Efrosinia Ruleva, interview, summer 1993.

29. Interestingly, she adds that her daughter also had an abortion with a village woman after she had had her first child; so, village abortionists continued to ply their trade even after abortion was again legalized. Elena Bobkova, interview, summer 1993.

30. Praskovia Korotchenkova, interview by Listova, Elizavetino, El'ninsk raion, Smolensk province, summer 1993.

31. Ibid. For other comments on the distaste and even hostility that women expressed against abortionists, see interviews with Fira Krugman, interview by Ransel, Leningrad, May, 12, 1990; and with Fina Iurenieva, interview by Ransel, Ethnographic Institute, Leningrad, June 5, 1990.

32. Efrosinia Ruleva, interview, summer 1993.

33. Anna P-va, interview by Glazunova and Ransel, Vvedenskoe, Moscow province, June 6, 1993. Pavel Grafov, interview by Glazunova and Ransel, Nazarovo, Moscow province, June 6, 1993. Zinaida Shumkova, interview by Glazunova and Ransel, Fedorovskoe, Moscow province, June 5, 1993.

34. Elizaveta Smirnova, interview by Glazunova and Ransel, Staroe Selo, Moscow province, June 7, 1993.

35. Anna Mikhaleva, interview by Listova, Inakovka 2, Tambov province, summer 1994.

36. Natalia Mikhaleva, interview by Listova, Inakovka 2, Tambov province, summer 1994.

37. Tamara Privalova, interview by Peshkova, Maminskoe, Sverdlovsk province, summer 1993.

38. Galina Mamina, interview by Peshkova, Maminskoe, Sverdlovsk province, summer 1993.

39. Anna Panacheva, interview by Peshkova, Maminskoe, Sverdlovsk province, summer 1993.

40. Efrosinia Ruleva, interview, summer 1993.

41. Elena Tsygankova,interview by Listova, Elizavetino, El'ninsk raion, Smolensk province, summer 1993.

42. Anna Varfolomeeva, interview, summer 1993.

43. Anastasia Kuzina, interview by Glazunova and Ransel, Vvedenskoe, Moscow province, June 6, 1993.

44. Anna Zueva, interview, spring 1990.

45. I. P. Il'ina, "Vliianie voin na brachnost' sovetskikh zhenshchin," in *Brachnost', rozhdaemost', smertnost' v Rossii i v SSSR,* ed. A. G. Vishnevskii (Moscow, 1977), 50–61. S. A. Novosel'skii, "Vliianie voiny na polovoi sostav rozhdaiushchikhsia," *Voprosy demograficheskoi i sanitarnoi statistiki* (Moscow, 1958), 191–98.

46. Anna Zueva, interview, spring 1990.

47. Tatiana Vorob'eva, interview by Peshkova, Maminskoe, Sverdlovsk province, summer 1993.

48. Antonina Ptichnikova, interview by Glazunova and Ransel, Kablukovo, Moscow province, June 8, 1993.

49. Valentina Lopatkina, interview by Glazunova and Ransel, Tsarevo, Moscow province, June 6, 1993.

50. Ibid.

51. Raisa Semenovna's testimony is included in the interview with her mother, Anastasia Shishanova, interview, summer 1993.

52. Valentina Shapovalova, interview by Listova, Korobets, El'ninsk raion, Smolensk province, summer 1993.

53. Antonina Abramova, interview, summer 1994.

54. Lia Brykina, interview by Listova, Inakovka 1, Tambov province, summer 1994; Anna Kasiakina, interview by Listova, Inakovka, Tambov province, summer 1994. Aleksandra Krivolapova, interview, summer 1994.

55. Anna Kasiakina, interview, summer 1994.

56. Evidently, Khatima's mother was not around to advise her, for, as mentioned in chapter 3, her mother broke under the stress of the famine of the early 1920s and gave up her six other surviving children to the children's home in Melikesa (later Dmitrovgrad) and left Khatima, the oldest, to fend for herself. Her father was also apparently absent and died soon after. Nizamova, interview by Shugaeva, Tatarskii Kalmaiur, summer 1993.

57. Garifabanu Abdullina, interview by Shugaeva, Tatarskii Kalmaiur, Ul'ianovsk province, summer 1993.

58. Zubarzhat Rezvanova, interview by Shugaeva, Tatarskii Kalmaiur, Ul'ianovsk province, summer 1993.

59. Sharifa Ialisheva, interview by Ransel, April 21, 1990, Leningrad. Follow-up interview by Ransel with relative Amina Teleshova, May 8, 1990, Leningrad.

60. See chapter 8 on child care and medical practices.

61. This woman's comments may have been influenced by her state of health: at the time of the interview, she was bedridden. Zatia Bagautdinova, interview by Shugaeva, Tatarskii Kalmaiur, Ul'ianovsk province, summer 1993.

62. Khatima Nizamova and others, women in mosque interview by Ransel, Tatarskii Kalmaiur, Ul'ianovsk province, July 16, 1990. Follow-up with Nizamova, interview by Shugaeva, Tatarskii Kalmaiur, Ul'ianovsk province, summer 1993.

63. Mariam Gimadeeva, interview by Shugaeva, Tatarskii Kalmaiur, Ul'ianovsk province, summer 1993.

64. Fakhiza Suleimanova, interview by Ransel, Simbirsk, Ul'ianovsk province, July 15, 1990.

65. Ibid.

66. Nurania Badrieva, interview by Shugaeva, Tatarskii Kalmaiur, Ul'ianovsk province, summer 1993.

67. Minzifa Mustafina, interview by Shugaeva, Tatarskii Kalmaiur, Ul'ianovsk province, summer 1993.

68. Roza Fakhrutdinova, interview by Shugaeva, Tatarskii Kalmaiur, Ul'ianovsk province, summer 1993.

69. Mariam Gimadeeva, interview, summer 1993.

70. Sofia Teleshova, interview by Ransel, May 31, 1990, Leningrad.

71. Khatima Nizamova, women in mosque interview, July 16, 1990.

72. Minzifa Mustafina, interview, summer 1993.

5. Giving Birth

1. Maksim Gorkii, "Rozhdenie cheloveka," *Polnoe sobranie sochinenii,* vol. 14 (Moscow, 1972), 143–53.

2. This type of effort at controlling spiritual forces may be common to many non-"modern" communities. Mary Helen Ayres, a midwife in Indiana, tells me that her Amish clients communicate with and about her and her co-workers in this same indirect way.

3. Semyonova Tian-Shanskaya, *Village Life in Late Tsarist Russia,* 11. See also Dm. Petukhov, "Babnichan'e," *Meditsinskii vestnik* 23 (1863), 215; and G. I. Popov, *Russkaia narodno-bytovaia meditsina,* 334–37.

4. Olga Mal'tseva interview by Ransel, Chernaia, Batetskii raion, Novgorod province, May 25, 1990.

5. Afanisa Sudakova explained that only one's mother should know about the start of labor, for if others found out, the birthing woman would suffer for a long time; interview by Listova, Barkanovskaia, Vozhegodskii raion, Vologda province, 1981. See also Udel'nyi Park interviews, by Shapovalova and Ransel, Leningrad, May 12, 1990, and references that follow in this chapter.

6. Anna Zueva, interview by Ransel, Chernaia, Batetskii raion, Novgorod province, May 24–26, 1990.

7. Natalia Skovorodina, interview by Listova, Cherniakovo, Tarnogskii raion, Vologda province, 1981.

8. Samuel C. Ramer, "Childbirth and Culture: Midwifery in the Nineteenth-Century Russian Countryside," in Ransel, *The Family in Imperial Russia,* 229–30.

9. Anfisa Sudakova, interview, 1981.

10. Dr. Vasilii Dobrynin, interview by Listova, Inakovka, Tambov province, summer 1994. Maria Ivanovna (born 1905), interview by Listova, Inakovka region, Tambov province, summer 1994.

11. In regard to the saying of "farewells," women were well aware of the dangers of death in childbirth. Anna Zueva and Olga Mal'tseva underscored this point and noted that each village had two or three families of orphans from the loss of a mother. Both women included in Olga Mal'tseva, interview, May 25, 1990.

12. Anna Reutova, interview by Listova, Inakovka 2, Tambov province, summer 1994.

13. Maria Malikova, interview by Listova, Inakovka 1, Tambov province, summer 1994.

14. This is the diminutive form of the word for a folk or granny midwife, *povitukha.*

15. For references in the ethnographic sources, see E. A. Pokrovskii, *Fizicheskoe*

vospitanie detei u raznykh narodov, preimushchestvenno Rossii (Moscow, 1984), 42–44; M. G. Rabinovich, *Ocherki etnografii russkogo feodal'nogo goroda* (Moscow, 1978), 249; and Semyonova Tian-Shanskaia, *Village Life in Late Tsarist Russia,* 16.

16. Anna Reutova, interview, summer 1994.

17. Marfa Malikova, interview by Listova, Inakovka 1, Tambov province, summer 1994.

18. Praskovia Krivolapova, interview by Listova, Inakovka 2, Tambov province, summer 1994.

19. See more on this interesting woman in chapter 6 on baptism.

20. The interviewer emphasized in her report to me that the mention of Jewish in referring to the doctor was not done in a discriminatory manner but merely by way of ethnic identification. Maria Malikova, interview, summer 1994.

21. See women in Udel'nyi Park, interview #2, May 12, 1990, Leningrad, in which a woman from Galich in Kostroma province born in 1918 tells of watching her mother give birth in this way. See also Popov, *Russkaia narodno-bytovaia meditsina,* 341; and Petukhov, "Babnichan'e," 216.

22. Maria Malikova, interview, summer 1994.

23. Anna Reutova, interview, summer 1994.

24. Praskovia Krivolapova, interview, summer 1994.

25. For more on this, see T. A. Listova, "Rebenok v russkoi sem'e. Rozhdenie, kreshchenie. 2-aia polovina XIX–XX v.," in *Obychai i obriady, sviazannye s rozhdeniem rebenka,* ed. T. A. Listova and T. P. Fedianovich (Moscow, 1995), 22–27.

26. Marfa Malikova, interview, summer 1994.

27. Praskovia Krivolapova, interview, summer 1994.

28. Anna Mikhaleva, interview by Listova, Inakovka 2, Tambov province, summer 1994.

29. Natalia Mikhaleva, interview by Listova, Inakovka 2, Tambov province, summer 1994.

30. Vasilii Dobrynin, interview, summer 1994.

31. Ibid.

32. Antonina Abramova, interview by Listova, Inakovka 2, Tambov province, summer 1994.

33. Lia Brykina (born 1932), a village schoolteacher, had her first two babies in the farm maternity ward and her third in Kirsanov. Anna Kasiakina (born 1939) had four children between 1963 and 1973, all in a maternity ward, and she received the normal work leaves before and after delivery. Lia Brykina and Anna Kasiakina, interviews by Listova, Inakovka 1, Tambov province, summer 1994.

34. Lia Brykina, interview, summer 1994; Antonina Abramova, interview, summer 1994.

35. Daria Fedosenkova, interview by Listova, Suglitsa, El'ninsk raion, Smolensk province, summer 1993.

36. The steam bath might even be used during labor if heat was thought to be needed; the heat of the steam was believed to soften the mother's body and thus facilitate the movement of the baby through her body. Popov, *Russkaia narodno-bytovaia meditsina,* 334–35.

37. The Russian is "Ne boisia rodov, a boisia prirodov." Tatiana Varfolomeeva, interview by Listova, Nikitino, El'ninsk raion, Smolensk province, summer 1993.

38. Among many prerevolutionary ethnographic accounts of this practice are Popov,

Russkaia narodno-bytovaia meditsina, 338–39; Petukhov, "Babnichan'e," 215; Afino-genov, *Zhizn' zhenskogo naseleniia,* 78–79; and Semyonova Tian-Shanskaya, *Village Life in Late Tsarist Russia,* 12.

39. Elena Sorokoumova, interview by Listova, Nikitino, El'ninsk raion, Smolensk province, summer 1993.

40. Efrosinia Ruleva, interview by Listova, Korobets, El'ninsk raion, Smolensk province, summer 1993.

41. The first male child of this new couple was named in honor of the fallen first husband and brother. Elena Bobkova, interview by Listova, El'ninsk raion, Smolensk province, summer 1993.

42. Anna Kirsanova, interview by Listova, Vititni, El'ninsk raion, Smolensk province, 1993. Though Anna's husband died when their youngest child was just seven, the couple gave their children a very good start in life; they all were educated and became successful.

43. Tsygankova described the work of the babka in the usual way: they tie up the umbilical cord, wrap the baby, and in some cases help out with the housework for two days. She did not fear the evil eye, and let people see her baby right away when they came to give small gifts. Elena Tsygankova, interview by Listova, Elizavetino, El'ninsk raion, Smolensk province, summer 1993.

44. Anna Varfolomeeva, interview by Listova, Nikiktino, El'ninsk raion, Smolensk province, summer 1993.

45. Valentina Shapovalova, interview by Listova, Korobets, El'ninsk raion, Smolensk province, summer 1993.

46. The transcript has some pronounal confusion here, but the overall sense connects the phrase to the birthing mother.

47. Pelagea Sharav'eva, interview by Peshkova, Maminskoe, Sverdlovsk province, summer 1993.

48. Aleksandra Guseva, interview by Peshkova, Maminskoe, Sverdlovsk province, summer 1993.

49. The figures compiled by the Princeton fertility project confirm the slower decline in fertility for this region generally. See Ansley J. Coale, Barbara Anderson, and Erna Härm, *Human Fertility in Russia since the Nineteenth Century* (Princeton, 1979), Tables 2.4–2.7.

50. Iulia Ortikova, interview by Peshkova, Maminskoe, Sverdlovsk province, summer 1993.

51. Galina Mamina, interview by Peshkova, Maminskoe, Sverdlovsk province, summer 1993.

52. Aleksandra Gibert, interview by Peshkova, Maminskoe, Sverdlovsk province, summer 1993.

53. Her first child was, however, stillborn.

54. Tamara Privalova, interview by Peshkova, Maminskoe, Sverdlovsk province, summer 1993. The youngest informant of this generation and region, Anna Panacheva, did not have her children in Maminskoe but in a remote village from which she moved to Maminskoe after her childbearing years. No medical services were available where she gave birth, and she, like all other women there, was attended in birth by a village midwife in the traditional way, the only difference being that she was released from work for a month before and a month after birth. Anna Panacheva, interview by Peshkova, Maminskoe, Sverdlovsk province, summer 1993.

55. Antonida Popova, interview by Peshkova, Maminskoe, Sverdlovsk province, summer 1993.

56. Valentina Tripapina, interview by Ransel, Laikovo, Moscow province, July 8, 1990.

57. Anastasia Shishanova, interview by Glazunova and Ransel, Tsarevo, Moscow province, June 6, 1993.

58. Praskovia and Tatiana Kurkova, interview by Glazunova and Ransel, Zhukovka, Moscow province, June 6, 1993.

59. Olimpiada Bakhmesterova, interview by Glazunova and Ransel, Staroe Selo Moscow province, June 7, 1993.

60. Anastasia Spiridonova, interview by Glazunova and Ransel, Lepeshki, Moscow province, June 7, 1993.

61. Lina Buldakova, interview by Glazunova and Ransel, Vvedenskoe, Moscow province, June 5, 1993.

62. Ekaterina Danilishina, interview by Ransel, Semashko Institute, Moscow, July 1, 1993.

63. Vera Belikova, interview by Glazunova and Ransel, Nazarovo, Moscow province, June 6, 1993.

64. Vasilii Shumkov, interview by Glazunova and Ransel, Fedorovskoe, Moscow province, June 5, 1993.

65. Ibid.

66. Zinaida Shumkova, interview by Glazunova and Ransel, Fedorovskoe, Moscow province, June 5, 1993.

67. Antonina Larshina, interview by Glazunova and Ransel, Orlovo, Moscow province, June 8, 1993.

68. This woman gave birth to her first and third children at home, but only because her husband was unable to locate a horse in time to get her to the hospital. An old and experienced neighbor woman did the deliveries, not asking for payment. Antonina Grafova, interview by Glazunova and Ransel, Nazarovo, Moscow province, June 6, 1993.

69. *Mat' i ditia, Meditsinskaia entsiklopediia,* and *Entsiklopediia domashnego khoziaistva* were the titles mentioned. Zoia Vovoshkina and Antonina Ptichnikova, interview by Glazunova and Ransel, Kablukovo, Moscow province, June 8, 1993.

70. Elizaveta Smirnova, interview by Glazunova and Ransel, Staroe Selo, Moscow province, June 7, 1993.

71. Anna Konobievskaia, interview by Glazunova and Ransel, Zhukovka, Moscow province, June 7, 1993.

72. It is worth noting that in the nineteenth century, stillbirths and perinatal mortality were unusually high among Tatars. Ershov attributed this at the time to "unnatural" marriages of the Tatars, in which the age differences between men and women were large. *Materialy dlia sanitarnoi statistiki sviiazhskogo uezda,* 111–12. This untested observation is scarcely credible. Modern anthropologists believe that this mortality is a function of the narrow pelvis of Tatar women, which is thought to be related to a diet poor in vitamins (vegetables are few) and their reluctance until recent times to seek medical help. Rickets is common, and Caesarean sections often have to be done on Tatar women. See comments by Mariam Gimadeeva, interview by Shugaeva, Tatarskii Kalmaiur, summer 1993.

73. A. A. Sukharev, *Kazanskie tatary,* 39, 47–50, observed Tatar women doing light

field work. N. I. Vorob'ev, "Kazanskie tatary," *Materialy po izucheniiu Tatarstana*, vol. 2, 162, writes that they ordinarily did not work in the fields. R. G. Mukhamedova, *Tatary-Mishari* (Moscow, 1972), 174, writes about Tatars whose women were relieved of field work in late pregnancy. See also Lev F. Zmeev, *Medikotopograficheskoe opisanie* (Moscow, 1883), 23, on the division of labor in Tatar households.

74. Garifabanu Abdullina, interview by Shugaeva, Tatarskii Kalmaiur, Ul'ianovsk province, summer 1993.

75. Khatima Nizamova, interview by Shugaeva, Tatarskii Kalmaiur, Ul'ianovsk province, summer 1993.

76. Women in mosque (principal informant was Khatima Nizamova, age 87, but also contributing were Emmegel'sem Aiukianova, age 87, and Merfuga Kaiumova, age 81), interview by Ransel, Tatarskii Kalmaiur, Ul'ianovsk province, July 16, 1990.

77. Mariam Gimadeeva, interview, summer 1993.

78. Women in mosque, interview, Ul'ianovsk province, summer 1990.

79. This was evidently a local Tatar folk belief, for it is not based in Islam, according to my colleague Nazif Shahrani. Women in mosque interview, Ul'ianovsk province, summer 1990.

80. Women in mosque interview, Ul'ianovsk province, summer 1990. This method is practiced throughout Central Asia, according to Shahrani.

81. Khatima Nizamova, interview, summer 1993.

82. Mariam Gimadeeva, interview, summer 1993.

83. Rkia Kamaletdinova, interview by Shugaeva, Tatarskii Kalmaiur, Ul'ianovsk province, summer 1993.

84. Women in mosque interview, Ul'ianovsk province, summer 1990.

85. The younger woman was Roza Fakhrutdinova (born 1933), interview by Shugaeva, Tatarskii Kalmaiur, Ul'ianovsk province, summer 1993.

86. Zeinab Gimatdinova, interview by Shugaeva, Tatarskii Kalmaiur, Ul'ianovsk province, summer 1993.

87. Sofia made this intervention during the interview with her sister. Fina Iurenieva, interview by Ransel, Ethnographic Institute, Leningrad, June 5, 1990.

88. See, for example, Ivan Blagovidov, *Materialy,* 13; Mil'kovich, "Byt i verovaniia tatar," 7–10; P. S. Nazarov, "K etnografii bashkir," 178–80; and A. A. Sukharev, *Kazanskie tatary,* 40–41.

89. Fakhiza Suleimanova, interview by Ransel, Simbirsk, Ul'ianovsk province, July 15, 1990.

90. Sofia's intervention in: Fina Iurenieva, interview, summer 1990.

91. Sofia Teleshova, interview by Ransel, Leningrad, May 31, 1990. Doctors working among the Tatars in the nineteenth century remarked with frustration on the refusal of Muslim women to allow doctors to examine them. See, for example, Blagovidov, *Materialy,* 15 and appendix; Dalinger, *Mediko-statisticheskoe issledovanie,* 124, 146, 166.

92. Garifabanu Abdullina, interview, summer 1993.

93. Her mother, who lived to age 95, gave birth to eight children between 1921 and 1943. Nurania Badrieva interview by Shugaeva, Tatarskii Kalmaiur, Ul'ianovsk province, summer 1993.

94. Garifabanu Abdullina, interview, summer 1993.

95. Zukhra Pozdniakova, interview by Ransel, Krasnoe Selo, Leningrad province, April 20, 1990. Khatima Nizamova, Zubarzhat Rezvanova, Mariam Gimadeeva, Rkia Kamaletdinova, Zeinab Gimatdinova, Zatia Bagautdinova, interviews, summer 1993.

96. Mariam Gimadeeva, Zeinab Gimatdinova, interviews, summer 1993.

97. Fakhiza Suleimanova, interview, summer 1990.

98. Fina Iurenieva, interview, summer 1990.

99. Zukhra Pozdniakova, interview, spring 1990; Roza Fakhrutdinova, interview, summer 1993.

100. Another woman mentioned the prayer "iangalif." Zubarzhat Rezvanova, interview, summer 1993. *"Iangalif"* is a combination and corruption of two words: *"ian,"* meaning soul, and *"alif,"* the first letter of the Arabic alphabet. The alif is like a thin stick and refers to the soul, having the sense that the birthing woman is fearful and in danger. Personal correspondence from the Tatar historian Guzel Ibneeva. My colleagues Devin DeWeese and Nazif Shahrani, specialists in Islam, had not heard of this prayer, which is apparently unique to Volga Tatars or a local variation or corruption.

101. Khatima Nizamova, interview, summer 1993.

102. Zatia Bagautdinova, Nurania Badrieva, interviews, summer 1993.

103. Women in mosque interview, Ul'ianovsk province, summer 1990.

104. Khatima Nizamova, interview, summer 1993.

105. Zukhra Pozdniakova, interview, spring 1990.

106. Sharifa Ialisheva, interview by Ransel, Leningrad, April 21, 1990.

107. Fina Iurenieva, interview, summer 1990.

108. Minzifa Mustafina, a milkmaid, was also concerned about the disruption in milk production that could come from losing contact with her cows. Interview by Shugaeva, Tatarskii Kalmaiur, Ul'ianovsk province, summer 1993.

109. Mariam Gimadeeva, interview, summer 1993.

110. Minzifa Mustafina, interview, summer 1993.

111. Roza Fakhrutdinova, interview, summer 1993.

6. Baptism and Equivalent Muslim Rites

1. For some examples of such letters see RGAE, f. 396, op. 2, d. 29, ll. 51, 52; ibid., op. 3, d. 71, ll. 57, 69–70. Exhortations to introduce Oktiabriny appeared regularly during the 1920s in the magazine *Krest'ianka.*

2. Glennys Jeanne Young, "Rural Religion and Soviet Power, 1921–1932" (Ph.D. diss., University of California, Berkeley, 1989), 190.

3. In a recent study, the Finnish scholar Arto Luukkanen attributes this campaign and much of the energy behind the early assaults on the church to the influence of Leon Trotsky and his followers. *The Party of Unbelief: The Religious Policy of the Bolshevik Party 1917–1929* (Helsinki, 1994), especially chapter 3.

4. Mikhail Heller and Aleksandr M. Nekrich, *Utopia in Power: The History of the Soviet Union from 1917 to the Present* (New York, 1986), 137. The sacred vessels confiscated during this "valuables crisis" evidently did not go to famine relief; the famine merely provided a pretext for the government to deprive the church of its wealth. Daniel Peris, "Storming the Heavens: The Soviet League of the Militant Godless and Bolshevik Political Culture in the 1920s and 1930s" (Ph.D. diss., University of Illinois at Urbana-Champaign, 1994), 31–33.

5. Functioning churches decreased from 46,457 in 1917 to 4,225 in 1939 and priests from 50,960 to 5,665. These figures include the Living Church sponsored by the regime. Wassilij Alexeev, "The Russian Orthodox Church 1927–1945: Repression and Revival," *Religion in Communist Lands* 7:1 (Spring 1979), 29.

6. Nothing is said about it in such well-known studies of the era as George W. Breslauer, *Khrushchev and Brezhnev as Leaders: Building Authority in Soviet Politics* (London, 1982); Edward Crankshaw, *Khrushchev: A Career* (New York, 1966); Carl A. Linden, *Khrushchev and the Soviet Leadership* (Baltimore, 1966); Michel Tatu, *Power in the Kremlin: From Khrushchev to Kosygin* (New York, 1968).

7. Michael Bourdeaux, "The Black Quinquennium: The Russian Orthodox Church 1959–1964," *Religion in Communist Lands* 9:1–2 (Spring 1981), 20, citing a study by Nadezhda Teodorovich.

8. Bourdeaux, "The Black Quinquennium," 20–21; Heller and Nekrich, *Utopia in Power,* 673.

9. Michael Aksenov Meerson, "The Russian Orthodox Church 1965–1980," *Religion in Communist Lands* 9:3–4 (Autumn 1981), 101–106.

10. Peris, "Storming the Heavens," 45–49. Young, "Rural Religion," 82, 135–39.

11. Peris, "Storming the Heavens," 45–59. Young, "Rural Religion," 165–67, relates typical incidents of vandalism.

12. Larry E. Holmes, "Fear No Evil: Schools and Religion in Soviet Russia, 1917–1941," in *Religious Policy in the Soviet Union,* ed. Sabrina Petra Ramet (Cambridge, 1993), 125–57.

13. Anastasia Vakhromeeva, interview by Glazunova and Ransel, Kablukovo, Moscow province, June 7, 1993.

14. She followed this comment with a story about how she had to haggle with the priest over the price of the baptism, a common occurrence in Russian villages, for the parish clergy supported themselves on farming and fees for service. Ekaterina Gerasimova, interview by Glazunova and Ransel, Tsarevo, Moscow province, June 6, 1993.

15. Zinaida Shumkova, interview by Glazunova and Ransel, Fedorovskoe, Moscow province, June 5, 1993.

16. Evdokia Sevriukova, interview by Listova, Suglitsa, El'ninsk raion, Smolensk province, summer 1993.

17. Nina Novozhilova, interview by Glazunova and Ransel, Nazarovo, Moscow province, June 6, 1993.

18. Tatiana Varfolomeeva, interview by Listova, Nikitino, El'ninsk raion, Smolensk province, summer 1993.

19. Praskovia Kurkova, interview by Glazunova and Ransel, Zhukovka, Moscow province, June 6, 1993. Valentina Tripapina in Moscow province mentioned that the church had a font that you could take home with you to have the baptism performed in your home; interview by Ransel, Laikovo, Moscow province, July 8, 1990.

20. Elena Sorokoumova, interview by Listova, Nikiktino, El'ninsk raion, Smolensk province, summer 1993.

21. Efrosinia Ruleva, interview by Listova, Korobets, El'ninsk raion, Smolensk province, summer 1993. For some other examples of early baptism, see G. M. Naumenko, *Etnografiia detstva,* 73–75.

22. Elena Tsygankova, interview by Listova, Elizavetino. El'ninsk raion, Smolensk province, summer 1993.

23. Olimpiada Bakhmesterova, interview by Glazunova and Ransel, Staroe Selo, Moscow province, June 7, 1993.

24. Examples of lay baptizers also mentioned by Anastasia Vakhromeeva, interview, summer 1993; and Valentina Lopatkina, interview by Glazunova and Ransel, Tsarevo, Moscow province, June 6, 1993.

25. Praskovia Korotchenkova, interview by Listova, Elizavetino, El'ninsk raion, Smolensk province, summer 1993.

26. Praskovia Korotchenkova, interview, summer 1993.

27. Nina Novozhilova, interview, summer 1993.

28. Vera Belikova, interview by Glazunova and Ransel, Nazarovo, Moscow province, June 6, 1993.

29. Zoia Vovoshkina, interview by Glazunova and Ransel, Kablukovo, Moscow province, June 8, 1993.

30. Antonina Ptichnikova and Zoia Vovoshkina, interview by Glazunova and Ransel, Kablukovo, Moscow province, June 8, 1993.

31. Valentina Lopatkina, interview, summer 1993.

32. This testimony is an example of how rural Russians could distinguish between formal adherence to dogma and actual belief in an afterworld and final reckoning. Anna Varfolomeeva, interview, summer 1993.

33. Ekaterina Gerasimova, interview, summer 1993.

34. With the presumed corollary that their spirits would haunt the woods and byways seeking a resting place. Juha Pentikainen, *The Nordic Dead-Child Tradition: Nordic Dead-Child Beings—A Study in Comparative Religion* (Helsinki, 1968). D. K. Zelenin, "K voprosu o rusalkakh (kul't pokoinikov, umershikh neestestvennoiu smert'iu u russkikh i u finnov)," *Zhivaia starina* 20 (1911), 357–424.

35. Anastasia Shishanova, interview by Glazunova and Ransel, Tsarevo, Moscow province, June 6, 1993.

36. Ekaterina Gerasimova, interview, summer 1993.

37. Antonina Grafova, interview by Glazunova and Ransel, Nazarovo, Moscow province, June 6, 1993.

38. Daria Fedosenkova, interview by Listova, Suglitsa, El'ninsk raion, Smolensk province, summer 1993.

39. Valentina Lopatkina, interview, summer 1993. This same concern about the failing effect of spells on unbaptized children was common in the villages we surveyed in the Urals, as confirmed by a personal note of one of the researchers, Elena Stepanova.

40. Anastasia Vakhromeeva, interview, summer 1993.

41. In fact, the mothers of the women interviewed in this region lost 45 percent of their offspring in childhood (of 52 reported births by these women, 29 children survived).

42. Praskovia Krivolapova, interview by Listova, Inakovka 2, Tambov province, summer 1994. Another woman pointed out that an unbaptized child was not furnished with a guardian angel. Maria Malikova, interview by Listova, Inakovka 1, Tambov province, 1994.

43. Pelagea Nikulina, interview, summer 1994; Praskovia Krivolapova, interview, summer 1994.

44. Pelagea Nikulina, interview, summer 1994; Anna Reutova, interview by Listova, Inakovka 2, Tambov province, summer 1994.

45. Maria Malikova, interview, summer 1994.

46. G. A. Nosova, "Traditsionnye obriady russkikh: Krestiny, pokhorony, pominki," *Rossiiskii etnograf* (Moscow, 1993), 49–52.

47. Nosova, "Traditsionnye obriady," 30–31.

48. Semyonova Tian-Shanskaia, *Village Life,* 15.

49. Anna Reutova, interview, summer 1994.

50. Evdokia Sevriukova, interview, summer 1993. See also comments by other women from this region. For example, Praskovia Korotchenkova, who had her children from 1941 to 1960, reported that families chose names either according to saints' days or their own personal preference: interview, summer 1993. Elena Bobkova, whose childbearing occurred from the early 1940s to the mid-1950s, said that names were no longer chosen by the saints' days but by personal preference: interview by Listova, Ezhevitsa, El'ninsk raion, Smolensk province, summer 1993.

51. Maria Malikova, interview, summer 1994.

52. See, for example, Natalia Mikhaleva, interview by Listova, Inakovka 2, Tambov province, summer 1994.

53. Anna Mikhaleva, interview, summer 1994. On the significance of churching and the requirement that women not enter the church or touch icons for forty days after a birth, Tatiana Varfolomeeva, interview, summer 1993.

54. Anna Kosiakova, interview by Listova, Inakovka 1, Tambov province, summer 1994.

55. Anna Kosiakova, interview, summer 1994.

56. There could be consequences for men as well, of course, when it was learned that they did not prevent their wives from baptizing their children. A woman from Moscow province reported that her husband, a teacher, received a reprimand when it became known that she had had their children (born in the 1940s) baptized. Klavdia Fateeva, interview by Listova, Kiiasovo, Stupinsk raion, Moscow province, spring 1994.

57. I should add that churching was a common experience of older village women in all the communities studied, not just in the Tambov villages. See, for example: Valentina Tripapina, interview, summer 1990; Anisia Gureeva, interview by Listova, Kiiasovo, Stupinsk raion, Moscow province, spring 1994; Olga Mal'tseva, interview by Ransel, Chernaia, Novgorod province, May 25, 1990.

58. Anna Kosiakova, interview, summer 1994.

59. She mentions elsewhere that her mother-in-law took care of the baptism of her children, another sign that she was avoiding any direct contact with the church, no doubt for professional reasons. Lia Brykina, interview by Listova, Inakovka 1, Tambov province, summer 1994.

60. See, for example, the report by Tatiana Varfolomeeva, who said that the children in her village wore crosses until they started to school but then had to remove them "because times were such that they would be bawled out for that"; interview, summer 1993.

61. Anna Kosiakova, interview, summer 1994.

62. Lia Brykina, interview, summer 1994.

63. An important part of baptism practice traditionally was the christening dinner. Although such dinners were reported and described by several women, the practice was not included in my questionnaire and consequently insufficient material was obtained to allow a mapping of changes in this aspect. I have therefore left it out of this discussion.

64. Women in mosque (principal informant was Khatima Nizamova but also contributing were Emmegelsem Aiukianova, Merfuga Kaiumova, and others), interview by Ransel, Tatarskii Kalmaiur, Ul'ianovsk province, July 16, 1990.

65. Fakhiza Suleimanova, interview by Ransel, Simbirsk, Ul'ianovsk province, July

15, 1990. My colleague Nazif Shahrani tells me that this early naming is done in Central Asia for fear of losing benefits that accrue to the parents on Judgment Day. They receive such benefits only if their child dies with a name.

66. Ibid.

67. Women in mosque, interview, Ul'ianovsk province, July 16, 1990.

68. Zeinab Gimatdinova, interview by Shugaeva, Tatarskii Kalmaiur, Ul'ianovsk province, summer 1993. Nazif Shahrani reports that seven years is a common interval nowadays in Central Asia.

69. Zeinab Gimatdinova and Mariam Gimadeeva, interviews, Ul'ianovsk province, summer 1993.

70. Fakhiza Suleimanova, interview, Ul'ianovsk province, summer 1990.

71. Sofia Teleshova, interview by Ransel, Leningrad, May 31, 1990.

7. Coping with Infant Death

1. Philippe Ariès, *Centuries of Childhood: A Social History of Family Life,* trans. Robert Baldick (New York, 1962), see especially 38–40. See also on the pre-modern period Jacques Gélis et al., *Entrer dans la vie: Naissances et enfances dans la France traditionelle* (Paris, 1978), 195–98.

2. The most powerful and compelling of these studies is about northeastern Brazil: Nancy Scheper-Hughes, *Death without Weeping: The Violence of Everyday Life in Brazil* (Berkeley, 1992). See also Susan C. M. Scrimshaw, "Infant Mortality and Behavior in the Regulation of Family Size," *Population and Development Review* 4:3 (September 1978), 383–403; Monica Das Gupta, "Selective Discrimination against Female Children in Rural Punjab, India," *Population and Development Review* 13:1 (March 1987), 77–100; Nancy E. Levine, "Differential Child Care in Three Tibetan Communities: Beyond Son Preference," *Population and Development Review* 13:2 (June 1987), 281–304.

3. A. M. Bol'shakov, *Sovremennaia derevnia v tsifrakh* (Leningrad, 1925), 100.

4. For a story about a cow being valued more than people, see K. Shidlovskii, "K kharakteristike narodnykh vozzrenii na etiologiiu, sushchnost' i terapiiu boleznei (Iz nabliudenii zemskogo vracha), *Meditsinskii vestnik* 52 (1883), 841. The same accusation of women giving better care to calves than to their own children is made in an article manuscript by R. Iakhina sent by the Office of Maternal and Child Welfare (OMM) in Moscow to the offices of *Krest'ianka* magazine in May 1924. RGAE, f. 396, op. 2, d. 29, l. 2. Reports of indifference to the death of children are many. A few examples are V. T. Demich, "Pediatriia u russkogo naroda," 11:2 (August 1891), 127–28; P. Griaznov, *Opyt sravnitel'nogo izucheniia,* 168 (reports of women who thanked God for taking their excess children); D. N. Zhbankov, *Vliianie otkhozhikh promyslov,* 85; *Otchet moskovskogo vospitatel'nogo doma za 1869 god* (Moscow, 1870), 29–31.

5. Praskovia Korotchenkova, interview by Listova, Elizavetino, El'ninsk raion, Smolensk province, summer 1993.

6. A. V. Balov, "Rozhdenie i vospitanie," 93–100; the same was true of babies who did not cry at their baptism, according to Balov. He also notes in another study ("Ocherki Poshekhon'ia," *Etnograficheskoe obozrenie* 14:4 [1901], 96, 100) the belief that babies born with their faces toward the ground (*litsom k zemle*) would not live long, a disturbing observation since most babies are born face down (that is, facing the mother's spine). If Balov had this right, it would signify a high degree of pessimism about the chances of an infant's survival. The belief does nevertheless fit with the notion of the

earth pulling the child back to itself, the women naturally reading the face toward the ground as a desire of the child to return to the moist mother earth of Russian mythology. Other examples are in A. O. Afinogenov, *Zhizn' zhenskogo naseleniia,* 338; and Naumenko, Etnografiia detstva, 54–55.

7. Praskovia Kurkova and Tatiana Kurkova, interview by Glazunova and Ransel, Zhukovka, Moscow province, June 6, 1993.

8. Elizaveta Nikolaeva, interview by Glazunova and Ransel, Tsarevo, Moscow province, June 6, 1993.

9. Anastasia Shishanova, interview by Glazunova and Ransel, Tsarevo, Moscow province, June 6, 1993.

10. Anastasia Spiridonova, interview by Glazunova and Ransel, Lepeshki, Moscow province, June 7, 1993.

11. Minzifa Mustafina, interview by Shugaeva, Tatarskii Kalmaiur, Ul'ianovsk province, summer 1993.

12. Nurania Badrieva, interview by Shugaeva, Tatarskii Kalmaiur, Ul'ianovsk province, summer 1993.

13. Garifabanu Abdullina, interview by Shugaeva, Tatarskii Kalmaiur, Ul'ianovsk province, summer 1993. See also Fina Iurenieva, interview by Ransel, Ethnographic Institute, Leningrad, June 5, 1990; Mariam Gimadeeva, interview by Shugaeva, Tatarskii Kalmaiur, Ul'ianovsk province, summer 1993.

14. Zeinab Gimatdinova, interview by Shugaeva, Tatarskii Kalmaiur, Ul'ianovsk province, summer 1993.

15. Valentina Tripapina, interview by Ransel, Laikovo, Moscow province, July 8, 1990.

16. This phrase borrowed with thanks from the title of Nancy Scheper-Hughes's outstanding study of northeastern Brazil.

17. Elena Bobkova, interview by Listova, El'ninsk raion, Smolensk province, summer 1993.

18. Anna Kirsanova, interview by Listova, Vititni, El'ninsk raion, Smolensk province, summer 1993.

19. Efrosinia Ruleva, interview by Listova, Korobets, El'ninsk raion, Smolensk province, summer 1993; Elena Tsygankova, interview by Listova, Elizavetino, El'ninsk raion, Smolensk province, summer 1993.

20. Rkia Kamaletdinova, interview by Shugaeva, Tatarskii Kalmaiur, Ul'ianovsk province, summer 1993.

21. Marfa Malikova, interview by Listova, Inakovka 1, Tambov province, summer 1994.

22. Pelagea Nikulina, interview by Listova, Inakovka, Tambov province, summer 1994. The information relates to the Inzhavinsk raion where she had lived most of her life.

23. Aleksandra Guseva, interview by Peshkova, Maminskoe, Sverdlovsk province, summer 1993.

24. Lia Brykina, interview by Listova, Inakovka 1, Tambov province, summer 1994.

25. This point is elaborated by T. A. Bernshtam, *Molodezh' v obriadovoi zhizni russkoi obshchiny XIX–nachala XX v.* (Leningrad, 1988), 262–63, where she also suggests that the Slavic root *mold* derives from the Indoeuropean morpheme *magh,* i.e., "to be able."

26. Vladimir Dal', *Tolkovyi slovar' zhivogo velikorusskogo iazyka,* vol. 4 (Moscow, 1955), 316–17.

27. "Eti startsy neredko khodiat s ryliami i poiut dumy, oni zhe sleptsy, khotia by i ne byli ni stary, ni slepy." Ibid., vol. 4, 317.

28. Anastasia had to endure yet another ordeal when she was not allowed to bury this child. "It was Soviet power then [the year was 1931]," she said, and they demanded an investigation to determine if she had murdered the child. The so-called nun was very helpful because she testified that the boy was mortally ill with diarrhea, vomiting, and convulsions. Anastasia Vakhromeeva, interview by Glazunova and Ransel, Kablukovo, Moscow province, June 7, 1993.

29. Zinaida Shumkova, interview by Glazunova and Ransel, Fedorovskoe, Moscow province, June 5, 1993.

30. George P. Fedotov, *The Russian Religious Mind,* vol. II: *The Middle Ages,* ed. John Meyendorff (Cambridge, Mass., 1966), 88–89.

31. *Krest'ianka,* 1926, no. 21 (November), 1.

32. Balov, "Rozhdenie i vospitanie detei," 99.

33. Anna Zueva, interview by Ransel, Chernaia, Batetskii raion, Novgorod province, May 24–26, 1990.

8. Child Care

1. John Rickman, "Russian Camera Obscura: Ten Sketches of Russian Peasant Life (1916–1918)," in *The People of Great Russia: A Psychological Study,* ed. Geoffrey Gorer and John Rickman (New York, 1949), 50–51.

2. Maria Somova, interview by Listova, Pakhotnyi ugol, Tambov province, summer 1994.

3. Marfa Malikova, interview by Listova, Inakovka 1, Tambov province, summer 1994. See also Anna Varfolomeeva, interview by Listova, Nikitino, El'ninsk raion, Smolensk province, summer 1993.

4. Anisia Gureeva, interview by Listova, Kiiasovo, Stupinsk raion, Moscow province, spring 1994.

5. Antonina Larshina, interview by Glazunova and Ransel, Orlovo, Moscow province, June 8, 1993.

6. Galina Mamina, interview by Peshkova, Maminskoe, Sverdlovsk province, summer 1993; Anna Zueva, reporting on women in northern Novgorod province, interview by Ransel, Chernaia, Batetskii raion, Novgorod province, May 24–26, 1990.

7. This was Pelagea Sharav'eva, interview by Peshkova, Maminskoe, Sverdlovsk province, summer 1993.

8. Natalia Mikhaleva, interview by Listova, Inakovka 2, Tambov province, summer 1994.

9. Antonina Abramova, interview by Listova, Inakovka 2, Tambov province, summer 1994.

10. Praskovia is speaking here of her early births (she had four children between 1941 and 1960) when she was living under the roof of her mother-in-law and suffered deprivation both because of the scarcity of the times in this war-devastated sector and the strict treatment she endured from her mother-in-law. The two younger children were reared when she was mistress in her own home and could provide better for herself. Praskovia Korotchenkova, interview by Listova, Elizavetino, El'ninsk raion, Smolensk province, summer 1993.

11. Anna Mikhaleva, interview by Listova, Inakovka 2, Tambov province, summer 1994.

12. Natalia Mikhaleva, interview by Listova, Inakovka 2, Tambov province, summer 1994.

13. Elena Tsygankova, interview by Listova, Elizavetino, El'ninsk raion, Smolensk province, summer 1993.

14. Two of her seven were foster children. Tatiana Vorob'eva, interview by Peshkova, Maminskoe, Sverdlovsk province, summer 1993.

15. Zakia Zagidullina, interview by Peshkova, Maminskoe, Sverdlovsk province, summer 1993.

16. Women in mosque (principal informant was Khatima Nizamova but also contributing were Emmegelsem Aiukianova, Merfuga Kaiumova, and others), interview by Ransel, Tatarskii Kalmaiur, Ul'ianovsk province, July 16, 1990.

17. Rosa Fakhrutdinova, interview by Shugaeva, Tatarskii Kalmaiur, Ul'ianovsk province, summer 1993.

18. Zeinab Gimatdinova, interview by Shugaeva, Tatarskii Kalmaiur, Ul'ianovsk province, summer 1993.

19. See chapter 1.

20. Sharifa Ialisheva, interview by Ransel, Leningrad, April 21, 1990; Mariam Gimadeeva, interview by Shugaeva, Tatarskii Kalmaiur, Ul'ianovsk province, summer 1993.

21. Amina Teleshova, interview by Ransel, Leningrad, May 8, 1990.

22. See Fakhiza Suleimanova, interview by Ransel, Simbirsk, Ul'ianovsk province, July 15, 1990; Fina Iurenieva, interview by Ransel, Ethnographic Institute, Leningrad, June 5, 1990; Sofia Teleshova, interview by Ransel, Leningrad, May 31, 1990.

23. The principal exponent of this "swaddling hypothesis" was Geoffrey Gorer. See Geoffrey Gorer and John Rickman, *The People of Great Russia: A Psychological Study,* 93–193.

24. Erik H. Erikson, *Childhood and Society,* 2nd edition (New York, 1963), 389–92.

25. Lawrence Stone, *The Family, Sex and Marriage In England 1500–1800,* abridged edition (New York, 1977), 267–70; Karin Calvert, *Children in the House: The Material Culture of Early Childhood, 1600–1900* (Boston, 1992), 61–65.

26. Ivan Betskoi, *Kratkoe nastavlenie vybrannoe iz luchshikh avtorov s nekotorymi fizicheskimi primechaniiami o vospitanii detei ot rozhdeniia ikh do iunoshestva* (St. Petersburg, 1766).

27. Valentina Tripapina, interview by Ransel, Laikovo, Moscow province, July 8, 1990.

28. Anna P-va, interview by Glazunova and Ransel, Vvedenskoe, Moscow province, June 6, 1993.

29. Anastasia Spiridonova, interview by Glazunova and Ransel, Lepeshki, Moscow province, June 7, 1993; Vera Belikova, interview by Glazunova and Ransel, Nazarovo, Moscow province, June 6, 1993. Anfisa Sudakova (born 1923) from northern Russia covered the crib with a sarafan to protect it from cold and the evil eye, and insisted that babies not be shown to outsiders for one year. Interview by Listova, Barkanovskaia, Vozhegodsk raion, Vologda province.

30. Antonina Larshina, interview, summer 1993.

31. *Cambridge World History of Human Disease,* 978–79.

32. Nina Novozhilova, interview by Glazunova and Ransel, Nazarovo, Moscow province, June 6, 1993.

33. Elizaveta Smirnova, interview, summer 1993.

34. Antonina Larshina, interview by Glazunova and Ransel, Orlovo, Moscow province, June 8, 1993.

35. Efrosinia Ruleva, interview by Listova, Korobets, El'ninsk raion, Smolensk province, summer 1993.

36. Elena Bobkova, interview by Listova, El'ninsk raion, Smolensk province, summer 1993.

37. Praskovia Korotchenkova, interview by Listova, Elizavetino, El'ninsk raion, Smolensk province, summer 1993.

38. Anna Varfolomeeva, interview, summer 1993.

39. Valentina Shapovalova, interview by Listova, Korobets, El'ninsk raion, Smolensk province, summer 1993.

40. Anna Mikhaleva, interview, summer 1994.

41. Only one informant, Maria Malikova, mentioned gendered clothing starting as early as age one and a half. Interview, summer 1994.

42. She was born in 1927. Anna Kosiakova, interview by Listova, Inakovka 1, Tambov province, summer 1994.

43. Elena Tsygankova, interview, summer 1993.

44. Natalia Mikhaleva, interview, summer 1994.

45. Lia Brykina, interview by Listova, Inakovka 1, Tambov province, summer 1994.

46. Anna Kasiakina, interview, summer 1994.

47. "Naji kuram" (in Tatar). Roza Fakhrutdinova, interview, Ul'ianovsk province, summer 1993.

48. Fakhiza Suleimanova, interview, Ul'ianovsk province, summer 1990.

49. Zatia Bagautdinova, interview by Shugaeva, Tatarskii Kalmaiur, Ul'ianovsk province, summer 1993.

50. The Urals and Novgorod sites yielded less information on the topics of this section.

51. Tatiana Kurkova, interview by Glazunova and Ransel, Zhukovka, Moscow province, June 6, 1993.

52. Olimpiada Bakhmesterova, interview by Glazunova and Ransel, Staroe Selo, Moscow province, June 7, 1993.

53. Vera Belikova, interview, summer 1993.

54. Anastasia Vakhromeeva, interview by Glazunova and Ransel, Kablukovo, Moscow province, June 7, 1993.

55. Lina Buldakova, interview by Glazunova and Ransel, Vvedenskoe, Moscow province, June 5, 1993.

56. Praskovia Korotchenkova, interview, summer 1993.

57. This family lost three of its eight children young. Natalia Mikhaleva, interview, summer 1994.

58. Marfa Malikova, interview, summer 1994.

59. This woman had one miscarriage and stillborn twins in addition to her other losses. Pelagea Nikulina, Bulgakovka, Inzhavinsk raion, interview by Listova, Tambov province, summer 1994.

60. Villagers had to be very sparing with fuel in this prairie region that depended largely on brushwood and grasses for burning. Praskovia Krivolapova, interview by Listova, Inakovka 2, Tambov province, summer 1994.

61. Maria Malikova, interview, summer 1994. Maria Abramova, interview, summer 1994.

62. Anna Kasiakina, interview, summer 1994.

63. Antonina Abramova, interview, summer 1994.

64. Natalia Mikhaleva, interview, summer 1994.

65. See her story in chapter 7 on coping with infant death.

66. A permanent medical station did not open in Tsarevo until 1960, but the village was on the main road to Krasnoarmeisk and only about five kilometers from that city's hospital.

67. Antonina Larshina, interview, summer 1993. Medical researchers had just recently discovered that the actual vector of the disease was body lice, and measures were taken by both sides in World War I to delouse soldiers, but the disease devastated Polish and Russian civilian populations after 1918. *Cambridge World History of Human Disease* (Cambridge, 1993), 1083.

68. Elizaveta Smirnova, interview, summer 1993; Klavdia Fateeva, interview by Listova, Kiiasovo, Stupinsk raion, Moscow province, spring 1994; Antonina Grafova, interview by Glazunova and Ransel, Nazarovo, Moscow province, June 6, 1993.

69. Tatiana Kurkova, interview, summer 1993.

70. Anastasia Shishanova mentioned placing children in the oven, a common enough treatment for many sorts of illnesses in Russia in the past, which usually involved partial insertion of the sick person in a baking chamber. Shishanova, interview by Glazunova and Ransel, Tsarevo, Moscow province, June 6, 1993.

71. See interviews by Glazunova and Ransel with Kuzina, Spiridonova, Buldakova, P-va, Shumkov, Novozhilova, and Vovoshkina.

72. Lina Buldakova (and daughter Tatiana Kachalkina), interview, summer 1993.

73. These remedies are still common in cities, too. I have been treated to them myself when I have taken ill during research trips to Russian archives and libraries; a kindly female archive worker would decide that her special concoction was the proper cure for my flu or food poisoning.

74. See chapter 7 on coping with infant death.

75. Maria Somova, interview, summer 1994.

76. Aleksandra Krivolapova, interview, summer 1994.

77. Natalia Mikhaleva, interview, summer 1994.

78. The death rate was well under 5 percent for an adequately nourished population, though in malnourished children in underdeveloped regions of the world it could rise to from 5 to 10 percent. *Cambridge World History of Human Disease*, 873.

79. Antonina Abramova, interview, summer 1994.

80. Anisia Gureeva, interview, spring 1994.

81. Valentina Lopatkina, interview by Glazunova and Ransel, Tsarevo, Moscow province, June 6, 1993.

82. Antonina Ptichnikova, interview by Glazunova and Ransel, Kablukovo, Moscow province, June 8, 1993.

83. Maria Abramova, interview, summer 1994.

84. Pelagea Nikulina, Marfa Malikova, interviews, summer 1994.

85. My comments here are based on studies of the moral economy in peasant society. See the classical texts by Edward C. Banfield, *The Moral Basis of a Backward Society* (New York, 1958), and George M. Foster, "Peasant Society and the Image of the Limited Good," *American Anthropologist* vol. 67 (1965), 293–315.

86. Jonas Frykman explains how this method was observed in some regions of nineteenth-century Sweden, where rickets in connection with the evil eye or evil touch

functioned to exclude women who engaged in unsanctioned sexual behavior. *Horan i bondesamhället* (Lund, 1977), 25–52.

87. Anastasia Vakhromeeva, interview, summer 1993.

88. Tatiana Kurkova, interview, summer 1993.

89. Ibid.; Anna Zueva, interview, spring 1990.

90. Anna Kirsanova, interview by Listova, Vititni, El'ninsk raion, Smolensk province, summer 1993.

91. Anna Varfolomeeva, interview, summer 1993.

92. Pelagea Nikulina, interview, summer 1994.

93. The woman taking her children to Kirsanov was Antonina Abramova. Interview, summer 1994. On folk healers, see also Lia Brykina, interview, summer 1994.

94. Maria Abramova, Maria Malikova, Antonina Abramova, and Lia Brykina, interviews, summer 1994.

95. Women in mosque interview, Ul'ianovsk province, July 16, 1990. Rkia Kamaletdinova, interview by Shugaeva, Tatarskii Kalmaiur, Ul'ianovsk province, summer 1993. "Work days" were a measure of collective farm effort, computed differently for different jobs. The net revenue of the farm at the end of each year was distributed to workers on the basis of their accumulated "work days."

96. Roza Fakhrutdinova, interview, Ul'ianovsk province, summer 1993.

97. Fina Iurenieva, interview, summer 1990.

98. Khatima Nizamova, interview by Shugaeva, Tatarskii Kalmaiur, Ul'ianovsk province, summer 1993; Garifabanu Abdullina, interview by Shugaeva, Tatarskii Kalmaiur, Ul'ianovsk province, summer 1993.

99. Zatia Bagautdinova, interview by Shugaeva, Tatarskii Kalmaiur, Ul'ianovsk province, summer 1993.

100. Nurania Badrieva, interview by Shugaeva, Tatarskii Kalmaiur, Ul'ianovsk province, summer 1993.

101. Roza Fakhrutdinova, interview, Ul'ianovsk province, summer 1993.

102. Khatima Nizamova, interview, Ul'ianovsk province, summer 1993.

103. Fakhiza Suleimanova, interview by Ransel, Simbirsk, Ul'ianovsk province, July 15, 1990. See also interview with Sharifa Ialisheva, interview, spring 1990.

104. Personal communication, September 28, 1999.

105. Sharifa Ialisheva, interview, spring 1990.

106. Another memorable case related by Sharifa was of a gypsy boy with the "falling sickness" (epilepsy). She at first refused to treat him because he was a gypsy, but after much importuning from his people, she treated him with her usual measures of spells and water and claimed that he did improve.

107. Zeinab Gimatdinova, Nurania Badrieva, interviews, Ul'ianovsk province, summer 1993.

108. Zeinab Gimatdinova, interview, Ul'ianovsk province, summer 1993.

109. Khatima Nizamova, Garifabanu Abdullina, Mariam Gimadeeva, interviews, Ul'ianovsk province, summer 1993.

110. Zubarzhat Rezvanova, interview by Shugaeva, Tatarskii Kalmaiur, Ul'ianovsk province, summer 1993.

111. Fakhiza Suleimanova, interview, Ul'ianovsk province, summer 1990.

112. Zatia Bagautdinova, Roza Fakhrutdinova, interviews, Ul'ianovsk province, summer 1993.

113. Zeinab Gimatdinova, interview, Ul'ianovsk province, summer 1993.

114. Zeinab Gimatdinova, Mariam Gimadeeva, interviews, Ul'ianovsk province, summer 1993.

115. Zatia Bagautdinova, interview, Ul'ianovsk province, summer 1993.

116. Marfa Malikova, interview, summer 1994.

9. Conclusion: Life and Loyalty in Hard Times

1. Zukhra Pozdniakova, interview by Ransel, Krasnoe Selo, Leningrad province, April, 20, 1990.

2. Ekaterina Gerasimova, interview by Glazunova and Ransel, Tsarevo, Moscow province, June 6, 1993.

3. See the stories of Lina Buldakova, interview by Glazunova and Ransel, Vvedenskoe, Moscow province, June 5, 1993; Sharifa Ialisheva, interview by Ransel, Leningrad, April 21, 1990; Efrosinia Ruleva, interview by Listova, Korobets, El'ninsk raion, Smolensk province, summer 1993; and women in Udel'nyi Park #2, interview by Shapovalova and Ransel, Leningrad, May 12, 1990.

4. Tatiana Varfolomeeva, interview by Listova, Nikitino, El'ninsk raion, Smolensk province, summer 1993. See also Praskovia Krivolapova, interview by Listova, Inakovka 2, Tambov province, summer 1994.

5. Vera Belikova, interview by Glazunova and Ransel, Nazarovo, Moscow province, June 6, 1993.

6. See, among others, the testimony of Lina Buldakova, interview, summer 1993; Elizaveta Nikolaeva, interview by Glazunova and Ransel, Tsarevo, Moscow province, June 6, 1993; and Maria Somova, interview by Listova, Pakhotnyi Ugol, Tambov province, summer 1994.

7. Fortunately, she owned two cows, which were a great help in feeding so many children. Ekaterina Gerasimova, interview by Glazunova and Ransel, Tsarevo, Moscow province, June 6, 1993.

8. Sharifa Ialisheva, interview, spring 1990. Lina Buldakova, interview, summer 1993. Anastasia Vakhromeeva, interview by Glazunova and Ransel, Kablukovo, Moscow province, June 7, 1993.

9. Marfa Malikova, interview by Listova, Inakovka 1, Tambov province, summer 1994.

10. Maria Malikova, interview by Listova, Inakovka 1, Tambov province, summer 1994.

11. See, among others, women in Udel'nyi Park, #1 and #2, interviews, May 12, 1990; Anna Konobievskaia, interview by Glazunova and Ransel, Zhukovka, Moscow province, June 7, 1993.

12. Indeed, the interviewer noted at the time that the stores in the market center of Korobets were altogether empty. Anna Varfolomeeva, interview by Listova, Nikitino, El'ninsk raion, Smolensk province, summer 1993.

13. Nina Novozhilova, interview by Glazunova and Ransel, Nazarovo, Moscow province, June 6, 1993.

14. Anna Kirsanova, interview by Listova, Vititni, El'ninsk raion, Smolensk province, summer 1993.

15. Antonina Larshina, interview by Glazunova and Ransel, Orlovo, Moscow province, June 8, 1993.

16. See chapter 2.

17. Anna Zueva, interview by Ransel, Chernaia, Batetskii raion, Novgorod province, May 24–26, 1990.

18. Valentina Lopatkina, interview by Glazunova and Ransel, Tsarevo, Moscow province, June 6, 1993.

19. Antonina Abramova, interview by Listova, Inakovka 2, Tambov province, summer 1994.

20. Nancy Ries, *Russian Talk,* esp. chapter 3.

21. Antonina Ptichnikova, interview by Glazunova and Ransel, Kablukovo, Moscow province, June 8, 1993.

22. See interviews with Zubarzhat Rezvanova, Zatia Bagautdinova, and Minzifa Mustafina, interviews by Shugaeva, Tatarskii Kalmaiur, Ul'ianovsk province, summer 1993.

23. Fakhiza Suleimanova, interview by Ransel, Simbirsk, Ul'ianovsk province, July 15, 1990.

24. Many history books have been appearing in recent years that tell the Tatars' side of the story of their encounter with the Russians and portray their centuries-long struggle to defend their culture and religion. A typical recent example is I. M. Lotfullin and F. G. Islaev, *Dzhikhad tatarskogo naroda: Geroicheskaia bor'ba tatar-musul'man s pravoslavnoi inkvizitsiei na primere istorii novokreshchenskoi kontory* (Kazan, 1998).

Bibliography

Note: This bibliography is limited to the works cited in the book. As is usual in any project of this size, hundreds of additional archival files and thousands of articles and books were consulted, but it would try the patience of readers and publisher to include them all here.

Oral Interview Materials

Indiana Oral History Research Center Archives

Archival Sources

Gosudarstvennyi Arkhiv Rossiiskoi Federatsii (GARF)
 fond 406 Narodnyi komissariat raboche-krest'ianskoi inspektsii RSFSR, 1920–1934
 fond 482 Ministerstvo zdravookhraneniia RSFSR, 1918–1991
 fond 4591
Rossiiskii Gosudarstvennyi Arkhiv Ekonomii (RGAE)
 fond 396 Redaktsiia: "Krest'ianskaia gazeta"
Tsentral'nyi Gosudarstvennyi Istoricheskii Arkhiv Sankt-Peterburga (TsGIA SPb)
 fond 8 Vospitatel'nyi dom
Rossiiskii Gosudarstvennyi Istoricheskii Arkhiv (RGIA)
 fond 515
 fond 767
Tsentral'nyi Gosudarstvennyi Arkhiv Sankt-Peterburga (TsGA SPb)
 fond 3007
 fond 4301

Printed Sources

Journals Cited Often

Krest'ianka, 1922–
Zhurnal akuzherstva i zhenskikh boleznei, 1887– (abbreviated as ZAZB)

Books and Articles

Afinogenov, A. O. *Zhizn' zhenskogo naseleniia Riazanskogo uezda v period detorodnoi deiatel'nosti zhenshchiny i polozhenie dela akusherskoi pomoshchi etomu naseleniiu.* St. Petersburg, 1903.

Aleksandrov, V. A. *Sel'skaia obshchina v Rossii.* Moscow, 1966.

Alexeev, Wassilij. "The Russian Orthodox Church 1927–1945: Repression and Revival." *Religion in Communist Lands* 7:1 (Spring 1979), 29–34.

Antonov, A. N. *Okhrana materinstva i mladenchestva. Posobie dlia vrachei.* Vol. 1, part 1. Leningrad, 1929.

———. *Podgotovka devochki k materinstvu.* Leningrad, 1929.

Ariès, Philippe. *Centuries of Childhood: A Social History of Family Life.* Trans. Robert Baldick. New York: Vintage Books, 1962.

Balashov, D. M., Iu. I. Marchenko, and N. I. Kalmykova. *Russkaia svad'ba: Svadebnyi obriad na Verkhnei i Srednei Kokshen'ge i na Uftiuge (Tarnogskii raion Vologodskoi oblasti).* Moscow, 1985.

Ball, Alan M. *And Now My Soul Is Hardened: Abandoned Children in Soviet Russia, 1918–1930.* Berkeley: University of California Press, 1994.

Balov, A. V. "Ocherki Poshekhon'ia." *Etnograficheskoe obozrenie* 14:4 (1901), 81–134.

———. "Rozhdenie i vospitanie detei v Poshekhonskom uezde, Iaroskavskoi gubernii." *Etnograficheskoe obozrenie* 2:3 (1890), 90–114.

Banfield, Edward C. *The Moral Basis of a Backward Society.* New York: Free Press, 1967. First pub. 1958.

Bekarevich, A. A. *K izucheniiu v mediko-topograficheskom i statisticheskom otnoshenii gubernskogo goroda Minska.* St. Petersburg, 1890.

Berberova, Nina. *The Italics Are Mine.* Trans. Philippe Radley. New York: Harcourt, Brace and World, 1969.

Berlin, M. *Ocherk etnografii evreiskogo narodonaseleniia v Rossii.* St. Petersburg, 1861.

Bernshtam, T. A. *Molodezh' v obriadovoi zhizni russkoi obshchiny XIX–nachala XX v.* Leningrad, 1988.

Betskoi, Ivan. comp. *Kratkoe nastavlenie vybrannoe iz luchshikh avtorov s nekotorymi fizicheskimi primechaniiami o vospitanii detei ot rozhdeniia ikh do iunoshestva.* St. Petersburg, 1766.

Binshtok, V. I., and S. A. Novosel'skii. *Materialy po estestvennomu dvizheniiu evreiskogo naseleniia v Evropeiskoi Rossii za 40 let (1867–1906).* Petrograd, 1915.

Blagovidov, Ivan. *Materialy k izledovaniiu* [sic] *zdorov'ia inorodtsev simbirskoi gubernii, Buinskogo uezda (Chuvash, Mordvy i Tatar), sobrannye posredstvom izmereniia rosta, okruzhnosti grudi, emkosti legkikh i vesa.* St. Petersburg, 1886.

Bol'shakov, A. M. *Derevnia 1917–1927.* Moscow, 1927.

———. *Sovremennaia derevnia v tsifrakh.* Leningrad, 1925.

Bonnell, Victoria E. "The Peasant Woman in Stalinist Political Art of the 1930s." *American Historical Review* 98:1 (February 1993), 55–82.

Bourdeaux, Michael. "The Black Quinquennium: The Russian Orthodox Church 1959–1964." *Religion in Communist Lands* 9:1–2 (Spring 1981), 18–23.

Breslauer, George W. *Khrushchev and Brezhnev as Leaders: Building Authority in Soviet Politics.* London: George Allen & Unwin, 1982.

Bridger, Susan. *Women in the Soviet Countryside: Women's Roles in Rural Development in the Soviet Union.* Cambridge: Cambridge University Press, 1987.

Busygin, E. P., et al. *Sel'skaia zhenshchina v semeinoi i obshchestvennoi zhizni.* Kazan, 1986.

Calvert, Karin. *Children in the House: The Material Culture of Early Childhood, 1600–1900.* Boston: Northeastern University Press, 1992.

Cambridge World History of Human Disease. Ed. Kenneth F. Kiple. Cambridge: Cambridge University Press, 1993.

Chubinskii, P. P. *Trudy etnografichesko-statisticheskoi ekspeditsii v zapadno-russkii krai.* St. Petersburg, 1872.

Clements, Barbara Evans. *Daughters of Revolution: A History of Women in the U.S.S.R.* Arlington Heights, Ill.: Harlan Davidson, 1994.

Coale, Ansley J., Barbara Anderson, and Erna Härm. *Human Fertility in Russia since the Nineteenth Century.* Princeton: Princeton University Press, 1979.

Crankshaw, Edward. *Khrushchev: A Career.* New York: Viking Press, 1966.

Czap, Peter, "Marriage and the Peasant Joint Family in the Era of Serfdom." In *The Family in Imperial Russia,* ed. David L. Ransel, 103–23. Urbana: University of Illinois Press, 1978.

Dal', Vladimir. *Tolkovyi slovar' zhivogo velikorusskogo iazyka.* 4 vols. Moscow, 1955.

Dalinger, A. *Mediko-statisticheskoe issledovanie tatarskogo naseleniia Astrakhanskogo uezda.* St. Petersburg, 1887.

Danilishina, E. I. "Okhrana zdorov'ia zhenshchiny-materi v gody velikoi otechestvennoi voiny." *Sovetskoe zdravookhranenie,* no. 3 (1986), 40–42.

Danilishina, E. I., and A. S. Fedoseev. "Deiatel'nost' organov zdravookhraneniia po okhrane zdorov'ia detei i podrostkov v gody velikoi otechestvennoi voiny." *Voprosy okhrany materinstva i detstva* no. 5 (1985), 13–18.

Das Gupta, Monica. "Selective Discrimination against Female Children in Rural Punjab, India." *Population and Development Review* 13:1 (March 1987), 77–100.

Demich, V. T. "Pediatriia u russkogo naroda." *Vestnik obshchestvennoi gigieny, sudebnoi i prakticheskoi meditsiny* 11:2 (August 1891), 125–45; 9:3 (September 1891), 187–212; 12:1 (October 1891), 66–76; 12:2 (November 1891), 111–23; 12:3 (December 1891), 169–86.

Dukes, Paul, ed. *Russia under Catherine the Great.* Vol. II: *Catherine the Great's Instruction (Nakaz) to the Legislative Commission, 1767.* Newtonville, Mass.: Oriental Research Partners, 1977.

Ely, Stanislaus Pinas. *Fiziko-medicheskie primechaniia o vrede proizkhodiashchem ot upotrebleniia rozhkov dlia kormleniia mladentsov, i o proistekaiushchikh ot togo chastiiu ves'ma zhestokikh, chastiiu zhe i smertonosnykh detskikh bolezniakh.* St. Petersburg, 1785.

Engelstein, Laura. *The Keys to Happiness: Sex and the Search for Modernity in Fin-de-Siècle Russia.* Ithaca: Cornell University Press, 1992.

Erikson, Erik H. *Childhood and Society.* 2nd ed. New York: W. W. Norton, 1963.

Ershov, Sergei. *Materialy dlia sanitarnoi statistiki sviiazhskogo uezda. Opyt sravnitel'noi demografii russkoi i tatarskoi narodnostei.* St. Petersburg, 1888.

Fedotov, George P. *The Russian Religious Mind.* Vol. II: *The Middle Ages.* Ed. John Meyendorff. Cambridge, Mass.: Harvard University Press, 1966.

Feitel'berg, I. *Opyt mediko-topograficheskogo opisaniia goroda Vindavy.* Iur'ev, 1894.

Foster, George M. "Peasant Society and the Image of the Limited Good." *American Anthropologist* 67 (1965), 293–315.

Frieden, Nancy Mandelker. *Russian Physicians in an Era of Reform and Revolution, 1856–1905.* Princeton: Princeton University Press, 1981.

Frierson, Cathy A. *All Russia Is Burning: A Cultural History of Rural Fire and Arson in Late Imperial Russia.* Forthcoming.

Frykman, Jonas. *Horan i bondesamhället.* Lund: LiberLäromedel, 1977.

Fuks, K. *Kazanskie tatary v statisticheskom i etnograficheskom otnosheniiakh.* Kazan, 1844.

Gélis, Jacques, et al. *Entrer dans la vie: Naissances et enfances dans la France traditionelle.* Paris: Gallimard, 1978.

Giliarovskii, F. V. *Issledovaniia o rozhdenii i smertnosti detei v Novgorodskoi gubernii*. Vol. I: Zapiski imp. russkogo geograficheskogo obshchestva po otd. statistiki. St. Petersburg, 1866.

Glebov, D. "Okhrana zdorov'ia zhenshchin i rebenka v kolkhozakh i sovkhozakh." *ZAZB* 41:2 (March–April 1930), 131–39.

Goldman, Wendy Z. "Alimony and the Peasant Dvor: the Gap between Family Law and Rural Life." Paper delivered at AAASS National Convention, New Orleans, November 1986.

———. *Women, the State and Revolution: Soviet Family Policy and Social Life, 1917–1936*. New York: Cambridge University Press, 1993.

Golynets, L. *K izucheniiu v mediko-topograficheskom i statisticheskom otnoshenii gubernskogo goroda Mogileva*. St. Petersburg, 1887.

Gorer, Geoffrey, and John Rickman, eds. *The People of Great Russia: A Psychological Study*. New York: W. W. Norton, 1949.

Gorkii, Maksim. *Polnoe sobranie sochinenii: khudozhestvennye proizvedeniia*. 25 vols. Moscow, 1968–1976.

Griaznov, P. *Opyt sravnitel'nogo izucheniia gigienicheskikh uslovii krest'ianskogo byta i mediko-topografiia cherepovetskogo uezda*. St. Petersburg, 1880.

Grigor'eva, N. N. "Sorok let okhrany materinstva i detstva v RSFSR." *Voprosy okhrany materinstva i detstva* 2:5 (1957), 5–14.

Heller, Mikhail, and Aleksandr M. Nekrich. *Utopia in Power: The History of the Soviet Union from 1917 to the Present*. New York: Summit Books, 1986.

Hoch, Steven L. *Serfdom and Social Control in Russia: Petrovskoe, a Village in Tambov*. Chicago: University of Chicago Press, 1986.

Holmes, Larry E. "Fear No Evil: Schools and Religion in Soviet Russia, 1917–1941." In *Religious Policy in the Soviet Union*, ed. Sabrina Petra Ramet (Cambridge: Cambridge University Press, 1993), 125–57.

Hutchinson, John F. *Politics and Public Health in Revolutionary Russia, 1890–1918*. Baltimore: Johns Hopkins University Press, 1990.

Iakovenko, M. G. *Materialy k antropologii evreiskogo naseleniia Rogachevskogo uezda Mogilevskoi gubernii*. St. Petersburg, 1898.

Iampol'skii, S. M. "'Kaplia moloka' i ee znachenie v bor'be s detskoi smertnost'iu i zabolevaemost'iu." *Vrachebnaia gazeta* 43 (1909), 1297–1301.

Il'ina, I. P. "Vliianie voin na brachnost' sovetskikh zhenshchin." In *Brachnost', rozhdaemost', smertnost' v Rossii i v SSSR*, ed. A. G. Vishnevskii (Moscow, 1977), 50–61.

Juviler, Peter H. "Family Reforms on the Road to Communism." In *Soviet Policy-Making: Studies of Communism in Transition*, ed. Peter H. Juviler and Henry W. Morton (New York: Praeger, 1967).

Kenigsberg, M. M. *Sanitarnoe sostoianie Orenburgskoi gubernii po dannym estestvennogo dvizheniia naseleniia za trekhletie 1897–1899 gg*. Orenburg, 1901.

Khotovitskii, Stepan. "O nekotorykh pogreshnostiakh i predrassudkakh kasatel'no soderzhaniia detei, v pervoe vremia ikh zhizni." In *Trudy sanktpeterburgskogo obshchestva russkikh vrachei*, part 1 (St. Petersburg, 1836), 160–66.

Konius, E. M. *Istoki russkoi pediatrii*. Moscow, 1946.

———. *Puti razvitiia sovetskoi okhrany materinstva i mladenchestva (1917–1940)*. Moscow, 1954.

Koshelev, V. V. *Mediko-topograficheskoe opisanie goroda Mogileva na Dnepre*. St. Petersburg, 1901.

Kudriavtsev, P. F. *Derevenskie iasli-priiuty v Simbirskoi gubernii letom 1899 g.* Syzran, 1900.

Kurkin, P. I. *Detskaia smertnost' v moskovskoi gubernii i ee uezdakh v 1883–1897*. Moscow, 1902.

Kurzon, V. M. *Okhrana materinstva i mladenchestva v SSSR*. Samara, 1928.

Lapidus, Gail Warshofsky. *Women in Soviet Society: Equality, Development, and Social Change*. Berkeley: University of California Press, 1978.

Leavitt, Judith Walzer. *Brought to Bed: Childbearing in Ameria, 1750–1950*. New York: Oxford University Press, 1986.

Levin, M. M. "K kharakteristike prichin iskusstvennogo vykidysha." *ZAZB* 42:3 (1931), 375–78.

Levine, Nancy E. "Differential Child Care in Three Tibetan Communities: Beyond Son Preference." *Population and Development Review* 13:2 (June 1987), 281–304.

Likhtenshtedt, I. R. *O prichinakh bol'shoi smertnosti detei na pervom godu zhizni i merakh k ee otvrashcheniiu*. St. Petersburg, 1839.

Linden, Carl A. *Khrushchev and the Soviet Leadership*. Baltimore: Johns Hopkins University Press, 1966.

Listova, T. A. "Rebenok v russkoi sem'e. Rozhdenie, kreshchenie. 2-aia polovina XIX-XX v." In *Obychai i obriady, sviazannye s rozhdeniem rebenka*, ed. T. A. Listova and T. P. Fedianovich (Moscow, 1995), 8–59.   ·

Liu, Lilian. "The Development of the Soviet Rural Health Care System and the Role of the Feldshers, 1917–1941." Ph.D. diss., University of Maryland, 1988.

Lotfullin, I. M., and F. G. Islaev. *Dzhikhad tatarskogo naroda: geroicheskaia bor'ba tatar-musul'man s pravoslavnoi inkvizitsiei na primere istorii novokreshchenskoi kontory*. Kazan, 1998.

Luukkanen, Arto. *The Party of Unbelief: The Religious Policy of the Bolshevik Party 1917–1929*. Helsinki: Finnish Historical Society, 1994.

Makkaveev, I. F. "Osobennosti organizatsii okhrany materinstva v Leningrade i puti dal'neishego razvitiia v etoi oblasti." *ZAZB* 41:1 (January–February 1930), 82–91.

Maksimovich-Ambodik, Nestor M. *Iskusstvo povivaniia ili Nauka o babichiem dele*. 6 vols. St. Petersburg, 1784–1986.

———. *Kratkoe ispytanie mnogikh zakosnelykh mnenii i predrazsuzhdenii kasatel'no bere-mennykh zhen, rodil'nits i novorozhdennykh detei*. St. Petersburg, 1786.

Malinovskii, L. N. *K izucheniiu v mediko-topograficheskom i statisticheskom otnoshenii g. Revelia*. Revel, 1891.

Meerson, Michael Aksenov. "The Russian Orthodox Church 1965–1980." *Religion in Communist Lands* 9:3–4 (Autumn 1981), 101–109.

Mil'kovich. *Byt i verovaniia tatar Simbirskoi gubernii v 1783 g. (iz zapisok uezdnogo zem-lemera Mil'kovicha)*, ed. N. Vinogradov. Kazan, 1905.

Mukhamedova, R. G. *Tatary-Mishari*. Moscow, 1972.

Naselenie SSSR za 70 let. Ed. L. L. Rybakovskii. Moscow, 1988.

Naumenko, G. M., compiler. *Etnografiia detstva*. Moscow, 1998.

Nazarov, P. S. "K etnografii bashkir." *Etnograficheskoe obozrenie* 2:1 (1890), 164–92.

Nikitenko, V. P. *Detskaia smertnost' v evropeiskoi Rossii za 1893–1896 god*. St. Petersburg, 1901.

Nikol'skii, D. P. *Obzor deiatel'nosti gubernskikh s"ezdov zemskikh vrachei*. Vyp. 1. St. Petersburg, 1888.

Nikol'skii, V. I. *Sanitarnoe issledovanie Penzenskoi gubernii. Statistika naseleniia gorodov i uezdov za 10 let (1880–89 gg.)*. Penza, 1893.

———. *Tambovskii uezd. Statistika naseleniia i boleznennosti (s tablitsami i diagrammami)*. Tambov, 1885.

Nosova, G. A. *Traditsionnye obriady russkikh: krestiny, pokhorony, pominki*. Published in the series *Rossiiskii etnograf*. Moscow, 1993.

Novosel'skii, S. A. *Smertnost' i prodolzhitel'nost' zhizni v Rossii*. Petrograd, 1916.

———. "Vliianie voiny na polovoi sostav rozhdaiushchikhsia." In *Voprosy demograficheskoi i sanitarnoi statistiki* (Moscow, 1958), 191–98.

"Ob organizatsii i sostoanii rodil'noi pomoshchi v RSFSR." *ZAZB* 44:3 (1933), xx.

Otchet moskovskovo vospitatel'nogo doma za 1869 god. Moscow, 1870.

Paperno, Irina. *Suicide as a Cultural Institution in Dostoevsky's Russia*. Ithaca: Cornell University Press, 1997.

Pentikainen, Juha. *The Nordic Dead-Child Tradition: Nordic Dead-Child Beings—A Study in Comparative Religion*. Helsinki: Folklore Fellows Communications, 1968.

Peris, Daniel. "Storming the Heavens: The Soviet League of the Militant Godless and Bolshevik Polticial Culture in the 1920s and 1930s." Ph.D. diss., University of Illinois at Urbana-Champaign, 1994.

Peskov, P. A. *Opisanie Durykinskoi volosti moskovskogo uezda v sanitarnom otnoshenii*. Moscow, 1879.

Petukhov, Dm. "Babnichan'e." *Meditsinskii vestnik* 23 (1863), 215–16.

Pokrovskii, E. A. *Fizicheskoe vospitanie detei u raznykh narodov, preimushchestvenno Rossii. Materialy dlia mediko-antropologicheskogo issledovaniia*. Moscow, 1884.

———. *Ob ukhode za malymi det'mi*. Moscow, 1899.

Popov, G. I. *Russkaia narodno-bytovaia meditsina*. St. Petersburg, 1903.

"Protiv gnilogo liberalizma v meditsinskoi pechati." *ZAZB* 43:1 (1932), 2–6.

Rabinovich, M. G. *Ocherki etnografii russkogo feodal'nogo goroda*. Moscow, 1978.

Rachinskii, N. I. "Glavnye momenty v istorii razvitiia akusherstva." *ZAZB* 15:3 (1901), 375–98.

Ramer, Samuel C. "Childbirth and Culture: Midwifery in the Nineteenth-Century Russian Countryside." In *The Family in Imperial Russia*, ed. David L. Ransel (Urbana: University of Illinois Press, 1978), 218–35.

Ransel, David L. "Culture, Childbirth, and Disease among Women in Belarus in the Late Imperial Period." Forthcoming in Belarussian.

———. "Mothering, Medicine, and Infant Mortality in Russia: Some Comparisons." Occasional Paper, Kennan Institute for Advanced Russian Studies, no. 236 (1990).

———. *Mothers of Misery: Child Abandonment in Russia*. Princeton: Princeton University Press, 1988.

———. "'Starye mladentsy' v russkoi derevne." In *Mentalitet i agrarnoe razvitie Rossii (XIX–XX vv.)*, ed. V. P. Danilov and L. V. Milov (Moscow, 1996), 106–14.

Rein, G. E. *Rodovspomozhenie v Rossii. Sbornik dokladov na IX Pirogovskom s"ezde*. St. Petersburg, 1906.

Reuterswärd, Elisabeth. *Kulturell intervention. Ett participatorisk experiment*. Lund: Sociologiska Institutionen, 1990.

Ries, Nancy. *Russian Talk: Culture and Conversation during Perestroika*. Ithaca: Cornell University Press, 1997.

Ritchie, Donald A. *Doing Oral History.* New York: Twayne Publishers, 1995.

Romanov, A. E. *O zabolevaemosti naseleniia kuznetskogo uezda v 1881 godu.* Penza, 1881.

————. *O zabolevaemosti naseleniia kuznetskogo uezda. Saratovskoi gubernii v 1882 godu i ob ospoprivivanii za etot zhe god.* Penza, 1883.

Rudenko, S. I. *Bashkiry. Opyt etnologicheskoi monografii.* 2 vols. Petrograd, 1916; Leningrad, 1925.

Scheper-Hughes, Nancy. *Death without Weeping: The Violence of Everyday Life in Brazil.* Berkeley: University of California Press, 1992.

Schiebinger, Londa. "Why Are Mammals Called Mammels?" *American Historical Review* 98:2 (April 1993), 382–411.

Schlesinger, Rudolf, ed. *The Family in the U.S.S.R.* London: Routledge and K. Paul, 1949, 1998.

Scrimshaw, Susan C. M. "Infant Mortality and Behavior in the Regulation of Family Size." *Population and Development Review* 4:3 (September 1978), 383–403.

Semenova, L. N. *Ocherki istorii byta i kul'turnoi zhizni Rossii, pervaia polovina XVIII v.* Leningrad, 1982.

Semyonova Tian-Shanskaya, Olga. *Village Life in Late Tsarist Russia,* ed. David L. Ransel. Bloomington: Indiana University Press, 1993.

Serebrennikov, P. N. *Opyt mediko-topograficheskogo opisaniia g. Irbiti Permskoi gubernii s planom goroda i diagrammami.* St. Petersburg, 1885.

Shidlovskii, K. "K kharakteristike narodnykh vozzrenii na etiologiiu, sushchnost' i terapiiu boleznei (Iz nabliudenii zemskogo vracha)." *Meditsinskii vestnik* 51–52 (1883); 2–3 (1884).

Shidlovskii, K. I. *Svod postanovlenii i rabot I–VI vserossiiskikh s"ezdov vrachei.* Moscow, 1899.

Shmelev, M. *Opyt meditsinskoi topografii iaroslavskoi gubernii.* St. Petersburg, 1868.

Smith-Rosenberg, Carroll. "The Female World of Love and Ritual: Relations between Women in Nineteenth-Century America." *Signs* 1 (1975), 1–29.

Snigirev, V. *O smertnosti detei na pervom godu zhizni. Opyt mediko-statisticheskogo issledovaniia v Stavropol'skoi gubernii s 1857 po 1862 god.* St. Petersburg, 1863.

Spasskii, N. *Ocherki po rodinovedeniiu. Kazanskaia guberniia.* 2nd ed. Kazan, 1912.

Stone, Lawrence. *The Family, Sex and Marriage In England 1500–1800.* Abridged ed. New York: Harper Colophon Books, 1977.

Sukharev, A. A. *Kazanskie tatary (uezd Kazanskii). Opyt etnograficheskogo i mediko-antropologicheskogo issledovaniia.* St. Petersburg, 1904.

Sussman, George D. *Selling Mothers' Milk: The Wet-Nursing Business in France, 1715–1914.* Urbana: University of Illinois Press, 1982.

Tatu, Michel. *Power in the Kremlin: From Khrushchev to Kosygin.* New York: Viking Press, 1968.

Teziakov, N. I. *Materialy po izucheniiu detskoi smertnosti v Saratovskoi gubernii s 1902 po 1904 gg.* Saratov, 1908.

Uden, F. (?) "O pervykh estestvennykh prikliucheniiakh novorozhdennogo cheloveka." *Sanktpeterburgskie vrachebnye vedomosti* (series running 1792–1794).

Urlanis, B. Ts. "Dinamika urovnia rozhdaemosti v SSSR za gody sovetskoi vlasti." In *Brachnost', rozhdaemost', smertnost' v Rossii i v SSSR,* ed. A. G. Vishnevskii (Moscow, 1977), 8–27.

Vorob'ev, N. I. *Kazanskie tatary (etnograficheskoe issledovanie material'noi kul'tury dooktiabr'skogo perioda).* Kazan, 1953.

————. "Kazanskie tatary." In *Materialy po izucheniiu Tatarstana,* vol. 2, ed. G. G. Ibragimov and V. I. Vorob'ev (Kazan, 1925).

Waters, Elizabeth. "The Modernization of Russian Motherhood." *Soviet Studies* 44:1 (1992), 123–35.

————. "Teaching Mothercraft in Post-Revolutionary Russia." *Australian Slavonic and East European Studies* 1:2 (1987), 29–56.

Wood, Elizabeth. *The Baba and the Comrade: Gender and Politics in Revolutionary Russia,* Bloomington: Indiana University Press, 1997.

Worobec, Christine D. *Peasant Russia: Family and Community in the Post-Emancipation Period.* Princeton: Princeton University Press, 1991.

Young, Glennys Jeanne. "Rural Religion and Soviet Power, 1921–1932." Ph.D. diss., University of California, Berkeley, 1989.

Zelenin, D. K. "K voprosu o rusalkakh (kul't pokoinikov, umershikh neestestvennoiu smert'iu u russkikh i u finnov." *Zhivaia starina* 20 (1911), 357–424.

Zhbankov, D. N. *Vliianie otkhozhikh promyslov na dvizhenie narodonaseleniia Kostromskoi gubernii po dannym 1866–1883 gg.* Kostroma, 1887.

Zhuk, A. P. *Razvitie obshchestvenno-meditsinskoi mysli v Rossii v 60–70 gg. XIX veka.* Moscow, 1963.

Zhuk, V. "Shkola sel'skikh povival'nykh babok." *ZAZB* 4:7–8 (1890), 485–520.

Zmeev, Lev F. *Medikotopograficheskoe opisanie i statisticheskii ocherk narodonaseleniia Bugul'minskogo uezda Samarskoi gubernii.* Moscow, 1883.

Zybelin, Semen. *Slovo o pravil'nom vospitanii s mladenchestva v razsuzhdenii tela, sluzha-shchem k razmnozheniiu v obshchestve naroda.* Moscow, 1775.

————. *Slovo o sposobe, kak predupredit' mozhno nemalovazhnuiu mezhdu prochimi med-lennogo umnozheniia naroda prichinu, sostoiashchuiu v neprilichnoi pishche, mladentsam davaemoi v pervye mesiatsy ikh zhizni.* Moscow, 1780.

Index

DAVID L. RANSEL is Professor of History and Director of the Russian and East European Institute at Indiana University, Bloomington. He has served as editor of the *Slavic Review* and the *American Historical Review*. He is author of *The Politics of Catherinian Russia: The Panin Party* and *Mothers of Misery: Child Abandonment in Russia*. He is also editor of *The Family in Imperial Russia: New Lines of Historical Research* and *Village Life in Late Tsarist Russia* (Indiana University Press), and co-editor (with Jane Burbank) of *Imperial Russia: New Histories for the Empire* (Indiana University Press).